Leadership, Ethics, and Policing

LEADERSHIP, ETHICS, AND POLICING

CHALLENGES FOR THE 21ST CENTURY

EDWIN MEESE III
The Heritage Foundation

P. J. ORTMEIER
Grossmont College
&
California State University

Foreword by
Leroy D. Baca
Sheriff, County of Los Angeles

Upper Saddle River, New Jersey 07458

Library of Congress Cataloging-in Publication Data

Edwin, Meese
Leadership, ethics, and policing: challenges for the twenty-first century/Edwin Meese III and P. J. Ortmeier.
p.cm.
Includes bibliographical references and index
ISBN 0-13-026871-2
1. Police ethics 2. Law enforcement—Moral and ethical aspects 3. Police training—Moral and ethical aspects 4. Law enforcement—United States 5. Police—United States I. Ortmeier, P.J. II. Title
HV7924.M44 2002
1741/.93632 21 2002044810

Editor-in-chief: Stephen Helba
Executive Editor: Frank Mortimer, Jr.
Assistant Editor: Sarah Holle
Production Editor: Ann Imhof, Carlisle Publishers Services
Production Liaison: Barbara Marttine Cappuccio
Director of Production & Manufacturing: Bruce Johnson
Managing Editor: Mary Carnis
Manufacturing Buyer: Cathleen Petersen
Creative Director: Cheryl Asherman
Cover Design Coordinator: Miguel Ortiz
Cover Designer: Miguel Ortiz
Cover Image: Koopman, Corbis/StockMarket
Interior Illustrations: Dorie Savage
Marketing Manager: Tim Peyton
Editorial Assistant: Barbara Rosenberg
Composition: Carlisle Communications, Ltd.
Printing and Binding: RR Donnelly & Sons

Pearson Education, LTD., *London*
Pearson Education Australia PTY. Limited, *Sydney*
Pearson Education Singapore, Pte. Ltd.
Pearson Education North Asia Ltd., *Hong Kong*
Pearson Education Canada, Ltd., *Toronto*
Pearson Educacíon de Mexico, S.A. de C.V.
Pearson Education-Japan, *Tokyo*
Pearson Education Malaysia, Pte. Ltd.

10 9 8 7 6 5 4
ISBN 0-13-026871-2

To August Vollmer, O. W. Wilson, and William H. Parker,
for their leadership, vision, and contributions to the
professionalism of the police service.

Contents

Foreword

There is no profession so universally scrutinized by the public in terms of leadership as law enforcement. People look to law enforcement agencies and individual peace officers for sound judgment, decisiveness, and courage in protecting public welfare and ensuring that our nation's federal, state, and local laws are fairly and consistently enforced. When citizens feel that they cannot trust their law enforcement representatives in terms of exercising wise and equitable judgment, public trust is forfeited and society as a whole suffers.

At its best, as exemplified by the extreme valor of those individuals who lost their lives trying to save others during the terrible events of September 11, 2001, law enforcement has shown that its institutions protect and defend the public during the worst, most heinous situations that life can offer.

On the other hand, issues such as racial profiling, internal and external discrimination and harassment, criminal misconduct by individual officers, and institutional corruption have galvanized the public in recent years, creating a crisis of confidence in law enforcement. Our communities' need for government leaders to account for and address these issues have compelled law enforcement professionals to critically evaluate core beliefs, codes of conduct, internal training methods, auditing systems, and use of corrective action against officers who violate law and policy. In addition, law enforcement leaders have been forced to examine and reevaluate their assumptions about the nature—and needs—of the communities they serve.

How can one come to terms with such a situation? Here is what the Chinese observed and understood. In ancient times, they developed a written language based on characters, each of which symbolized a separate idea. Within that system, the characters were often combined to create completely new ideas. The symbol for "crisis" was such an amalgamation. It combined the character representing "danger" with the character representing "opportunity," resulting in a symbol showing that *crisis provides opportunity as well as danger.*

As mentioned above, we truly are at a point of crisis in terms of the public's confidence in the efficacy of law enforcement. Law enforcement agencies can view the situation as one dangerous to the credibility of police institutions and the safety of the general populace. Law enforcement can also view the situation as an opportunity to make positive changes toward the future, utilizing basic principles of leadership as a guide.

What should principles of leadership require of us? At their very core, such principles should motivate all law enforcement representatives to have the courage to stand up for what is right, challenge what is wrong, and apply common sense and fairness in all that we do. These principles also require us to partner with the communities we serve in order to secure and promote public safety and trust. Finally, principles of leadership should require that we be accountable to those communities in terms of our job performance and conduct.

In *Principle-Centered Leadership,* author Stephen R. Covey states that true leaders put service first:

> Those striving to be principle-centered see life as a mission, not as a career. . . . In effect, every morning they "yoke up" and put on the harness of service, thinking of others.

The motto of the Los Angeles County Sheriff's Department is "A Tradition of Service." "Service" is the operative word here, pointing to the reality of any law enforcement officer's primary mission and task—that "yoke of service" that can only be born with the officer's acknowledgment that the officer's institution will also bear the responsibility and accountability that come through true leadership.

Leroy D. Baca

Sheriff, County of Los Angeles

PREFACE

To meet and resolve the conflicts, issues, and challenges contemporary police officers encounter, radical rethinking and restructuring of the police service is necessary. Traditional incident-driven policing must be supplemented, and in some cases replaced, with proactive, problem-oriented policing. Furthermore, proactive policing and rapidly changing circumstances demand unprecedented police officer skills. Although great strides have been made in many police education and training arenas, particularly in the areas of cognitive and psychomotor skill development, affective competency development is woefully inadequate, even nonexistent in some police departments. Affective competencies include leadership skills as well as those associated with appropriate values, integrity, ethics, and a sense of morality, all of which are essential for police officers in the twenty-first century.

Leadership, Ethics, and Policing: Challenges for the Twenty-First Century addresses and stresses the need for ethical leadership competence for all police officers. Although the central theme of the book focuses primarily on leadership, the approach integrates theory and practice as it explores the concepts and principles of leadership as well as those of values, morality, and ethics, and their relationship to police work. This book also functions as a suggested guide for the creation of a police human resource selection and development strategy that will recruit and equip officers with essential ethical leadership competencies. The authors do not endorse nor do they promote any specific ethical leadership approach. Rather, the concepts and discussions presented in this work provide information that can be used by the reader to discover and develop a leadership style and an ethical orientation that meet individual and societal needs.

The ethical leadership principles presented in this book apply in virtually any situation, especially in policing and other criminal justice and public safety environments. Its content is also applicable to community-oriented government, an approach that views the citizen both as a customer and a participant. Therefore, this book is appropriate for non-police as well as police personnel. The book is essential reading for practitioners as well as students and can be used as a primary text in leadership and ethics-oriented courses or as a supplemental text in any police, criminal justice, or public safety course. The book is a critical ingredient in each step of leadership development for entry-level personnel. It is also appropriate for seasoned police professionals, individuals who are preparing for promotion, or any criminal justice or community-oriented government practitioner.

ORGANIZATION OF THE BOOK

Chapter 1 reintroduces the reader to Robert Peel's principles for policing and addresses the challenges facing the police service in the twenty-first century. Chapter 2 profiles the importance of, and presents an argument for, ethical leadership competence for all police officers. Chapter 3 presents concepts and dynamics of leadership. Included is an overview of leadership theory. Ethics, morality, and their relationship to leadership are the subject of Chapter 4. Definitions and the theoretical basis for ethics are presented along with explanations for the relationship among ethics and virtue, morality, choice, and professional conduct. Chapter 5 addresses policing as a profession. Emphasis is placed on the identification of unprofessional conduct as well as policies and procedures for prevention and correction of unethical conduct.

Chapter 6 is the first of four chapters devoted entirely to specific ethical leadership competencies. Chapter 6 focuses on the art, science, and skills associated with effective communication. Chapter 7 discusses the importance of motivation skills. Emphasis is placed on police officer attitudes, individual differences, behavioral assumptions, and motivating leadership styles. Chapter 8 addresses ethical decision making and problem solving. The reader is introduced to ethical decision-making concepts and problem-solving methodology. Chapter 9 completes the problem-solving cycle by addressing the competencies and mechanics of planning, implementation, organization, and evaluation.

Chapter 10 presents ethical leadership in the context of a policing environment. Emphasis is placed on the importance of ethics and leadership in community policing: the philosophy and strategy that address what policing is all about. Chapter 11 peers into the future, identifying some of the issues facing the police, and hopes to assist the reader in the creation of a vision for policing in the twenty-first century.

Each chapter begins with a set of learning objectives. Key terms and concepts are highlighted in the text and listed for review at the end of the chapter. Also included are discussion questions and scenario-based exercises.

ABOUT THE AUTHORS

Edwin Meese III Edwin Meese III holds the Ronald Reagan Chair in Public Policy at The Heritage Foundation, a Washington-based public policy research and education institution. He is also a Distinguished Visiting Fellow at the Hoover Institution, Stanford University, California, and a Distinguished Senior Fellow at The University of London's Institute of United States Studies. Mr. Meese also lectures, writes, and consults throughout the United States on a variety of subjects.

Mr. Meese served as Governor Ronald Reagan's Executive Assistant and Chief of Staff in California from 1969 through 1974 and as Legal Affairs Secretary from 1967 through 1968. Before joining Governor Reagan's staff in 1967, Mr. Meese served as Deputy District Attorney in Alameda County, California. From 1977 to 1981, Mr. Meese was a Professor of Law at the University of San Diego, where he served as Director of the Center for Criminal Justice Policy and Management. During this time he also served as Vice Chairman of California's Organized Crime Control Commission.

Mr. Meese supervised President-elect Ronald Reagan's transition effort following the November 1980 election. During the presidential campaign, he served as Chief of Staff and Senior Issues Advisor for the Reagan-Bush Committee. From January 1981 to February 1985, Mr. Meese held the position of Counselor to the President, the senior position on the White House Staff, where he functioned as the President's chief policy advisor.

Mr. Meese served as the 75th Attorney General of the United States from February 1985 to August 1988. As the Nation's Chief Law Enforcement Officer, he directed the U.S. Department of Justice and led international efforts to combat terrorism, drug trafficking and organized crime. As Attorney General and as Counselor, Mr. Meese was a member of the President's Cabinet and the National Security Council. He served as Chairman of the Domestic Policy Council and as Chair of the National Drug Policy Board.

In addition to his background as a lawyer, educator, and public official, Mr. Meese has been a business executive in the aerospace and transportation industry, serving as Vice President for Administration of Rohr Industries, Inc. in Chula Vista, California. He left Rohr to return to the practice of law, engaging in corporate and general legal work in San Diego County.

Mr. Meese is the author of *With Reagan: The Inside Story*, which was published by Regnery Gateway in June 1992, and is co-editor of *Making America Safer*, published in 1997 by The Heritage Foundation.

Mr. Meese is a graduate of Yale University and holds a law degree from the University of California at Berkeley. He is a retired Colonel in the United States Army Reserve. He is active in numerous civic and educational organizations and currently serves on the boards of the Landmark Legal Foundation, the Capital Research Center, and the National College of District Attorneys, and is the chairman of the governing board of George Mason University in Northern Virginia.

P. J. Ortmeier P.J. Ortmeier holds bachelor's and master's degrees in Criminal Justice and a Ph.D. in Educational Leadership with an emphasis in Public Safety Training and Development. He is a U.S. Army veteran, a former police officer, and served as the coordinator of a criminal justice program at a midwestern college for ten years. He has developed and implemented numerous courses and degree programs in law enforcement, corrections, and public safety. As a member of a California Commission on Peace Officer Standards and Training (POST) steering committee, Dr. Ortmeier participated in the creation of a plan to integrate leadership, ethics, and community policing concepts and skill development throughout the entire basic academy for entry-level peace officers.

Currently, Dr. Ortmeier is the Coordinator of the Administration of Justice Program at Grossmont College in El Cajon, California. He also holds teaching positions at California State University, San Marcos, The Union Institute and University, and Webster University in San Diego.

Dr. Ortmeier is the author of *Public Safety and Security Administration*, *Policing the Community: A Guide for Patrol Operations*, and *Security Management: An Introduction*, as well as several articles appearing in journals such as *The Police Chief*, *California Security*, *Police and Security News*, and *Security Management*. His writing focuses on professional career education, management, leadership, and competency development for public safety personnel.

Dr. Ortmeier is a member of the Academy of Criminal Justice Sciences, the American Society for Law Enforcement Training, the California Association of Administration of Justice Educators, and the American Society for Industrial Security. His current interests include the development of leadership skills and career education pathways for law enforcement and other public safety professionals.

ACKNOWLEDGMENTS

Although it would not be possible to thank all those who were involved in the development of this book, the authors wish to express appreciation to several individuals and organizations. Gratitude is extended to many friends at Prentice Hall: Executive Editor Frank Mortimer, Assistant Editor Sarah Holle, Executive Business Development Manager Ramona Sherman, Marketing Manager Tim Peyton, Production Liaison Barbara Cappuccio, and former Executive Editor Kim Davies for her patience, encouragement, and support. At Carlisle Production Services, thanks go to Production Manager Ann Imhof and copyeditor Julie Kennedy.

The authors greatly appreciate the helpful comments, suggestions, and valuable insights contributed by the manuscript reviewers: Lt. John Buckovich, Richmond Police Department, Richmond, VA; Vincent Benincasa, Hesser College, Concord, NH; Ellen Cohn, Florida International University, Miami, FL; Steve Egger, University of Springfield, Springfield, IL; George Coxey, Owens Community College, Perrysburg, OH; and Mike Grabowski, Prairie View University, Waller, TX. The authors are also deeply indebted to Los Angeles County Sheriff Leroy D. Baca for the Foreword, to Dorie Savage for her assistance with the creation of the illustrations, and to Elizabeth Reid for her coordination activities. Special thanks to the agencies and organizations that provided photographs: the New York Police Department, the Chicago Police Department, the Los Angeles Sheriff's Department, the San Diego Police Museum, the Portland, Oregon, Bureau of Police, and the Cobb County, Georgia, Police Department.

Leadership, Ethics, and Policing

Chapter 1

The Challenge for Modern Policing

Learning Objectives

After completing this chapter, the reader should be able to:

- describe Robert Peel's Principles of Policing and relate these principles to twenty-first-century policing.
- explain the imperative for change in modern policing.
- articulate the challenges facing the police service that emulate from the requirements of community policing, advancements in technology, and the need for professionalism and accountability.
- discuss and analyze the need for ethical leadership in policing.

Introduction

To effectively meet and overcome the issues and challenges that face the police in the twenty-first century, major rethinking (Goldstein, 1993) and restructuring of police services will be necessary. To accomplish their mission, police officers of all ranks must possess ethical leadership competence. Further, the traditional model of policing must be modified by a redefinition of the ways in which the police provide services to the public (Goldstein, 2001; Peak & Glensor, 2002). The basic police mission—to protect and serve—will not change. However, the culture and methodology in and through which police services are provided must change radically. Without substantive progress in defining the goals and priorities of the police service, the police mission will remain wedded to meaningless phrases (Fyfe, 1996). As fluid societal dynamics pose new challenges, the police must rise to meet new and ever-changing public service requirements. Many traditional policing strategies, in and of themselves, are no longer appropriate.

Some police administrators and their departments are pioneering new styles and concepts of policing. In many law enforcement agencies, innovation and change have been accompanied by a reduction in crime and the creation of safer communities. But the test of new ideas and increased effectiveness is determined by how they will permeate the police profession more broadly—throughout the thousands of police departments in the United States. More deeply, innovation and change must take place, not only at the command level but throughout the agency hierarchy to the line officer on the street.

To secure and maintain public support, which is an essential ingredient for police success, police agencies must strive to deploy high-quality personnel who possess integrity and leadership skills. Resistance to change must also be overcome if the police are to keep pace with changing demographics and the challenges posed by new problems. The police themselves are in the best position to orchestrate new policing philosophies and strategies to meet twenty-first century challenges and requirements. However, to accomplish this, police officers of all ranks must possess ethical leadership skills as well as technical competence.

PRINCIPLES OF POLICING

Peel's Principles

It is perhaps ironic that while strategies, management systems, and operating mechanisms may change, some basic doctrines remain the same. **Sir Robert Peel,** the founder of modern policing, established nine "Principles of Policing," when he organized the London Metropolitan Police in 1829. Peel's principles are still relevant today and have gained even greater validity as the ideas of community policing spread throughout the United States. Peel decreed that:

1. The basic mission for which police exist is to prevent crime and disorder as an alternative to the repression of crime and disorder by military force and severity of legal punishment.
2. The ability of the police to perform their duties is dependent upon public approval of police existence, actions, behavior, and the ability of the police to secure and maintain public respect.
3. The police must secure the willing cooperation of the public in voluntary observance of the law to be able to secure and maintain public respect.
4. The degree of cooperation of the public that can be secured diminishes, proportionately, the necessity for the use of physical force and compulsion in achieving police objectives.

5. The police seek and preserve public favor, not by catering to public opinion, but by constantly demonstrating absolutely impartial service to the law, in complete independence of policy, and without regard to the justice or injustice of the substance of individual laws; by ready offering of individual service and friendship to all members of the society without regard to their race or social standing; by ready exercise of courtesy and friendly good humor; and by ready offering of individual sacrifice in protecting and preserving life.
6. The police should use physical force to the extent necessary to secure observance of the law or to restore order only when the exercise of persuasion, advice, and warning is found to be insufficient to achieve police objectives; and police should use only the minimum degree of physical force that is necessary on any particular occasion for achieving a police objective.
7. The police at all times should maintain a relationship with the public that gives reality to the historic tradition that the police are the public and that the public are the police; the police are the only members of the public who are paid to give full-time attention to duties that are incumbent on every citizen in the interest of the community welfare.
8. The police should always direct their actions toward their functions and never appear to usurp the powers of the judiciary by avenging individuals or the state, or authoritatively judging guilt or punishing the guilty.

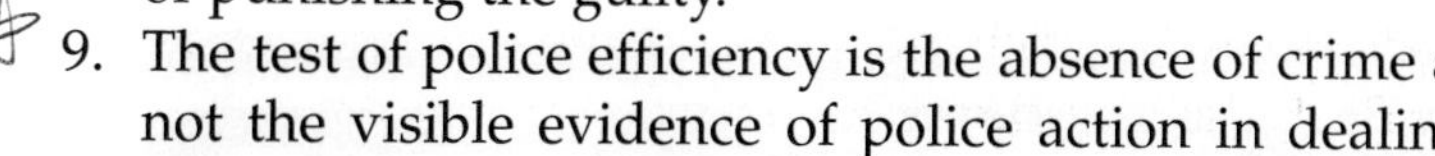

9. The test of police efficiency is the absence of crime and disorder, not the visible evidence of police action in dealing with them (Lee, 1901).

Peel's efforts led to the passage of the London Metropolitan Police Act in 1829, creating the first recognizable police force.
Sir Robert Peel (1788-1850)

The Modern Application of Peel's Principles

Reviewing Sir Robert Peel's nine principles of policing, almost two centuries later, reveals that the principles still form the foundation of policing and particularly modern concepts of police-community relations. Peel viewed the police mission as the *prevention* of crime and disorder. Success of police agencies, therefore, should be measured in terms of safer communities (the absence of crime and disorder), not merely the number of arrests made or traffic citations issued (the visible evidence of police action). This fundamental maxim is consistent with the relationship that should exist, according to Peel, between the police and the citizens they serve. His references to the need for "public approval of police action" and for "securing the willing cooperation of the public in voluntary observance of the law" are the basis for today's version of successful police-community relationships.

Peel's belief in the citizenry's responsibility for crime control and public safety ("the historic tradition that the police are the public and that the public are the police . . . ") is the very foundation of neighborhood participation in community policing. Finally, the mandate that police use force only when absolutely necessary, and in a proportionately appropriate manner, is not only essential to the previous themes, but is directly relevant to one of the most serious problems faced by many law enforcement agencies today. In short, the extent to which Peel's principles are followed by modern police departments can serve as a barometer of successful police-citizen relationships and the respect and cooperation that is received from the public the police serves.

THE CHANGE IMPERATIVE

The **change imperative** alters lives, transforms societies, and creates enourmous leadership challenges for the police. While certain principles, such as those set forth by Robert Peel, are enduring, a powerful mandate for change still exists. Tom Peters, one of America's leading management experts, wrote that change is the only constant in the contemporary world of public and private organizations. Further, he stated that change is not a strong enough word because the acceleration in the pace and scope of change makes what one does and how one works the subjects of nothing less than a revolution. The ability to respond and adapt to change in society, and to utilize change as a constructive force, increasingly makes the difference between success and failure (Peters, 1994).

People and organizations change through two non-mutually exclusive processes. In many cases, surprising and, sometimes, abrupt chaotic events and circumstances create a need for change. Alternatively, other situations involve an evolutionary process through which change occurs gradually over time. In scientific circles, the former process is often referred to as complexity theory while the latter is referred to as evolutionary theory. Both theories apply to how change occurs. Successful people and organizations exhibit superior performance when they are able to combine both processes to continuously reinvent themselves (Brown & Eisenhardt, 1998). For example, police officers must react quickly and instinctively in complex crisis situations. This is illustrative of complexity change theory in action. Police organizations, on the other hand, evolve gradually. The gradual shift from traditional to community policing is an example of evolutionary change theory in action. Thus, some change must involve an evolutionary process (Ford, Boles, Plamondon, & White, 2000).

Change in modern society poses particular problems for the police service, which traditionally has experienced difficulty in keeping pace with new developments in the social, economic, and political conditions of the citizenry it serves (Earle, 1988). In the three decades from 1950 through the 1970s, extensive change characterized most communities in America. Increased urbanization, dramatically expanding crime rates, significant demographic change, and inner-city deterioration were all part of this societal turbulence. But conventional methods of policing changed little during this period, despite the increased threats to public safety. The typical police response was often reactive and bureaucratic—concentrating on methods and procedures, with little imaginative or strategic thinking to affect results. Management and efficiency received more attention than leadership and effectiveness. Such inflexibility can block creativity (Harris, 2002).

Change presents opportunity (Harr & Hess, 2003). Beginning in the latter half of the 1980s, new concepts of police leadership began to be explored and old concepts were resurrected. The exploration and resurrection turned problems into opportunities and obstacles into challenges. Imaginative experimentation, increased acceptance of responsibility, as well as new relationships with the people served have provided the basis for a beneficial transformation in policing that extended into and will progress throughout the twenty-first century.

Three major areas of change signify this potential for improvement: community policing, technological progress, and professionalization and accountability. Together these phenomena provide the foundation for a new style of leadership in policing that can and will permeate the entire police service, from the top echelons of police management, through the various levels of command and supervision, to—perhaps most importantly—the officers on the street who come into daily contact with individual citizens and the neighborhoods in which citizens live.

Community Policing

As the crime rate throughout the nation continued to rise from the 1960s until the early 1980s and as deteriorating social conditions and urban strife increasingly threatened ordinary citizens, all aspects of the criminal justice process came under closer scrutiny. State and local authorities, legislative and judicial bodies, citizen groups, and national commissions asked serious questions about why governments at all levels were failing in their primary responsibility: to protect the lives and property of their citizens. In the 10 years between 1965 and 1975 no less than five major national studies involved assessments of the state of policing. The studies emanated from the President's Commission on Law Enforcement and the Administration of Justice (1965–1967), the National Advisory Commission on Civil Disorders (1968), the National Advisory Commission on the Causes and Prevention of Violence (1969), the President's Commission on Campus Unrest (1970), and the National Advisory Commission on Criminal Justice Standards and Goals (1971–1973) (Goldstein, 1990; Schmalleger, 2001; Senna & Siegel, 2001).

These, and other studies that continued over the next two decades, came to the same conclusion: the traditional model of policing that had grown up since the 1950s, which involved police officers riding in cars, removed from day-to-day contact with citizens, responding to radio calls after a crime had been committed, and dealing primarily with crime victims and criminals, was not a satisfactory means of dealing with either the crime problem or the public safety needs of citizens living and working in their unsafe neighborhoods (Goldstein, 2001; Peak & Glensor, 2002). As one police expert described the situation, the police devoted most of their resources to responding to calls instead of acting on their own initiative to prevent or reduce community crime and disorder problems. As a result, the rank-and-file officer's time and talent was not being used effectively. At the same time, the police were neglecting the community itself as a major resource with enormous potential for problem identification and resolution (Goldstein, 1990). Other scholars began making similar points in their communities (Moore & Stephens, 1991; Scott, 2000). As this thinking became more prevalent, and as far-sighted law enforcement executives and criminal justice scholars came together to explore new methods of responding to the challenges of crime, disorder, and public safety, what has been described as a quiet revolution began to reshape policing in America (Kelling, 1988).

Although there is no single, universally accepted model of policing (Cohen, 1996), the police service is becoming more community-oriented. Under a variety of names—strategic policing, problem-oriented policing, and neighborhood policing, among others—police agencies are applying **community policing** concepts to reinvigorate old ideals and develop new methods to better satisfy the demands and needs of the citizens they serve. In the course of the self-examination and creative thinking that is taking place, fundamental questions have been raised about the basic purpose and responsibilities of the police, the capabilities they possess, the types of contributions they can make to society, the optimum methods of their organization and deployment, and the relationship that they have with the communities that employ them. In contrast to a philosophy of business as usual, police executives sense the need to redeploy the resources and authority entrusted to them in hopes that their organizations will provide greater value for society (Moore & Trojanowicz, 1988; Newton, 2002).

While many different labels have been applied to community policing and a variety of innovative organizational and procedural models have been initiated to implement it, virtually all have two essential principles in common: a primary focus on community engagement and problem solving (Community Policing Consortium, 1994); and a more effective use of line police officers, relying on their creativity and expertise, and involving them more closely and directly with the public (Goldstein, 2001; Spelman & Eck, 1987).

Although some suggest that implementation of community policing can be problematic (Crank, 1998; Crank & Caldero, 2000; Klockars, 1991; Manus, 2002; Mastrofski & Worden, 1991), comprehensive community policing activities can achieve legitimate community and societal goals. Critical to the success of community policing as democracy in action is the need to gain the support of traditional rank-and-file officers (Crank & Caldero, 2000). Additionally, agencies must deploy police officers who possess the requisite ethical orientation as well as critical thinking, problem solving, and leadership skills necessary to engage law-abiding citizens and

Community policing attempts to reconnect the police with the citizens they serve.
Photo courtesy of Los Angeles Sheriff's Department

assist them with the identification of, and the creation of solutions to, problems that plague individual communities (Goldstein, 1990, 2001; Haberfeld, 2002; Meese, 1993; Meese & Kurz, 1993; Ortmeier, 1996, 1997, 2002; Peak & Glensor, 2002). Community policing represents a new vision of the role of the police in a democratic society (Skolnick, 1994).

Advancements in Technology

Nowhere has the acceleration of change been more pronounced than in the field of technology. **Technological advancements** in computers, communications, medicine, genetics, transportation, and numerous other areas related to policing has been so rapid and pervasive that it provides tremendous opportunities for improvement in virtually every aspect of crime prevention, control, and investigation. Likewise, similar technological changes in the rest of society will affect both criminals and law-abiding citizens, thus having a direct impact on how police officers carry out their duties. Cybercrime through the use of the Internet, computer crime involving theft and fraud, electronic finance, global mobility, and digitized communications, all present new opportunities for criminals and new risks for society (Lyman, 2002; Peak & Glensor, 2002; Ramsey, 2002; Tafoya, 1991).

Biosensors, lasers, nonlethal weapons technology, computerized information and identification systems, bionic surveillance equipment, and behavior-altering drugs offer great promise to crime fighters (Muraskin & Roberts, 2002). The police must learn to apply technology correctly and ensure that the use of technology does not separate the police from the communities they serve (A LEN interview with Police Chief Mark A. Kroeker of Portland Ore., 2002).

Early police communications centers were primitive by today's standards.
Photo courtesy of San Diego Police Museum

Police communications centers became more sophisticated during the mid-20th Century.
Photo courtesy of San Diego Police Museum

Modern police communications centers incorporate computer technology.
Photo courtesy of San Diego Police Museum

How police agencies respond to technological advancements will mark the test of effective leadership, both in utilizing constructively the advantages to law enforcement presented by technology (i.e., crime analysis and DNA profiling) and in coping with its misuse by the criminal element and the law enforcement community itself (National Commission on the Future of DNA Evidence, 2000). Although new crime prevention and suppression tools created through technological advancements can enhance justice system personnel effectiveness, the same tools expand the potential for abuse. Invasions to privacy, for example, must be prevented and civil rights must be insulated from the misuse of technology (Muraskin & Roberts, 2002).

Strategic thinking and innovative conceptualization are the hallmarks of the type of leadership needed to use technology effectively and appropriately. Some futurists describe such imaginative planning as thinking outside the box. Noted management expert Peter Drucker wrote dramatically in the *Harvard Business Review* that every organization has to prepare for the abandonment of everything it does (Drucker, 1992). People are living in an age of social transformation (Drucker, 1994). Tom Peters described it in even more vivid terms. He stated that the world is turning upside down. This upheaval is of the once-every-two-centuries sort. The technology revolution is speeding up to coincide with the arrival of the global village. And, there is no place to hide, no place in which one can sit this one out (Peters, 1992).

Early police radio cars were not technologically advanced.
Photo courtesy of San Diego Police Museum

Police radio car communications systems were improved during the 1960s and 1970s.
Photo courtesy of San Diego Police Museum

Modern police vehicles are equiped with two-way radios, mobile data computers (MDCs), mobile data terminals (MDTs), cellular phones, and global positioning systems (GPS).
Photo courtesy of San Diego Police Museum

Such proclamations may sound strange to police officers and agency chief executives who have spent two decades or more hearing about how things have been done a certain way, but the predictions of Drucker and Peters more accurately reflect the mind-set of many of the citizens and community leaders who will be evaluating the performance of the police officer and the officer's agency. Indeed, successful law enforcement agencies are already demonstrating how to harness technology for their own use and are working to neutralize its exploitation at the hands of the criminal (Boni & Kovacich, 2000; Coleman, 1994; Global crime cartels are tech savvy, 2000; Muraskin & Roberts, 2002; Thurman, Zhao, & Giacomazzi, 2001). The appropriate and effective use of information technology, automated identification devices, mobile computer and communication systems, and other modern technological developments will necessitate personal mastery in adaptation to changes in technology and will pose continuing ethical and leadership challenges to the modern police officer (Peak & Glensor, 2002).

Professionalism and Accountability

Professionalism has been the ostensible goal of policing for several decades, as expressed by police executives as well as police union and fraternal organizations (Byers, 2000; Goldstein, 1990, 2001; Kleinig, 1996b; Perez & Moore, 2002; Vollmer, 1936; Wilson, 1968). Law enforcement agencies have pursued the professionalism objective by trying to develop their technical skills through discipline, training, and apprenticeship, as well as through the use of increasingly sophisticated methods and equipment. While these strategies represent an important ingredient for developing police competence, they do not go beyond the effort required for virtually any complex trade or vocation. Despite the persistent rhetoric associated

Computers are used to analyze crime data, identify problems that require police attention, and deploy police resources efficiently and effectively.
Photo courtesy of Chicago Police Department

Centralized public safety command centers enhance communication, coordination, and decision making.
Photo courtesy of New York Police Department

with police professionalism, widespread achievement of professional status is very difficult for an occupation that lacks national cohesion (Kleinig & Zhang, 1993). The police claim professional status, although a common body of knowledge (an element of a profession) does not exist (Goldstein, 2001). Thus, more is required of the police to satisfy the developing philosophy and strategies of modern policing and to meet the heightened expectations of the community that is served.

Professionalism, then, as far as the police service is concerned, focuses on the values that the profession must adopt, the status of the officers in the organization and the community, and the manner in which the police are held accountable for their professional performance. It is a matter of self-image and of community perception. The commitment to constitutional and legal values, to mutual respect, and to service to the community, combined with self-reliance and self-motivation, are the indication of an authentic police professional (Meese, 1993; Meese & Moffit, 1997).

The issue of police **accountability,** as an aspect of professionalism, took on new meaning during the 1990s, initially due to the experience of New York City under the leadership of Police Commissioner William J. Bratton. From 1993 to 1996, reported criminal incidents decreased by nearly 50 percent. One significant factor in this crime reduction was that police leadership accepted responsibility for doing something about crime conditions in the city (Parshall-McDonald & Greenberg, 2002). This was not always the case. Somehow, in the 1960s and in the increasingly permissive society of the 1970s, the police were excused from having any responsibility for the prevention of crime. Many experts began to proclaim that too many causes of crime were beyond the control of police. How could the police be held accountable for preventing crime when so many of its causes were beyond the control of the police? (Bratton, 1997).

Through changes in organization, strategy, and management—but particularly by accepting the fact that the police department could, and should, take action to prevent and reduce crime, New York City reduced its crime rate and provided an example for police departments throughout the nation. By using computer technology to develop a multifaceted computer-driven crime statistics **(CompStat)** operations management model, local precinct commanders were held accountable for crime conditions within the boundaries of their commands (Parshall-McDonald & Greenberg, 2002). They and their officers were given greater flexibility in the use of resources, were encouraged to try new initiatives, and were required to regularly explain their strategies and the results they produced.

As this type of professionalism and accountability is adopted by other police agencies across the United States, it becomes established as an accepted practice of modern police leadership (Jones & Carlson, 2001; Lyman, 2002; Walker, 2001; Whisenand & Ferguson, 2002). Yet, as the police pursue the common good, they must be ever mindful of civil rights and temper their actions to ensure legal and ethical practices. The nature of policing constantly places officers in situations in which good ends can be achieved through illegal and unethical means (Crank & Caldero, 2000; Klockars, 1991). Therefore, officers must remember that police work involves broad values concerning how people treat one another. Traditional management principles provide little guidance in such circumstances (Crank, 1998). This is a genuine dilemma that requires effective ethical leadership skills at the street level as well as in the command structure.

THE ETHICAL LEADERSHIP CHALLENGE

Rapid change is the most striking feature of contemporary society. Many, if not most, strategic initiatives (such as crime reduction) fail to account for the need to manage change. Strategies fail because their creators overemphasize the ability to predict the future and underemphasize the importance of executing, with flexibility in mind, the strategy that is chosen. Given the pervasiveness of rapid change, the key to strategic success involves managing change. Success occurs in a rapidly changing environment when people and organizations reinvent themselves continuously to meet new challenges and redefined goals. At the most progressive level, managing change is about leading change. Rather than reacting to change (i.e., an increase in gang activity), progressive leaders create change (proactively seek out ways to prevent gang activity from occurring). This means that progressive people and organizations not only react to and anticipate change, but they are ahead of or even create the rules that dictate change. The best performers are those that lead change in their personal and professional lives. As leaders, progressive people establish the rhythm and pace for change and they create the environment for positive outcomes to occur. Managing change is not easy. The direction of change is often very uncertain. Neither can participants focus exclusively on change or wait for the future to unfold. Rather, participants must balance preservation of the status quo with future demands (Brown & Eisenhardt, 1998).

The dynamic nature of modern society will continue to confront the police and establish the intellectual climate within which the police must operate. Critical issues facing the police as well as changes in philosophy, organization and practice (community policing), changes in tangible resources (technology), and changes in expectations of performance (professionalism and accountability) establish parameters for analysis, planning, and decision making. These new dimensions for policing create an **ethical leadership challenge** and require effective ethical leadership skills for the twenty-first century.

The importance of ethical leadership development for all police officers cannot be overemphasized. A review of the literature, as well as research and expert opinion regarding attitudes, behaviors, and capabilities required of police officers, suggest that ethical leadership skills are absolutely essential (Anderson, 2000; Baca, 2002; Baker, 2000; Goldstein, 1990; Haberfeld, 2002; Jones & Carlson, 2001; Kokkelenberg, 2001; Meese, 1993; Meese & Kurz, 1993; Ortmeier, 1995, 1996, 1997, 2002; Pollock, 1998; Stevens, 2002; Vinzant & Crothers, 1998; Walker, 2001). However, police officers are not the only individuals who must change the way they think. Police organizations, governance structures, and the public must reconceptualize the role of the police in general and the role of the individual frontline police officer in particular.

To fully appreciate the benefits of line officer ethical leadership skill development, police organizations themselves must reorient their understanding of, and commitment to, line officers. Each police officer must be treated as a responsible decision maker, not simply as one who implements agency policy. As former New York City Police Commissioner William Bratton stated, "Police work is by nature decentralized and discretionary. The cop in the field, the front-line supervisor, the precinct commander—these are the real decision makers in day-to-day police work" (Bratton & Andrews, 1999, pp. 14–27).

Additionally, police organizations must carefully reconsider recruitment standards. Although police recruits are not generally better equipped than the rest of the population to make difficult and complicated decisions (Cohen & Feldberg, 1991), police agencies must carefully recruit and select individuals who possess or can develop ethical leadership skills. After new officers are selected, they should undergo extensive formal and experiential training that emphasizes values, ethics, and diagnostic skills that assist with the identification of the peculiar characteristics of a given situation, the articulation and attainment of goals, and the ability to alter behaviors to achieve desired outcomes. Many regions of the United States have implemented or developed plans to integrate the study of leadership and ethics into basic as well as advanced police officer training programs (California State Commission on Peace Officer Standards and Training, 2002; Massachusetts Criminal Justice Training Council and the Regional Community Policing Institute of New England, 1997). Some college criminal justice programs already have leadership and ethics courses in place or plan to offer courses on these subjects (California Association of Administration of Justice Educators, 2002; California State Commission on Peace Officer Standards and Training, 2001; Jones & Carlson, 2001; Komives, Lucas, & McMahon, 1998).

Police organizations must redefine and redesign performance evaluation processes. Traditional police performance measures emphasize adherence to rules and the accomplishment of discrete tasks. While important, traditional evaluation measures may prove inadequate. As leaders, police officers are best evaluated by determining the appropriateness of the goals they set and the steps taken to achieve those goals (Fyfe, 1996; Goldstein, 1990, 1993, 2001).

Police organizations must also change how line officers are supervised. With the acquisition of leadership skills, line officers and their supervisors must change their expectations. Supervisors should expect that subordinates can and will make appropriate decisions and assume responsibility for their actions. Subordinates can expect that supervisors recognize that the line officer is in a more direct vantage point to evaluate and respond to situations and problems (Vinzant & Crothers, 1998). A leadership culture must permeate the entire organization. Officers must possess the skills necessary to lead and supervise themselves (Baca, 2002). Finally, agencies must reconsider the nature and types of rewards given to police officers. Recognition of a job well done as well as the expression of appreciation for a police officer's contributions as a public servant are critical to officer morale and job satisfaction (Vinzant & Crothers, 1998).

As the result of the very nature of rapid change in the twenty-first century, the police are forced to confront and view policing philosophy, strategy, and tactics from radically different perspectives. In addition to the need to deploy highly educated, quality personnel, the police community will be required to develop greater expertise, face new and emerging threats, participate with global policing networks, and become involved with revolutionary changes besieging the workplace as well as society (Anderson, 2000; Peak & Glensor, 2002; Tafoya, 1991). The social problems that threaten the character of a democracy will increase, not decrease (Goldstein, 1993).

Finally, attitudes toward the police as government workers must also change if the full positive impact of police leadership development is to be realized. Society holds contradictory views on police discretion and decision making (Cohen & Feldberg, 1991; Fyfe, 1996; Kleinig, 1996a). Some people suggest that discretionary decision making, which is consistent with leadership ideals, is inconsistent with the role of bureaucratic government employees in a democratic society. Given the potential for abuse, it is easy for some to argue in favor of limiting discretion rather than expanding it and viewing it as a welcome by-product of ethical and creative leadership activity. To change these basic assumptions, the police must work to change the notion, well-established in popular culture, that government workers are often incompetent and that government itself is the subject of waste and abuse. Political leaders can use their power of persuasion to change attitudes and support new concepts and perceptions of who the police are and what they do (Vinzant & Crothers, 1998). The police, as a component of community-oriented government, can promote a vision through which citizens are viewed as customers and the police view themselves as service providers (Peak & Glensor, 2002).

SUMMARY

Major rethinking and some restructuring of police agencies is necessary to meet and overcome issues and challenges faced by the police in the twenty-first century. The police mission will not change. However, the police culture and methods for providing services must change. As a supplement to, or as a total replacement for, traditional policing methods, community policing will become the norm.

The nine principles of policing, proclaimed by Sir Robert Peel in the founding of the London Metropolitan Police, are still relevant today, but must be adapted to modern conditions and requirements. Peel's emphases on a constructive relationship between the police and the citizens, on the responsibility of the public for crime prevention and control, and on limiting the use of force are the bases for enlightened police leadership today.

The change imperative will require that the police restructure operations through community policing, incorporate and use more technology, and demonstrate professionalism and accountability. Furthermore, to meet the challenges of the twenty-first century, all police officers must demonstrate effective and ethical leadership competence.

KEY TERMS AND CONCEPTS

Define, describe, or explain the importance of each of the following:

accountability
change imperative
community policing
CompStat
ethical leadership challenge
professionalism
Sir Robert Peel
technological advancements

DISCUSSION QUESTIONS AND EXERCISES

1. Review the nine principles of policing, as developed by Sir Robert Peel in 1829. How does each of Peel's principles apply in the twenty-first century?
2. How do people and organizations change?
3. What problems do societal changes pose for the police service? How should the police respond to these problems?
4. Discuss how changes in police organization and deployment (community policing), advancements in technology, and the need for professionalism and accountability affect the police service.
5. Is ethical leadership a challenge to police officers? Explain.

CHAPTER 2

THE IMPORTANCE OF ETHICAL LEADERSHIP

LEARNING OBJECTIVES

After completing this chapter, the reader should be able to:

- define ethical leadership.
- articulate the importance and need for ethics and leadership skills in policing.
- explain why ethical leadership is every police officer's responsibility.
- describe the role of values, discretion, and goal accomplishment in policing.
- distinguish between leadership qualities and competencies.
- analyze the qualities as well as the competencies of a police officer as a leader.
- recognize essential police leadership competencies.

INTRODUCTION

Competence as ethical leaders equips police officers with the tools necessary to face twenty-first-century issues and challenges (Anderson, 2000; Ford, Boles, Plamondon, & White, 2000; Haberfeld, 2002; Meese, 1993; Meese & Kurz, 1993; Ortmeier, 1995; 1996, 1997, 2002; Whisenand & Ferguson, 2002). Leadership skills and ethical behavior are essential to policing a democratic society. The police have a duty to serve the law as well as the public and, since the police possess tremendous authority over an individual, officers have a responsibility to perform their duties in an ethical manner. Coupled with effective leadership ability, high moral and ethical behavior places the police in the position of a powerful force to secure and maintain public safety and order.

Ethical leadership is not restricted to a few with rank and privilege (Johnson, 2001). On the contrary, sharing command is inevitable in a democratic society and it is necessary to accommodate the ever-changing demographics and expectations of society. Ethical leadership skills are especially critical for the frontline officer, the person responsible for implementing police strategy consistent with social order expectations. Line officers are forced to assume leadership roles whether they want to or not. The police officer on the street necessarily exercises broad discretion and is the public official with whom most citizens have direct contact (Cohen, 1996; Cohen & Feldberg, 1991; Crank & Caldero, 2000; Fyfe, 1996; Goldstein, 1990, 2001; Kleinig, 1996a, 1996b). Appropriately empowering all police officers with ethical leadership skills enhances the public's perception of the police and enables officers to assist with the creation of solutions to community problems (Stevens, 2002). Successful people and organizations of the future will be those who take personal growth and leadership development seriously (Anderson, 2000). Through appropriate education, training, and experience in leadership, ethics, and policing, the ethical police officer can lead others to set high standards, and improve the quality of life for the police practitioner, the citizen-consumer, and the community.

WHY ETHICAL LEADERSHIP?

Role of Values and Discretion

Progress in any profession is based on the ability to predict and control. But predictions are influenced by assumptions based on theory. Thus, theory and practice are inseparable. Control involves selective adaptation to human nature rather than attempting to control human nature itself. Yet, control implies and raises reasonable apprehensions about possible manipulation and exploitation of people (Kleinig & Zhang, 1993). Therefore, professionals pursue objectives and goals only to the extent that human values are preserved and protected. Professionalism implies that the professional will act ethically in pursuit of objectives and goals (McGregor, 1960).

Freedom of choice makes ethical considerations—the judgments about whether human behavior is right or wrong—an important element of leadership (Johnson, 2001). Thus, leadership involves values. Because it has a moral dimension, leadership demands that anyone who assumes a leadership role develop an awareness of how one's values and ethics define leadership (Northouse, 2001). At its foundation, policing involves values that govern how people are treated (Crank, 1998). Furthermore, due to their status as representatives of the people (government), police officers assume a leadership role. As such, officers can use information regarding values and the theories and practices of leadership and ethics to better understand themselves, strengthen their leadership capabilities, motivate and influence others appropriately, and do the right thing at the right time (Lyman, 2002).

Legislators possess the authority to define behavior as criminal activity and prescribe a penalty for the activity's commission. The rationale for the creation of a criminal law is usually based on a public safety issue. However, legislators also employ moral definitions when deciding what types of behavior might be considered criminal. Certainly, arguments in favor of laws prohibiting behavior defined as murder, burglary, and robbery use traditional moral definitions as well as public safety as their foundation. Some laws, however, are based primarily on legislative definitions of morality. For example, laws prohibiting behavior in the form of prostitution, liquor sales on Sunday, and gambling often have morality as their primary source for legitimacy (Pollock, 1998).

As part of the executive branch of government, the police are responsible for preventing crime and disorder and enforcing legislatively enacted statutes. With civil authority granted to them by the people, the police enforce society-wide rules over the dissent of individuals (Reinman, 1990). Yet, as society's peacekeepers and law enforcers, the police can exercise a considerable amount of discretion to carry out their mission (Cohen & Feldberg, 1991). Thus, the police, through the exercise of discretion, decide who to stop and cite for a traffic violation, who to investigate, and who to arrest. As professional law enforcement officers, the police also have a duty to serve the law, support constitutional safeguards such as due process and equal protection, and serve the public. Due process protects individuals from erroneous government deprivation of life, liberty, or property, and equal protection provisions protect against arbitrary and discriminatory use of authority (Pollock, 1998). As public servants, the police are supposed to be service-oriented, objective, accountable, democratic, and respectable. Although discretion expands and contracts depending on the situation, police officers possess the ability to wield more discretion in situations on a daily basis than any other justice professional. Further, because police officers are human beings with enormous discretionary power (Cohen, 1996; Cohen & Feldberg, 1991; Fyfe, 1996; Goldstein, 1990, 2001; Kleinig, 1996a, 1996b; Meadows, 2002; Pollock, 1998; Souryal, 1992), they may be tempted to take advantage of their position, show favoritism, and demonstrate less than the highest standard of exemplary behavior. Therefore, the police must be sensitive to ethical issues. As professionals charged with the enforcement of the law and maintenance of public order, police officers must exercise enlightened moral judgment and high ethical standards, especially as judgment and ethics relate to discretionary decision making, use of force, constitutional due process, and equal protection (Lyman, 2002; Massachusetts Criminal Justice Training Counsel & the Regional Community Policing Institute of New England, 1997; Ortmeier, 2002; Pollock, 1998; Whisenand & Ferguson, 2002). Values-led ethical leadership in policing maximizes effort by integrating prized community values into an agency's mission, vision, strategy, operating plans, and services (Whisenand & Ferguson, 2002).

A Means to Accomplish Goals

Whether or not frontline police behavior is appropriate and legitimate depends, to a certain extent, on the goals officers are expected to achieve as well as the standards by which they are evaluated. In many situations, the police mission is reduced to a meaningless phrase—"to protect and serve"—because goals and priorities for the police are absent or not clearly defined (Fyfe, 1996). Additionally, politicians, community leaders, citizens, academics, as well as the police themselves often set goals and subsequently criticize the police if those goals are not achieved. The critics may fail to recognize that the police work in an environment that is politically, socially, and practically problematic. Thus, the police may be doomed to fail from the start, particularly when officers function without appropriate ethical leadership skills (Ford, Boles, Plamondon, & White, 2000; Vinzant & Crothers, 1998).

Police officers are forced to confront some of the most critical and difficult problems facing society. In the course of a single work shift, an officer may be faced with people in crisis, personal injuries, criminal suspects, traffic collisions and violators, domestic violence situations, a natural or environmental disaster, lost or abused children, juvenile delinquents, and angry citizens (California State Commission on Peace Officer Standards and Training, 1998). Not only is there great variability and unpredictability with the situations faced by the officer (Goldstein, 1993, 2001), the situations are often multifaceted and emotionally charged. Thus, the police officer is forced to make critical, sometimes life-or-death decisions that are complicated, situational, discretionary, and laden with the possibility of negative repercussions for and from the officer and people involved, the agency, coworkers, the community, the courts, the law, and the media. Within this context, police officer decisions are made in an environment containing a multitude of direct and indirect influences that shape what officers do and how they do it (Cohen & Feldberg, 1991; Crank & Caldero, 2000; Goldstein, 1993, 2001; Kleinig, 1996b; Klockars, 1991; Souryal, 1992; Vinzant &

Crothers, 1998). Ethical leadership skills provide the foundation for effective integration of discretionary decision making, legitimacy of action, and accountability (Lyman, 2002; Whisenand & Ferguson, 2002).

Despite the problems associated with defining what ethical leadership is, the concepts and skills of ethics and leadership provide a compelling and useful framework for understanding and facing the challenges of the line police officer. First, ethical leadership skills encompass a wide variety of behaviors that, when exercised appropriately, allow the leader to employ numerous approaches to accomplishing goals. Second, concepts of ethical leadership demand consideration of values and ethics and provide a link between an officer's authority and power, and the legitimacy of the officer's actions. Third, ethical leadership concepts and models provide standards by which police officer actions can be evaluated. Fourth, the language of leadership and ethics present powerful and positive tools and address the role of the police officer within the larger context of the community and society. Fifth, leadership and ethics theories provide a useful framework for understanding and directing the exercise of police discretion. Accordingly, police officers are required to perform ethically and demonstrate different types of leadership in diverse situations (Vinzant & Crothers, 1998).

The exercise of discretion is appropriate when influenced by ideals in relation to a specific set of circumstances. The value of ethical leadership competence and skill development is not just in changing what police officers do but how they think about what they do. The acquisition and exercise of ethical leadership skills will help police officers to better conceptualize and articulate their activities in a complex world, assist them with defining their role in positive terms, enhance their sense of competence, and highlight the importance of what they do. Further, ethical leadership skills help police officers to understand the complex nature of their work, to redefine their self-images, and to demonstrate to other people the interconnectedness of law enforcement with other dimensions of the social governance system (Lyman, 2002; Whisenand & Ferguson, 2002).

WHO IS AN ETHICAL LEADER?

Ethical Leader Defined

An **ethical leader** is one who possesses a philosophical moral foundation upon which decisions and behavior are based. Without the foundation, behavior will fluctuate as circumstances and personal preferences change. An ethical leader is trustworthy and possesses good character, competence, and commitment. The ethical leader challenges the process, inspires shared vision, encourages and enables others, provides a model of appropriate behavior, and maintains accountability, personal perspective, and balance. Although imperfect, an ethical and credible leader aspires to demonstrate virtue in speech and action, publicly and privately, at all times. Moral authority is not established through publicity or speeches. Rather, ethical leadership is developed through consistent action and the development of a credible reputation, usually in a relatively small group or community. From the humble beginning in the small environment, the influence of ethical leadership can be multiplied. Mother Teresa was internationally known as a virtuous person, yet she rarely appeared in the media. Some politicians, on the other hand, spend an enormous amount of time, energy, and money in failed media attempts to establish their moral credibility (Hawkins, 2000).

Unethical leaders are deceitful. They deny having knowledge, withhold information followers need, use information for personal benefit only, violate rights of others, release information to the wrong people, and place followers in ethical binds. Unethical leaders are inconsistent, misplace and break loyalties, are irresponsible, and abuse privilege and power (Johnson, 2001).

The morally correct way to proceed is not always obvious in police work (Crank & Caldero, 2000). The conflict arising from ambiguous situations can be agonizing (Kleinig, 1996b). Politically motivated government officials, for example, may require the police to selectively enforce some laws while improperly ignoring others. Yet, the ethical leader avoids improper behavior while assuming additional responsibility for influencing the actions of others through example. In doing so, the police officer as an ethical leader is: committed to the law and professional standards of behavior, responsive and sensitive to changing circumstances and needs of others, and knowledgeable and skilled regarding trends and means for accomplishing a mission. Finally, the ethical leader avoids conflicts of interest and takes affirmative steps to encourage ethical behavior and to correct unethical behavior (Hellriegel, Jackson, & Slocum, 2002; Pollock, 1998).

The police are the first line of defense against tyranny and violations of constitutional and legal safeguards. Police officers take an oath to uphold and support the U.S. and state constitutions, and enforce laws fairly. Police behaviors, tactics, and strategies must be consistent with the oath, lest the officers betray the public's trust and the authority granted to them (the police) by the citizens of a society.

The role of leadership in maintaining ethical credibility cannot be overestimated nor can it be abdicated. Leaders must take preventive and corrective action toward misconduct and demonstrate a commitment to excellence. As ethical leaders, police officers should be intimately familiar with the moral (right versus wrong) dimensions of police work (Cohen & Feldberg, 1991) and should demonstrate ethical behavior (conform conduct to acceptable moral standards). An ethical person exhibits certain moral traits and bases behaviors, including decision making, on ethical principles. The traits most often associated with ethical leadership are honesty, trustworthiness, and integrity (Hellriegel, Jackson, & Slocum, 2002). The test for effective police officer leadership competence in the twenty-first century will remain focused on morality, integrity, and ethical behavior (California State Commission on Peace Officer Standards and Training, 2002; Cohen & Feldberg, 1991; Kleinig, 1996b; Ortmeier, 2002; Reiman, 1990).

Good character, values, and ethics form the foundation for competence as a leader. This foundation influences attitude, thought processes, decision making, and behavior, and guides an individual to do the right thing at the right time. Leaders have a heavy burden of responsibility. Without a firm ethical foundation, leaders cannot guide others (Baker, 2000; Hellriegel, Jackson, & Slocum, 2002).

Ethical Leadership Is Every Officer's Responsibility

The chief executive officer (CEO) of a police agency is probably the most important strategic initiator. Whether a sheriff, chief, superintendent, director, commissioner, or other person in charge of a police agency, the CEO plays a significant role in defining the organization's philosophy, values, vision, mission, and priorities. The CEO is instrumental in creating the climate conducive to successful change and positive outcomes. The CEO is in the best position to view the relationship between the police agency and the community as a whole, and to assist with the creation of a vision for the future.

Upper and middle managers (deputy chiefs, captains, lieutenants) should lead as well as manage. Rather than insulate themselves from line supervisors and officers, upper and middle managers should interact with subordinates, assisting the latter through mentoring, coaching, and team building. Upper and middle managers are in an excellent position to act as conduits, monitoring for and adjusting the pace of change. Some people are attracted to supervisory positions for the wrong reasons. They are attracted by the power and control that comes with a position of authority. However, true leadership is not so much the exercise of power as it is the empowerment of others. Leadership is service to others that requires tremendous commitment, energy, patience, humility, and selflessness.

Line supervisors (primarily sergeants) are in a pivotal leadership position to facilitate the achievement of goals. These supervisors help line personnel achieve accountability and performance objectives. It has been stated that the quality of police service to a community may be linked di-

The front line officer has the most contact with the public and is in the best position to directly impact the lives of the citizens.
Photo courtesy of Los Angeles Sheriff's Department

rectly to the quality of supervision. Line supervisors are in the best position to assume a leadership role in reviewing officer productivity and citizen contact, making recommendations for improvement and taking corrective action when appropriate (Baker, 2000).

Finally, regardless of the size of a police agency, the territory it covers, or the number of levels of authority or supervision, it is the line officer who has the most direct role in serving the mission of the agency. The line officer has the greatest contact with the citizenry and is in the best position to directly impact the lives of the people who are served. Thus, considerable training and education resources should be expended to develop ethical leadership competencies in police recruits as well as senior officers. Further, ethical leadership development should be viewed as a lifelong process, not an event (Anderson, 2000; Johnson, 2001; Kokkelenberg, 2001; Meese, 1993; Ortmeier, 1995, 1996, 1997, 2002; Stevens, 2002; Vinzant & Crothers, 1998).

ETHICAL LEADERSHIP DEVELOPMENT

Fear of crime, police responses to social unrest, and citizen perceptions of police effectiveness contribute to the rise or decline of community support for the police. Although experts in a study conducted in 1995 determined that police training and education programs do an excellent job of assisting police officers in the development of cognitive, procedural, and technical skills, these programs often do little to promote the development of essential nontechnical competencies and qualities such as effective judgment, leadership, and integrity, all of which improve police performance and help generate community support for the police (Ortmeier, 1996).

The rationale in support of ethical leadership competence for all police officers can be summarized as follows:

- A community receives the type of police service it supports (see also, Wilson, 1968).
- Community support is absolutely vital to successful law enforcement and this support is dependent upon a positive police public image (see also, Coffey, 1990).
- The police public image is dependent upon the public's confidence in the integrity and judgment of the police as well as the process and outcomes of human interaction between the individual police officer and citizens.
- Police behavior is determined not only by the physical and psychological dynamics of the nature of the work, but also by the preservice and in-service training police officers receive in basic academies, college classrooms, and by senior fellow officers on the street (Peak & Glensor, 2002). Simply stated, bad habits and bad attitudes—or their exemplary opposite—can be passed on from one generation of police officers to the next (Ortmeier, 1997).
- Most existing curricula in police academies, college-level criminal justice programs, even on-the-job training programs, generally lack the focus necessary to develop the affective skills required for development of a proper attitude and competence in communications, human relations, critical thinking, problem solving, leadership, and integrity, which are absolutely essential to success in contemporary law enforcement (As costs soar, questions of quality dog Mass. college for cops program, 2001; Brown, 2001; Haberfeld, 2002; Meese, 1993; Meese & Kurz, 1993; Ortmeier, 1995, 1996, 1997, 2002; Whisenand & Ferguson, 2002).
- To secure and retain the trust of the citizenry, police officers must maintain the highest standards of personal and professional conduct by demonstrating ethical leadership (Anderson, 2000; Meese, 1993; Ortmeier, 1995, 1996, 1997, 2002).

Ethical leadership skills are among the most important competencies required of a line police officer. Yet, leadership skill development is often reserved for the higher-level ranks in the police service. Many reasons for this phenomenon exist. One is the false assumption that the line officers simply follow the lead presented by their superiors. But experience demonstrates that this is not necessarily true. Considerable attention must be given to providing line officers with competencies, such as leadership, that traditionally have been associated with higher ranks (Carter, Sapp, & Stephens, 1989). Line officer leadership skills are not likely to develop without education and training. If leadership competencies are to emerge from within the police establishment, incentives must be developed that afford police officers the opportunity to acquire a broad-based education that supports leadership development (As costs soar, questions of quality dog Mass. college for cops program, 2001; Baro & Burlingame, 1999; California State. Community College Chancellor's Office, 1996; Carlon, 1999; Michelson & Maher, 1993; President's Commission on Law Enforcement and Administration of Justice, 1967; Scott, 1986; U.S. Congress, 1968). Police officers, particularly in a twenty-first-century policing environment, must develop leadership competencies to grasp a vision, transmit it, and help translate it into constructive action (Meese, 1993; Ortmeier, 1995, 1996, 1997, 2002; Souryal, 1981).

Although ethical leadership is a dynamic phenomenon requiring integration of numerous attributes, qualities, and skills, it is, essentially, a means to influence, mobilize, or motivate others to accomplish common goals (California State Commission on Peace Officer Standards and Training, 1990). Skolnick and Bayley (1986) reinforced the importance of leadership skills to the success of policing by stating that these skills are necessary to create a sense of purpose for police officers and for the operation of a police agency. This sense of purpose emphasizes civic responsibility, self-knowledge, and a global perspective (Green, 1988). Utilizing this sense of purpose, citizens should be viewed as customers and the police should be viewed as leaders providing a community service (Meese & Kurz, 1993).

With the passage of the Omnibus Crime Control and Safe Streets Act of 1968, literally billions of dollars were spent on law enforcement training and education. As a result, the United States witnessed a proliferation of college-level education programs for pre-service as well as in-service law enforcement personnel. Through the Law Enforcement Education Program (LEEP), funded by the 1968 legislation, the number of undergraduate criminal justice-related degree programs rose from 39 in 1967 to 376 in 1977 (Walker, 1983). The programs were established on the belief that a higher level of formal education would produce a police officer who was more responsive and accountable to the public, an officer who could deal more effectively with crime and thus improve the quality of life for American citizens.

Some have argued that there is no correlation between highly educated police officers and a reduction in crime rates, since the crime rate continued to increase at a rapid pace during the late 1960s and into the 1970s (U.S. Department of Justice, Federal Bureau of Investigation, 1997) while the LEEP program was in full operation. Some writers contend that a college education for police officers might actually be counterproductive (Carter, Sapp, & Stephens, 1989; Sherman & Bennis, 1977). This sentiment, however, was discounted by expert opinion and studies that discovered enhanced performance and more appropriate judgment is demonstrated by college-educated police officers (Brown, 2001; Meese & Kurz, 1993; Roberg, 1978; Vodicka, 1994). Furthermore, college-educated police officers tend to promote to higher ranks more rapidly than their counterparts without college degrees (Polk & Armstrong, 2001). Yet, many agencies are waiving college education requirements for recruits because of a limited applicant pool (NJSP gambles on the viability of its college degree requirement, 2000; Pressed for applicants, NYPD waives two-year college standard, 2000; Strapped for personnel, Portland kills four-year degree requirement for recruits, 2001).

In 1994, Congress passed, and the president signed, another multibillion dollar crime bill (U.S. Congress, 1994). Federal dollars were again budgeted for law enforcement training and education. However, several questions remain. Aside from technical training and education, how should these dollars have been spent? Do police training and education programs assist officers in the development of the nontechnical competencies, such as those associated with ethics and leadership, required of police officers in contemporary society? More specifically, which skills are required of the police so they may restore and improve public confidence and lead communities to identify and solve problems? (As costs soar, questions of quality dog Mass. college for cops program, 2001; Meese, 1993; Meese & Kurz, 1993; Ortmeier, 1995, 1996; Whisenand & Ferguson, 2002).

ETHICAL LEADERSHIP COMPETENCIES

Although the study of leadership originally focused on traits or inbred qualities that a person possessed since birth, today it is believed that leadership skills can be acquired or modified extensively through learning. These skills include competence to: keep communication channels open and functioning effectively; interact socially; solve problems; plan; initiate action; and accept responsibility. Such skills are not inherited, they are learned (Anderson, 2000; McGregor, 1960; Ortmeier, 1996, 2002). Also, critical to the success of the leader are skills in facilitation of team interaction, effective team problem solving, and training (Miskin & Gmelch, 1985), with substantial attention being paid to the ability to communicate (K. L. Clark, 1994).

More specifically, an effective and ethical leader is likely to demonstrate excellent communications and interpersonal skills. A highly rated leader is likely to be both relations-oriented and task-oriented, manage conflict successfully, and mobilize and direct individuals toward higher objectives (Bass, 1981). Bisesi (1983) suggested that successful leaders are willing to negotiate and have a high sense of organizational responsibility. Orton (1984) cited the importance of quality decision making, commitment, implementation, and the ability to employ situational strategies. The inability to communicate and relate to other individuals may lead to conflict or incompatibility between the leader and those who are led (Smith & Peterson, 1990).

A number of experts have discussed the motivational aspects of leadership. Motivational or person-oriented behaviors tend to promote follower satisfaction although they may not always contribute to group productivity (Bass, 1981). McGregor (1966) suggested that people already possess motivation and desire full responsibility. Yukl (1971) postulated that, whereas leader initiation increases subordinate task skill, leader consideration increases subordinate motivation. In turn, enhanced subordinate skill and motivation improve the subordinate's effectiveness.

Leadership competencies have also been addressed in terms of the ability to plan, organize, and set goals. Bennis (1961) suggested a revision in leadership theory to include participation in joint consultation between the leader and others to allow for integration of individual as well as organizational goals. Leaders must create clear-cut and measurable goals based on the advice from all elements of a community. Likert (1961) discovered that high-producing leaders make clear what the objectives are and give people freedom to complete the task. Argyris (1964) suggested that it is in an individual's nature to be self-directed and seek fulfillment through the exercise of initiative and responsibility. Hersey and Blanchard (1982) suggested that leadership, depending on the situation, involves goal setting, organizing, setting time lines, directing, and controlling.

Knickerbocker (1948) suggested that the functional relationship called leadership exists when a leader is perceived by a group as controlling the means for the satisfaction of their needs. Group members make contributions and continue to interact because the members find social exchange mutually rewarding (Homans, 1958). Changing the expectations for rewards changes the motivation of the individual or the group (Bass, 1960). Evans (1970) suggested that the leader can determine the follower's perception of the abundance of the rewards available. Scott (1977) emphasized positive reinforcement as a means of bringing out desired behavior.

CONTEMPORARY VIEWS ON LEADERSHIP COMPETENCIES

Studies have shown that a high-priority leadership attribute is that which relates to leadership skills or competencies (Kouzes & Posner, 1993). Leadership competencies should not be confused with **leadership qualities.** Although critical to effective and ethical leadership, qualities such as understanding, courage, compassion, respectfulness, and genuineness (Anderson, 2000) are difficult to measure by any objective standard. Competencies (skills), however, can be learned and competency acquisition and practice can be measured objectively (Stevens, 2002). Accordingly, contemporary authors often focus on **leadership competencies**—that is, the abilities to *do* things rather than *feel* things. The objective measurement standard is based on observable behavior and demonstrated knowledge acquisition rather than an attempt to measure subjective human emotions. Bennis (1984, 1993a) identified four competencies of leadership:

- management of attention—the ability to attract followers;
- management of meaning—the ability to communicate one's viewpoint or vision;
- management of trust—reliability;
- management of self—the ability to know one's skills and use them effectively.

Daniel (1992) identified 13 leadership competencies. They include the following:

- goal orientation;
- bottom-line orientation;
- communicates and enforces standards;
- initiative;
- strategic influence;
- communicates confidence;
- interpersonal sensitivity;
- develops and coaches others;
- gives performance feedback;
- collaboration and team building;
- systematic problem solving;
- image and reputation;
- self-confidence.

Kotter (1993) stated that good leaders: articulate a vision; involve people in decision making; provide coaching, feedback, and role modeling; and recognize and reward success. Drath and Paulus (1994, pp. 22–23) refer to leadership as "a social meaning-making process that takes place as a result of activity or work in a group." They went on to state that leaders must be trained to participate in, rather than exercise, leadership by learning community-oriented, meaning-making capacities, such as the capacity to understand oneself as both an individual and as a socially embedded being, the capacity to understand systems in general as mutually related and interacting and continually changing, the capacity to take the perspective of another, and the capacity to engage in dialogue. Leaders must be flexible (Bridges, 1994) and demonstrate initiative, integrity, and the ability to empower others (Davids, 1995). They must give support, communicate, facilitate interaction, listen actively, and provide feedback (Hersey & Blanchard, 1982).

In the final analysis, there is no great divergence in central themes or philosophies regarding ethical leadership, only differences in opinion with respect to the effectiveness of leadership approaches and the application of competencies (Wolfson, 1986). The real test of leadership lies in the performance of the groups being led (Bass, 1981) and the competencies required depend on the situation, the people involved, the action to be taken, and the desired results (Byrnbauer & Tyson, 1984). In a technologically advanced knowledge society, leadership competence must be open to, and required of, all workers (Drucker, 1994). The police service is no exception. Thus, all police officers must possess leadership skills as well as ethical competence (Anderson, 2000; Baca, 2002; Baker, 2000; Meese, 1993; Meese & Kurz, 1993; Ortmeier, 1995, 1996, 1997, 2002).

POLICE OFFICER LEADERSHIP COMPETENCIES

Meese and Kurz (1993) aptly described the individual qualities needed for success in a community-based, problem-oriented policing environment:

> Among the qualities which are radically different than those required for the traditional "crime fighting" officer are: proactive problem solver, peacekeeper and developer of cooperative relationships, guided by values and goals. Other traits include personal accountability, self-reliance, self-motivation, and capability as a mediator, negotiator, and community mobilizer. . . . Finally, the police officer will be more often a professional with a college degree (p. 296).

Police officer competencies relate to the officer knowledge and skills necessary to function effectively and appropriately in a policing environment. Officers must think creatively and independently. They must communicate well in their interactions with others (Harr & Hess, 2003). They must be able to create a vision and develop appropriate steps for solving problems. Instead of reacting primarily to incidents, the officer is forced to analyze, plan, and take initiative (Meese, 1993). Furthermore, recruitment, selection, training, and education programs must be modified to develop a core of officers with the instinct and leadership competencies necessary for working with the community (Anderson, 2000; California Association of Administration of Justice Educators, 2002; California State. Commission on Peace Officer Standards and Training, 2001, 2002; Fleissner, Fedan, & Klinger, 1992; Meese, 1993; Meese & Kurz, 1993; Ortmeier, 1995, 1996, 1997, 2002; Peak & Glensor, 2002; Whisenand & Ferguson, 2002). One must remember that it is the individual patrol officer who has the greatest freedom, discretional authority and ability to work directly with the public and who is perceived as the primary representative of the police department (Goldstein, 1990; 2001). It is this officer who has the most direct contact with the public and its problems.

In 1967, the President's Commission on Law Enforcement and the Administration of Justice observed that physical strength and aggressiveness reflected the popular image of what the police do. The commission also observed that this image was inconsistent with a careful analysis of the job requirements. It further noted that one incompetent officer could trigger a riot, permanently damage the reputation of a citizen, or alienate a community against a police department. In a contemporary policing environment, brute strength and aggressiveness give way to a new breed of officers who are better educated, self-managed, creative, guided by values and purposes, and who are not constrained by rules and excessive supervision (Meese, 1993). This does not suggest that brute strength and aggressiveness are not appropriate when circumstances warrant. But most police work does not involve physical confrontations. Most police activity requires situation management and ethical leadership. Officers must be team players, not subordinates, and supervisors must act as facilitators (J. R. Clark, 1994). Even the day-to-day, seemingly routine, decisions officers make about their own conduct and actions have potentially far-reaching consequences and must be guided by individual introspection about values, integrity, principles, and ethics (Boehm, 1988; Lyman, 2002; Ortmeier, 2002; Whisenand & Ferguson, 2002).

Police departments must deploy the most innovative, self-disciplined, and self-motivated officers directly into the community as outreach specialists and community problem solvers, not soldiers (Peak & Glensor, 2002; Trojanowicz & Carter, 1990; U.S. Department of Justice, 1992, December). As such, police officers must be sensitive to public perceptions and possess complex critical thinking skills (California State Community College Chancellor's Office, 1992). They must be able to adapt to changing community needs (McKinnie, 1995; Wycoff & Oettmeier, 1994) and utilize a human relations approach to communicate, identify and solve problems, and look toward service to the community (California State Assembly, 1991; Coffey, 1990; Meese, 1993; Spelman & Eck, 1987). There is also a need to develop collaborative, multidisciplinary approaches to community problems by including members of civil rights groups, and health, education, social service, and child welfare agencies as well as business and industry (Lyman, 2002; Ortmeier, 2002; U.S. Department of Justice, 1993; Whisenand & Ferguson, 2002).

Skill and competency requirements for police personnel are changing to meet the challenges of the twenty-first century. Many police departments are searching for a new breed of officer—the *customer-oriented cop.* Police agencies from New York to San Diego; Largo, Florida, to Lawrence, Michigan; and Los Angeles to Edneyville, North Carolina; are recruiting and training police officer candidates who are oriented toward, and committed to, community policing. Additionally, training programs that emphasize leadership, ethics, and the community orientation are being implemented for officers already in service (California State. Commission on Peace Officer Standards and Training, 2001, 2002; Ortmeier, 2002; *Selecting a New Breed,* 1999).

Research on Police Leadership Competencies

During the 1990s, several studies were conducted to identify essential police leadership competencies. Most of the studies focused on the supervisory-level and management-level leadership while a few addressed leadership skills required of frontline-level officers. In 1995, Ortmeier conducted a study to identify essential frontline-officer leadership competencies. The Ortmeier study is believed to be the first study to address leadership skills at the street officer level (Ortmeier, 1996). In 1996, Anderson and King conducted two studies through the Justice Institute of British Columbia. The purposes of the Anderson and King studies were to identify necessary leadership skills for supervisors and managers in the police community and public justice and safety sectors in British Columbia (Anderson & King, 1996a, 1996b). Similar studies were subsequently conducted with the Vancouver, British Columbia, police, and the San Diego, California, Police Department.

In 1997, through a project sponsored by the **International Association of Chiefs of Police (IACP),** the Federal Law Enforcement Training Center (FLETC), in conjunction with the Royal Canadian Mounted Police (RCMP), developed a list of leadership competencies for all police officers. The FLETC/RCMP list includes core leadership values that were identified as the foundation for the core leadership competencies. The FLETC/RCMP core values list includes integrity, honesty, professionalism, compassion, respect, accountability, fairness, and courage. The FLETC/RCMP core leadership competencies list are categorized in eight major competency groups: change management, communication, relationship building, service orientation, sharing power and creating opportunity, and inspiration and motivation (Anderson, 2000).

The study conducted by Ortmeier in 1995 searched for answers to questions regarding the need for police leadership development at the operational (frontline officer) level. The study focused on the leadership competencies perceived as essential for police practitioners in an environment that emphasizes community participation, engagement, and problem solving—all of which are essential ingredients to effective policing. For purposes of the study, a competency was defined as a highly specialized knowledge or skill that relates directly to the mastery of specific capabilities of a police officer that can be measured objectively. Leadership was defined as the ability to influence or mobilize individual citizens, groups, businesses, and public and private agencies to act together and participate in activities designed to discover and implement solutions to community problems. Leadership competency was defined as the skill, or set of skills, necessary to promote community engagement, participation, and problem solving (Ortmeier, 1996).

Among others, the panel of participants in the study included Herman Goldstein, who is considered the father of problem-oriented policing, former U.S. Attorney General Edwin Meese III, police executives and line officers throughout the United States as well as law enforcement scholars from Harvard and Stanford Universities, the John Jay College of Criminal Justice, and other academic institutions. Ultimately, the results of the study can be used to develop a strategy for increasing the quality of law enforcement practice through the improvement of law enforcement leadership training and education, leadership competence in individual officers, and police effectiveness. In essence, the strategy will connect the police to the community through enhanced ethical leadership practices. Implementation of the strategy may also promote behaviors consistent with twenty-first-century policing requirements and will assist officers in the development of the leadership competencies necessary to effectively connect with the public and implement problem-oriented community policing.

The research design for the study was qualitative, utilizing the Delphi Technique. The benefit of qualitative research, and probably its greatest strength, is that it not only provides information to make decisions but also uncovers additional questions that need to be answered (Levine, 1982). The study uncovered information for curriculum decisions necessary in the development of a police leadership training and education strategy. Current literature demonstrates a recognition for the unique responsibilities of police personnel and the difficulty of quantifying skills for the qualitative law enforcement job tasks. The police hold a unique position with respect to public trust and responsibility. Furthermore, decision making in police work includes the added dimension of unquantifiable judgment. Therefore, a qualitative research design and the Delphi Technique were well suited to this study.

The procedures utilized in the study included a series of three questionnaires that were consistent with those typically followed in the Delphi process. Three rounds of data were collected and analyzed. After every round the ratings for each item were tabulated and a composite rating was computed. Subsequently, the composite rating for each item was included on the next questionnaire so all panel members could view the composite rating of the group as well as their own individual ratings. At no time during the process were panelists informed of the identity of the other panel members or how other individual members of the panel rated these items.

Essential Police Leadership Competencies

The **essential police leadership competencies** identified in the Ortmeier study are grouped into five major categories. The **communications and related interpersonal competencies** category addresses one's ability to communicate with diverse populations. Through **motivational competencies,** a person demonstrates the ability to encourage others and build proactive relationships. **Problem-solving competencies** focus on problem identification, critical and analytical thinking, and situation analysis. **Planning and organizing competencies** are used to create a vision, prioritize, delegate, and define goals and objectives. **Actuation-implementation competencies** address the ability to implement a vision and evaluate results. The categories and competencies grouped within them are as follows.

Communications and Related Interpersonal Competencies

A police officer should be able to:

- demonstrate effective verbal communication skills.
- demonstrate effective listening skills.
- demonstrate effective counseling skills.
- demonstrate knowledge of different ethnic and racial cultures.
- demonstrate empathy in a multicultural society.
- facilitate interaction.
- maintain group cohesiveness and member satisfaction.
- demonstrate effective public speaking skills.
- prepare effective, clear written communications.

Motivational Competencies

A police officer should be able to:

- encourage creativity and innovation.
- act as a catalyst and arouse proaction.
- engage in team building.
- develop cooperative relationships.
- demonstrate persistence and continuity.
- demonstrate enthusiasm.
- demonstrate commitment to assignment.
- recognize and encourage responsible leaders.
- demonstrate intellectual curiosity.

Problem-Solving Competencies

A police officer should be able to:

- analyze situations.
- identify and evaluate constituent needs.
- identify problems.
- analyze problems.
- employ situational strategies.
- demonstrate ability to mediate/negotiate.
- provide means for goal attainment.
- demonstrate diagnostic and hierarchical prescriptive skills.

Planning and Organizing Competencies

A police officer should be able to:

- promote change.
- create and maintain a vision.
- define objectives and maintain goal direction.
- prioritize tasks.
- demonstrate ability to organize resources.
- assign tasks effectively.
- create and maintain a psychologically safe environment to encourage open communication.
- provide for and maintain group process.
- demonstrate effective delegation skills.

Actuation-Implementation Competencies

A police officer should be able to:

- implement a vision into action.
- complete multiple projects on schedule.

- evaluate measurable individual and group goals.
- demonstrate capacity to represent interests and concerns of others.
- demonstrate knowledge of, and articulate the reality of, an organization's impact.
- demonstrate ability to learn from mistakes (Ortmeier, 1996).

Overall, the results of the study indicate that skills in effective verbal communication, listening, and demonstration of empathy or understanding in a multicultural society are essential. The ability to identify problems, make commitments, understand the reality of the police impact on crime, analyze situations, demonstrate persistence, employ situational strategies, and recognize solutions to problems are also essential competencies. Summarily, the ability to identify problems, think critically, and engage in team building and group problem solving are highly rated leadership competencies necessary for the police officer (Ortmeier, 1996).

In essence, the underlying concepts for leadership in policing generally support frontline officer competencies that assist a community in the creation of a vision for its future. They support the creation of a process through which the community can assist itself in the identification and development of solutions to problems. In addition, the community is encouraged to take action to solve those problems.

Traditionally, reporting of crime and other problems to the police has been the most frequent method by which the police become aware that someone has been victimized or traumatized by criminal or other problematic activity. It is important, then, that citizen reporting and police efficiency is encouraged and improved through effective leadership in policing (U.S. Department of Justice, Bureau of Justice Statistics, 1992). Effective leadership also increases the public's confidence in the integrity and judgment of the police as well as improves the process and outcomes of human interaction between the individual police officer and the citizens.

Leadership is viewed as a management function by some authorities. However, these skills are also required of the line officer to improve public confidence and lead communities to identify and solve problems. Officers must be able to create and sustain community interest and activity in the law enforcement effort by fostering an environment that reinforces positive behavior and results. In essence, management follows leadership but does not supersede it. Contemporary policing requires competencies beyond those traditionally taught in police academies and college classrooms. Efforts should and are being made to incorporate affective competencies, such as those associated with leadership and ethics, into basic police academies, in-service training, and college curricula (Anderson, 2000; As costs soar, questions of quality dog Mass. college for cops program, 2001; Brown, 2001; California Association of

Administration of Justice Educators, 2002; California State Commission on Peace Officer Standards and Training, 2001, 2002; Crank & Caldero, 2000; Meese, 1993; Meese & Kurz, 1993; Ortmeier, 1995, 1996, 1997, 2002).

Additionally, police recruitment efforts must focus on individuals who possess the psychological profile as well as the background, educationally and experientially, to develop leadership skills appropriate to policing. The potential for ethical leadership as well as the ability to develop leadership competence must be an essential ingredient in the police officer candidate screening process.

Police officer ethics and leadership competency development can no longer be ignored. A review of the literature, expert opinion, and study results support the premise that ethical leadership competencies are essential for contemporary police officers. Some experts suggest that the traditional paramilitary structure and attitudes of the police service are inconsistent with contemporary community needs (Champion & Rush, 1997; Lyman, 2002; Peak & Glensor, 2002). The paramilitary automatons of the present must be transformed or replaced with self-contained human leadership agents who can guide communities safely through the twenty-first century (Anderson, 2000; Brown, 2001; California State Commission on Peace Officer Standards and Training, 2001, 2002; Ortmeier, 1995, 1996, 1997, 2002).

A Word of Caution

People who develop and exercise ethical leadership skills should not be surprised if others do not react to leadership behaviors in a positive way. Leadership is a difficult task and individuals are cautioned to expect some resistance when assuming a leadership role. The public is often confused by and suspicious of people who identify themselves as ethical leaders. The public is confused because leadership and ethics mean different things to different people. Furthermore, the public may be suspicious because some self-proclaimed ethical leaders have self-destructed because of their own moral and ethical failure. Additionally, many leaders desire unquestioning followers rather than use leadership skills to assist and empower the followers to own and solve their own problems. Thus, misguided leadership and ethical confusion often contribute to the mistrust and the cynical critique of leaders, rather than promote a more positive view among the citizenry that prizes and demands ethical leadership of those in authority.

Ethical leaders often face difficult challenges and are forced to make unpopular decisions and choices that are personally costly. During the course of a career, ethical leaders may encounter several occasions when they must choose between personal loss and an ethically compromised situation. Ethical leaders choose to maintain their integrity rather than succumb to expediency and personal gain (Hawkins, 2000).

SUMMARY

Police officers necessarily must assume a leadership role because of their status as representatives of the people. As leaders, police officers are uniquely situated to influence and motivate others to achieve legitimate and noble public interests. Furthermore, with the authority and power to enforce law, the police are in a position to exercise enormous discretion with respect to the means utilized to accomplish public safety goals. Legitimate exercise of authority and discretion necessitates an ethical foundation upon which police behavior must be based lest the police abuse their authority.

Ethical leadership is every police officer's responsibility and ethical leadership competencies are among the most important skills an officer can possess. Officers with such ethical leadership skills demonstrate enhanced performance, reduce liability, and generate public trust and support. Essential police leadership skills can be categorized as communications and related interpersonal, motivational, problem solving, planning and organizing, and actuation-implementation competencies.

KEY TERMS AND CONCEPTS

Define, describe, or explain the importance of each of the following:

actuation-implementation competencies
communication and related interpersonal competencies
essential police leadership competency
ethical leader
International Association of Chiefs of Police (IACP)
leadership competency
leadership qualities
motivational competencies
planning and organizing competencies
problem-solving competencies

Discussion Questions and Exercises

1. Why are ethics and leadership important in policing?
2. Who is an ethical leader?
3. Is leadership development important for all in the police profession? Why, or why not?
4. What is an ethical leadership competency?
5. Distinguish leadership qualities from leadership competencies or skills. How can ethical leadership skills be developed?

Chapter 3

Concepts and Dynamics of Leadership

Learning Objectives

After completing this chapter, the reader should be able to:

- formulate a definition for leadership.
- discuss approaches to the study of leadership.
- list and describe leadership theories.
- differentiate various theories of leadership.
- identify and analyze leadership behaviors.
- compare and contrast leadership with management.

Introduction

Effective and ethical leadership is essential in policing and leadership competence is required at all ranks. Yet, leadership itself is difficult to define and is often misunderstood. Definitions and theories of leadership vary and the process for leadership development can be vague. As exemplified by this chapter's discussion of leadership definitions, concepts, dynamics, and theories, the study of leadership may appear abstract, confusing, dull, and uninteresting. However, broad-based knowledge of leadership provides the foundation for leader development. Moreover, substantial evidence suggests that education and training in, as well as the practice of, leadership skills are essential for all police officers in contemporary society. This chapter outlines and briefly describes various leadership theories. Subsequent chapters will address the practical application of leadership theories and concepts.

LEADERSHIP DEFINED

The universal phenomenon called leadership has been the subject of a great deal of research from both the theoretical and the practical points of view. However, leadership defies a common definition. There are about as many definitions of leadership as there are people to define it (Northouse, 2001; Vinzant & Crothers, 1998) and the range of definitions reveals considerable differences among the various views on leadership (Anderson, 2000).

Leadership has been defined and described variously as: a trait, the focus of group process, the art of inducing compliance, an exercise of influence, a kind of behavior or act, a form of persuasion, a power relationship, an instrument for goal attainment, an effective interaction, a differentiated role, and an initiation of structure (Bass, 1990). Leadership is a power relationship because leaders are in power positions. Coercive, reward, and legitimate powers are linked to position or rank. Expert and referent powers are linked to individuals. Coercive power is based on penalties, reward power depends on the ability to deliver something of value, and legitimate power is based on position or rank. Knowledge, education, credentials, and skills build expert power. Referent (role model) power is based on the admiration one has for another. Followers appear to

LEADERSHIP DEFINED

Leadership has been defined as:

- a trait (characteristic or quality).
- the focus of group process.
- the art of inducing compliance.
- the ability to influence or motivate.
- a behavior or act.
- a form of persuasion.
- a power relationship.
- an instrument or process for goal attainment.
- an effective interaction.
- a differentiated role.
- the initiation or maintenance of structure.
- the process of arranging a situation (facilitation).
- the ability to direct or coordinate relationships.
- an activity that mobilizes people.
- a social meaning-making process.

be more satisfied and productive when leaders rely on expert and referent power (Johnson, 2001; Whisenand & Ferguson, 2002).

Leadership has also been defined in terms of acts or behaviors (Carter, 1953), an act that results in others acting or responding in a shared direction (Shartle, 1956), the process of arranging a situation so as to achieve common goals (Bellows, 1959), and the initiation and maintenance of structure in interaction and expectation (Stogdill, 1959). It has been defined as directing and coordinating work relationships while showing consideration (Fiedler, 1967), an activity that mobilizes people to do something (Heifetz, 1994), a social meaning-making process that takes place as a result of activity or work in a group (Drath & Paulus, 1994) and as a process through which a person influences others to achieve a common goal (Northouse, 2001). Within the context of community policing, leadership for police officers has been defined as the ability to influence or mobilize individual citizens, groups, businesses, and public and private agencies to act together and participate in activities designed to discover and implement solutions to community problems (Ortmeier, 1996, 2002).

APPROACHES TO THE STUDY OF LEADERSHIP

For many years, the most common approach to the study of leadership concentrated on leadership traits, suggesting that there were certain characteristics or superior qualities that differentiated the leader from nonleaders (Stogdill, 1948). Bernard (1926) explained leadership in terms of traits of personality and character. Thus, a leadership trait (leadership quality) was defined in terms of inborn characteristics unique to an individual. However, a review of the research using the trait approach to leadership has revealed few significant or consistent findings (Stogdill, 1948).

Early in the twentieth century, definitions of leadership viewed the leader as a focal point for group change activity and process. According to this view, the leader is always the nucleus of the group (Cooley, 1902). Frederick Taylor (1911), a major theorist of the scientific management movement, viewed people as instruments or machines to be manipulated by their leaders. In essence, the scientific management movement emphasized the concern for output. Sigmund Freud (1922), a psychoanalytical theorist, saw the leader as a father figure, a source of love or fear, as the embodiment of the superego, and as the emotional outlet for followers' frustrations and destructive aggression.

Early theories of leadership viewed the leader as the focal point of group activity.
Photo courtesy of San Diego Police Museum

In the 1920s and 1930s, the human relations movement emerged. According to human relations theorists, the group or organization is developed around the members and the leader is attentive to human feelings and attitudes. The main focus, contrary to the scientific management movement, was on the needs of the individual rather than the needs of the group or organization (Mayo, 1945).

Cowley (1928) defined a leader as a person who has a specific agenda and is moving toward an objective with the group in a definite manner. Schenk (1928) suggested that leadership involves persuasion and inspiration rather than direct or implied threat of coercion. Bogardus (1929) suggested that leadership, as a social process, is a social inter-stimulation that causes people to set out toward an old goal with new zest or a new goal with hopeful courage. Through this view, leadership was not the cause of group action, but was an effect of it. J. F. Brown (1936) proposed five field-dynamic laws of leadership. According to Brown, leaders must: have membership character in the group they are attempting to lead; represent a region of high potential in the social field; adapt themselves to the existing field structure; realize long-term trends in field structure; and recognize that leadership increases in potency at the cost of a reduction in the freedom of leadership.

Barnard (1938) declared that theories of leadership behavior cannot be constructed in a vacuum. The theories must contain elements about situations as well as persons. In other words, leadership must focus on the interaction between the situation and the individual. The focus in the situational approach to leadership is on observed behavior, not on hypothetical inborn or acquired traits (Hemphill, 1949). For Fiedler (1967), the effectiveness of a given pattern of leader behavior is actually contingent on the demands imposed by the situation. And, according to Pfeffer (1977), understanding a leader's behavior involves exploring the leader's mind in order to determine what the leader is thinking about the situation in which leadership occurs.

Both trait theorists and situational theorists attempted to explain leadership as the impact of a single set of forces. The interactive effects of individual and situational factors were overlooked (Bass, 1981). Leadership, therefore, appeared as a manner of interaction involving behavior by and toward an individual who is lifted to a leadership role by other individuals (Jennings, 1944) and is defined in terms of the origination of interaction based on the basic variables of action, interaction, and sentiments in a situation (Homans, 1950). Each participant in this interaction is said to play a role—one person, the leader, does the influencing and the other people in the group respond (Gordon, 1955).

Describing leadership in terms of the ability to motivate, influence, or persuade has been viewed as a major step in the direction of defining leadership. Nash (1929) suggested that leadership implies influencing change in the conduct of people. Cleeton and Mason (1934) suggested that leadership indicates the ability to influence people and secure results through emotional appeals rather than through the exercise of authority. Tead (1935) defined leadership as the activity of influencing people to cooperate toward some goal they may come to find desirable. Copeland (1942) maintained that leadership is the art of dealing with human nature—it is the art of influencing a body of people, by using persuasion or example, to follow a line of action. Stogdill (1950) defined leadership as the process or act of influencing activities of an organized group in its efforts toward goal setting and goal achievement.

Tannenbaum and Schmidt (1958) believed that leaders could influence followers by either of two methods. They could tell their followers what to do and how to do it. Alternately, they could share their leadership responsibilities with their followers by involving them in the planning and the execution of the task. Blake and Mouton (1965) conceptualized leadership in terms of a managerial grid in which an individual's concerns for *people* were compared to concerns for *production*. An individual who rated high in both areas developed followers who are committed to accomplishing goals in a relationship of trust and respect. Likert (1967) suggested that leaders must take the expectations, values, and interpersonal skills of others into account. Leaders could build group cohesiveness and motivation for productivity by providing freedom for responsible decision making and exercise of initiative.

Hersey and Blanchard (1972) synthesized Blake and Mouton's managerial grid and suggested that leader behavior is related to the maturity of the people being led. Maturity was defined in terms of the nonleaders' experience, achievement, motivation, willingness, and ability to accept responsibility. As the maturity of nonleaders increased, the leader's involvement decreased. Finally, Osborn and Hunt (1975) suggested that leadership theory must take into account and be sensitive to the larger environment of which leaders and nonleaders are a part.

An important breakthrough in understanding the concept of leadership occurred with the publication of *Leadership* by James MacGregor Burns. He characterized leaders either as **transactional** (when one person takes the initiative, making contact with others for the purpose of the exchange of valued things) or **transformational** (when one or more persons engage with others in a way in which the leader and nonleader raise one another to higher levels of motivation and morality) (Burns, 1978). Examples of transactional leadership through a contingent reward approach can be found in *The One Minute Manager* (Blanchard & Johnson, 1992). A function of transactional leadership is to maintain the group's or organization's operation rather than to change it (Burns & Becker, 1988). Transformational leadership, on the other hand, focuses on the three behavior patterns of charisma, intellectual stimulation, and individualized consideration (Bass, 1985). Finally, Tichy and Ulrich (1984) presented the transformational leader as the model for future leadership excellence. They cited three identifiable activities associated with transformational leadership: creation of vision—view of a future state, mobilization of commitment—acceptance of the new mission, and institutionalization of change—new patterns of behavior adopted to embrace change (Ortmeier, 1996, 2002; Tichy & Ulrich, 1984).

LEADERSHIP THEORIES OVERVIEW

As demonstrated in the discussion of definitions and approaches to the study of leadership, the topic of leadership is itself subject to a great deal of debate. The debate can confuse experts on the topic, not to mention the student of leadership. Leadership definitions and approaches are derivatives of theories that were and are developed to explain the concepts and dynamics of leadership. As with leadership definitions, there are about as many **leadership theories** as there are theorists to describe the leadership phenomenon. To place leadership theories into some form of logical, easily understood framework, this section of the book is devoted to a brief description of many of the theories of leadership. For sake of simplicity, the leadership theories presented are categorized in three major groups: leader-centered theories, follower- and context-centered theories, and leader-follower interactions-centered theories.

LEADERSHIP THEORIES OVERVIEW

Leader-Centered Theories

- Trait Theories
- Behavior Theories
- Personal-Situational Theory
- Interaction-Expectation Theory

Follower- and Context-Centered Theories

- Situational Theory
- Contingency Theory
- Path-Goal Theory

Leader-Follower Interactions-Centered Theories

- Leader-Follower (Member) Exchange Theory
- Transformational Theory
- The Psychodynamic Approach

Leader-Centered Theories

Leader-centered theories focus on a leader's traits, behaviors, personal characteristics and their relationship with the environment (situation), and ability to initiate and fulfill expectations of group members.

Trait Theories

Probably the earliest approach to the study of leadership is **trait theory** (Vinzant & Crothers, 1998), which represents one of the first systematic attempts to examine leadership. In the early 1900s, great leaders were studied to identify traits that made them successful. Often referred to as "great man" theories, trait approaches to leadership focused on identifying the innate qualities and characteristics possessed by great political, military, and social leaders (Anderson, 2000; Northouse, 2001). According to trait theory, individual and, predominately psychological, inborn characteristics in human beings form the ingredients for leadership ability. Individual traits such as popularity, originality, self-confidence, judgment, sociability, humor, aggressiveness, desire, adaptability, assertiveness, decisiveness, intelligence, alertness, insight, initiative, persistence, and the ability to cooperate, among others, combine to inspire others and cause them to follow a leader's agenda (Bass, 1990; Northouse, 2001; Vinzant & Crothers, 1998).

In the mid-1900s, trait theory was challenged by research that questioned the universality of leadership traits (Northouse, 2001). Stogdill (1948) suggested that no consistent, uniform, group of traits distinguished leaders from nonleaders across a variety of situations. A leader in one situation may not be a leader in another. Stogdill reconceptualized leadership. Rather than focus on qualities or characteristics a leader possessed, Stogdill focused on relationships between people (Stogdill, 1948). Personal traits continued to be important, but researchers believed traits should be considered as relative to the requirements of a given situation (Northouse, 2001). Although certain inborn traits may increase the likelihood of leadership effectiveness (Bennis, 1984), especially by demonstrating vision and charisma (Bass, 1990), mere possession of certain traits does not assure that a person will, in fact, become a leader (Stogdill, 1948; Northouse, 2001).

The primary value of trait theories is that they highlight the importance of personal qualities and characteristics in a leadership venue. However, personal traits are only one group of factors that could influence behavior in others. Thus, any reliance on trait theories provides an incomplete picture of leadership and does not account for numerous other contributing factors. Trait theories focus too heavily on high-level personnel in organizations and society, fail to account for the circumstances within which a leader operates, and do not make the leader's behavior legitimate. Additionally, trait theories fail to account for one's ability to learn and demonstrate leadership skills. Leadership competence can be developed although the leader candidate was not born with any of the innate qualities suggested in trait theories. Finally, trait theories fail to distinguish between individuals who are demonstrating true leadership and those who are merely exercising power because of their status (Vinzant & Crothers, 1998).

Although trait theories may help to explain differences in personal and professional successes of individuals, trait theories of leadership do not adequately account for the complexities of the context in which leadership is required. Individuals function in a complex system of laws, customs, organizations, and cultures. Since the environment in which leadership is required is complex and multifaceted, trait theories do not fully apply (Vinzant & Crothers, 1998).

Behavior Theories

Behavior theories are very different from trait theories of leadership. Trait theories emphasize personal qualities and characteristics of the leader rather than conduct. Sometimes referred to as the style approach, behavior theories focus on what leaders do and how they act (Northouse, 2001). Behavior theories of leadership suggest that circumstances can cause an individual to rise to a leadership role (Anderson, 2000). Effective leaders engage in behaviors that are likely to achieve desired results. Some behavior theories of leadership emphasize the importance of follower- or worker-centered and participative forms of leadership (Argyris, 1964; Likert, 1961; Vinzant & Crothers, 1998).

Scholars and researchers who study the behavior approach to leadership focus on two general types of behaviors: task (initiating structure) behaviors that facilitate goal accomplishment and relationship (consideration) behaviors that assist others with the development of comfortable feelings about themselves, other people, and the situation they are in. Central to the behavior theory is the leader's ability to combine task and relationship behaviors to influence others to achieve a goal. Although not a refined theory, perhaps the most famous of the behavior approaches was promoted by Blake and Mouton (1965) through their Managerial Grid, later renamed the Leadership Grid. The grid is designed to demonstrate how leaders help organizations achieve goals through concern for production as well as concern for people (Blake & Mouton, 1965; Northouse, 2001).

Behavioral leadership models grew out of research programs in the 1940s and 1950s conducted at Ohio State University and the University of Michigan. Utilizing questionnaires to observe the behavior of leaders, researchers at Ohio State determined that leadership behaviors fell into two categories: initiating structure (leader structures role of self and others to accomplish task) and consideration (the leader demonstrates concern for and supports others in the group). In the Michigan studies researchers used a similar research approach and focused on production-oriented and employee-oriented behaviors. The Michigan group discovered that effective leaders engage in both task-oriented and relationship-oriented behaviors. Research supports the behavioral approach because leaders who consider the needs of and provide support for others tend to build follower satisfaction, trust, and loyalty, all of which enhance performance and goal achievement (Likert, 1961, 1967; Vinzant & Crothers, 1998).

Behavior (style) theories of leadership do not focus on how leaders should behave but rather on a description of the major components of leader behavior. The approach reminds leaders that leadership behavior has both a task and a relationship dimension. Depending on the circumstances, the leader may find it necessary to be more task oriented, whereas in others, the leader may be more relationship oriented.

Behavior theories of leadership broaden the scope of leadership research beyond the limitations of trait theories and are validated by a wide range of studies (Blake & Mouton, 1965). However, behavior theories are not without critics. Researchers have not been able to establish a consistent link between behaviors and outcomes. Furthermore, the behavior approach fails to identify a universal leadership style that could be effective in most situations (Northouse, 2001).

Personal-Situational Theory

The **personal-situational** leadership **theory** was the first to focus on the complex factors involved in the development of leadership. The theory was also the first to be studied by serious research efforts. This theory proposes that a complex combination of intellectual, affective, and action characteristics, as well as specific conditions in the leader's environment, operate to create successful leadership. The success is dependent on the leader's ability to understand the followers and the environment in which the followers function, and react appropriately as the followers and the situation change (Anderson, 2000). Accordingly, Bennis (1961) recommended that numerous human characteristics and environmental conditions should be considered when developing leadership theory. Bennis suggested that theories on leadership should consider: the value of the person in relation to productivity, a measurement of rationality, the impact of interpersonal relations and the informal organization, and the positive influence of benevolence as a superior-subordinate relationship builder. Further, Bennis suggested leadership theory should address: task enlargement and follower-centered supervision that promotes self-development, and participation that allows for the integration of individual and group or organizational goals (Anderson, 2000; Bennis, 1961).

Interaction-Expectation Theory

According to the **interaction-expectation** orientation to leadership **theory,** leadership involves the act of initiating a structure that is supported by group members. The group supports the effort because the structure helps solve mutual problems, positively transforms or conforms to group norms, and causes group members to expect that success in their endeavors will result if they follow the leader of the initiative (Adler, 2002; Vroom, 1964). Thus, according to interaction-expectation theory, leadership involves initiating as well as fulfilling the expectations of others. The credibility of the leader is enhanced when expectations generated by the leader are fulfilled (Anderson, 2000; Homans, 1950; Stogdill, 1959).

Follower- and Context-Centered Theories

Follower- and context-centered leadership **theory** development reflected a significant advance over simplistic, universal, one-way leadership models (Anderson, 2000).

Situational Theory

The situational approach to the study of leadership—developed, refined, and revised by Hersey and Blanchard (1982)—focuses on leadership in particular situations. As one of the most widely recognized approaches to the study of leadership, **situational theory** operates on the premise that different situations demand different styles of leadership. Thus, to be effective, a leader must be able to adapt leadership style as situations change. Situational leadership has directive (task) and supportive (relationship) dimensions, and each dimension is applied proportionately to the demands of the situation. To determine what proportion of each dimension is required in a particular situation, the leader must first assess and evaluate follower or group member competence (skills) and commitment (motivation) to a given task or goal. Based on the assumption that follower or member competence and commitment change over time, the situational leader changes the degree of directive and supportive behaviors to meet the needs of followers or group members. According to situational theory, the most effective leaders are those who match the competence and commitment of others and recognize and adapt to changing follower and group member needs (Northouse, 2001; Vinzant & Crothers, 1998).

The dynamics of situational leadership theory are best understood by studying its bifurcated parts: leadership style and the development levels of followers. Leadership style refers to leader directive and supportive behaviors. Directive, or task, behaviors assist group members with goal achievement through directions, establishing goals and evaluation methods, defining roles, demonstrating how goals can be achieved, and setting time limits. Supportive behaviors help increase follower comfort levels. Development level refers to follower competence and commitment—the follower's mastery of the skills necessary to complete a task and a positive attitude toward the task. Effective leaders, according to the situational theory, correctly diagnose follower developmental level and match the leadership style to the level of development based on the situation at hand.

The situational leadership approach is practical, is easily understood, is prescriptive (tells one what to do) rather than descriptive, emphasizes leader flexibility, and underscores the importance of unique follower needs. The approach has broad applications and is used extensively in practitioner training and development arenas. Situational leadership theory also has its critics, however. Few research studies have been conducted that would justify the assumptions in the approach. The model is somewhat ambiguous—it is not clear how competence is combined with commitment. Further, the approach does not identify how leader style should be matched to follower development level nor does it address the issue of whether the leader should match style to the group or individual members of the group. Finally, situational leadership questionnaires designed to accompany training associated with the model force respondents to choose predetermined, situational leadership-favoring responses rather than other leadership behaviors not described in the model (Northouse, 2001).

Contingency Theory

The **contingency theory** of leadership supports the idea that leadership is situational in nature, with a wide range of variables contained in a particular situation. According to the theory, directive leaders may be more effective in certain situations than supportive leaders, and vice versa (Anderson, 2000; Fiedler, 1967). Through the application of the contingency theory, an attempt is made to match the leader to the situation. It posits that leader effectiveness depends on how well the leader's style fits the context of the situation (Northouse, 2001).

In contingency theory, leadership styles are described as task motivated (concerned with goal achievement) and relationship motivated (concerned with developing close interpersonal relations). The theory suggests that situations can be categorized by assessing three situational variables: leader-follower relations, task structure, and position power. Leader-follower relations refer to the degree of confidence, attraction, and loyalty followers have for their leader. Task structure refers to the degree to which the requirements of a task are clear. Structural tasks afford more control to the leader. Ambiguous tasks decrease leader influence. Position power refers to the amount of authority a leader has to punish or reward a follower. According to the theory, when a Least Preferred Coworker (LPC) instrument, developed by Fiedler, is used in conjunction with a determination of the three situational variables, a leader's effectiveness in a given context can be predicted.

Contingency theory is predictive and supported by empirical research, has broadened the understanding of situations on leaders, recognizes that leaders cannot be effective in all situations, and is useful when developing leadership profiles. The theory has been criticized because it is not totally explanatory. Furthermore, the LPC instrument is cumbersome and does not correlate well with other leadership measures. Finally, the theory does not provide options when leaders are mismatched with situations. Thus, the theory fails to support teaching or learning leader adaptive skills that are necessary in changing situations (Northouse, 2001).

Path-Goal Theory

The **path-goal theory** was formulated by House (1971) and others in the early 1970s. The approach suggests that the leader's role is to enhance follower performance and goal achievement through motivation and increasing rewards for achievement of goals (Anderson, 2000; House, 1971). Unlike situational theory, which suggests leaders must adapt to follower developmental level, and contingency theory, which suggests a match between a leader's style and situational variables, the path-goal approach emphasizes the relationship between leader style and follower and environmental characteristics. According to path-goal theory, leaders should use a style that meets follower motivational needs. Followers are motivated when they believe that they are capable, that efforts will help achieve a planned goal, and that rewards for results are worthwhile (Northouse, 2001).

Path-goal theory focuses on directive, supportive, participative, and achievement-oriented behaviors in an effort to select a leadership style that is appropriate to a follower's needs and situation. Directive leadership, similar to initiating structure and task behavior, characterizes the leader as one who assigns a task and directs clear standards of performance. Supportive leadership, similar to relationship and consideration behaviors, strives to make the task pleasant. Supportive leaders treat followers as peers. Through participative leadership, a leader invites followers to participate in the decision-making process. Achievement-oriented leadership is characterized by leader challenges for followers to perform at the highest possible level. Leaders may demonstrate any or all of these styles depending on the follower and the situation.

In practice, path-goal theory is applied according to follower needs and environmental variables. If, for example, a task is structured, yet boring or frustrating, the leader may choose to use supportive leadership behaviors. Participative leadership behaviors can be used when followers tend to work alone and must exercise independent judgment. Through participative leadership, followers feel a need to be in control and respond more favorably when they are involved with making decisions relating to performance standards and goal achievement. Although path-goal theory is complex and not the subject of many leadership-training programs, the theory does offer valuable insight and recommendations for leaders of all levels as well as for all types of tasks and situations (Northouse, 2001).

Leader-Follower Interactions-Centered Theories

Some leadership theories emphasize the process involved in the interactions of leaders and followers or group members. These **leader-follower interactions-centered theories** are discussed here.

Leader-Follower (Member) Exchange Theory

Citing a process involving interactions between leaders and followers (members), **leader-follower exchange theory** represents a departure from theories that focus on what leaders do toward their followers. Early research on the theory focused on the vertical linkages (relationships) of leaders and followers. Researchers discovered two types of linkages: in-group, based on expanded and negotiated role responsibilities, and out-group, based on defined roles such as those found in employment contracts. Followers whose performance went beyond what was expected and expanded their roles with leaders became part of the in-group. Followers who achieved only what was asked of them were part of the out-group. Later research on leader-follower exchange theory added the dimension of organizational effectiveness: how the quality of the exchange related to positive outcomes for leaders, followers, groups, and organizations. Results of the research indicated that good leader-follower exchanges (relationships) produce greater gains for organizations as well as for an organization's members (Northouse, 2001).

Current research on leader-follower exchange theory focuses on how leader-follower relationships can be used for leadership development. This approach suggests that leaders should develop good relationships with all followers as well as create partnership networks throughout the organization. The leadership development relationship between leader and follower progresses from stranger through acquaintance to mature partner. As partners, the leader and follower are bound together in ways other than the traditional hierarchically defined relationship.

Leader-follower exchange theory makes the relationship the focal point of a leadership process in which effective communication is critical. Although the model promotes trust building, commitment, and respect, it fails to explain how one develops high-quality relationships (Graen & Uhl-Bien, 1995; Northouse, 2001).

Transformational Theory

Although the term transformational leadership was first introduced by Downton (1973), it was James MacGregor Burns who popularized the theory in his book, *Leadership* (1978). Burns distinguished between two types of leadership: transactional and transformational. According to Burns (1978), most leadership models utilize a transactional approach through which exchanges occur between leaders and followers. Politicians make promises in exchange for votes, employers promise salary increases in exchange for high employee productivity, college professors exchange grades for student work, prosecutors exchange a reduction in a criminal charge for defendant cooperation (plea bargaining), and police officers may exchange a verbal warning (as compared to a traffic citation) for a motorist's civility during a stop for a motor vehicle code violation. Thus, through transactional leadership, leaders provide followers with something of value in exchange for performance or support on the part of the followers. The exchange is, therefore, a transaction (Anderson, 2000; Burns, 1978).

In contrast, the transformational leader focuses effort and makes choices based on goals, values, and ideals that the leader determines the group or organization wants or ought to advance (Vinzant & Crothers, 1998). As Burns (1978) stated:

> Transforming leadership, while more complex, is more potent. The transforming leader recognizes and exploits the existing need or demand of a potential follower. But, beyond that, the transforming leader looks for potential motives in followers, seeks to satisfy higher needs, and engages the full person of the follower. The result of transforming leadership is a relationship of mutual stimulation and elevation that converts followers into leaders and may convert leaders into moral agents of change.
>
> . . . Moral leadership emerges from and always returns to the fundamental wants and needs, aspirations, and values of the followers. I mean the kind of leadership that can produce social change that will satisfy follower's authentic needs (Burns, 1978, p. 4).

Transformational leadership involves a process through which a leader engages others and creates a connection that raises the level of motivation and morality in the leader as well as the followers (Northouse, 2001). The leader's exercise of power over the followers is a component of the process. However, the leader's use of power is grounded and legitimized by the underlying values, goals, and ideals of the individuals, groups, organizations, and communities being led. Thus, according to transformational leadership theory, the leader strives to advance shared values and needs (Burns, 1978; Johnson, 2001).

In some cases, transformational leadership is closely aligned with charisma. House (1976) suggested that some leaders act in ways that have charismatic effects on followers. According to House, charismatic leaders often display personal characteristics such as dominance, a desire to influence others, self-confidence, and a strong sense of moral values. Through their actions, charismatic leaders are also role models, are competent to followers, articulate goals with moral overtones, communicate high expectations to followers, exhibit confidence in follower ability, and arouse task-relevant motives in followers. As a result, followers trust, accept, and identify with the leader and develop emotional involvement with achievement of goals (House, 1976).

Bass (1985) expanded the concepts of transformational leadership presented by House (1976) and Burns (1978). Bass described transactional and transformational leadership as a single continuum, and gave more attention to followers by suggesting the theory could apply even when outcomes were not positive. Bass suggested that transformational leadership motivates followers to produce more than expected by raising follower consciousness about the importance and value of certain goals, encouraging followers to transcend self-interest for the sake of the group or organization, and motivating followers to address higher needs (Bass, 1985).

Transformational leaders possess strong internal values and motivate others to act above self-interest. Transformational leadership is attractive to people because it is easily understood and leaders are seen as providing a vision for the future. Transformational leadership meets leader as well as follower needs, treats leadership as a process in which needs and growth of others are central, and places emphasis on values and morality (Bass, 1985; Burns, 1978; Northouse, 2001). The concepts of transformational leadership are viewed by some as applicable to community policing environments because communities and their relationships with the police are constantly evolving and transforming (Ford, Boles, Plamondon, & White, 2000).

Transformational leadership theory may have several weaknesses also. The theory lacks clarity because of vague references to motivation, vision, trust, and nurturing. It is often interpreted too simplistically and the theory often treats leadership as a personality trait rather than as a behavior that can be learned. The application of transformational leadership is also subject to abuse and risk. Since the process involves changing follower values and moving them toward a new vision for the future, followers could be steered in the wrong direction. The leader's values and vision may not be appropriate (Northouse, 2001). For example, criminal gang leaders have values and vision, but their motivation and actions are often inconsistent with morality and the law.

One of the most influential critics of transformational leadership and other modern leadership theories is James Rost, a retired professor of leadership studies from the University of San Diego. Rost contends that most current theories of leadership are based on an industrial model in which leaders function as super managers who influence followers to get things done. Rost believes the industrial model is ill-suited for a postindustrial age, which places greater value on diversity, consensus building, collaboration, and participation. Rost emphasizes the relationship and interaction between leader and follower. According to Rost, the leader-follower relationship should be based on persuasion (not coercion), influence flowing in both directions, follower choice to participate, and joint goal creation. He believes that ethical leadership occurs when leaders and followers freely agree that intended changes fairly reflect mutual purposes (Johnson, 2001; Rost, 1991). However, Rost's postindustrial leadership model, which rejects transformational leadership because it glorifies leaders at the expense of followers, fails to recognize that leaders may, on occasion, be required to use coercive rather than persuasive power (Johnson, 2001).

The Psychodynamic Approach

The **psychodynamic approach** is aptly named because it represents an approach to leadership rather than a coherent theory. According to the psychodynamic approach to leadership, leaders are more effective if they have insight into the psychological makeup of themselves and their followers. The approach is distinguished from trait, behavioral, or situational theories. In trait theory, personal characteristics are assumed to be important. Behavioral theories stress the style of the leader. Situational theories emphasize the match between leader and follower.

The psychodynamic approach makes none of the assumptions presented in trait, behavioral, or situational leadership theories. The psychodynamic approach does not presume that a particular personality type is best suited for leadership. Nor does the approach presume to match style to followers or a particular situation. Value is placed on the leader's and follower's awareness of their own personality characteristics so they understand how and why they respond the way they do to each other. Thus, an important function of a leader is to facilitate insight acquisition and personal needs identification in self and others. The approach also places emphasis on learned and deep-seated emotional responses rather than immediate awareness. An underlying assumption in the approach is that personality characteristics are ingrained and difficult to change in any significant way. The personality characteristics develop over time and depend, to a great extent, on variables such as family background, maturation, dependence or independence, repressed feelings, and the nature of one's relationships. The key is acceptance of one's own personality features and quirks as well as the features and quirks of others (Stech, 2001).

Since its conception with Sigmund Freud (1938), the psychodynamic approach to human development was intended to produce change in a person. The intention has led to the development of countless self-improvement programs and the publication of numerous books on the subject. The approach takes into account that both leaders and followers have needs and feelings, not all of which are consciously available. The approach's greatest strength lies in the results of the analysis of the leader-follower relationship. Additionally, the approach encourages self-assessment and insight development on the part of the leader and discourages manipulative techniques in leadership. Criticisms of the approach include the subjective nature of insight development. Furthermore, research on the approach relies primarily on the clinical observations of psychologists and psychiatrists, whose opinions may be biased in favor of the approach. And, although the approach emphasizes personal growth, especially of leaders, the approach does not account for organizational variables that might influence behavior (Stech, 2001).

LEADERSHIP IS NOT MANAGEMENT

Leadership should not be confused with position or rank, although leaders often occupy positions of authority (Johnson, 2001). Nor should leadership be confused with management. Leadership and management are interrelated, yet different (Anderson, 2000; Baker, 2000). Both represent distinct concepts even though management and leadership may be exercised or exhibited by the same individual. In spite of the considerable amount of overlap between leadership and management, the two concepts should not be confused with each other (Northouse, 2001; Stojkovic, Kalinich, & Klofas, 2003). Leadership, which is broader than management, occurs anytime one attempts to motivate, influence, or mobilize an individual or a group. **Management,** on the other hand, involves directing people toward organizational goals (Hersey & Blanchard, 1982). Leadership produces change by establishing direction, aligning people, motivating, and inspiring. Management brings a measure of order and consistency to organizations by planning and budgeting, organizing and staffing, and controlling (Kotter, 1990). Leaders do not operate in a vacuum. They are accountable to others within the context of values, norms and expectations (Vinzant & Crothers, 1998). Leadership is an art based on a philosophy. Management involves analysis, sequencing, and application. In other words, management follows leadership (Covey, 1998).

When considering the distinction between leadership and management, one must examine two different courses of life history: leadership development through socialization, which prepares the individual to guide institutions and maintain the existing balance in social relations, versus leadership development through personal mastery, which impels an individual to struggle for psychological and social change. Society produces its managerial talent through the first course of life history while leaders emerge through the second course (Zaleznik, 1993). Bennis (1993b, p. 214) distinguished management from leadership through the following comparisons:

- The manager administers; the leader innovates.
- The manager is a copy; the leader is an original.
- The manager maintains; the leader develops.
- The manager focuses on systems and structure; the leader focuses on people.
- The manager relies on control; the leader inspires trust.
- The manager has a short-range view; the leader has a long-range perspective.
- The manager asks how and when; the leader asks what and why.
- The manager has an eye on the bottom line; the leader has an eye on the horizon.

- The manager accepts the status quo; the leader challenges it.
- The manager is the classic good soldier; the leader is unique.
- The manager does things right; the leader does the right thing.

True leadership is for the benefit of the followers, not the enrichment of the leaders (Townsend, 1970). As one author stated, the leader is the one who climbs the tallest tree, surveys the situation, and cries out, "Wrong jungle!" The manager responds with, "Shut up! We are making progress." (Covey, 1998).

SUMMARY

Definitions and theories of leadership vary. Therefore, the study of leadership and its development may appear to be abstract and confusing. However, leadership skills are necessary for all contemporary police officers. Leadership is not management. Leadership occurs through motivation, influence, and mobilization of any individual or group. Management focuses on directing people toward organizational goals.

Approaches to the study of leadership have focused on inborn leadership traits as well as skills or competencies that can be developed through learning. Leadership theories include those that are leader-centered (trait, behavior, personal-situational, and interaction-expectation theories), follower- and context-centered (situational, contingency, and path-goal theories), and leader-follower interactions-centered (leader-follower exchange, transformational, and psychodynamic theories). Knowledge and application of leadership is essential to police practice and to the design of effective ethical leadership education and pre-service as well as in-service training programs for police officers.

KEY TERMS AND CONCEPTS

Define, describe, or explain the importance of each of the following:

behavior theory
contingency theory
follower- and context-centered theories
interaction-expectation theory
leader-centered theories
leader-follower interactions-centered theories
leader-follower (member) exchange theory
leadership

leadership theory
management
path-goal theory
personal-situational theory
psychodynamic approach
situational theory
trait theory
transactional leadership theory
transformational theory

DISCUSSION QUESTIONS AND EXERCISES

1. Create a definition of leadership.
2. Why is the study of leadership difficult?
3. Compare and contrast leadership with management.
4. Early approaches to the study of leadership focused on leadership traits or qualities while more recent approaches address leadership competencies. Should leadership traits be discounted in favor of leadership competencies? Explain.
5. Review the theories of leadership presented in this chapter. Can one best theory be identified as applicable in all leadership scenarios? Explain.

CHAPTER 4

ETHICS, MORALITY, AND LEADERSHIP

LEARNING OBJECTIVES

After completing this chapter, the reader should be able to:

- define ethics, morality, values, and virtue.
- describe the theoretical basis for ethics.
- explain the relationship between ethics and morality.
- describe the importance of choice as it relates to ethical decision making.
- evaluate situations that involve unprofessional conduct.
- articulate the foundation for codes of ethics and behavior.
- integrate concepts of ethics with concepts of leadership.

INTRODUCTION

The study of ethics and morality is difficult, especially as it relates to leadership. From the standpoint of a criminal justice practitioner, ethical issues are often encountered when situations involve: the use of discretion, force, or deceptive practices; assurance of rights to due process; and loyalty to peers. Concrete answers to ethical issues in these situations are often elusive. No policy manual or code of ethics can identify correct action or provide a moral formula to determine what action to take in every situation. However, moral and ethical issues can be approached in a rational manner if a person has learned of, and is prepared to act in a manner consistent with, morality and ethics. As a morally and ethically informed person, an individual can use moral reasoning abilities to separate poor responses to ethical questions from those with plausible ethical answers (Close & Meier, 1995). This chapter is devoted to a discussion of ethics and its relationship to morality and leadership. As the reader encounters personal and professional situations that require morally and ethically correct responses, it is hoped that the material presented in this chapter will prove helpful.

ETHICS DEFINED

Ethics is the study of the principles of good conduct and systems of moral values. **Ethical behavior** relates to conduct that conforms to accepted principles of morality and good conduct. The word *ethics* is derived from the Greek word *ethos,* meaning character, conduct, or custom as well as the derivative phrase *ta ethika,* which Plato and Aristotle used to describe their studies of Greek values. Ethics involves a concern for the virtuousness and character of a person as well as a concern for the character of a society, which is called its *ethos.* Ethics is the participation in and understanding of the character of a society, an ethos as well as the social values and rules (morality) that exist to guide a societal member's behavior. Ethics concerns right and wrong, moral duty and responsibility, and personal character. Thus, ethics involves the study of standards of conduct and moral judgment. Ethical behavior is that which is consistent with acceptable standards of conduct and morality (Close & Meier, 1995; Jones & Carlson, 2001; Northouse, 2001; Solomon, 1996).

Ethics is often the subject of disagreement because general agreement regarding basic ethical principles and practices apparently does not exist in every situation. It is, however, important to appreciate differences of opinion and listen to the views of others. Ethics does not depend on a finding of factual justification for morality as a whole (Close & Meier, 1995; Cohen & Feldberg, 1991; Kleinig, 1996b; Solomon, 1996). The process of searching for moral and ethical standards is, by itself, a worthwhile personal and professional endeavor.

Typically, ethics is learned sporadically from early childhood through adulthood, as people acquire values and participate in a societal system. Ethics is concerned with living well, being a good person, doing the right thing, getting along with others, and wanting the right things. Ethics is essential to living in any society. Ethics refers to the study of values and their justification as well as to the actual values and rules of conduct by which people live.

Any study or understanding of ethics is complicated because ethical standards are not based on universal agreement. People behave (or misbehave) according to the complex and—at least in the minds of some—continually changing rules, customs, and expectations. Consequently, people are forced to reflect on their conduct and attitudes to justify and, sometimes, to revise them. During World War II, for example, the attitude of most young men drafted into the military was that of unquestioning acceptance. During the Vietnam War, however, many who resisted the draft were hailed by some as moral heroes (Solomon, 1996).

Numerous ethical challenges arise in culturally diverse environments that often do not occur in homogenous cultures. Globalization has given rise to massive migration, immigration, international travel and business activities, and satellite communications systems. The resulting cultural diversity makes ethical decision making more difficult because of differing cultural values. In some cultures, bribery is permissible (Africa, Middle East), providing false information is not considered deceptive (Mexico), theft of intellectual property is not illegal (Thailand, Indonesia, Malaysia), and gender inequality is the norm (Middle East, Japan) (Johnson, 2001).

Cultures are dense in values, beliefs, and habits. Cultures, therefore, process information in value-laden ways (Crank, 1998). As people merge from single cultures to form multicultural heterogenous societies, some conflict is almost inevitable. Conflicting community standards and desires can only be resolved by appealing to broad principles of morality and ethics. Thus, seemingly competitive theories about values, morality, and ethics may be combined to form an ethical pluralism that can be used to resolve an ethical dilemma (Johnson, 2001). In other words, knowledge of these theories may assist with creating a common sense of right thinking and correct action for a multicultural society.

THEORETICAL BASIS FOR ETHICS

The theoretical basis for ethics is derived from two areas of analysis: **metaethics** and **normative ethics.** Metaethical analysis attempts to discover the reasons for making a moral judgment about life. One approach to metaethics is referred to as absolutism, an approach through which unchanging reasons for a course of action are based on knowledge that is considered to be true. Individuals may develop a belief that is based on false assumptions. For example, a person may believe that all police officers are abusive, and accept this belief as truth. Another approach to metaethics is referred to as relativism. According to relativism, what is moral, right, or wrong depends on the group or culture within which the behavior takes place. Criminal gangs have a value system and certain ethical standards are accepted within the gang. Thus, gang members may possess ideas of morality that are relative to the group, but not society.

Normative ethics considers more concrete questions. For example, what types of acts are morally right or morally wrong? There are two approaches or theories involved in normative ethics. One is referred to as **deontological ethics,** which is duty driven. In this approach, the means through which one acts count more than the ends. A person acts according to duties, rights, and sense of responsibility. Deontological theories are often referred to as nonconsequentialist or formalist theories of ethics. They typically do not consider the consequences of one's actions to be morally significant. Although they do not ignore consequences entirely, deontological theories of ethics focus on the quality of what one does rather than what one's actions produce (Close & Meier, 1995; Johnson, 2001). Deontological theories are divided into act and rule-based theories. Act theories focus on the morality (right versus wrong) of an action. Rule-based theories address ethical decision making on the basis of rules promulgated to prescribe correct behavior.

Act-based deontologism is further divided into conscience (moral intuition) and situational ethics. Conscience ethics is often based on a religious belief that humans possess a uniform set of moral intuitions and that right and wrong actions are identified by examining one's conscience. Although moral intuition has value in ethical reasoning, a review of history reveals differing views regarding what is morally acceptable behavior. Through situational ethics, by contrast, every situation is viewed as unique and, consequently, rules and other moral guides are useless or of little value. One must apply one's own moral intuition in light of circumstances that exist in the current situation. Since every situation is unique, consistency in decision making is not expected. The fatal flaw in situational ethics is the lack of consistency, uniformity, and reliability, the plausible requirements for any ethical theory or system that can reliably guide human behavior.

Rule-based deontologism is subdivided into three strands: Kantianism, divine command theory, and the Golden Rule. **Kantian theory** is based on the work of Immanuel Kant (1724–1804). Kant attempted to identify a foundation for morally correct action that is free of erratic and varying psychological motivations. Kant proposed that morally correct action is performed based on duty alone. Kant's supreme principle of morality, the categorical imperative, was based on what one must do. According to Kant, one must act to treat self and others as a means as well as an end. Thus, people cannot be "used" as a means to a good end. The impact of decisions on others must always be considered (Close & Meier, 1995; Johnson, 2001; Solomon, 1996).

Divine command (theological voluntarism) **theory** is also a form of rule-based deontologism. According to the theory, a person's actions are morally correct if they conform to the commandments or teachings of a religious person's deity (God, Yahweh, Jehovah, Allah, Shiva, Krishna, or

OVERVIEW OF MAJOR THEORIES OF ETHICS

METAETHICS: Attempts to discover reasons for making moral judgments.

- **Absolutism:** reasons for decision are unchangeable and based on what is believed to be true.
- **Relativism:** Morality (right vs. wrong) depends on group within which behavior takes place.

NORMATIVE ETHICS: Focuses on morality of actions.

- **Deontological theories (nonconsequentialism):** duty driven; means count more than ends (consequences).
  - **Act-based deontologicalism:** focus on morality (right vs. wrong) of an action.
    - **Conscience (moral intuition) ethics:** moral principles are uniform; actions based on uniform set of moral intuitions human beings should possess.
    - **Situational ethics:** situation determines behavior.
  - **Rule-based deontologicalism:** rules prescribe correct behavior.
    - **Kantianism:** correct action based on duty; what one must do.
    - **Divine command theory:** actions are morally correct if they conform to the will of a deity.
    - **Golden Rule:** treat others as one would treat self; based on concept of equal treatment.
- **Teleological theories (consequentialism):** goal driven; ends (consequences) justify the means used.
  - **Utilitarianism:** promotes the greatest good for the greatest number; actions are ethical when good outcomes (consequences) outweigh bad outcomes.
    - **Act utilitarianism:** seeks to determine morality of specific acts.
    - **Rule utilitarianism:** actions are morally correct if they conform to rules that are morally right. Rules are morally right if they promote the greatest good for the greatest number.
  - **Ethical egoism:** actor promotes greatest good (consequences) for self.

Satan). Thus, morality of action originates with what is understood to be the will of the deity.

The third rule-based deontological ethics theory is based on the principle of the **Golden Rule**—Do unto others as you would have them do unto you. The Golden Rule is based on the concept of equal treatment, a principle associated with teleological rule utilitarianism as well as deontology. The Golden Rule theory of ethics is the subject of criticism because it cannot

PRINCIPLES OF ETHICS

- **Nonmaleficence:** to refrain from harming oneself or another. It occurs when an individual or group is in a position to cause harm but does not.
- **Beneficence (bringing about good):** occurs when an individual or group benefits others.
- **Fidelity (promise-keeping):** occurs when an individual or group makes and keeps an explicit or implicit promise to another.
- **Veracity:** occurs when an individual or group is in a position to deceive someone but communicates the truth.
- **Justice:** occurs when an individual or organization distributes benefits among individuals or groups in society who have legitimate claims to the benefits.
- **Reparation:** occurs when an individual or group wrongs another and makes reparation for the wrong.
- **Gratitude:** occurs when an individual or group is the thankful beneficiary of another's kindness.
- **Confidentiality:** occurs when an individual or group does not harm another with inappropriate disclosure of information (Close & Meier, 1995; Ortmeier, 1999; Solomon, 1996).

be applied consistently in practical settings. One cannot always treat others as one would choose to be treated. A police officer could not consistently apply the Golden Rule since the officer is often legally bound to arrest and incarcerate other persons, something not wanted for oneself. Thus, consistent and uniform application of the Golden Rule is often unrealistic (Close & Meier, 1995).

The other approach to normative ethics is referred to as **teleological ethics.** This approach is goal driven. Ends count and concern focuses on consequences. The teleological approach is often referred to as the consequentialist approach. The term "teleological" is derived from the Greek *telos,* which means goal or end. The most popular variety of teleological ethics is utilitarianism, a principle that promotes the greatest good for the greatest number of people. According to utilitarianism, actions are ethical when good outcomes (consequences) outweigh the amount of bad outcomes produced. Thus, teleological ethical theory is an inherently quantitative moral theory, counting the amount of good outcomes. Similar to deontological theories of ethics, teleological utilitarianism can be divided into act and rule-based theories. Act utilitarianism refers to the morality of a specific action. Since it could take years to determine if some acts are morally correct—a court-ordered execution, for example—act utilitarianism lacks practicality. Rule utilitarianism seeks to overcome the impracticality. According to rule utilitarianism, an action is morally correct if it is based on any rule (law, policy, value) that is morally right (produces the greatest good for the greatest number). A serious problem associated with utilitarianism is the devaluation, even violation, of certain moral principles such as fairness and equal treatment.

The other approach to teleological ethical theory is called **ethical egoism.** Through ethical egoism, the actor promotes the greatest good (consequences) for self. The difficulty with the ethical egoist approach, however, is the conflict that can arise if all people pursue their own self-interests without regard to others (Close & Meier, 1995; Jones & Carlson, 2001; Solomon, 1996).

Several basic ethics principles can be derived from the theories of ethics. These principles include nonmaleficence, beneficence, fidelity, veracity, justice, reparation, gratitude, and confidentiality.

ETHICS AND VIRTUE

The vast majority of people share respect for certain fundamental traits and dispositions of good character commonly referred to as **virtues.** Virtues tend to govern personal and social lives (Kleinig, 1996b). Virtues form a foundation for morality. The primary virtues, as identified by Plato and Aristotle, include prudence (discretion), justice (rightness, integrity), courage (strength in face of adversity), and self-restraint (temperance). Christians added faith, hope, and love. Additional virtues have been derived from the original seven (Johnson, 2001). Thus, virtues also include honesty, compassion, perseverance, self-discipline, responsibility, friendship, loyalty, generosity, modesty, gentleness, thriftiness, and industriousness (Bennett, 1993; Kleinig, 1996b; Pollock, 1998).

Generally, virtue refers to who a person is, while ethics refers to what a person does. Individuals may possess some virtues and not others. A person could be completely honest but not compassionate. To the extent to which people possess virtues, some people may be more virtuous than others. In some cases, especially in the professions, virtues may be in conflict (Perez & Moore, 2002; Pollock, 1998). In law enforcement, for example, it is legally permissible (and common practice) to be dishonest with a criminal suspect during an interrogation. In an attempt to solicit a confession, the interrogator may inform the suspect that other inculpatory (incriminating) evidence exists although it actually does not. The interrogator is "doing the right thing" in an attempt to solicit a confession. Accordingly, at times it

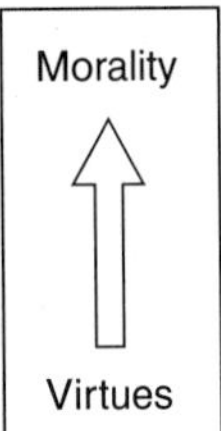

FIGURE 4–1 Virtues and Morality

may be necessary for individuals to consider the primacy of virtues, prioritizing them according to standards of ethical behavior. Thus, when one considers the ethics of virtue, the principle of doing the right thing (doing good) may take precedence over being good.

Ethics and Morality

The terms "ethics" and "moral" have similar root meanings. The Greek word *ethos* and the Latin word *moralis* both pertain to custom or character. The plural of moralis, *mores* (pronounced "mor-ayz"), still exists in English, referring to customs or common practices of human beings (Close & Meier, 1995).

The ability to identify situations with moral content is a very important ingredient in the ethics equation. Yet, it is often difficult to distinguish between situations that have moral and nonmoral content. Ethics is concerned with one's moral duty, the duty to act according to what is morally right. However, the term "duty" also has nonmoral applications (Close & Meier, 1995). For example, a police officer may have a responsibility to check a duty roster to learn about a future work schedule. However, this responsibility is not a moral responsibility unless it leads to a failure to report for duty; a failure that results in poor staffing and negatively impacts public safety.

While ethics includes a wide range of acceptable behaviors in a society, morality is more specific. Morality is a subset of ethics that transcends the

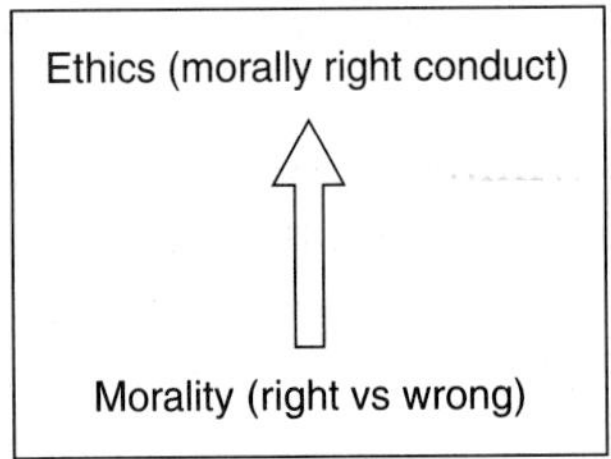

FIGURE 4–2 Morality and Ethics

boundaries of any particular ethos or situation. Ethics focuses on an individual's sense of self and place in a society. **Morality** focuses on the universal, inviolable rules in *any* society. Accordingly, ethics is concerned with existing values and acceptable standards of behavior in a particular society, while morality is concerned with rational and objective decision making based on what is universally acceptable behavior anywhere. An essential ingredient in morality is consideration for the best interests of others over one's own interests (Cohen & Feldberg, 1991; Kleinig, 1996b; Pollock, 1998; Solomon, 1996).

An appropriate foundation for understanding and evaluating the framework for morally correct police decision making is provided by the social contract theory articulated by two English political writers, **Thomas Hobbes** (1588–1679) and **John Locke** (1632–1704) (Cohen & Feldberg, 1991; Kleinig, 1996b). Hobbes and Locke each envisioned government as the outcome of an agreement (social contract) among citizens. Hobbes (1649/1950) argued that political authority emanated from the presumed consent of the governed. Locke (1690) stated that the trust, power, and authority are vested in a magistrate (forerunner of police officer or judicial official) to use for the good of people in society (Gough, 1976; Hobbes, 1649/1950; Kleinig, 1996b; Locke, 1690; Pollock, 1998; Reiman, 1990).

Those who wrote the American Declaration of Independence and the U.S. Constitution were greatly influenced by Locke's concept of a social contract through which a limited government functioned as an agent of the citizens with their consent (Cohen & Feldberg, 1991; Gough, 1976; Locke, 1690). As the most visible agents of government, with power and authority vested in them by the social contract to act as referees, police officers should remain neutral as they make decisions to enforce the law, keep the peace, and maintain public order (Cohen & Feldberg, 1991).

Some ethicists, called relativists, reject the idea of universal moral principles. These ethicists argue that morality is relative to a culture or society. What is moral in one culture or society may not be moral in another (Solomon, 1996). The relativist theory could be expanded to cover different types of situations a human may encounter. Thus, behavior appropriate to one situation may be inappropriate in another. The authors concur with experts who suggest that relativist thinking may be misguided and dangerous. If a police officer strives to rid society of criminals, it does not follow morally that the officer may use any means necessary to eradicate the criminal element (Cohen & Feldberg, 1991; Crank & Caldero, 2000; Kleinig, 1996b; Klockars, 1991). If police officers are willing to do almost anything to achieve good ends, they have corrupted themselves and their profession (Crank & Caldero, 2000). Certain behaviors are simply wrong and violate the essential nature of morality, that is, doing the right thing in the right way at the right time.

ETHICS AND CHOICE

The premise of virtue ethics is simple—people with high moral character make good moral choices. Virtues are not easily developed or discarded. They persist over time. Virtuousness makes a person sensitive to ethical issues and encourages them to act morally. Virtues operate independent of a situation. Virtuous leaders do not abandon their principles to please others (Johnson, 2001).

In spite of efforts to regulate police behavior through codes of ethics and conduct, officers still retain broad discretion to make choices when performing police work. The ability to exercise discretion comes with responsibility and police officers, for the most part, are held accountable for their actions (Cohen & Feldberg, 1991). However, a fundamental axiom of policing involves what some refer to as the noble cause. The **noble cause** is a commitment to do something to prevent illegal human behavior and apprehend criminal offenders. It inspires officer values and, for some officers, justifies their actions. As the police exercise authority to ensure public safety, the noble cause becomes a central ends-based initiative. The initiative is corrupted when police officers violate the law themselves on behalf of personally held moral values and a desire to "put the bad person away" (Crank & Caldero, 2000; Klockars, 1991; Perez & Moore, 2002). Yet, police officers are not recruited from the ranks of morally superior beings. Nor would it be wise to create police officers who are viewed as morally superior, lest their judgment be considered above any right versus wrong test (Cohen & Feldberg, 1991).

A genuine **moral dilemma** occurs when a police officer is in a situation from which the officer cannot emerge innocent, no matter what the officer does. When arresting an extremely dangerous person can be achieved only through the use of unethical means, the officer faces the dilemma. To what extent does a morally good end justify the use of an unethical, even illegal, means to achieve this end? Can falsifying probable cause for a stop or search ever be justified? Could failure to use unethical means to apprehend an inherently dangerous person lead to moral disrepute of the officer? Could inaction lead to a lawsuit by a victim of the dangerous person who was not apprehended because ethical means were not available? Hopefully, when confronted with these types of decisions, officers will make the morally and ethically correct choices (Klockars, 1991).

The practice of community policing itself may create unique ethical problems for a police officer. First, creative policing, customized to meet the needs of a particular community, accompanied by expanded officer discretion, could set the stage for discriminatory enforcement and assignment of officers. In addition, certain individuals or specific groups of people in a community may be more vocal than others. The more vocal people might present themselves as community spokespersons. Officers must recognize that all those who assert leadership status in the community are not necessarily motivated by what is in the best interest of the community (Crank & Caldero, 2000; Mastrofski & Worden, 1991).

The importance of choice in ethics is often confused with the notion that values are subjective and people merely choose their own set of values. This assumption is misleading because most ethical decisions involve a choice between already established possibilities. Personal values are rarely one's own values alone. By their very nature, values are shared and exist outside those who embrace the values. A person does not choose the alternative. Rather, the person chooses among alternatives (Solomon, 1996).

Most people live in a pluralist society, an environment with no single code of ethics but several sets of values emanating from a variety of cultures and subcultures (Solomon, 1996). Members of a criminal gang may subscribe to a particular set of values or code of ethics. They may not believe it unethical to kill a rival gang member. A police officer may not intervene to stop a fellow officer's misbehavior because a "blue code of silence" is maintained in the police subculture. The individual challenge is to choose and follow an appropriate set of values.

Certain cognitive processes and socialization with others reinforce unethical conduct and influence the onset and proliferation of undesirable behavior. Thus, psychological and social forces help produce police misconduct. However, one should not lose sight of the role of choice when police officers engage in unethical and unprofessional conduct. Given a police officer's position of public trust, unethical, even illegal, behavior results when an officer makes a conscious decision to act in a way that is not appropriate to the situation. While circumstantial reasons, peer pressure, loyalties, social factors, or psychological problems may exist, the fundamental ingredient for unethical conduct by the police is a conscious decision to abuse authority or engage in misconduct. Although the other factors may help perpetuate, justify, or excuse unethical conduct, it is an individual officer's conscious decision-making process that is ultimately determinative (Byers, 2000).

ETHICS AND PROFESSIONAL CONDUCT

Two police officers respond to the reported robbery of a convenience store. Upon arrival at the scene, the officers determine that the suspect has fled the area. Appropriate police procedure is followed by both officers.

However, while interviewing the victim-clerk, the first officer observes the second officer take a candy bar and, without paying for it, leave the store. Has an ethical standard been violated? Should the first officer intervene? If so, how should a police officer respond to another officer's unethical or inappropriate conduct? If the first officer does not intervene, is minding one's own business a valid excuse? If an appropriate intervention does not take place, is the first officer as unworthy of the badge as the second? Peace officers are sworn to uphold the law. Yet, professionalism involves more than effective law enforcement and courtesy toward the general public (Dempsey, 1992). Officers have a legal as well as a moral obligation to act legally, responsibly, and ethically.

Ethics involves moral principles and focuses on the concept of right and wrong and standards of behavior. Unlike law or organizational policy, which is formally prescribed and enforced by a controlling authority, ethics is based on moral standards, rather than strict legality alone. These moral standards, or ethical values, are formed through the influence of others. These standards are concerned with the relationships between people and how they exist in peace and harmony.

Values are fundamental beliefs on which personal decisions and conduct are based. Societal values are based on the norms of the community. Organizational values represent the beliefs of an organization. Professional values are reflected by an occupation or discipline. Personal values are based on individual beliefs. Values may be ethical or unethical. Gang members have values but their behavior may be unethical. Behavior may be unethical, yet not illegal. Therefore, ethics assumes a special meaning and involves the systematic reflection on, and analysis of, morality. It takes on a specific form when someone assumes the role of a professional.

Values are enduring yet changeable beliefs that certain conduct and goals are personally or socially preferable over opposite conduct and goals. Generally, values are learned (programmed) in human beings through imprinting, modeling, and socialization. Imprinting is dominant during a human's formative years (birth to school age), in which key figures induce parents, guardians, and significant others. Modeling occurs from early school age to one's early teens, a period during which human beings begin to identify with internal (family) and external "heroes." From early teenage years until the early twenties (adolescence), socialization with peers dominates human values acquisition. In adulthood, values learned in early childhood through adolescence remain unless changed through a significant emotional event or profound dissatisfaction with existing conditions (Whisenand & Ferguson, 2002).

Ethical standards dictate behavior even when law or precedent, which may prescribe rules of conduct, do not exist. Whenever one possesses the power of discretional decision making, the decision should conform to what one ought to do, even though specific law, policy, or precedent is not available. The ends do not always justify the means. Conducting oneself according to an acceptable ethical standard, whether the profession has a code of ethics or not, means doing the right thing at the right time. This ability to act properly is formed by careful thought and study on the subject of ethics.

Police officers engage in unethical conduct when they accept gratuities, misuse the badge of office, practice racism and discrimination, misuse privileged communications and confidential information, misappropriate property, obstruct justice, engage in inappropriate off-duty behavior, and evoke a code of silence with respect to another officer's misbehavior (California State Commission on Peace Officer Standards and Training, 1999).

Some argue that there can be a distinction between one's public and private morality. Yet, although private lapses in moral judgment do not necessarily lead to similar lapses in one's public affairs, it seems artificial to compartmentalize private and public ethics. One's private tendencies can cross over into one's public decisions. Fostering virtuous behavior and ethical leadership is a lifelong process. It involves understanding morality, learning from hardship, cultivating good habits, the identification of role models, and clarification of values (Johnson, 2001; Kleinig, 1996b).

Potential ethical problem areas in policing include corruption, discrimination, violation of rights to privacy, violation of rights under the Constitution, entrapment, negligence, use of excessive force, uncivil conduct, violation of agency policies or procedure, or violations of the professional code of ethics. Each of these areas should be addressed in recruit and in-service training programs (Ortmeier, 2002).

With the possible exception of presidential candidates, police officers are more closely scrutinized and possibly subject to more misinformed and biased criticism than any other occupational group (Fuller, 2001). Although real or imagined unethical behavior, let alone criminal conduct, on the part of the police involves a very small number of police officers, the negative impact that such acts have on the public's image of the police can be devastating.

LAW ENFORCEMENT CODES OF ETHICS AND CONDUCT

The goals of moral education and adherence to codes of ethics and conduct seek to provide a foundation on which police officers can act as autonomous moral agents (Parker, 1957; Close & Meier, 1995). Although police officers do not have moral insight or powers of analysis greater than

THE LONE RANGER CREED

Clayton Moore, as the star of television's *Lone Ranger* series in the 1940s and 1950s, crusaded against villains on his horse, Silver, accompanied by his trusty sidekick, Tonto. In his personal as well as his professional life, Clayton Moore attempted to live up to the provisions of the Lone Ranger Creed.

- A person must be a friend to have one.
- All people are created equal and have within them the power to make the world a better place.
- God created firewood, but every person must gather and light it.
- Everyone must be prepared physically, mentally, and morally to fight for what is right.
- People should make the most of what they have.
- Democracy shall live always.
- Sooner or later, all people must settle with the world for what they have taken from it.
- All things change but the truth, and truth lives on forever (Germain, 1999).

anyone else (Cohen & Feldberg, 1991), officers can hopefully make moral decisions based on personal moral values independent of what other persons believe. For most people, personal moral values are those held because they are believed to be universally true and correct. Thus, these values are part of a single system of universal ethical standards that should be present in every officer's personal and professional life (Close & Meier, 1995; Parker, 1957).

Codes of ethics have a long history. The Decalogue of Judeo-Christian tradition, the Eightfold Path of Buddhism, the Code of Hammurabi, and the 400 B.C. Oath of Hippocrates are a few examples of ancient codes. However, professional codes of ethics did not assume a prominent public role until the nineteenth century. Codes of ethics and conduct did proliferate in the early twentieth century but they did not become popular in policing until the 1950s. Yet, early police agencies often incorporated ethics material in their instructions, rules, and regulations issued to officers (Kleinig & Zhang, 1993).

Whether they are referred to as canons, standards, tenets, credos, declarations, principles, or statements of professional responsibility, codes of ethics and conduct prescribe how professionals should pursue the ideals that are implicit in their activities. Healthcare and peacekeeping are examples of these activities. The public's assurance in the integrity of the activity is at stake. The codes are not viewed as comprehensive. Rather, they

CODE OF ETHICS

As a law enforcement officer, my fundamental duty is to: serve the community; safeguard lives and property; protect the innocent against deception, the weak against oppression or intimidation and the peaceful against violence or disorder; and respect the constitutional rights of all to liberty, equality and justice.

I will keep my private life unsullied as an example to all and will behave in a manner that does not bring discredit to me or to my agency. I will maintain courageous calm in the face of danger, scorn or ridicule; develop self-restraint; and be constantly mindful of the welfare of others. Honest in thought and deed both in my personal and official life, I will be exemplary in obeying the law and the regulations of my department. Whatever I see or hear of a confidential nature or that is confided to me in my official capacity will be kept secret unless revelation is necessary in the performance of my duty.

I will never act officiously or permit personal feelings, prejudices, political beliefs, aspirations, animosities or friendships to influence my decisions. With no compromise for crime and with relentless prosecution of criminals, I will enforce the law courteously and appropriately without fear or favor, malice or ill will, never employing unnecessary force or violence and never accepting gratuities.

I recognize the badge of my office as a symbol of public faith, and I accept it as a public trust to be held so long as I am true to the ethics of police service. I will never engage in acts of corruption or bribery, nor will I condone such acts by other police officers. I will cooperate with all legally authorized agencies and their representatives in the pursuit of justice.

I know that I alone am responsible for my own standard of professional performance and will take every reasonable opportunity to enhance and improve my level of knowledge and competence.

I will constantly strive to achieve these objectives and ideals, dedicating myself before God to my chosen profession. . . law enforcement (International Association of Chiefs of Police, 1991a).

form a perspective through which professional services are rendered. Since significantly vulnerable people place their fragile trust in a police officer's hands, codes of ethics provide the public with some reasonable assurance that the trust will not be exploited or betrayed (Kleinig & Zhang, 1993).

Codes of ethics and **conduct** are common among long-established professional groups. The codes provide a means through which professionals can assess their own behavior (Kleinig & Zhang, 1993). Persons who adhere to such codes exhibit certain qualities or traits. Professionals exhibit honesty, trustworthiness, integrity, fairness, tolerance, empathy, respect,

CODE OF CONDUCT

All law enforcement officers must be fully aware of the ethical responsibilities of their position and must strive constantly to live up to the highest possible standards of professional policing.

The International Association of Chiefs of Police believes it [to be] important that police officers have clear advice and counsel available to assist them in performing their duties consistent with these standards, and has adopted the following ethical mandates as guidelines to meet these ends.

Primary Responsibilities of a Police Officer

A police officer acts as an official representative of government who is required and trusted to work within the law. The officer's powers and duties are conferred by statute. The fundamental duties of a police officer include serving the community, safeguarding lives and property, protecting the innocent, keeping the peace and ensuring the rights of all to liberty, equality and justice.

Performance of the Duties of a Police Officer

A police officer shall perform all duties impartially, without favor or affection or ill will and without regard to status, sex, race, religion, political belief or aspiration. All citizens will be treated equally with courtesy, consideration and dignity.

Officers will never allow personal feelings, animosities or friendships to influence official conduct. Laws will be enforced appropriately and courteously and, in carrying out their responsibilities, officers will strive to obtain maximum cooperation from the public. They will conduct themselves in appearance and deportment in such a manner as to inspire confidence and respect for the position of public trust they hold.

Discretion

A police officer will use responsibly the discretion vested in the officer's position and exercise it within the law. The principle of reasonableness will guide the officer's determinations, and the officer will consider all surrounding circumstances in determining whether any legal action shall be taken.

Consistent and wise use of discretion, based on professional policing competence, will do much to preserve good relationships and retain the confidence of the public. There can be difficulty in choosing between conflicting courses of action. It is important to remember that a timely word of advice rather than arrest—which may be correct in appropriate circumstances—can be a more effective means of achieving a desired end.

Use of Force

A police officer will never employ unnecessary force or violence and will use only such force in the discharge of duty as is reasonable in all circumstances.

Force should be used only with the greatest restraint and only after discussion, negotiation and persuasion have been found to be inappropriate or ineffective. While the use of force is occasionally unavoidable, every police officer will refrain from unnecessary infliction of pain or suffering and will never engage in cruel, degrading or inhuman treatment of any person.

Confidentiality

Whatever a police officer sees, hears or learns that is of a confidential nature will be kept secret unless the performance of duty or legal provision requires otherwise.

Members of the public have a right to security and privacy, and information obtained about them must not be improperly divulged.

Integrity

A police officer will not engage in acts of corruption or bribery, nor will an officer condone such acts by other police officers.

The public demands that the integrity of police officers be above reproach. Police officers must, therefore, avoid any conduct that might compromise integrity and thus undercut the public confidence in a law enforcement agency. Officers will refuse to accept any gifts, presents, subscriptions, favors, gratuities or promises that could be interpreted as seeking to cause the officer to refrain from performing official responsibilities honestly and within the law. Police officers must not receive private or special advantage from their official status. Respect from the public cannot be bought; it can only be earned and cultivated.

Cooperation with Other Police Officers and Agencies

Police officers will cooperate with all legally authorized agencies and their representatives in the pursuit of justice.

An officer or agency may be one among many organizations that may provide law enforcement services to a jurisdiction. It is imperative that a police officer assist colleagues fully and completely with respect and consideration at all times.

Personal-Professional Capabilities

Police officers will be responsible for their own standard of professional performance and will take every reasonable opportunity to enhance and improve their level of knowledge and competence.

continued

Through study and experience, a police officer can acquire the high level of knowledge and competence that is essential for the efficient and effective performance of duty. The acquisition of knowledge is a never-ending process of personal and professional development that should be pursued constantly.

Private Life

Police officers will behave in a manner that does not bring discredit to their agencies or themselves.

A police officer's character and conduct while off duty must always be exemplary, thus maintaining a position of respect in the community in which he or she lives and serves. The officer's personal behavior must be beyond reproach (International Association of Chiefs of Police, 1991b).

responsibility, loyalty, accountability, and self-control. Professionals consistently pursue excellence in carrying out their duties (California State. Commission on Peace Officer Standards and Training, 1999).

Virtually every profession establishes a code of ethics and sets forth standards of behavior for its members. It is not uncommon for a profession to have two versions of its professional code—a short promissory version for public display and a longer version that outlines and explains statements of principle. Numerous police-related codes of ethics and conduct exist (Kleinig & Zhang, 1993). The International Association of Chiefs of Police (IACP) developed a Code of Ethics and a Code of Conduct for law enforcement officers.

CODES OF ETHICS—PROS AND CONS

Since no universal set of moral rules exists that is accepted by everyone, many professions and organizations attempt to regulate member conduct by enumerating which actions are morally permissible or impermissible. The moral rules are usually contained in the codes of ethics or behavior, or in ethical canons (Kleinig & Zhang, 1993). Rarely, however, is any attempt made at a rational justification for the rules in the codes. Thus, codes or canons of ethics are not ethical theories. Rather, the codes or canons of ethics are often used to protect the occupation or organization's members from external review or regulation. Additionally, codes of ethics rarely state a hierarchy indicating the order in which the rules should be followed. Consequently, codes and canons of ethics may conflict and often fail to correlate with practical situations. A police code of ethics, for example, typically requires honesty while insisting that officers relentlessly pursue criminals. Does this mean, then, that officers cannot deceive a suspect during an interrogation (Close & Meier, 1995)?

The IACP Code of Ethics has been criticized by some as irrelevant to the realties of most police officers because it specifies perfect behavior. In spite of the criticism, the code does project an ideal toward which officers can strive. Since the code describes the highest standard of behavior, police agencies should develop behavior-related policies that can be more objective and enforceable. Although police officers are human and thus, by the very nature of humanity, subject to imperfect behavior and judgment, this code of ethics provides an aspiring standard against which officers can measure their own behavior. All police officers should strive to conform their behavior to the central themes in the IACP Code of Ethics.

The central themes in the law enforcement code of ethics are: justice, fairness, and equality; service to the community; the supremacy of the Constitution and the law; and maintenance of a standard of conduct that is consistent with a police officer's public position (Pollock, 1998). While many legal precepts already prescribe or imply the themes of justice, fairness, and equality contained in codes of ethics (Rawls, 1971), the codes are often created because of a heightened sense of moral and social accountability. They are commonly justified because they explicitly describe desirable behavior (Kleinig & Zhang, 1993). Together with other moral principles based on rational grounds, codes of ethics can provide a compass to orient a police officer's sense of moral direction.

ETHICS AND LEADERSHIP

True leaders have followers regardless of the leader's rank or title. Thus, leadership is not confined to supervisors and managers. Leadership is an individual responsibility. Ethical behavior is also an individual responsibility. Ethical leadership of self must occur before one can ethically lead others. Everything a leader does through competence, skills, and abilities is influenced by who a leader is, and who a leader is depends on individual character, values, morals, and attitudes (Kokkelenberg, 2001).

The principles of ethical leadership provide a sound foundation for those who assume or are placed in leadership roles. Although not inclusive, these principles include respect, service, justice, honesty, and community. The origin of these principles can be traced to Aristotle and the importance of these principles has been addressed in a variety of disciplines (Northouse, 2001). Ethical leadership has been researched and discussed in relation to business (Beauchamp & Bowie, 1988), counseling psychology (Kitchener, 1984), biomedicine (Beauchamp & Childress, 1994), and leadership education and training (Komives, Lucas, & McMahon, 1998).

Ethical leaders respect others and treat them as ends in themselves rather than means to an end (Beauchamp & Bowie, 1988). Ethical leaders find unconditional worth and valuable differences in others (Kitchener, 1984). Ethical leaders nurture others, assisting them with creating an awareness of their own values and goals. The leader's nurturing leads to the integration of follower values and needs with those of the leader's (Burns, 1978; Northouse, 2001).

Ethical leaders serve others. Ethical leaders coach, mentor, empower, build teams, and promote citizenship. Public service providers, such as police officers, have a duty to help others pursue legitimate interests. Service to others is the primary building block to moral and ethical leadership (Beauchamp & Childress, 1994; Covey, 1990; Kouzes & Posner, 1995; Northouse, 2001).

Ethical leaders are fair and just. They treat others equally, without discrimination. No one receives special treatment except when unique circumstances require special consideration. Differential treatment must be based on sound ethical standards (Northouse, 2001; Rawls, 1971). Police officers should strive for equal treatment of all based on fairness and justice. Supervisory decisions should be based on one or any combination of the principles of equality, need, individual rights, effort, societal contribution, and merit (Beauchamp & Bowie, 1988).

Ethical leaders are honest and trustworthy. Deliberate and illegitimate misrepresentations of reality create distrust (Northouse, 2001). Corruption, false testimony, dishonest reporting, and other illegitimate deceptions weaken relationships, destroy credibility, and lead to withdrawal of support. The public's trust in the integrity and honesty of police officers is an essential ingredient to effective policing. In fact, honesty among police officers has been cited as one of the most desirable characteristics a police officer can possess (Harr & Hess, 2003). Dishonesty causes citizens to lose faith in the police service.

Ethical leaders build communities by searching for goals compatible with everyone's best interests. The ethical leader strives for the common good of the community. By doing so, leaders as well as followers are raised to a higher level of productivity, social consciousness, and moral purpose (Burns, 1978). In a community policing environment, a police officer's ability to engage and solicit participation from community members is critical to the development and implementation of solutions to community problems. The positive consequence of community building is an improvement in the quality of life of the leader as well as the followers.

Ethics assumes an important position in regard to leadership. Ethical leadership concerns itself with who leaders are, how they think, and how they behave. In the decision-making process, ethical issues are involved (Jones & Carlson, 2001). The choices people make in a particular situation, as persons in positions of leadership are required to do, are informed and directed by their ethics.

Theories of ethics relating to leadership fall into two broad categories: those that focus on conduct and those that focus on character. Further, ethical theories that focus on the conduct of leaders are viewed from two perspectives: theories that stress the consequences, results, or outcomes of leader actions and those that emphasize the duty or rules governing leader actions.

In assessing consequences of choices and actions, there are different approaches to making morally correct decisions. Ethical egoism postulates that an individual should act to create the greatest good for self (Northouse, 2001). A decision made by police officers to achieve crime reduction goals established by their agency in order to gain promotion or reward is an example of a decision based on ethical egoism.

A second consequence-based approach, **utilitarianism,** states that people (leaders) and societies should strive to create the greatest good (happiness) for the greatest number of people. As articulated by the English philosopher and political scientist **Jeremy Bentham** (1748–1932), utilitarianism proposes that correct (or morally right) action creates the greatest balance of good consequences over bad consequences for all of those who might be affected by the action (Bentham, 1789/1973; Close & Meier, 1995; Harrison, 1967; Northouse, 2001). Budgeting more resources for community crime prevention rather than for response to reported crimes is an example of the utilitarian approach. "The ends justify the means" is also an example of utilitarianism (Close & Meier, 1995; Klockars, 1991).

Closely associated with utilitarianism and at the opposite end of the spectrum from ethical egoism, is altruism, an approach that suggests that actions should be based on concern for the best interests of others (Northouse, 2001). If a police officer enters a burning home to search for and save the lives of fire victims, the officer demonstrates an altruistic approach to ethical behavior. The officer's behavior is contrary to self-interest.

Rather than simply looking at consequences (outcomes), some ethical theories address an individual's duty to perform the right actions. This perspective seeks to identify goodness or rightness in one's actions, independent of the consequences. Being respectful of and fair toward others, telling the truth, and keeping promises are examples of this perspective.

The second broad category of ethical theories focuses on a person's character, placing emphasis on who the person is rather than what the person does. Character theories are virtue-based. Further, it is believed that good character can be developed and that virtues and moral ability are not innate but can be learned (Northouse, 2001). Character-based theories argue that a moral person demonstrates the virtues of temperance, courage, self-control, generosity, honesty, social ability, modesty, fairness, and justice (Velasquez, 1992).

The relationship between leadership and ethics is extremely important. Ethics takes on a critical dimension for leaders. In a sense, effective leadership and ethics are inseparable. A critical ingredient in many definitions of leadership is the ability to influence others. A leader's influence can have a tremendous impact on the lives of those being led. Thus, in the process of leading others, a person assumes an enormous ethical burden and an increased level of responsibility. Because leaders are often in a position of control, they must be sensitive to the effect their attitudes, communications, and behaviors have on the values, beliefs, and actions of others. Although all persons have an ethical responsibility to treat others with dignity and respect, leaders have a special responsibility. Thus, ethics is central to leadership because of the authority and influence such a position confers (Burns, 1978; Heifetz, 1994; Johnson, 2001; Northouse, 2001).

SUMMARY

The study of ethics and morality is difficult because concrete solutions to ethical problems are often elusive. An ethic is a principle of good conduct. Ethics is the study of the principles of good conduct and systems of moral values. Ethical behavior relates to conduct that is consistent with accepted principles of morality. Numerous theories attempt to describe the basis for ethics. Virtue refers to who a person is, while ethics focuses on personal behavior. Morality is a subset of ethics that encompasses universal rules of behavior applicable to any society. Ethical decisions are based on preferable values and appropriate, correct choices. Professional conduct emanates from correct choices. Codes of ethics and behavior provide personal guides to ethical leadership behavior.

KEY TERMS AND CONCEPTS

Define, describe, or explain the importance of each of the following:

act-based deontologicalism
code of conduct

code of ethics
deontological ethics
divine command theory
ethical behavior
ethical egoism
ethical leader
ethics
Golden Rule
Jeremy Bentham
John Locke
Kantian Theory
metaethics
moral dilemma
morality
noble cause
normative ethics
rule-based deontologicalism
teleological ethics
theories of ethics
Thomas Hobbes
utilitarianism
values
virtue

DISCUSSION QUESTIONS AND EXERCISES

1. Should police officers be held to a higher moral and ethical standard than the populations they serve?
2. The law enforcement code of ethics states that officers should not act officiously. What does this statement mean? How can officers function without acting officiously?
3. What types of off-duty, private behavior discredit the police profession? Should police agencies regulate private, off-duty behavior?
4. How should a police officer respond if the officer witnesses the unethical behavior of another officer?
5. Two officers respond to the scene of a reported robbery at a convenience store. While the first officer is interviewing the victim, the second officer is observed by the first officer taking candy without paying for it. What should the first officer do?

CHAPTER 5

POLICING AND PROFESSIONAL CONDUCT

LEARNING OBJECTIVES

After completing this chapter, the reader should be able to:

- discuss the common characteristics of professions and professionalism.
- distinguish between ethical and unethical conduct.
- describe the consequences of unethical behavior.
- analyze the role of the police subculture as a mechanism for self and group protection.
- create policies and procedures for prevention and correction of unethical conduct.
- evaluate the need for a police officer bill of rights.
- formulate and choose ethical courses of action.

INTRODUCTION

Under the best of circumstances, policing can be an extremely difficult task. The police encounter dangerous situations and officers are often expected to solve problems they did not create and are beyond their capacity to resolve. A democracy's ideological conflict between the norms governing order maintenance and the principle of accountability surrounding the rule of law sets the stage for numerous demands on the police. Almost simultaneously, a police officer is expected to be a parent, friend, moralist, public servant, rule and law enforcer, street fighter, and sharpshooter (Skolnick, 1994).

As evidenced by numerous publicized accounts of their activities, police officers often have a high profile and are scrutinized more than any other occupational group in society. There is probably a good reason for this phenomenon. No other professional group in society is entrusted with the power to protect persons as well as property and to arrest, detain, question, and use force against citizens (Byers, 2000). Although the vast majority of law enforcement officers practice their profession in an exemplary manner, without engaging in any form of unprofessional behavior, it is police misconduct that makes front-page news. Accounts of incidents involving police abuse of discretion and authority, use of excessive force, discriminatory practices, and dishonesty appear more frequently in the media than do accounts of police successes. Additionally, hindsight is considerably easier to formulate than foresight, and criticism is not difficult after the fact. Obviously, police officers who engage in unethical and unprofessional conduct should be criticized and held accountable for their actions. It is also possible to learn more from police failures than from police success stories. As a means for prescribing appropriate police behavior, much of this chapter highlights what the police should not do. The presentation will focus on unethical and unprofessional conduct as the type of behavior police officers should avoid.

Trust, honesty, and appropriate behavior are ingredients to a successful relationship. The police and the community are partners in a collaborative relationship designed to keep the peace and respond to crime and disorder. Since the police are continually the targets of ethical evaluation (Byers, 2000), they must act responsibly and professionally to gain and maintain the public's trust and support. Additionally, the police are in a unique leadership position that can be used to assist communities as they seek to address crime and disorder problems and improve the quality of life. Above all else, police officers should do no harm.

POLICING AS A PROFESSION

Professionalism is often invoked as the solution to the conflicts among a police officer's roles and tasks. Most importantly, professions seek to infuse work with moral values and sanction those who do not uphold these moral values (Skolnick, 1994). Historically, however, the police service has not enjoyed the high status associated with some traditional professions such as medicine or law. Police officers are usually recruited from groups with modest economic, educational, and social status (Cohen & Feldberg, 1991; Kleinig, 1996b). Further, entry-level qualifications for police officers have focused on physical characteristics and abilities, not intellectual prowess or moral vision. However, significant progress toward professionalism status was achieved during the twentieth century (Kleinig, 1996b).

Beginning with August Vollmer's *The Police in Modern Society* (1936), the call for recognition of policing as a profession has gained in prominence (Kleinig, 1996b). In 1968, James Q. Wilson summarized a new vision for police professionalism. He stated that the characteristics of the professional police officer include the exercise of "wide discretion alone and with respect to matters of the greatest importance" and that this ability is based on a status "conferred by an organized profession" that "certifies the member has acquired by education certain information and by apprenticeship certain arts and skills that render [an officer] competent" to "handle emergency situations, to be privy to guilty information, and to make decisions involving questions of life and death or honor and dishonor." He also stated that a professional "is willing to [be] subject to the code of ethics and sense of duty to colleagues" (Wilson, 1968, pp. 29–30).

It is unlikely that any credible evidence can be produced that would suggest that policing has not become more professional over the past several decades (Byers, 2000). However, a common body of police knowledge does not exist (Goldstein, 2001) and at least one critical question must be answered: If law enforcement is a profession, have police officers acquired the wide range of skills necessary to police communities in a modern democratic society? In a nationwide FBI study conducted for the purposes of determining law enforcement training needs, police officers themselves did not view police training regarding relations with community as a high priority (Phillips,

The call to recognize policing as a profession gained prominence during the 20th century. *Photo courtesy of San Diego Police Museum*

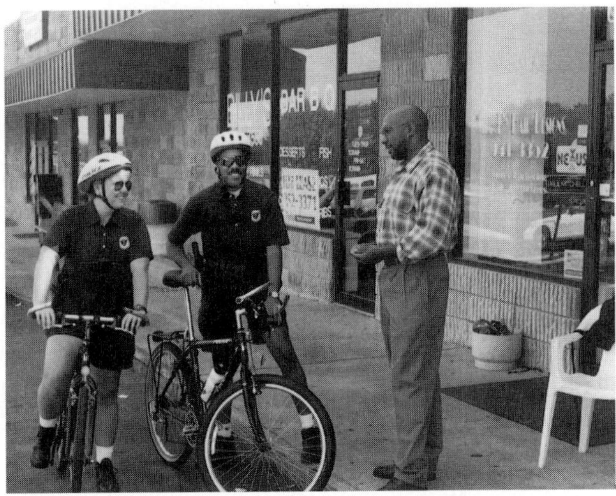

A close working relationship with the community is essential to the success of any policing stategy. *Photo courtesy of Cobb County, Georgia, Police Department*

1988). An effective and close working relationship with the community is essential to the success of any policing strategy. To function effectively within a community, policing requires officers to acquire nontraditional police skills so they may involve the community as a coparticipant in the control of crime and maintenance of order (Goldstein, 2001; Raffel Price, 1995).

In addition, because most police activity is situational, discretionary, and agency-specific, the skills required of the police officer are "more akin to occupational attributes which are developed through the melding milieu of education, training, and police experience" (Carter, Sapp, & Stephens, 1988, p. 13). As one court observed:

> Few professionals are so peculiarly charged with individual responsibility as police officers. Officers are compelled to make instantaneous decisions, often without clear-cut guidance from the legislature or departmental policy, and mistakes of judgment could cause irreparable harm to citizens or even the community (*Davis v. City of Dallas*, 1985, p. 215).

The term **profession** implies that its members adhere to certain ethical standards of behavior and achieve a minimum level of competence to be employed in a particular discipline or occupation. Common characteristics of professions and professionalism include:

- a code of ethics and standards of conduct.
- a public service orientation.
- common goals and principles.
- a recognized body of knowledge relative to the profession.

- a system for credentialing or licensing its members.
- an organization that promotes high standards and the interests of the profession.

In the quest for professional status, most members of the law enforcement community work hard to conform behavior to the characteristics of a profession. Numerous examples highlight police service endeavors toward professionalism. Some form of pre-service training is required and standards for selection and retention of peace officers have improved greatly. Common goals are reflected in the police mission. Criminal justice and law enforcement education has emerged as a discipline and helped to create a recognized body of knowledge. Codes of professional conduct have also developed (Kleinig & Zhang, 1993) and a system for licensing police officers exists in all states. Still, police misconduct in some areas indicates that there are police officers who do not subscribe to or strive toward professional standards.

POLICE MISCONDUCT

It is unreasonable to suggest that the police service is permeated with graft, criminal activity and abuse of authority by officers, corruption, occupational deviance, and other forms of illegal and unethical behavior (Byers, 2000). Unethical police behavior is not systemic. On the other hand, one could not deny that police misconduct is displayed by some individual officers, groups of officers, or even by a few police agencies.

Police misconduct can manifest itself in many forms. Examples of such misconduct are presented here, beginning with a sampling of incidents occurring over a 10-year period.

1992 Police officers were charged and subsequently convicted of beating a man. One officer received 25 years in prison, the other officer received 8 to 18 years.

1995 A police officer, testifying during the O. J. Simpson trial, committed perjury by lying about his use of a racial slur.

1996–1999 Sixty-one officers were terminated from a large urban police department for using excessive force, lying, drug use, theft, domestic violence, and improper relationships with minors and drug dealers.

1996 Sheriff's deputies were videotaped beating illegal immigrants following a high-speed freeway chase.

1997 A New York City police officer was charged (and convicted in 1999) of sodomizing a Haitian immigrant with a broken broomstick. In 2001, the City of New York and the police union agreed to pay $9 million in an out-of-court settlement to the immigrant. Three other NYPD officers received criminal convictions in connection with the case: one for violation of the immigrant's civil rights and obstruction of justice, and two for obstruction of justice for lying to cover up the incident. In 2002, the Second U. S. Court of Appeals reversed the convictions of the three officers, citing inadequate legal counsel and insufficient evidence to sustain the convictions.

1997 Prosecutors knowingly relied on perjured testimony and false information from paid informants.

1997 Allegations of improper conduct in the handling of informants within a gang prosecution unit were publicized.

1998 Two patrol officers were investigated for leading a gambling ring.

1998 A seven-year highway patrol veteran was arrested by the Drug Enforcement Administration (DEA) on suspicion of selling drugs to an informant.

1998 An off-duty police officer, drinking in a bar, drew a firearm on a patron during a fight in which the officer had become involved.

1998 A federal agent was arrested in a child pornography case.

1998 A police officer was arrested for computer thefts in a burglary he investigated.

1998 Rogue deputies were investigated for beating jail inmates.

1998 A police officer, working off duty in the construction business, threatened a customer using the authority of his official position.

1998 Over 300 FBI employees were disciplined for offenses ranging from major felonies to stealing office supplies. Thirty-two FBI employees, including 11 special agents, were fired from the bureau.

1999 A police officer was charged with thefts from wallets of traffic violators he stopped.

1999 A sheriff was convicted of filing false travel expense claims with the county.

1999 Seven prosecutors and sheriff's deputies were charged with conspiring to frame an innocent man.

2000 Four police officers from a major urban police department were indicted by a federal grand jury on charges connected with an elaborate scheme to profit from the sale of stolen plumbing fixtures. Dozens of unwitting fellow officers purchased at least $100,000 worth of the stolen goods. One of the indicted officers was also indicted on illegal drug charges.

2000 A U.S. Border Patrol agent and an immigration detention officer were convicted of stealing U.S. government auto parts.

2001 A grand jury indicted a white Cincinnati police officer on charges of negligent homicide and obstruction of official business in connection with his fatal shooting of an unarmed black man. Civil unrest subsequent to the shooting and prior to the indictments led to the worst riots in Cincinnati since the violence in the aftermath of the assassination of Martin Luther King Jr. in 1968.

2001 Two men in their late sixties were finally exonerated of their murder convictions after a judge concluded that the FBI hid evidence that would have proven their innocence. One had spent over 33 years in prison for his conviction and the other 30 years before they were freed.

2001 Five present and former agents of the DEA claimed they routinely falsified arrest records in the agency's Caribbean office. The office claimed credit for hundreds of arrests that were actually made by local police. The arrest records were inflated in an effort to receive more resources for the office.

2001 A few members of the 3,350 American police officer delegation recruited to serve with the International Police Task Force (IPTF) in Bosnia were removed for sexual misconduct and exceeding their authority. Others were forced to resign under suspicion of committing statutory rape, abetting prostitution, and accepting gifts from Bosnian officials.

2001 Four officers from a large police department were charged with more than 60 felonies and misdemeanors for assault, kidnaping, and falsifying police reports.

2002 Former FBI special agent Robert Hanssen was sentenced to life in prison for spying for the Russians during and after the Cold War. Hanssen joined the FBI in 1976 and began spying for the Soviets three years later, soon after he was assigned to a counterintelligence unit in the New York office. Except for self-imposed suspensions of his espionage activities in the early 1980s and 1990s, Hanssen spent 25 years spying for the Soviet military intelligence agency and the KGB.

2002 A California highway patrol officer was convicted in the theft of 650 pounds of cocaine from an evidence locker. The officer's co-conspirator in the theft was his half brother, a state Bureau of Narcotics Enforcement agent.

Nearly every major police force in the United States has experienced some form of unethical or illegal police behavior (Byers, 2000). A 1998 U.S.

government report cited examples of publicly disclosed drug-related police corruption in Atlanta, Chicago, Cleveland, Detroit, Los Angeles, Miami, New Orleans, New York, Philadelphia, Savannah, and Washington, D.C. On-duty police officers conducted unconstitutional searches and seizures, stole money and illegal drugs, sold illegal drugs, protected drug operations, gave false testimony, and submitted false crime reports. In addition to the profit motive, one city discovered its corrupt officers were also motivated by vigilante justice and the ability to exercise authority over others. Since 1995, 10 officers in a single major city police district were charged with illegal drug activity and abuse of power. In another major city, 11 officers were convicted for accepting $100,000 from undercover agents to protect a cocaine warehouse. The undercover operation was terminated when a witness was killed under orders from one of the city's police officers (U.S. General Accounting Office, 1998).

Numerous corruption investigations focused on a single police department. The NYPD is the largest and one of the oldest police departments in the United States. Yet, six investigations of corruption within the NYPD have taken place over a 100-year period (Chin, 1997). These investigations include the following:

1895	Lexow Committee
1913	Curran Committee
1932	Seabury Investigation
1955	Helfand Investigation
1972	Knapp Commission
1994	Mollen Commission

In one of the most disturbing police misconduct scandals to hit an urban police department in decades, a corruption probe into the Los Angeles Police Department in 1999 uncovered a wide range of serious allegations. A few officers in the department's Rampart Division were accused of beating suspects, planting evidence, fabricating testimony, and unjustifiably killing a suspect in 1996. Some police officers were alleged to have rented an apartment for on-duty sexual liaisons with prostitutes who were also enlisted by the officers to sell drugs that the officers stole from drug dealers. In at least one incident, a defendant was forced to plead guilty to a crime he did not commit. In another alleged incident, two officers wounded a suspect, then planted a rifle on the suspect. The officers later arranged to have the suspect prosecuted and convicted for shooting at them. The imprisoned suspect was subsequently released when one of the officers involved in the shooting incident revealed the truth about what happened. Almost two dozen LAPD officers were relieved of duty, terminated, or resigned in connection with the corruption probe. In 2000, three LAPD officers were convicted on charges stemming from the scandal. The officers' convictions were later reversed on appeal. The investigation may lead to the release of numerous prison inmates and probationers as they appeal convictions resulting from approximately 3,000 cases involving the allegedly corrupt officers (Krasnowski, 2000).

Media accounts of police misconduct as well as reports of abuse and corruption within the police service lead many citizens to stereotype all or most police officers as "bad cops." This perception cannot be further from the truth. Yet false assumptions persist, which help to create an environment of mistrust between the public and the police. Trust and integrity are at the very core of any good and effective relationship. It is incumbent upon every police officer to promote a code of conduct and demonstrate ethical behavior that helps to establish a climate of trust.

The **consequences of unethical behavior** and police misconduct include miscarriages of justice, nonenforcement of the law, and a poor police public image. The officer and the agency may be sued in federal and state courts, regardless of the intent of the officer (Crank & Caldero, 2000), and damages can run into the millions of dollars. Individual officers involved in unethical conduct may receive a reprimand, disciplinary action, or termination, or may be prosecuted criminally. Public embarrassment, humiliation of family and friends, increased stress, and loss of respect are also negative by-products of unethical conduct (California State Commission on Peace Officer Standards and Training, 1999; Crank & Caldero, 2000). As stated in the President's Crime Commission report on policing in 1967, unethical police behavior undermines public confidence. According to the commission, the police are entrusted with the enforcement of the fundamental rules that guide a society's conduct. Thus, illegal, dishonest, and inappropriate police behavior can destroy the public's trust and respect for the police generally, even though only a few police officers dishonor the authority vested in them. Nothing undermines public confidence and support for the police more than unethical conduct (President's Commission on Law Enforcement and Administration of Justice, 1967).

ROLE OF THE POLICE SUBCULTURE

A **subculture** is an enclave within a culture that is characterized by a distinct, integrated network of attitudes, beliefs, and behaviors. Subcultures often develop as a mechanism for self-protection and as a tool for the protection of others within the subculture. In the context of a workplace, a subculture is often characterized by attitudes, values, and unwritten rules, the purpose of which is to assist the worker to survive in the occupational environment. Subcultures develop in all occupations (Jones & Carlson, 2001).

Some argue that human beings tend to adopt the values and ethics of those with whom they associate, especially peers or colleague groups. Alternately, to resist the values and ethics and to fail to behave in ways that are consistent with one's colleague group place the resister at some risk. The nature of the work and the need for a support group may be particularly true in the field of law enforcement (Crank, 1998; Kleinig, 1996b; Pollock, 1998; Jones & Carlson, 2001; Skolnick, 1994). As Arthur Niederhoffer wrote in the 1960s, a police officer can become extremely cynical over time (Niederhoffer, 1967). The cynicism can spread to an officer's sense of morality, detaching moral constraints that would normally control individual officer or police group behavior (Kleinig, 1996b).

Early in a career, a police recruit learns to be sensitive to, and adopt the attitudes and beliefs of, peers and superiors. Once the novice enters the police subculture, the new officer is confronted with a set of values (Crank & Caldero, 2000) and norms, and is expected to conform to the requirements of the group (Champion & Rush, 1997; Desroches, 1986). To survive in the group, a police officer learns early that acceptance by peers does not lend itself to independent thinking about moral or ethical dilemmas encountered on the job (Crank, 1998; Jones & Carlson, 2001).

The personal bonding that occurs in a subculture can be dangerous if it inhibits, or even prohibits, individual moral and ethical decision making. Pressure is exerted by the group and some within the group, may lose the ability to regulate their individual behavior. In a sense, individuals within a group are victimized by the group. If individuals do not participate in unethical behavior, they may, at the very least, condone the behavior by failing to intervene or report inappropriate conduct. Taken to an extreme, unethical, even illegal, police conduct may be tolerated by nonparticipant officers. Thus, an environment exists where participant officers are not held to account for their actions. When the Mollen Commission investigated police corruption in New York City in the 1990s, former NYPD officer Bernard Cawley was called to testify before the commission. Cawley, already convicted for crimes committed while on duty, was asked why he did not fear detection. His response was indicative of the impermissible conduct tolerated within some subcultures. Cawley replied that he and his peers were not afraid of the police because *they were the police* (Jones & Carlson, 2001).

The major distinction between subcultures in the law enforcement workplace and other types of occupational environments is often the degree to which values and beliefs are informally promulgated and adhered to. Occupation-related stressors probably provide the most significant distinguishing characteristics between police work and many other occupations. The presence of danger in police work and similarly dangerous occupations reinforces the subculture and fosters remarkable **group**

solidarity. An individual officer's welfare may depend on the availability and response of other officers. Thus, mutual support, group solidarity (unity of purpose), and loyalty are critical to survival. Loyalty to the group and peers often extends beyond dangerous situations. To protect others within the subculture, officers may remain loyal to other officers involved in unethical, even criminal, conduct (Cohen & Feldberg, 1991; Jones & Carlson, 2001; Skolnick, 1994; Walker, 2001). As discussed elsewhere in this book, the police subculture may also be a defense mechanism against perceived threats from criminals, the public, the courts and defense attorneys, the media, friends, family, even the agency's administration (Crank, 1998; Kleinig, 1996b).

The unwritten, informal code of conduct in a subculture is governed by a set of expectations as well as perceived threats to members of the group. Subcultures are generally characterized by expectations the group has regarding member behavior. As attitudes, beliefs, and informal rules are conveyed, punishments are imposed for nonconformity and rewards are distributed for conformity. Accordingly, appropriate "backup" for an officer in need of help may be delayed if the officer is a nonconformist. Similarly, a conforming officer may be supported by the group even when the officer demonstrates or is accused of unethical or criminal behavior.

A subculture, along with its group solidarity and loyalty, also develops because of perceived threats. As discussed earlier, perceived threats to police practitioners emanate from practically anyone who is not a police officer. In some cases, media coverage critical of the police or the public's antipolice sentiments may lead officers to believe they are under siege by an overwhelming number of enemies. As a result, the police view themselves as misunderstood warriors who do their best to protect the ungrateful critics from hordes of bad people. As the list of enemies expands to cover virtually all non-law-enforcement people, the police subculture is galvanized into a single impenetrable unit.

Many experts on policing agree that the single greatest obstacle to achieving accountability for police behavior is the **police subculture** (Walker, 2001). In support of this contention, the results of a national survey of police officers conducted in 1998 indicated that slightly more than half of those questioned agreed that officers tend to do nothing when they observe misconduct on the part of other officers. Nine hundred police officers from various agencies throughout the United States participated in a telephonic survey designed to address police attitudes toward use of excessive force. Although the respondents indicated it was not acceptable to use more force than is legally permissible to control a person who assaulted an officer, the respondents reported that it is not unusual for officers to ignore improper conduct by fellow officers. Reporting fellow officers was considered risky.

Although a majority of the respondents did not support silence as necessary to effective policing, they maintained that reporting peers for use of excessive force was not worth the consequences within the police subculture (Byers, 2000; Weisburd, Greenspan, Hamilton, Williams, & Bryant, 2000).

Another study was conducted in 1998 to determine police officer attitudes toward police misconduct. The study used input from 3,235 officer respondents from 30 agencies throughout the United States. Each participant was provided with 11 scenarios describing various types of police misconduct. Each participant was asked to respond to six questions intended to measure the officer's inclination to resist temptation to abuse rights and privileges associated with their occupation. Although the results of the study revealed little tolerance for "serious" misconduct, and indicated vast differences among agencies with respect to the environment for integrity, the study results consistently revealed that most officers would not report a fellow officer for "less serious" types of misconduct (such as accepting free meals and driving under the influence). Police officer participants in the study discounted the less serious forms of misconduct even though many members of society would identify the behavior as unacceptable (Byers 2000; Klockers, Ivkovich, Harver, & Haberfeld, 2000). With regard to promoting accountability for behavior, a possible solution is to transform the police subculture from one that tends to be self-protective to one that is self-policing (Walker, 2001).

Although the police subculture is often discussed in terms of its negative qualities and consequences, positive subcultural by-products also emanate from the group. The group solidarity formed in a police subculture can elevate morale through esprit de corps, and it can promote fellowship and mutual responsibility among those who share danger and stress (Skolnick, 1994). In crisis situations, loyalty and mutual support are critical to success. Through training, teamwork, and group solidarity, the police can prevent and de-escalate conflict and violence. Subsequent to a crisis situation, the mutual support provided by members of the police subculture are essential to the emotional and psychological health of the officers involved in the crisis (Jones & Carlson, 2001). Especially in officer-involved death cases, whether it is the death of a criminal suspect or another officer, group support is absolutely essential to the mental health of the officers (Jones & Carlson, 2001; Pollock, 1998).

There is no way to avoid the moral dimensions of police work (Cohen & Feldberg, 1991). At times, police officers are confronted with particularly difficult and challenging dilemmas (Crank, 1998; Klockars, 1991). Officers may be called upon to decide between group solidarity and loyalty to others versus the need to prevent, intercept, or report unethical behavior. This is especially true when officers witness unprofessional conduct on the part of other officers. Police officers know right from wrong. However, they must strive to retain their sensitivity toward thinking and behaving in a morally and ethically correct manner regardless of the perceived personal and professional consequences. The virtue test for the police subculture itself may lie in its ability to support attitudes, values, and behaviors that are consistent with doing the right thing at the right time. Only then will positive, rather than negative, qualities and consequences emanate from the moral struggle within the police subculture (Walker, 2001).

PREVENTION AND CORRECTION OF UNETHICAL CONDUCT

Unethical behavior patterns usually do not develop quickly. Rather, distinctive patterns of behavior develop over a period of time. Typically, these patterns are exemplified by symptoms that can be identified by police management as well as the **problematic officer**'s peers. Symptoms include an unusually high number of citizen complaints and use of force and resisting arrest incidents, as well as chronic performance problems. Obviously, officers who receive an abnormally high number of citizen complaints usually warrant closer observation. Although complaints against a hard-working police officer are not uncommon, substantial evidence suggests that in almost all police departments, a single officer or a small group of officers account for a disproportionate number of citizen complaints. The officers are usually involved in an abnormally high number of use of force and resisting arrest incidents. In addition to citizen complaints, problem officers are usually well known within the agency as officers with chronic performance problems. Utilizing **early warning symptom reporting systems** to identify problem officers can result with timely corrective interventions. Counseling, additional training, or closer supervision designed to correct officer behavior could play a very effective role in reducing the incidence of police misconduct (Walker, 2001; Walker, Alpert, & Kenney, 2001).

Most law enforcement officers demonstrate ethical behavior, especially if the officers know what is expected of them. Unethical behavior can be prevented if police agencies select the right people, communicate professional values through effective training, and deal appropriately with individuals who violate codes of conduct. Adherence to a code of ethics and standards of conduct is enhanced when officers are held accountable for their actions. When unethical conduct occurs, corrective action is necessary to retain the public's trust, maintain the integrity of the agency, and prevent misconduct in the future. Ethical officers must intervene to prevent and respond to inappropriate or criminal conduct demonstrated by other officers. Police officers must clearly communicate their values in advance, intervene verbally or physically if the situation requires immediate action, and report violations once discovered. The United States Constitution, state constitutional and statutory provisions, and case law support such intervention. Police agencies may take corrective action through internal integrity disciplinary proceedings (California State Commission on Peace Officer Standards and Training, 1999).

Adherence to a code of ethics and standards of conduct is sometimes difficult. Police practitioners confirm the existence of an officer subculture that is characterized by an unwritten informal code of ethics that influences officer conduct. The norms of the informal code include a requirement that officers remain loyal to their peers (Cohen & Feldberg, 1991; Crank, 1998; Kleinig, 1996b; Walker, 2001). As discussed earlier, perceived disloyalty may result in unpleasant consequences (Jones & Carlson, 2001). Although solidarity and loyalty are important ingredients to survival in virtually every occupation, maintenance of the public's trust demands adherence to standards of ethical behavior.

Evidence also suggests that many police agencies fail to appropriately discipline officers who are guilty of misconduct (Walker, Spohn, & DeLone, 2002). In response, some agencies are developing discipline guidelines. In March 2001, the LAPD and the agency's police union released a 13-page penalty guide that highlights sanctions for officer misconduct. A month earlier, Los Angeles Mayor Richard Riordan challenged police officials to act on LAPD's sinking officer morale. The new penalty guide was developed to replace the broad discretionary authority of supervisors to discipline officers, a primary source of resentment among the officers. The penalty guide includes 14 infractions grouped in 14 categories. The penalty guide distinguishes between first, second, and third offenses, and five levels of punishment for misconduct. Among others, the infractions include discourtesy, ethnic bias, driving violations, domestic violence, driving under the influence (DUI), sexual harassment, insubordination, theft, false imprisonment, and lying under oath. According to the penalty guide, the purposes of the guide are to eliminate uncertainty associated with disciplinary action; modify offender behavior; set expectations for others; ensure accountability, fairness, and consistency; and inspire public trust. Deviations from the penalty guide are allowed, but only in rare instances when a supervisor has justification for the exception. Other areas addressed by the LAPD include giving more discretion to supervisors to streamline disciplinary procedures by rejecting frivolous complaints against officers (You can get it in writing, 2001).

Disciplinary action must be based on legitimate infractions and balanced to render fairness and justice to individual cases. Sometimes, the strict enforcement of policies and rules designed to prevent or correct unethical conduct can produce negative side effects. Police officer morale and productivity can decline if officer behavior is unreasonably questioned and scrutinized, especially as a result of what an officer identifies as a frivolous citizen complaint (Police morale falls sharply, 2000).

Regarding police officer attitudes toward, and recommendations for, the prevention and correction of unethical conduct, one study revealed that serious incidents of police abuse are rare and that agencies generally do not tolerate abusive behavior. Further, the respondents to the study reported the problem of police abuse, where it exists, could be reduced through improved supervision, administrative sanctions, and training in ethics, interpersonal skills, and cultural awareness (Byers, 2000; Weisburd, Greenspan, Hamilton, Williams, & Bryant, 2000).

At least one expert on policing suggests that response to police misconduct must go beyond intervention with the officer or officers involved (Walker, 2001). Counseling, disciplining, terminating, or prosecuting a few police officers may produce a measure of symbolic justice. However, a focus on individual offenders fails to recognize and change the conditions that may have tolerated the unethical behavior or possibly allowed the misconduct to take place. Consequently, systemic change in the police service must focus not only on the conduct of individuals but also on the organizational culture of police agencies (Crank, 1998; McNamara, 2000; Peak & Glensor, 2002; Walker, 2001). Maintaining an ethical standard of conduct is an individual as well as an organizational responsibility. A positive ethical culture can be established and maintained through ethical leadership by example (inspiration), unifying individuals in support of ethical behavior (collaboration), ethics education and training, and ethics integration into personal and professional lives (Whisenand & Ferguson, 2002).

POLICE OFFICER RIGHTS

When discussing the issues of ethics and police misconduct, it is important to keep in mind that the vast majority of police officers are honest, ethical, and industrious people who spend their entire careers in exemplary service to the public. However, officers who demonstrate exemplary service are not typically those who appear on the front page of a newspaper or at the beginning of a television news broadcast. Most of the information the media presents relates to officer misconduct and exemplary officers pay an incredible emotional price for the few who warrant decreased confidence and increased scrutiny from the public (Pollock, 1998).

In an effort to protect the rights of police officers, some states, such as California, have enacted public safety officers' procedural bill of rights acts.

Commonly referred to as a **police officer bill of rights,** the purpose of such laws is to expressly provide police officers and other public safety personnel with statutory rights protecting them from arbitrary disciplinary or punitive action (Ortmeier, 2002; Peak, 1995). Generally, these laws provide that police officers:

- cannot be prevented from engaging in political activity, including seeking election to a school board.
- are entitled to due process when under investigation or being interrogated.
- cannot be subjected to punitive action or denied promotion for choosing to exercise rights under the statute.
- may not have adverse comments entered into a personnel file without notice and an opportunity to review the comments and sign the document containing the information.
- shall have 30 days to respond to any adverse comments entered into a personnel file.
- cannot be compelled to submit to a polygraph or similar examination nor can a refusal to submit to such an examination be used against the officer.
- cannot be compelled to disclose information regarding personal assets or income unless such disclosure is necessary to determine suitability for assignment to a specialized enforcement activity.
- shall not have agency owned or leased personal locker or storage space searched unless the search is conducted in the officer's presence, or with the officer's consent, or the officer is informed that a search will take place under the authority of a valid search warrant (Adams, 2001).

While police officer bills of rights may be appropriate to ensure fair treatment of officers and to support morale, they should not be designed or utilized to shield the incompetent, brutal, or corrupt individual from appropriate investigation and punishment. In fashioning such statements of rights, the legitimate functions of police executives to protect the integrity of the department, must be preserved.

Numerous court decisions support police management rights to enforce policy and control officer conduct (Peak, 1995; Whisenand & Ferguson, 2002). During internal investigations into noncriminal police officer misconduct, for example, the officer must respond to management's questions under penalty of disciplinary action. In *Garrity v. New Jersey* (1967), the U.S. Supreme Court reversed conspiracy to obstruct justice convictions against police officers who, during the course of an internal criminal misconduct investigation, were given a choice to incriminate themselves or forfeit their police jobs. The officers chose to make confessions. The Court held that the confessions were coerced in violation of the Fourteenth Amendment because the officers were not granted immunity from prosecution for statements given. In a subsequent decision, the U.S. Supreme Court affirmed that a police officer could be terminated for refusing to answer questions during a criminal investigation, provided the officer was informed that the responses could not be used later in a criminal prosecution (*Gardner v. Broderick,* 1968). However, in an internal noncriminal investigation of officer misconduct, an officer could be terminated from employment for failure to answer questions related to the investigation.

SUMMARY

Although the majority of police officers demonstrate ethical behavior and perform their work in an exemplary manner, some officers do engage in unprofessional conduct. Abuse of discretion and authority, use of excessive force, discriminatory practices, dishonesty, and unprofessional behavior are illustrative of officer misconduct. As a profession, the police service must strive to attract talented individuals, train them well, and assist with the maintenance of officer integrity.

The police subculture plays a critical role as a behavior control mechanism. As an officer grows to depend on other officers as a support group, the subculture helps to create a psychologically and physically dependent environment. Research supports a contention that the police subculture represents the single greatest obstacle to police accountability. However, positive side effects also emanate from the police subculture. Mutual support and teamwork can assist individual officers emotionally and help the police prevent and de-escalate conflict and violence.

Utilizing information from fellow officers, legitimate citizen complaints, and early warning symptom reporting systems, unethical behavior prevention and corrective intervention programs can be developed. Disciplinary policies and procedures should be clearly defined and communicated. Prevention of police misconduct involves improved supervision and training in ethics, interpersonal skills, and cultural awareness. Prevention goes beyond intervention with individual officers. The organizational culture of law enforcement must change also. Finally, without jeopardizing legitimate rights of police agency management, police officer rights must be protected so productivity and morale do not suffer.

KEY TERMS AND CONCEPTS

Define, describe, or explain the importance of each of the following:

consequences of unethical behavior
early warning symptom reporting system
group solidarity
police misconduct
police officer bill of rights
police subculture
problematic officer
profession
professionalism
subculture
unethical behavior pattern

DISCUSSION QUESTIONS AND EXERCISES

1. The term **profession** implies that its members adhere to ethical standards of behavior and achieve a minimum competence level to be employed in a particular occupation or discipline. Based on this definition, is law enforcement a profession? Explain your answer.
2. What are the consequences of police misconduct and unethical behavior?
3. What role does the police subculture play in the perpetuation of police misconduct?
4. How can police misconduct be prevented? Corrected?
5. What purpose does a police officer bill of rights serve?
6. Officers Smith and Jones are discussing recent events and Officer Jones shares details of a falsified police report Jones filed in an arrest Jones made a day earlier. How should Officer Smith respond?

Chapter 6

Communication: Key to Interpersonal Relations

Learning Objectives

After completing this chapter, the reader should be able to:

- describe the importance of effective verbal and interpersonal communications in a policing environment.
- evaluate techniques for communication in various situations.
- demonstrate verbal communications skills appropriate to the situation.
- integrate knowledge of cross-cultural communications in one-on-one or group communication environments.
- manage communication conflict.
- demonstrate effective tactical communications skills.
- describe the importance of good notes and reports.
- demonstrate effective written communication skills appropriate to policing.
- articulate the ethical dimension of the communication process.
- identify and utilize sources of information.

Introduction

Up to 70 percent of a police officer's working time is spent in communication with others. Therefore, proficiency in the art of communication, verbal or written, is critical to all police officers (Wallace, Roberson, & Steckler, 2001; Whisenand & Ferguson, 2002). However, one study indicated that fewer than one in three people who claimed to be good communicators could actually demonstrate effective communication skills during a live competence assessment. Even fewer of those assessed were able to demonstrate complicated and difficult-to-learn counseling, coaching, and consultative skills (Anderson, 2000). The results of another study indicate that policing experts tend to agree on one point: Effective communication skills are critical to officer success in contemporary law enforcement (Ortmeier, 1996).

An effective leader is a good communicator. Skills associated with listening, verbal and nonverbal communication, building and sustaining trust, promoting understanding, empowering others, and building teams are critical to successful leadership (O'Hair, Gustav, & Dixon, 2002). The ability to listen and communicate effectively to individuals and groups, verbally and in writing, facilitates interaction and helps maintain group cohesiveness and citizen satisfaction. Excellent communication also assists in any advisory effort, promotes harmony between and among different ethnic groups, and helps to create empathy in a multicultural society. Notions about crime and justice are related to an individual's view of the world. A good communicator can facilitate understanding. Effective communication between the police and the public reduces victim distress and encourages citizen crime prevention activities. It de-escalates emotion during crisis situations, which are reflective of a high percentage of police incidents. Policing requires that people be brought together to identify and solve community problems. Communication is the key to positive interaction and dialog and is an important ingredient in problem-solving efforts. Communication skills are also critical to officer self-management (Kidd & Braziel, 1999; Lyman, 2002; Ortmeier, 1995, 1996, 1997, 2002).

COMMUNICATION DEFINED

As many as 100 different definitions of communication exist. In its most basic form, **communication** is a process, rather than an event, that involves at least two people who engage in the process for the purpose of exchanging information (Wallace, Roberson, & Steckler, 2001). Communication involves the process of transmitting, receiving, and sharing ideas, facts, attitudes, values, and opinions. Through encoding (translating information to a communication medium), the sender transmits a message to a receiver who decodes the message. The receiver provides feedback to the sender based on the receiver's perception of the message's meaning (Hellriegel, Jackson, & Slocum, 2002; Stojkovic, Kalinich, & Klofas, 2003).

Communication can be verbal or nonverbal. In fact, all nonverbal behavior has communicative value. Yet, nonverbal communication can be ambiguous, bound by culture and relationships, and differ between genders. Nonverbal communication emanates from body orientation (stance), posture, gestures, facial expression, eye movement, voice inflection, touch, physical attractiveness, clothing, distance, territoriality, the physical environment, and time (Adler & Towne, 2002).

THE CONTEXT FOR COMMUNICATION

The presence or absence of communication can affect physical health. Communication shapes a person's identity (self-concept), fulfills a social need, and assists with the transmission of thought. Communication can be intentional or unintentional once transmitted. It is irreversible and unrepeatable (Adler & Towne, 2002). The context for communication is the totality of the circumstances in which communication occurs: the environment, the roles of the participants, acceptable standards of behavior for the situation, and the reason for the gathering (Kidd & Braziel, 1999)

Communication is a medium for the transmission of thought and meaning. The human mind is primarily a creative instrument, it processes and reacts to a communication based on the information presented and how the information is communicated. Additionally, how a person receives and processes a transmission depends on the receiver's intelligence, education, training, experiences, and the context in which the thought is transmitted by the communicator. Thus, successful communication involves effective thought and meaning transmission rather than information transmission. To communicate effectively for the purpose of influencing others, the communicator must transmit thought in the most concise and specific language possible (Fournies, 2000; Kidd & Braziel, 1999).

There is no one single ideal method of communication. The transactional process of communication depends on the situation, the relationship between or among the parties, and the communication competence (skill) of the parties involved. Competent communicators exhibit a wide range of communication behaviors, choosing and performing the behaviors that are appropriate to the situation and the relationship (Adler & Towne, 2002).

Communication takes place through a variety of mediums, each of which has relevance in policing. During the intrapersonal communications process, one thinks, reasons, evaluates, and speaks with oneself. Through **interpersonal communications,** individuals interact with each other, learning about one another's feelings, beliefs, and desires. In group communication, a limited number of people share ideas, identify and solve problems, and often develop new ideas through the synergism of the group. Through public communication (public speaking), individuals address an audience and attempt to inform or influence others to think and act in a particular manner. During the mass communications process, the media is used to persuade or entertain huge audiences. Machine-assisted communication utilizes technology and cyberspace to converse and exchange information (Gamble & Gamble, 1999).

A competent communicator makes the correct assumptions: Meanings are not in words alone, more communication is not always better, no single person or event causes another's reaction to a communication, and effective communication will not solve all problems (Adler & Towne, 2002). Yet, there are many myths and false assumptions associated with the communication process (Brilhart & Galanes, 1998).

- Many people believe they are good communicators when they are not. Most people do not reflect on their own communication deficiencies and, therefore, do little or nothing to improve.
- Another false assumption is that "all human problems are communications problems." Human beings are encumbered in many ways—only one of which is poor communication. For example, citizens and officers in a policing environment may wish to improve the quality of life in a ghetto neighborhood. However, many quality-of-life issues and mechanisms, such as economic conditions, are beyond the control of the police.
- "Good communication techniques guarantee good communication." This myth fails to account for a critical ingredient to effective communication—attitude. Communication is enhanced when one demonstrates sincerity and willingness to improve. People will forgive communication mishaps when the communicator's basic intentions are good.
- "The receiver misunderstood the communication." This myth fails to account for the two-way process involved in communications. Both sender and receiver must cooperate to promote unambiguous, mutually understood messages. If a message is misunderstood, both sender and receiver must share the responsibility for the misunderstanding.
- "Good communication on both sides always results in understanding." This is another myth. Perfect communication and understanding are not possible. Some communication is intended to be misleading. During an interrogation, for example, a police officer may wish to convince a suspect that a codefendant has already confessed. In other cases, the communicator may be trying to avoid hurting another's feelings. Clearly, however, when the intended outcome is mutual understanding, participants in the communications process should strive for perfection (Brilhart & Galanes, 1998).

Obstacles to communication include the presence of emotional and physical barriers, ineffective listening, and lack of a common meaning in a word or phrase (semantic problems) (Wallace, Roberson, & Steckler, 2001). Thus, effective communication is a complex process. The source of a message (the sender) formulates a mental image of the thought to be communicated, converts the thought to an appropriate transmission medium (verbal, physical expressions or gestures, or writing), and transmits the message to a receiver. If the message is properly formulated and transmitted, and if the receiver understands the message, the communication process is complete. Very often, however, differences in gender, age, intelligence, education, personal biases, and vocation, as well as language barriers and adverse circumstances, may inhibit the communication process. Intended meanings can be distorted through improper or inappropriate communication (Kidd & Braziel, 1999).

The effectiveness of communication is also determined by the circumstances in which the communication takes place. Noise distorts and interferes with the ability to send and receive messages. The context, or manner, in which the communication is presented can affect the receiver's interpretation of the message. Positive or negative feedback (and, of course, no feedback) influences future thoughts and courses of action (Gamble & Gamble, 1999).

Subsequent to the terrorist attack on New York's World Trade Center on September 11, 2001, an inquiry revealed that communication failures contributed to many police, fire, and other emergency personnel deaths. Officials at the incident command center were unaware of the severity of the incident, commanders lost track of who entered the buildings, and responding agencies did not receive appropriate instructions (Dwyer, 2002; Fire, police experts cite communication failures during Trade Center response, 2002).

Finally, as people communicate, they are changed in a way that influences what follows. Communication, therefore, has an effect on the participants in the process. This effect may manifest itself emotionally, physically, or cognitively (Gamble & Gamble, 1999). Since communication, once transmitted, is irreversible and unrepeatable, it cannot be taken back nor  can it be repeated in exactly the same fashion as before. Thus, the impact of poor communication cannot be erased.

Because the consequences may be severe, police officers must be aware of the importance of a proper attitude during the communication process, and the avoidance of a medium that may be derogatory, misleading, or illogical. According to the International Association of Chiefs of Police (1985), practitioners in the law enforcement community can avoid miscommunication if care is exercised to: gather reliable and sufficient evidence, distinguish fact from opinion, avoid generalizations and haste, and avoid misleading statistics. Police officers should also guard against illogical statements, make careful comparisons, and guard against faulty thinking.

Many of the qualities that apply to an effective message sender also apply to the message receiver. In fact, listening skills have been identified by police experts as essential for the police officer (Ortmeier, 1996). Listening, as a process, involves more than passively absorbing a communicator's words. Listening involves hearing, attending (paying attention), understanding (making sense of the message), responding (observable feedback), and remembering what was communicated. Poor listening may result from preoccupation with other thoughts, lack of effort, external noise, hearing problems, faulty assumptions, lack of training, speaking more than listening, and message overload (too much information). Keys to effective listening include speaking less, eliminating distractions, keeping an open mind, searching for ideas, asking questions, paraphrasing a speaker's message, and analyzing the information communicated (Adler & Towne, 2002; Whisenand & Ferguson, 2002).

According to Hess and Wrobleski (1993), listening capability can be improved if one maintains the proper attitudinal, behavioral, and mental orientation. A listener's attitude should show interest in the person and the message (be empathetic). A listener should not be self-centered, resist distractions, not let personal biases interfere, and listen with a clear mind. Behaviorally, the listener should be responsive with body language, encourage the subject, look at the subject, not interrupt, and take notes as appropriate. Mentally, the listener should ask appropriate questions, not change the subject, listen for ideas as well as facts, separate facts from opinions, and pay attention to content, not delivery. A listener should look for main points, avoid jumping to conclusions, concentrate, and use excess time to summarize the speaker's main ideas. An effective listener maintains an open mind, periodically clarifies what has been communicated, and is attentive to body language.

In recent years, through efforts to reconnect the police with the community, many police and other public safety agencies have adopted the philosophy, strategy, and practices associated with community policing and problem solving. Community policing requires individual police officers to engage citizens and groups within a community in an effort to assist them with local problem identification and solution development. Police officers are required to speak to citizens and address community gatherings. Therefore, public speaking skills have become increasingly important in police work (Kidd & Braziel, 1999).

In the final analysis, virtually all police business is a human relations business. The police are in the people business. Whether communicating with a crime suspect, attending to the injured, interviewing witnesses and victims, or speaking to a group of citizens, the ability to communicate is a critical component and necessary ingredient to effective policing. Every police contact with another human being should be viewed as an opportunity

Every police contact with another human being should be viewed as an opportunity.
Photo courtesy of Los Angeles Sheriff's Department

to enhance the law enforcement agency's ability to gather information and provide a foundation for the furtherance of the police mission to serve the community well (Ortmeier, 2002).

SPEECH AND INTERPERSONAL COMMUNICATIONS

As mentioned previously, effective interpersonal communication skills are essential in society generally, and in police work specifically. Experts on the subject of policing ranked effective communications skills number one out of sixty-two competencies essential to effective policing (Ortmeier, 1996). In another survey, 1,000 personnel managers in the United States ranked effective speech communication as the number one ingredient to obtaining employment and performing well once employed (Hanna & Wilson, 1998). High technology makes good communications skills even more critical, given the nature of the overwhelming amount of information available through electronic media.

One-on-One Conversations

Face-to-face communication with individuals has many advantages. It is normally fast and easy to control, provides instantaneous feedback, and adds a personal touch to the communications process. Interviewing witnesses and subjects is a large and extremely critical part of police work.

Good communications skills enhance the ability to gather information and obtain admissions and confessions from suspects.

Every communication includes both task and relationship dimensions. The task dimension refers to the people, events, and phenomena that occur outside the communicator. If one says, "Please describe, in your own words, what happened," the receiver will know what task is expected. At the same moment, the communication also involves a relationship dimension. If the parties have a strained relationship, or the message is poorly framed or misunderstood, the communication process may be ineffective (Hanna & Wilson, 1998). If, for example, a negative relationship exists, such as between a police officer and a victim who distrusts the police, the victim may not be willing to provide any information. Likewise, if the request is presented as a demand or the victim does not understand the language through which the request is made, the receiver may resist or not understand what is being requested.

A key to effective communication is to overcome defensiveness on the part of the subject being communicated with. When a verbal or written message is sent in a strong or violent manner, the listener becomes defensive. On some occasions, such as when a subject (or suspect) is incorrigible and refuses to obey a lawful order from a police officer, strong language may be necessary. During most encounters with others, however, forceful language and behavior may not be appropriate.

Behavior that increases defensiveness in others includes: judgment (or prejudgment) of others, control or manipulation, neutrality (showing little or no concern), superiority, certainty (rigid commitment to a point of view), and insincerity. Behavior on the part of the communicator that tends to reduce defensiveness by others includes: treating others with respect; cooperation and collaboration in a problem-solving effort; demonstrating empathy (identifying) with another's thinking; minimizing differences in status, authority, and power; willingness to accept additional information that may result in a change of mind; and candid, straightforward expression of attitudes and beliefs (Gibb, 1961).

Meetings

Meetings can be useful communications tools (O'Hair, Gustav, & Dixon, 2002). Yet, one should not have a meeting just for the sake of having a meeting. Not all meetings are justified. A meeting is not necessary if: there is no reason for it; a phone call, memo, fax, or e-mail will do; key people cannot attend; time is limited; and members are not prepared.

Meetings are necessary when the participant's tasks are interdependent, more than one decision needs to be made, and misunderstandings are likely without a meeting. Good meetings: have an agenda specifying the date, time, location, participants, items for discussion, goals, and pre-meeting work outlined; start on time and end on time; are as short as possible; stay on track; and achieve the goal(s) of the meeting (Adler & Elmhorst, 1996; Kidd & Braziel, 1999).

Working in Teams and Task Forces

The specific goals to be achieved by work teams and task forces vary among teams and organizations. Work teams tend to be more productive than individuals working alone. **Teamwork** tends to promote innovation and creative thinking, increase the speed with which tasks are accomplished, lower operating costs, and enhance the quality of services and products. Teams can be formed to solve problems in virtually any environment. Functional work teams are used to solve problems common to team member areas of responsibility and expertise. Multidisciplinary work teams consist of people from different functional areas and several organizational levels. Self-managing work teams, functional or multidisciplinary, operate with relative autonomy, selecting and training new members, setting goals and work schedules, and designing processes to accomplish objectives (Hellriegel, Jackson, & Slocum, 2002).

All working groups are not teams (Whisenand & Ferguson, 2002). Committees are not necessarily teams. A committee's purpose may be the representation of various constituencies. Teams and **task forces** are created to fulfill a need for interdependence and support. Effective teams are made up of highly independent individuals who work together to produce a result. Basic to the nature of teams are the assumptions that: the talent necessary to achieve results is already present in the group; every member knows what needs to be accomplished; the team's potential is limited only by the self-imposed team member limitations; and teamwork can be exciting and challenging (Whisenand & Rush, 1998).

Teamwork is essential in contemporary multi-jurisdictional policing activity as well as community policing environments where citizens, community groups, and the police must work together to identify and develop solutions to local problems. These teams may not have designated leaders. Although informal leaders may emerge, some teams may be self-directed groups or task forces responsible for working together to complete a task. Effective communication among team members occurs when participants: recognize team as well as personal goals, promote desirable norms of behavior, make sure all functional roles and expectations are fulfilled, and promote cohesiveness. In addition, team members should avoid excessive conformity, encourage creativity, and positively reinforce accomplishment.

In ideal environments, people wish to participate on teams. They need not be forced or manipulated into serving on them. One expert suggests that two basic questions should be asked before teams are created (Caroselli, 1997). Who knows? Who cares? In response to the first question, probable team members include those who are truly knowledgeable about the reasons for establishing the team. If the team has been created to function as a task force to solve a problem, team members should be intimately knowledgeable of the circumstances surrounding the problem. With regard to the second question, team members should be selected because they are committed to solving the problem. People who know about the reason for the team and are committed to the outcomes of team effort will communicate more effectively (Whisenand & Ferguson, 2002).

Poor work team performance can result from several factors. Team design, including the team size, and location are important factors. Optimal team size is four to eight members. Understaffed teams tend to outperform overstaffed teams. With respect to location, teams apparently perform well when they are removed from the daily activities of an organization. Bureaucracy and politics can restrict creativity. Additional factors contributing to poor team performance include the social and organizational culture within which teams work, inappropriate team member selection and training, and lack of a reward system tailored to the needs of team members (Hellriegel, Jackson, & Slocum, 2002).

Public Speaking

Public speaking is used as a vehicle to inform, persuade, and rally members around a common cause. In any public speaking situation the speaker should: have a clear and realistic goal; analyze the audience and the occasion; and organize ideas so the presentation solicits the listener's attention and the material is presented in a clear, brief, and orderly fashion without excluding necessary detail. Public speakers should: use supporting material and audiovisual aids when appropriate; present the material with enthusiasm, sincerity, confidence, and credibility; dress and act appropriately for the occasion; and use time effectively and efficiently (Adler & Elmhorst, 1996).

Many times throughout a law enforcement officer's career, the officer will be required to speak to the general public (Kidd & Braziel, 1999). The public speaking event may take place before an unruly crowd or an informal gathering of citizens, at a community meeting, before peers or command staff, in classroom settings, or at ceremonial activities such as graduations and banquets.

Public speaking events can be very intimidating for some individuals. Some agonize over the development of a speech and fear presentations before large groups of people. However, anxieties and fears may be overcome through planning, practice, and experience. In anticipation of a public speaking engagement, a presenter should develop an outline of topics to be discussed, create a narrative of the speech based on the outline, and practice speech delivery. In addition, the presenter should: be knowledgeable on the topic, understand the nature of the audience, use humor only when appropriate, dress appropriately, and be on time. A public speaker should: not read a speech verbatim; use visual aids, if possible; be cognizant of the time constraints; rehearse the presentation as often as possible; and request honest feedback from the audience after the presentation (Wallace, Roberson, & Steckler, 2001).

SPECIAL CHALLENGES IN COMMUNICATIONS

Special challenges in communication arise when people are non-English speaking or are hearing or visually impaired. When language barriers exist, bilingual officers or citizen translators can assist in the communication process. Officers can also learn the basics of non-English languages through either credit or noncredit courses offered at local colleges. Other techniques that may be used to communicate with a non-English-speaking or hearing-impaired person include the following:

- obtain the person's attention.
- be certain the person understands the nature of the message content.
- keep speech slow and clear; use short sentences.
- make eye contact with the person.
- keep all items, such as pens, out of the mouth when speaking.
- do not stand in front of lights.
- use paper and pen to communicate if necessary.
- use facial expressions and body language.
- learn basic sign language.
- remember that the subject person may not have understood the message even if speech or body language indicates the message was understood (Gamble & Gamble, 1999).

Visually impaired people also require special attention. Initially, a police officer must be identified by the visually impaired person. An officer may place the impaired person's hand on a badge to communicate identity (Ortmeier, 2002). Numerous communications problems also arise because advanced societies now exist in an information age. Although technological advances seek to control and provide ready access to information, the impersonal nature of information technology can impact information flow and the interpersonal communications process in a negative manner (Whisenand & Ferguson, 2002).

CROSS-CULTURAL COMMUNICATION

The **cross-cultural communication** process occurs whenever a person from one culture sends a message to, and receives messages from, a person in a different culture. Misunderstandings are possible during this process because people from different cultures often perceive, interpret, and evaluate situations and people differently. To communicate effectively in a multicultural environment, people must recognize and adapt to the differences (Adler, 2002).

Within a communications context, culture may be defined as a pattern of a group's behavior, including its members' beliefs, language, actions, and artifacts (Kidd & Braziel, 1999; Putnam & Pacanowski, 1983). Culture is not what a group has. Rather, culture involves what a group is. Cultures, whether formal or informal, ethnic or organizational, form basic assumptions about what the culture represents. Often the culture operates under the assumption that it is superior to other cultures or groups (Pasquali, 1997).

Culture involves more than ethnic and racial similarities or common themes based on nationality or socioeconomic status. Organizations also tend to develop a unique culture. Organizations that develop customs and enlist new members to an institution often adopt preexisting attitudes, beliefs and habits associated with their predecessors in the organization. During the 1990s, a major urban police department attempted to reduce the amount of racism, sexism, and bigotry in the department by actively recruiting women and minorities. The strategy did little to change the organizational culture or the ways in which its members viewed themselves. The new recruits did not change the organization, rather the organization changed the recruits as they adapted to the organizational climate and adopted preexisting attitudes and beliefs.

When a person moves from the comfort zone of one culture into a culture that is foreign or different, a natural anxiety emerges. The transition into an unfamiliar culture may cause fear and mistrust. When the cultural change is severe, the person making the transition may experience **culture shock.** This phenomenon occurs during the early stages of the transition and is accompanied by feelings of stress and anxiety (Dodd, 1998). The symptoms of culture shock include irritability, loneliness, paranoia, upset stomach, and sleeplessness. Communication-based symptoms include excessive complaining, withdrawal, frustration, and defensive communication. Thus, cultural change and culture shock present challenges to effective communication in multicultural environments.

Culture shock may also occur in relatively homogeneous populations. In rural areas, for example, one might assume that members of the community tend to retain common beliefs, and think and act alike. However, even in remote areas, the difference in the degree of affluence between or among neighbors may be quite severe. Poor people may exist in a culture that is radically different from that of their wealthy neighbors. Religious beliefs may be quite different also and radical ideas, even violent behavior, may radiate from individuals who are isolated from mainstream society.

Adapting to new cultures and environments involves working through the culture shock first. According to Dodd (1998), culture shock can be overcome if a person is patient with others and does not overreact, meets and greets new people, explores unfamiliar culture-specific customs, and mentally reflects on the new culture. Additionally, a person entering a new culture can think positive thoughts, write about experiences, observe the body language and habits of members of the new culture, and learn the host culture's verbal language.

Working with people in a new environment involves overcoming the stress associated with the new experience. Long-term adaptation also involves the stress-growth-acculturation dynamic. Effective communication is extremely important to the process of facilitating the adaptation. Police officers who are cognizant of cultural differences and who focus on assimilating into the host culture will be more effective and less stressed when working in a multicultural environment.

Competency in cross-cultural communications leads to positive professional job task performance (Wulff, 2000). Success on the job is the result of the recognition of, and successful adaptation to, different cultures. Successful interpersonal relationships signal effective outcomes. Competence in cross-cultural communication leads to high technical and professional performance, resourcefulness, and the ability to innovate. Cross-cultural communication competence also promotes effective organizational communications, goal development, and task completion.

One might ask, so what? Is a focus on intercultural communication effectiveness simply another feel-good, politically correct strategy with no valued practical application? Not likely. There is a great deal of research that suggests that intercultural communication competence leads to successful outcomes (Wulff, 2000). Since police officers are required to work with and for people from a wide cultural range, the necessity for developing competence in this area cannot be underestimated. From a police recruiting standpoint, screening for psychological barriers or mental maladjustments that may inhibit cultural adaptation and relationship building may result in fewer interpersonal problems with an officer. The screening may also reduce the likelihood of misunderstandings, use of excessive force, and indifference, which could lead to a poor public image and organizational liability for an officer's actions. Psychological testing (MMPI, 16PF, Myers-Briggs, Taylor-Johnson Temperament Analysis, etc.) may be used as a screening device to eliminate candidates who are not psychologically fit to perform the duties of a contemporary police officer.

From an individual officer's point of view, cross-cultural communication competence may reduce negative job-related stress, help to maintain good health, eliminate barriers to effective job or task performance and promotion possibilities, and generate fewer citizen complaints. Effective cross-cultural communications skills are no panacea, nor are they substitutes for understanding and a sincere appreciation for differences among human beings. The development and application of these skills promote positive interpersonal relationships, an essential ingredient for effective policing in the twenty-first century.

Given the apparent need for intercultural communication competence, what can one do to acquire and develop the necessary skills? Dodd (1998) suggests the following:

- emphasize areas of similarity with others. Search for commonality rather than differences.
- practice acceptance of differing opinions. Remain open and receptive to other points of view. Dogmatism blocks effective communication.
- ensure that verbal messages are consistent with nonverbal messages. In the long run, a mixed message discredits the sender.
- avoid dominating conversations. Listen and hear as well as speak. People who spend most of their time speaking tend to bore others and are less credible.
- avoid submissiveness in conversations. Being overly submissive can be as harmful as domination. People respect others who have something worthwhile to contribute.
- recognize and affirm communication from others. Avoid being overly critical. People appreciate understanding more than they do criticism.

Police officers are often recruited from population groups who are different from the citizens the officers are ultimately sworn to protect and serve. Even when recruited from the same population group, such as an inner-city area, the officers may establish residence in suburbia and commute to work. Rarely does a police officer reside in the same area of a community where the most serious problems associated with crime and urban decay exist. Conflicts may result, therefore, when a police officer resides in one culture and works in another. These conflicts can be prevented. To understand the culture of a group is to understand how and why a group thinks, acts, and reacts to messages and events within its environment (Ortmeier, 2002).

MEDIA RELATIONS

The police and the news media are often viewed as two enduring adversaries (Gaines, Kaune, & Miller, 2001). The police criticize the media for reporting, as front-page news, police corruption and brutality. The media criticizes the police for being too insensitive. The law enforcement community is well advised to accept the fact that police data and operations are news. Crime statistics, officer-involved shootings, and high-speed pursuits always make the evening news. One often hears the phrase, "If it bleeds, it leads" (*Measuring What Matters,* 1997).

The police want favorable press; that is, accounts of officer bravery and low crime rates. However, because the relationship between the news media and the police is strained in many jurisdictions, the adversarial nature of the relationship may lead the press to report unfavorable news about the police. If police officers and agencies wish to receive more favorable press coverage, they should promote a relationship based on trust and inclusiveness. Where appropriate, the media may be included in background briefings and the police may share information that demonstrates how the law enforcement agency sets and meets goals in support of the agency mission and the community's vision for the future. The police will never be able to control the media. On the contrary, it should not. A free and open press is absolutely vital in a democracy. However, through good relationships, the police may be able to positively influence the thinking of those who report the news.

Reporters' jobs are to get and tell a story. They look for conflict, changes, and information of interest to the public. The police should develop a close working relationship with the press before a crisis occurs. Every police agency should have a designated public information officer to act as a liaison between the media and the agency. Honesty and openness is the best policy. It is better for the agency to release bad news about itself first. Officers must avoid confrontations with the media, admit problems and mistakes, and avoid police jargon, officious speech, and off-the-record statements. Responding to a reporter with "No comment" raises a red flag. Reporters generally assume the officer or agency is hiding something. It is better to respond with, "Due to its status as an open investigation, it is not appropriate to comment at this time" (Otto, 2000).

MANAGING COMMUNICATION CONFLICT

Conflict has been variously defined as a clash, a state of disharmony, opposition, strife, and war. Conflict and the words used to define or describe it often create an image that is so powerful that people become stressed and are unable to function appropriately in conflict situations. Conflict, however, is pervasive, frequent, and inevitable. It is not a product. It is a process in human nature. It is neither good nor bad; it simply is (Hanna & Wilson, 1998). Conflict serves an important interpersonal and organizational purpose. Therefore, one must learn to cope with, analyze, and manage conflict to reach appropriate goals.

Inevitably, even the best efforts at establishing and maintaining open lines of communication between parties and groups can result in conflict. The notion of balanced relationships suggests that the people involved either like or dislike the same things. A relationship may become unbalanced when people like each other but do not like the same things or when they like the same things, but do not like each other. Sound like a common occurrence? It is. Each person, or group, sifts perceptions of the other through the filter of cultural stereotypes (Dodd, 1998). Americans tend to dislike conflict and view it as negative. However, conflict can be productive as well as destructive. Conflict is productive when participants are satisfied with the outcome. When participants think they have gained as a result of the conflict and a balance has been struck between cooperation and competition, the conflict is productive. In contrast, conflicts are destructive when participants escalate them and winning becomes more important than gaining. Winning at all costs can even be deadly.

Conflict can stem from a variety of sources (Kidd & Braziel, 1999). Expressed struggle between or among people, perceived incompatible goals or scarce rewards, interdependence and interference can cause conflicts internally and between individuals. Conflict is a natural by-product of life and can, at times, be beneficial if positive consequences result from the conflict. People cope with conflict by applying different conflict reduction styles. Through nonassertive behavior, individuals cope by demonstrating inability or unwillingness to express their thoughts during a conflict. They may avoid conflict altogether or accommodate by giving in to another's pressure. In contrast, some people cope by using direct aggression. They may attack one's character or competence. The aggressor may attack physically, ridicule, threaten, tease, or swear. Passive aggression occurs when a communicator expresses hostility in some obscure manner. Passive aggressive people harbor feelings of resentment, rage, and anger.

Through indirect communication, the communicator conveys a message without hostility. The indirect communicator is interested in self-protection and may suggest that someone do something rather than direct the person to do it. Assertive communication occurs when the communicator clearly expresses needs and desires without resorting to judgment or dictating to others. Assertive communicative behavior is the most direct, honest, and aggression-free (Adler & Towne, 2002).

Conflict management and resolution are a major part of police work, especially when one considers cross-cultural communication conflict. Police officers can be very effective conflict de-escalators and managers if they understand and practice communicative leadership styles that offer solutions in conflict situations. These leadership styles often differ, depending on the situation and the context in which the situation occurs. When interviewing the victim of a serious crime, an officer may utilize a tactful, caring, and empathetic style that facilitates interaction and information flow. When searching a building for a possible armed suspect, the officer may utilize a highly structured, organized, conservative, and controlled leadership communication style. Working with a neighborhood group to identify and solve community-based problems, the officer may communicate in an open, participative, creative, resourceful, and politically aware leadership style. Finally, when effecting an arrest, the communicative leadership style may be task oriented, decisive, assertive, and authoritarian (Ortmeier, 2002).

TACTICAL COMMUNICATION

Major goals in police work involve soliciting information without being confrontational and generating voluntary compliance from law violators without resorting to physical force. **Tactical communication** is a message delivered through words and actions, which can be used to accomplish these goals. Officers should always convey a professional demeanor, speak with a respectful and neutral attitude, and display mannerisms that demonstrate control of the situation. In all cases, officers should keep in mind that any encounter is potentially dangerous. For example, with angry, hostile, hysterical, or emotionally unstable individuals, officers should remain calm and determine the cause of the hostility or hysteria. Speaking in a harsh or demeaning manner is inappropriate. With very young or very old individuals, officers should be patient and calm. Young people are easily frightened and often confused. The elderly are easily upset and often misunderstand instructions.

Voluntary compliance through tactical communication may be achieved by adhering to the following:

- ask. If practical to do so, give the subject the opportunity to comply voluntarily.

- explain the legal context. Explain the law and/or reason for the request.
- present options. Explain options to the subject, outlining possible courses of action and consequences of each.
- request cooperation. Provide the subject with one final opportunity to comply.
- take action. If the subject does not comply with officer requests, appropriate action must be taken that is consistent with the law and agency policy.

When confronted with noncompliant individuals, police officers are often subjected to verbal, if not physical, abuse. Officers can deflect and redirect verbal abuse by remaining calm and not becoming emotionally involved with the subject. Officers should also demonstrate respect for the subject. Disrespect promotes escalation of the conflict. When tactical communication fails, police officers must use the force option that is reasonably necessary to gain compliance. The degree of force used should be consistent with the degree of resistance and should be based on the circumstances in the situation (California State Commission on Peace Officer Standards and Training, 1999).

Hostage Situations

Hostage situations arise from a variety of circumstances. They may arise from terrorist activity, at the scene of prison riots, when a crime is in progress, or when the police respond to a domestic disturbance. Hostage takers may be mentally unstable individuals, criminals who use a bystander as a shield, riotous demonstrators, political extremists, or religious zealots.

Police response and styles of control in hostage situations typically fall within three broad categories: do nothing and wait out the hostage taker; attack or assault the hostage taker's position; or negotiate with the hostage taker. To do nothing invites injury to the hostage and generates negative publicity for the law enforcement agency. Assaults on hostage taker positions are rarely successful. Almost 80 percent of the attacks on hostage takers result in death to hostages (Hess & Wrobleski, 1993). The most desirable and successful option in a hostage situation is to negotiate. Hostage negotiations benefit the situation because stalling for time allows the initial state of high emotion to subside and the scene can be isolated and contained. As time passes, the lives of the hostages become more secure as the hostage taker realizes the value associated with human life and the hostages' continued safety. The hostage taker might even develop affection for the hostages.

Most large police organizations have trained hostage negotiators. Since a majority of police agencies have fewer than 20 sworn officers, the patrol officer or a dispatcher may be required to assume the responsibilities of a negotiator. Regardless of the personnel used, the incident commander and the negotiator should not be the same person. The commander must devote full attention to the entire situation. If the hostage taker realizes the negotiator is in charge, the taker knows the negotiator does not need to seek another's approval to grant requests. Additionally, hostage negotiators must remember that weapons are not negotiable items, that negotiators should never offer to substitute themselves for hostages, and that they should be truthful whenever possible. Furthermore, deadlines should be avoided, relatives and friends should not be allowed to negotiate, and negotiators should not converse with hostages because this increases the hostages' value to the hostage taker. Intelligence on the hostage taker should be gathered. Face-to-face negotiations are best, but telephones, radios, and bullhorns are safer (Maher, 1989).

Hostage negotiations often cover an extended period of time. Negotiators should be patient, talkative, and able to suspend judgment of the hostage taker. Virtually all police officers are potential hostage negotiators. Therefore, basic training in hostage negotiations for most police officers may be beneficial.

Barricaded Subjects

Many, if not all, of the guidelines and techniques used in hostage situations are also appropriate when confronted with barricaded subjects. These subjects may not be a threat to others. They may be suicidal. However, unlike hostage situations, if no threat to human life exists, it may be best to wait out a barricaded subject (Hess & Wrobleski, 1993).

If the subject is barricaded due to a suicide attempt or crisis situation, police officers should demonstrate an empathetic attitude, secure the scene, safeguard people and property, establish rapport with the subject, and reassure the subject. Officers should also: determine the reason for the crisis; comply with requests, if possible; and follow procedures for mental evaluation, if appropriate, when the crisis is over (Russell & Beigel, 1990).

NOTE TAKING AND REPORT WRITING

Many police officers dread the thought of **note taking** and **report writing.** Since police officers tend to be people of action, they do not appreciate the slow, deliberate process demanded by good writing (Thaiss & Hess, 1999). However, a police officer's ability to document facts surrounding an incident, interview, accident, investigation, or criminal activity not only reflects on the officer's professionalism, but also on the criminal justice system's ability to process a case (California State Commission on Peace Officer Standards and Training, 1999; Peak & Glensor, 2002). Probably no other single activity in law enforcement is more important than the need for effective documentation, comprehensive notes, and quality reports. Yet, police recruits tend to have poor writing skills and many fail the report-writing section of the police academy. Individual officers and some agencies also place writing skill development low on their priority lists.

Police officers are required to perform documentation tasks on a continuous basis. Documentation is often accomplished through traditional note-taking and report-writing methods. If physical, technical, and legal requirements permit, documentation may occur through the use of audiotape, videotape, stenography, or computer-assisted recording devices. If computers are used to generate notes or reports, care must be exercised to ensure that confidentiality is maintained and access is restricted to a need-to-know basis. Computer disks that have been erased still retain information that can be retrieved through technical means. Additionally, other electronic mediums, such as e-mail and the Internet, are often not secure from message interception by outsiders (Ortmeier, 1999, 2002).

Field Notes

Field notes are notations created by an officer in the field while gathering information or investigating an incident. These notes become the primary source document for any subsequent official report. Field notes should be made contemporaneous to an incident. In other words, notes should be made during the course of the activity or immediately after an incident occurs. These notes are often referred to as field notes because they are recorded on the job in the field (Parr, 1999). Since memories fade and are often imperfect, notes must be written and maintained in the course of a police officer's occupation. Written communication skills are extremely important in the world of police work. Notes are personal to the note taker and may be used: to refresh one's memory; as the foundation for an official report; and as supporting evidence. Although notes are generally written for the note taker's use only, caution must be exercised when writing notes because any recording may be subject to review by another person or agency.

The most effective way to document information acquired in the field is to follow a systematic process. An officer should separate the parties involved; establish rapport; listen attentively to what the subject is communicating; take notes and ask appropriate questions (what, when, where, who, how, and why); and verify the information recorded by reviewing the information given with the subject. Care must be exercised to separate facts from opinions and conclusions (California State Commission on Peace Officer Standards and Training, 1999; Lyman, 2002).

Reports

Reports often become part of an official record, which forms the foundation for the history of an event. Reports may be viewed by peers, supervisors, the media, social service agencies, attorneys, the courts, insurance companies, and other criminal justice and public safety agencies. They may be scrutinized in the judicial process, provide evidence for litigation against the report writer, support a petition, or provide an officer with a defense against a lawsuit or criminal charge. Reports are used to determine future courses of action and as the basis for promotion, discipline, and evaluation. They can have negative as well as positive consequences and should be taken seriously. Reports with misspelled words, poor grammar, punctuation errors, inaccuracies, or omissions are potentially costly. Defective reports also cast doubt on the professionalism of the report writer.

Reports vary in form and content, yet each report has one common purpose: to communicate information in a clear, concise, and accurate manner. They should always be written with the audience or potential readers in mind. Effective report writing is a matter of reducing to writing the pertinent facts concerning an issue or event in much the same way and in much the same order that a story would be told verbally.

Report writing skills are critical in police work.
Photo courtesy of San Diego Police Museum

The types of reports used by an agency depend on the nature of the organization's activity and its documentation requirements. Most existing police organizations have reporting forms and formats in place. New agencies seeking to develop report forms and procedures should consult with existing agencies for information. Many publishers also market report form books and form tools in computer software packages.

General Report-Writing Principles

To be considered acceptable, a report must meet certain criteria. The writing must be reasonably fluent, well developed, and well organized, showing a sufficient command of the language to communicate the information. All essential information must be included in the report (who, what, where, when, how, why). The report must be free of mechanical errors (i.e., typing, grammar, punctuation, spelling, and word choice) that diminish its evidentiary value or usefulness. The time required to complete the report must be reasonable and consistent with the expectations of the job.

As previously stated, most existing police agencies have reporting forms and formats in place that guide the report writer so relevant and important information is not inadvertently excluded. Occasionally, however, a specific report form may not be available. To ensure that the report is complete, the report writer should strive to include the following information in any report:

- administrative data: include the date of the report, file or case number (if applicable), subjects involved, type of report, and complainant (if any).
- name and identification of the person writing the report.
- office or agency of origin.
- report status: open; pending; supplemental; closing (typically completed by supervisior).
- distribution: include those individuals to whom the report is to be sent.
- synopsis: a brief description of the case and/or investigation.
- details of the report: a narrative, including all facts acquired and all developed leads.
- conclusions and recommendations: this is the place for opinions and personal recommendations.
- undeveloped leads: follow-up necessary.
- enclosures list: for photographs, sketches, copies of documents, evidence receipts, computer disks (Lyman, 2002; O'Hara & O'Hara, 1994; Ortmeier, 2002).

THE EFFECTIVE REPORT

To write an effective report, the writer should:

- conduct a proper inquiry into the subject material of the intended report.
- take complete, accurate, readable notes.
- use the proper format, depending, naturally, upon for whose use the report is intended.
- choose the correct language.
- use proper sentence structure.
- be completely accurate with all the facts.
- not omit facts.
- distinguish facts from hearsay, conclusions, judgments, and personal opinions.
- strive for clarity.
- be concise.
- be absolutely fair.
- be complete.
- record the sequence of events in chronological order.
- record the names, addresses, and, if possible, social security and/or I.D. numbers of all involved.
- include an introduction, body, and conclusion in all narratives.
- check for spelling, punctuation, and capitalization errors.
- review the report to ensure that it adequately answers the questions of who, what, when, where, how, and why.
- write in past tense.
- proofread the report.

At a minimum, investigative reports should contain introductory information describing how the officer became involved in the situation; an identification of the offense, if any; and the facts necessary to establish the elements of the offense. Investigative reports should contain the identification of all parties involved, such as suspects, victims, witnesses, as well as the person(s) who reported the incident. Specific information regarding the parties includes full names, aliases, gender, ethnicity, dates of birth, residence addresses and phone numbers, work or school locations and phone numbers, and the parties' roles in the incident. Statements of parties involved should be recorded verbatim, if possible. Specifics relative to the scene of the incident should be included. This includes descriptions of physical evidence, the property damaged or stolen, and actions taken by the officer(s) at the scene (California State Commission on Peace Officer Standards and Training, 1999).

In an attempt to sound official, police personnel often adopt a writing style and use language that is elaborate, redundant, obscure, and full of jargon and legalese (Adams, 2001). Clear, concise, simple, commonly used vocabulary is best. Word and sentence length determine readability and understanding. Long words and sentences tend to increase the need for a higher reading level. In report writing, the author of the report should present accurate information utilizing brevity and clarity as guides to readability. Writers should avoid using words of more than two syllables and sentences should not exceed 10 words. In addition, when giving an interview to the media, officers often use the word "the" inappropriately. "The" with a long e is used appropriately only when the word following begins with a vowel.

Correct spelling and word usage, as well as proper punctuation and capitalization, are also essential ingredients to good report writing. Mistakes in these areas may lead the reader to believe that the writer is undereducated, poorly trained, careless, and unprofessional. The writer should not rely on computer spell-check programs either. The following are examples of inappropriate words that would not be identified by a spell-checker software program (Hess, 1997):

- He went to the *sight* of the accident.
- The *breaks* on the car did not work.
- She was identified as a drug *attic.*
- It was a *miner* incident.
- He injured his left *feet.*
- She did not *no* where the suspect went.
- The item was found in the car's *truck.*
- The suspect fell into a *whole.*
- He was unable to *here.*

Reports should be written to express a thought, not impress the reader. The language used in normal conversation should be the language used in the report. The vocabulary and style used should approximate what and how the writer would communicate if telling a story or explaining what happened during an incident. Active, rather than passive, voice is recommended in police report writing. For example, an officer should write, "I asked the witness for identification" rather than, "The witness was asked for identification."

Report writers should not attempt to replicate the writing style of someone else. If the author of the report is required to testify in court, the language used in the report should be the same as is presented verbally on the witness stand. First person, singular pronouns are recommended for describing what the report writer did, saw, or experienced. It seems more

AVOID USE OF JARGON

Examples of jargon and wordy phrases and their concise simple English counterparts include the following:

- in the vicinity of (near)
- verbal confrontation (argument)
- inquired (asked)
- proceeded to the location (went to ___)
- terminate (end)
- approximately (about)
- initiated (began)
- related (said)
- party (person)
- in view of the fact that (because)
- for the purpose of (to)
- conducted an investigation (investigated)
- upon an individual basis (individually)
- unit (car)
- pursuit of alleged perpetrator (ran after suspect)
- deceased (dead)
- maintained visual contact (watched)
- exited the vehicle (got out of the car)

natural to state "I" did something rather than "Officer Smith" or "this report writer" did something (Ortmeier, 2002).

Sources of Information

Common sources of information for an investigation include physical evidence, specialized databases, victims, witnesses, suspects, records, and informants.

Records, Documents, and Informants

Records include local, state, and federal law enforcement and other government data. Private individual and business records as well as various publications may also be valuable sources of information. Access to records may be gained through permission, the legal process, the information's status as a public record, and through computerized databases.

PHYSICAL DESCRIPTION PROTOCOL

For Human Subjects

- name, if known.
- gender.
- race and nationality, if known.
- age (estimated or exact, if known).
- height (approximate).
- weight (approximate).
- hair (color, style, length, baldness).
- eyes (color, shape).
- complexion (color, acne, freckles, birthmarks).
- other physical features (scars, tattoos, sideburns).
- eyeglasses.
- cap or hat.
- shirt and tie (color, style).
- coat or jacket (color, style).
- trousers, shorts, or dress (color, style, fabric).
- shoes or boots.
- jewelry.

Informants are also an important source of information. Informants are indispensable in many criminal investigations. When informants are utilized, care should be exercised to evaluate their motives, as well as the information provided, to ensure reliability. In a criminal prosecution, the reliability of informant information is critical. Failure to test the reliability of informant-supplied information could result in the suppression of evidence derived from the informant's information.

Victim and Witness Interviews

Police officers and investigators should be aware that the perceptive faculties and observations of victims and witnesses depend on external as well as internal factors. External factors that may distort an object or observation include: distance from, or proximity to, the object or event; lighting; weather; noise; and other environmental conditions. Other external factors that may distract victims and witnesses include the size of an object, movement, odors, and similarities between the observer and a subject. If a victim or witness observes a characteristic on a subject that is similar to a characteristic of the observer such as both wear mustaches, the observer is likely to recall the mustache as the most outstanding characteristic.

Internal factors that may affect a victim or witnesses' observations include personal characteristics of the observer such as physical condition, eyesight, hearing, and other perceptive capabilities. In addition, an individual's ability to observe and recall another human being, object, or event accurately depends on internal factors other than sensory capabilities. Emotional and psychological problems, experience and educational level, personal prejudices and bias, moods affected by color, and memory capacity impact observation and perceptive faculties (Adams, 2001).

Standard formats are generally used to describe persons. Adherence to a standard enhances uniformity of practice and helps to assure completeness in reporting. Victims and witnesses should first be asked to describe something unique about the subject or recall any similarities between the subject and the observer. After the victim or witness provides unsolicited information, the officer or investigator should ask for additional descriptive data (O'Hara & O'Hara, 1994; Adams, 2001).

Computerized Databases

A wealth of information is available to the contemporary law enforcement officer through **computerized databases.** Many of these databases are accessible through the dispatch center or in police vehicles equipped with mobile data terminals (MDTs) or mobile data computers (MDCs). Major databases include the following:

- **National Crime Information Center (NCIC).** Established in 1967, this system is maintained by the FBI and services all 50 states, federal law enforcement agencies, Puerto Rico, the U.S. Virgin Islands, the District of Columbia, and Canada. Organized into 17 databases, it contains a great deal of information including data on: missing and wanted persons; stolen vehicles, aircraft, and vessels; and stolen vehicle license plates. It also provides criminal history information and serves as a link to many other computerized information systems. Connections are available to other countries through the International Police Organization (INTERPOL).
- **NCIC 2000.** This enhanced NCIC system utilizes optical scanners to read fingerprint patterns. Officers may identify missing persons or fugitives by placing their fingers on a scanner port. The image is transmitted to the FBI's NCIC computer, which replies to the officer if the subject's fingerprints are on file. NCIC 2000 has improved data quality. It also searches all derivatives of names and contains mugshots and data on sexual offenders, probationers, parolees, and persons incarcerated in federal prisons.
- **Automated Property System (APS).** Utilizing the NCIC's APS article file, officers can process identification numbers and descriptions of

Many databases are accessible from police vehicles equipped with mobile data terminals (MDTs) or mobile data computers (MDCs).
Photo courtesy of Portland, Oregon, Bureau of Police

suspected stolen objects if the identification numbers are registered in the system.

- **National Incident-Based Reporting System (NIBRS).** This system is a function of the FBI's Uniform Crime Report (UCR) system. The NIBRS replaces the UCR Part I and Part II offenses with Categories A and B offenses. The new categories are much more comprehensive and up-to-date, including offenses that did not exist when the UCR was originally developed in the 1930s. The NIBRS and the UCR contain information regarding offenses reported to the police and subsequently reported to the FBI. However, the NIBRS provides more detailed information about the nature and scope of reported crimes.

  The FBI introduced the NIBRS in January 1989. The traditional UCR system presented the total number of reported occurrences of Part I offenses as well as arrest data for Part I and Part II offenses. As an alternative to summary reporting, the new enhanced UCR (or NIBRS) was developed to deal with the volume, diversity, and complexity of crime. The NIBRS requires more detailed reports. Agencies collect data regarding individual crime incidents and arrests and submit them in reports detailing each incident. This incident-based reporting provides much more complete information about crimes than do the summary statistics of the traditional UCR system.

  Among the major changes introduced in the NIBRS is the substitution of Part I and Part II offenses with Group A and B offenses. While the existing Part I crimes focus on street crimes, the new Group A is

NIBRS GROUP A OFFENSES

1. arson
2. assault offenses
3. bribery
4. burglary/breaking and entering
5. counterfeiting/forgery
6. destruction/damage/vandalism of property
7. drug/narcotic offenses
8. embezzlement
9. extortion/blackmail
10. fraud offenses
11. gambling offenses
12. homicide offenses
13. kidnaping/abduction
14. larceny/theft offenses
15. motor vehicle theft
16. pornography/obscene material
17. prostitution offenses
18. robbery
19. sex offenses, forcible
20. sex offenses, nonforcible
21. stolen property offenses
22. weapons law violations

more inclusive and widens criminological interest to crime in the suites such as white-collar crime.

Detailed information is provided for each of these crimes. Included among the 52 data elements collected is information detailing the crime circumstances, offender characteristics, arrestee data, victim information, and offense and property data (U.S. Department of Justice, 1988). Less detailed information is required for the 11 Group B offenses.

Other features of the NIBRS include new offense definitions. Rape, for example, in addition to cases involving force, has been expanded to include cases in which consent was not given due to temporary or permanent mental or physical incapacity. NIBRS uses new UCR codes and eliminates the hierarchy rule (all crimes occurring during the same incident are recorded). NIBRS introduces a new category called crimes against society. The additional category complements the existing crimes against property and crimes against persons categories

NIBRS GROUP B OFFENSES

1. bad checks
2. curfew/loitering/vagrancy violations
3. disorderly conduct
4. driving under the influence
5. drunkenness
6. family offenses/nonviolent
7. liquor law violations
8. peeping tom offenses
9. runaway offenses
10. trespass of real property
11. all other offenses

and includes crimes such as gambling, prostitution, and drug sales and use. NIBRS also establishes mechanisms for distinguishing between attempted versus completed crimes and expands data on the victim-offender relationship.

The NIBRS was intended to be fully operational by 1999 (Schmalleger, 2002). However, as of January 2002, fewer than 50 percent of the states were certified and several states had not yet developed or tested the new reporting system (National Incident-Based Reporting System, 2002).

- **Automated Fingerprint Identification System (AFIS).** This system utilizes optical scanners to record and electronically transmit fingerprints to a state or FBI fingerprinting identification (ID) database. It is designed to replace manual fingerprinting ID systems currently used by most agencies.
- **Stolen Vehicle System (SVS).** Stolen vehicle identification numbers (VINs) and stolen vehicle components with identification numbers are recorded and retrievable within this system.
- **Criminal Justice Information System (CJIS).** This is a state-based system that provides a wide range of information on wanted persons, guns, and stolen property. Many CJIS databases provide information on the progress of criminal cases from arrest through conviction and final disposition. Officers may access CJIS for follow-up information.
- **Automated Statewide Auto Theft Inquiry Service (AUTO STATIS).** This state-based system operates in conjunction with the NCIC and specializes in information regarding stolen, impounded, and repossessed vehicles.

- **Restraining Order System (ROS).** This California state-based system tracks restraining orders issued against individuals as a result of domestic violence or family court orders (Ortmeier, 2002; Payton & Amaral, 1996; Schmalleger, 2001; Senna & Siegel, 2001).

In addition to the computerized data described above, some law enforcement agencies are taking advantage of new computerized crime mapping technology. **Geographical Information Systems (GIS)** technology enables law enforcement agencies to analyze and correlate various data sources to create a detailed view of crime incidents and related factors within a specific geographic area. The crime-related data are plotted against a digitized map of a community, city, or region. Crime incident data are geocoded (assigning x and y coordinates to an address so information can be coded to a map) by using either street centerlines or parcels of land to identify a geographic location. Crime mapping analysis can be used for geocoding offense (arrest and incident) data, calls for service, and vehicle recovery information. Police agencies that utilize crime mapping report improvements in information dissemination, evaluation, and administration. Specifically, crime mapping data can be used to inform police personnel of crime incident locations, make resource allocation decisions, and evaluate intervention strategies. Crime mapping data can also inform citizens about crime activity, and identify hot spots and locations with repeat calls for service.

Although a majority of police departments engage in some form of crime analysis, usually compiling statistical reports to fulfill UCR requirements, only about 15 percent of police departments surveyed utilize any computerized crime mapping. Larger departments, with dedicated crime analysis staff primarily responsible for performing computerized inquiries, are more likely to utilize the latest technology. Significant financial resources, time, and training are necessary to establish a computerized crime mapping operation. Since most police departments in the United States are small, few police patrol officers currently use computerized crime mapping. However, use is likely to increase over time since mapping has been shown to be a valuable tool for law enforcement (Mamalian & LaVigne, 1999).

Computerized databases have made the process of collecting, storing, analyzing, and retrieving vast amounts of data much simpler and faster (Peak & Glensor, 2002). However, any system is only as strong as its weakest link. Since the data are contained in an electronic medium, unauthorized access, system collapse, and inadequate linkages between databases often create obstacles to effective information retrieval and exchange. The United States Immigration and Naturalization Service's IDENT system, for example, failed to identify Raphael Resendez-Ramirez as a suspected serial killer on the FBI's Ten Most Wanted List. Resendez-Ramirez was accused of eight murders, four of which occurred after the United States Border Patrol released him to return to Mexico on June 2, 1999. IDENT is an electronic system designed to store fingerprints and photographs of people who are apprehended after entering the United States illegally. Apparently, however, the IDENT system was self-constrained and did not have appropriate linkages to other databases that would have allowed the Border Patrol to discover Resendez-Ramirez's wanted status (Stern, 1999).

ETHICS IN COMMUNICATION

The moral and ethical dimensions of communication should be studied from a broad perspective. Without a broad perspective, the result of a communication may be immoral. In other words, if the ethical code of a single culture or group determines right and wrong, the perspective of that group is single-minded and would not produce authentic morality in a multicultural society (Pasquali, 1997). Police officers who view the world from a single perspective, usually their own, possess an image that is often distorted. Thus, the officers and the citizens with whom the officers are attempting to communicate rarely converse through a common medium. Intended meaning is not received, resulting in ineffective communication or no communication at all.

Further, most people live in a communications era that appears to be devoid of morality and ethical principles. This is often demonstrated by the relationship between public opinion and abuse by mass media personnel. Many commentators commit a "social felony" by misrepresenting the facts and misusing their power when communicating through the mass media (Pasquali, 1997). This creates a need for a new understanding of the importance of communication. But how can an individual police officer or even an entire police agency make a difference? What can a police corp of approximately 700,000 do to shape the public image of the police when the mass media can address a substantial portion of the almost 300 million U.S. residents in a single broadcast? The answers lie in the countless communications decisions a police officer makes on a daily basis. These decisions carry ethical considerations and are so very important, not only to the police public image, to the effectiveness of the police in a democratic society.

A core value associated with **ethical communication** behavior is honesty, the foundation of truthfulness. However, although honesty is desirable in principle, situations arise in which complete and full disclosure result in undesirable consequences. As alternatives to full disclosure, people revert to lying, equivocating, and hinting (Adler & Towne, 2002).

People use alternatives to full disclosure for many reasons. People lie to save face, avoid conflict, guide social interaction, expand or cease relationships, or gain power over others. Equivocal language consists of statements that contain more than one common definition. An equivocation is often used as an alternative to telling a lie. In response to an apology, an angry person may reply with, "Do not mention it," rather than lie about actual feelings. Hinting is more direct than equivocation. Hints are used to solicit desirable behavior. Rather than condemn inappropriate behavior of another outright, a person might suggest that the misbehaving person change behavior. Whether lying, equivocating, or hinting, the ethical challenge is to determine if the deceit provides an ethical alternative to full disclosure. Some ethicists suggest that deceit is not always unethical. They argue that the communicator's motive, rather than the deceit itself, ought to be judged, and, in some cases, the positive effects of the deception may outweigh negative consequences (Adler & Towne, 2002).

As a general principle, honesty is the best policy. Police officers should communicate the truth. Often, however, the very nature of police work confuses the issue of honesty and truthfulness because circumstances may dictate a deceptive course of action. Being absolutely honest may do more harm than good. Deception used to trick a suspect into a confession may be a legally and morally correct course of action. Honesty does not mean that all truth must be revealed. Telling a parent who was critically injured in a motor vehicle accident (and is receiving life-saving medical attention) that the parent's passenger children are dead may not be appropriate. To tell the truth prematurely may have devastating consequences. Likewise, communication behavior that is appropriate in one situation may not be appropriate in another. Confidentiality of police records must be maintained except as provided by constitutional law and freedom-of-information statutory provisions (Wallace, Roberson, & Steckler, 2001).

Absolutes in communication ethics rarely exist. However, an awareness of the positive or negative consequences of communication behavior that may arise can assist with making the appropriate communication decision at the appropriate time. When practiced continuously, ethical communication becomes habitual in most people.

Several guidelines to ethical communication can assist with communication decision making. First, communicators should maintain candor (truthfulness, honesty, frankness) and avoid deception, if possible. Messages should be accurate (free of errors) and consistent (not contradictory). Good communicators also maintain confidences, cultivate empathetic listening, and ensure the timeliness of messages sent. Finally, ethical communicators confront those who engage in unethical communication behavior (O'Hair, Gustav, & Dixon, 2002).

SUMMARY

Communication is a complex process, rather than an event, through which information is exchanged. It involves mediums for the transmission of thought and meaning, each of which has relevance in policing. Those involved in the communication process must strive to overcome myths and false assumptions regarding communication.

Effective communication skills are critical to the police officer. Proper attitudes and behaviors contribute to effective communication. Speech and interpersonal communications may involve one-on-one conversations, meetings, working in teams or on task forces, and public speaking. Police officers should be aware of the special challenges associated with communication as well as the processes for cross-cultural communication, managing conflict, and tactical communication.

Proper documentation through the use of appropriate writing skills is critical in police work. Officers must be familiar with and able to acquire information from a variety of sources. Finally, absolutes in communication ethics rarely exist. However, an awareness of the principles of communication ethics can assist with the development of appropriate communication decisions.

KEY TERMS AND CONCEPTS

Define, describe, or explain the importance of each of the following:

communication
computerized database
conflict management
cross-cultural communication
culture shock
ethical communication
field notes
Geographic Information System (GIS)
interpersonal communication
National Incident-Based Reporting System (NIBRS)
note taking
public speaking
report writing
special challenges in communication
tactical communication
task force
teamwork

DISCUSSION QUESTIONS AND EXERCISES

1. Why are communication skills important in a law enforcement environment?
2. Discuss how verbal communication and listening skills can be used to de-escalate conflict and reduce the need to use physical force.
3. What role does attitude play in the communication process?
4. Why is knowledge of different cultures important to effective communication in police work?
5. How should communication conflict be managed? Should approaches to conflict differ? Why, or why not? Can conflict be productive? If so, when?
6. What is tactical communication? When should it be used?
7. Why is documentation vital to police work?
8. A police officer is interrogating a criminal suspect. During the interrogation the police officer falsely states that an accomplice to the crime under investigation has already confessed. Is the officer's lack of truthfulness unethical? Explain your response.

Chapter 7

Motivation: Key to Personal and Professional Success

Learning Objectives

After completing this chapter, the reader should be able to:

- explain why motivational skills are important for a police officer.
- define motivation.
- distinguish between intrinsic and extrinsic motivators.
- compare and contrast theories of motivation.
- analyze behavioral assumptions about motivation as they relate to leadership style.
- describe the ethical leader as motivator.
- select a motivational leadership style appropriate to a situation.

Introduction

The motivation of and by police officers is vital to the success of any policing effort (Baker, 2000). Motivation provides the reason for a course of action. As stated by numerous experts on policing, motivation acts as a catalyst to arouse proaction in others (Ortmeier, 1996). It is part of the service mission of police work. Motivational skills are required to encourage creativity and innovation, engage in community team building, develop cooperative relationships, recognize and encourage responsible leaders, and demonstrate persistence as well as a continual commitment to the tasks at hand. In a community policing environment, a police officer must inspire and motivate others until someone other than the police can facilitate individual and community action. The unleashing of energy for the common good is a positive by-product of exercising motivational skills. Community-centered policing requires the motivation to develop relationships with numerous public and private agencies and organizations. Police officers who demonstrate intellectual curiosity and enthusiasm help to create an atmosphere of contagious commitment to a community good (Ortmeier, 1996).

THE CONTEXT FOR MOTIVATION

Practitioners, researchers, and academics have long sought to discover what motivates people, particularly as **motivation** relates to what causes people to achieve certain goals. Some theorists focused on individual characteristics such as personality traits, basic needs, and desires. Referred to as **humanistic, content, or need motivational theorists,** their orientation was toward satisfying an individual's internal needs. **Behavioralistic or process theorists,** on the other hand, focused on environmental factors such as the nature of work and peer groups. Behavioralists attempt to explain motivation in terms of learned behavior and external reinforcement, discounting internal drives. Behaviorists believe the process of reward and punishment determine future behavior (Thurman, Zhao, & Giacomazzi, 2001). More recently, theorists emphasize both individual and environmental factors, arguing that characteristics of the individual combine with environmental factors to direct motivational energy. Therefore, one must consider the individual person as well as the context within which the person is sought to be motivated.

Broadly defined, **context for motivation** refers to features in the achievement environment (workplace, organization); cultural factors (ethnicity, nationality); and numerous social situations (peer groups, family) in which people operate. In addition, one must search within developmental and historical arenas to identify contexts. Thus, when all contextual factors for motivation are considered, the ingredients and elements necessary to achieve motivation are extremely complex. Yet, the variety of contexts within which people operate must be considered when motivation to achieve is attempted (Urban, 1999). The various contextual influences have a profound effect on motivational techniques used in a particular set of circumstances. In a leadership role, the leader must consider the contextual factors and apply motivational techniques appropriate to the individual and the situation.

Additionally, a leader must consider the role of intrinsic (internal) and extrinsic (external) achievement motivators. Whenever people engage in achievement-related activities, their behavior is energized by a combination of intrinsic and extrinsic motivators. **Intrinsic motivation** involves a natural human propensity to explore and learn new ideas and to exercise one's own capabilities. Under appropriate conditions, human beings possess considerable intrinsic motivation and engage in an activity because of the inherent satisfaction (joy) it provides. Through intrinsic motivation, people unconsciously satisfy two psychological needs that accompany action. They experience autonomy, the sense of organizing action from within themselves, and efficacy (competence), the sense of having an effect on or mastering their own environment. Circumstances that facilitate self-determination and an internal locus of control, as perceived by the person motivated, will enhance intrinsic motivation. Factors that facilitate intrinsic motivation include the provision of personal choice, internal rewards (new learning and experiences), empathy from others, relevant feedback, and optimal challenges. People who are intrinsically motivated tend to enjoy activities more, feel more confident, experience less anxiety, and look forward to new challenges (Adler, 2002; Herzberg, 1959; Ryan & LaGuardia, 1999; Stojkovic, Kalinich, & Klofas, 2003).

Through **extrinsic motivation,** a person engages in an activity because the behavior provides a means to an end. The behavior is not inherently satisfying. Rather, the person engages in the behavior to receive a reward such as praise or money, or to avoid punishment, such as disciplinary action or loss of employment. The value of the activity is not determined by the self but by some external force. Extrinsic motivators include external regulation, introjection, identification, and integration. Through external regulation, a person engages in behavior to receive an externally offered reward. Through introjection, a person performs to avoid guilt or anxiety or to experience an ego-enhancement such as approval. Identification involves the

Motivation depends on the individual and the environment.
Photo courtesy of Los Angeles Sheriff's Department.

conscious acceptance of the worth or value of a goal. Identification allows a person to derive a sense of meaning or importance from an activity that fosters persistence, effort, and enhanced performance. Through integration, goals and activities are internalized, fully self-endorsed, and consistent with the actor's own goals and relationships. Each form of extrinsic motivation (external regulation, introjection, identification, and integration) represents an increasingly internalized (self-motivating) style of personal engagement to achieve. The more a person internalizes the reasons to engage in an activity or reach a goal, the more the person moves from extrinsic to intrinsic motivation (Ryan & LaGuardia, 1999).

ATTITUDE AND MOTIVATION

An **attitude** is a predisposition to respond favorably or unfavorably to persons, places, or objects in an environment. Attitude is reflected in behavior (Porter & Lawler, 1968; Whisenand & Ferguson, 2002). A police officer's attitude is an important factor both in terms of personal satisfaction with the job and the officer's relationships with others. In many venues, especially in some urban areas where police activity is high, officers may be so overwhelmed with calls for service that they become discouraged and lose sight of the larger goal of serving a noble ethical cause. Regardless of the workload, police officers should reflect on the meaning of the authority vested in them and the power inherent in the criminal justice system. The appropriate exercise of authority and power depends on each person's ability to maintain the highest standards of ethical behavior. After all, it is the people who work within the criminal justice system that make it just or corrupt (Pollock, 1998). In some police agencies an attitude of superiority creates arrogance and complacency among officers that stymies innovation and lowers productivity. Rigid, centralized command and overly strict adherence to departmental rules also helps to create an organizational culture based on apprehension and mistrust. Control is maintained through extrinsic fear of punishment for rule violations (Cortrite, 2000). The climate of mistrust and the authoritarian command and control management style lead to poor morale, problems with motivation, bad attitudes, and lack of accountability.

As criminal justice practitioners and professionals with discretionary decision-making ability, police officers exercise a tremendous amount of power over the lives of other people (Meadows, 2002; Palacios, Cromwell, & Dunham, 2002). Belief in the value of ethics and the practice of ethical behavior do not appear fortuitously. Nor does training and education in ethics and leadership necessarily create ethical leaders. Learning a body of knowledge and developing skills do not, in themselves, provide individuals with the moral sense necessary to use knowledge and skills wisely. The greatest protection against the corruption of power is the formation of an attitude or mind-set that is committed to ethical behavior. As an ethical leader, the police officer must be committed to the democratic process and all it entails. If constitutional provisions, the law, and ethical behavior are viewed by the police officer as impediments or irrelevant to the prevention and control of crime and disorder, the officer is not fulfilling the highest ideals of a public servant. Rather, the officer is a discredit to the professional community and does not belong in the police service (Pollock, 1998).

One of the greatest enemies of the police officer is an improper attitude. Effective policing requires a proper attitude: a mental commitment to integrity, ethics, community service, professionalism, and the police mission (Miller, 1995; Trautman, 2002). Despite popular belief, police work is not the most physically dangerous job in the world (Perry, 1994). Miners, construction workers, taxi drivers, firefighters, and 24-hour convenience store clerks all have higher work-related death rates. However, policing is extremely taxing, emotionally, mentally, and physically. Although police work can be 80-percent boredom, 20 percent can be sheer terror. Police officers must deal with dangerous people as well as the uncivil behavior of normally good citizens.

Some research suggests that police officers are not significantly different from the general population in terms of their psychological profiles and attitudes. In other words, police agencies do not recruit psychologically unfit individuals. However, research also suggests that there may be a significant difference between attitudes and behavior. Thus, the selection, training, and development of police officers must emphasize proper attitude as well as behavior (Walker, Spohn, & DeLone, 2002).

Today, the public demands and expects mature behavior and judgment on the part of its police officers. Policing is not the career field for immature, self-centered, overly aggressive, or abusive people. The psychological dynamics of police work generates stress, which must be dealt with effectively (Swanson, Territo, & Taylor, 1998). The officer must not allow stress to manifest itself in uncivil conduct toward normally law-abiding citizens, use of excessive force on criminal suspects, inappropriate behavior in the officer's personal life, officer suicide, or improper attitudes toward other people or the job itself.

In addition to maintaining a proper attitude, the police officer must recognize that the public, as well as the officer's agency and peers, has certain expectations of a law enforcement professional. These expectations are used to evaluate an officer's performance. The public's evaluation is based on how an officer appears and behaves as well as how the officer handles crises and problem situations. The public expects an officer to know a community's perceived needs, prevent crime, maintain order, provide service, and demonstrate equal and unbiased enforcement of the law. An officer's peers expect technical competence, physical backup when appropriate, and emotional support. An officer's motivation to do the right thing at the right time is critical in police service. Additionally, the ability to motivate others assists police officers in the fulfillment of their public safety mission.

Individual Differences and Motivation

Individuals differ in many ways because people have different values, personalities, needs, and abilities. These individual differences affect motivation in different ways. Although numerous studies have been conducted to improve the understanding of these differences, many suggest that an individual's needs (strong feelings of deficiency that create an uncomfortable tension) provide the basis for differences in motivation. The tension created by need becomes the motivating force and the individual takes action to reduce the tension by satisfying the need, thus diminishing the intensity of the motivating force (Hellriegel, Jackson, & Slocum, 2002). Ultimately, the factors that motivate others depend on the culture and situation at hand (Adler, 2002; Hellriegel, Slocum, & Woodman, 2001). However, several theories, which illustrate how individual differences affect motivation, are useful to police officers in understanding the reactions of the people with whom they come in contact.

Maslow's Hierarchy of Needs

Through his classic research and writings on motivation, Abraham **Maslow** arranged individual motivational factors according to a **hierarchy of needs**. Maslow identified five types of human needs: physiological (the most basic), security, affiliation, esteem, and self-actualization (at the top of the needs hierarchy). Physiological needs include those that are basic to human survival: food, water, shelter, and clothing. Security needs address the desire for stability, safety, good health, and the absence of threats or pain. In an employment situation, security needs may be satisfied if employment is stable and expands employee competence and confidence of long-term employability. Affiliation needs include the desire for friendship, belonging, and love. When a person's affiliation needs are not met, dissatisfaction may lead to low productivity, absenteeism, stress-related behaviors, and psychological problems. Esteem needs include the desire for self-respect, personal achievement, and recognition from others. To satisfy esteem needs, people desire prestige, status, and opportunities to demonstrate their competence and worth. Self-actualization needs, the highest level on

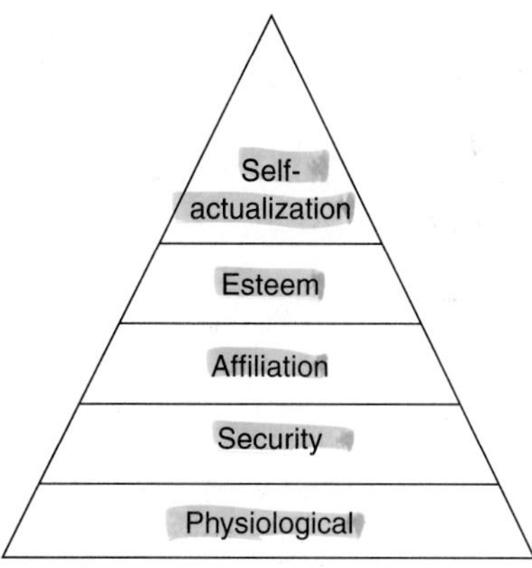

FIGURE 7–1 Maslow's Hierarchy of Needs. *Illustration by Dorie Savage.*

Maslow's need hierarchy continuum, are achieved when one's desires for personal growth, self-fulfillment, and reaching one's full potential are realized. Maslow suggested that as one need is satisfied, motivation shifts to satisfying the next higher level of need (Maslow, 1970).

Maslow's original formulation of the need hierarchy reflected his belief that movement in the hierarchy was upward only. In later formulations, Maslow suggested that movement in the hierarchy could be in both directions. Through his satisfaction-progression hypothesis, Maslow proposed that a need is a motivator until it is satisfied. Once satisfied, another need emerges. Additionally, low-level needs must be satisfied before higher level needs appear as motivators (Maslow, 1970; Hellriegel, Jackson, & Slocum, 2002).

Alderfer's ERG Theory

Clay Alderfer (1972) also viewed motivation from an individual needs perspective. In contrast to Maslow's five-level hierarchy of needs, however, Alderfer suggested three categories of need: existence, relatedness, and growth (Alderfer, 1972). Alderfer named his formulation existence, relatedness, and growth (ERG) theory. Similar to Maslow's physiological needs, Alderfer's existence needs included the desire for water, food, shelter, good working conditions, and other factors contributing to physical well-being. Relatedness needs, similar to Maslow's affiliation needs, referred to desires to establish and maintain good interpersonal relationships. Similar to Maslow's esteem and self-actualization needs, Alderfer's growth needs included desires for creativity, productivity, and personal development (Alderfer, 1972).

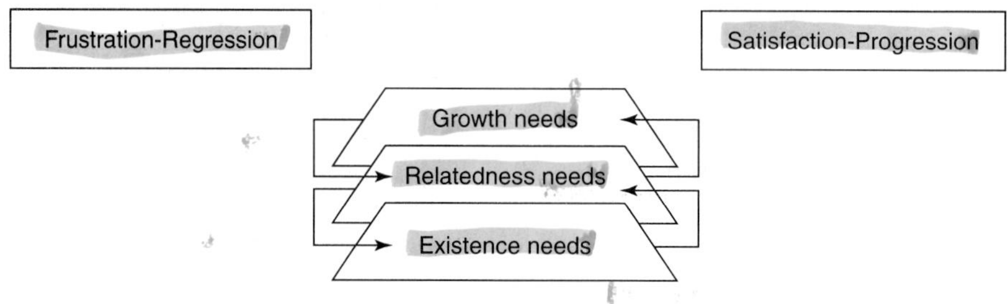

FIGURE 7–2 Alderfer's ERG Model of Motivation.
Illustration by Dorie Savage.

Alderfer's ERG theory recognized Maslow's satisfaction-progression hypothesis, but the ERG theory also contains an additional dimension called the frustration-regression hypothesis. The frustration-regression hypothesis suggests that frustration (obstacles) encountered when seeking to meet higher-level needs leads to a reemergence of lower-level needs. According to Alderfer, leaders should strive to identify and remove follower frustration that serves as an obstacle to productivity and growth. If frustrations cannot be removed, Alderfer suggests that leaders attempt to redirect a follower's energy toward a more satisfying need category (Alderfer, 1972; Hellriegel, Jackson, & Slocum, 2002).

Members of a community may be restricted economically because of poor earning potential. Thus, their desire for personal growth may be frustrated. As leaders, however, police officers assigned to the community could employ community policing strategies and tactics to bring community members together in a collaborative effort to improve the quality of life in their neighborhood, regardless of the member's personal economic condition. Thus, high achievement and satisfaction may be realized in the relatedness needs and existence needs categories.

McClelland's Learned Needs Theory

In his **learned needs theory,** David **McClelland** (1971) suggested that people develop needs through interaction with the surrounding environment. Thus, social contexts influence the learning of motivational needs. This theory contrasts with Maslow's theory that a needs hierarchy is inherent to human beings (Hellriegel, Jackson, & Slocum, 2002). According to McClelland, understanding the differences among individual motivators depends on the presence of three key motives: affiliation, achievement, and power (McClelland, 1971). The affiliation motive relates to one's desire to develop and maintain satisfying interpersonal relationships. The

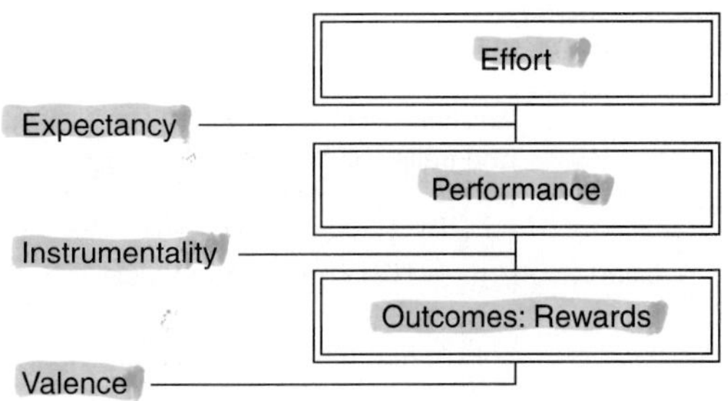

FIGURE 7–3 Expectancy Theory.
Illustration by Dorie Savage.

achievement motive focuses on the human desire for success. An individual's desire to control and influence others and the environment is emphasized by the power motive. As a person progresses through life, one or more of the motives becomes dominant. If more than one motive dominates an individual's personality, conflict between or among motives may arise. A person's desire for friendships (affiliation motive) on the job may conflict with the person's desire to produce and seek promotion (achievement motive). Leaders should strive to recognize and balance individual follower motives as they (the leaders) seek to motivate followers (Hellriegel, Jackson, & Slocum, 2002; McClelland, 1971).

Expectancy Theory

According to **expectancy theory,** an individual, given choices, selects options that are perceived to provide the greatest rewards. Thus, the expectancy theory or model suggests that motivation to perform is based on an understanding of the relationship between performance and effort and the perception of the desirability of outcomes associated with different performance levels (Vroom, 1964). Expectancy is linked to instrumentality and valence. Expectancy is the belief that a certain level of effort will result in a certain level of performance. Instrumentality involves an individual's belief that a specific level of performance will lead to a desired outcome. Valence is the importance (value) an individual attaches to various outcomes. For motivation to be high, the valence (value of the outcome) must be high. Although complex, expectancy theory represents one of the most comprehensive motivation models as it seeks to explain or predict task-related behavior (Lewis, Goodman, & Fandt, 2001; Vroom, 1964).

By adding elements to basic expectancy theory, the integrated expectancy model suggests that people who perform well are more satisfied if their performance is rewarded appropriately. However, satisfaction is not

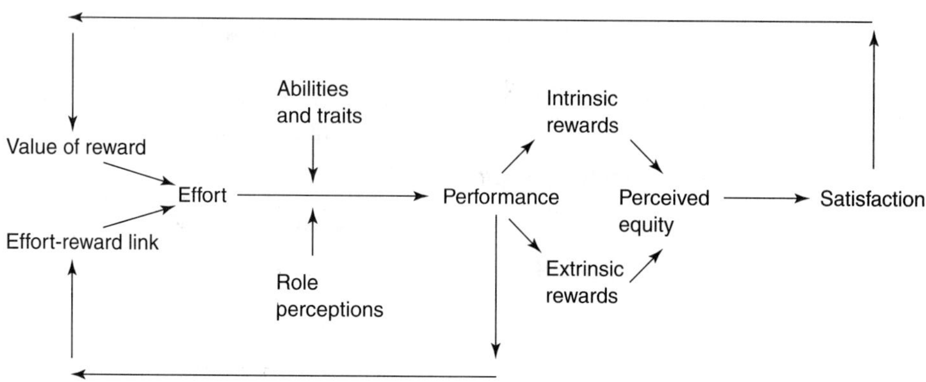

FIGURE 7–4 The Integrated Expectancy Model.
Illustration by Dorie Savage.

viewed as the cause of performance. Rather, the integrated expectancy model adds elements that can cause expectancies and instrumentalities to be lower than desired.

Elements or factors that affect expectancy include individual ability (competencies), traits (personality characteristics), and role perceptions (individual experiences and interactions with others). Elements that affect instrumentalities include extrinsic rewards (compensation, status, security) and intrinsic rewards (personal satisfaction). Integrated expectancy theory suggests that individual satisfaction depends on the difference in the rewards received as compared to what the individual believes should be received. A perception of unfair treatment will lower commitment and productivity (Hellriegel, Jackson, & Slocum, 2002).

Behavioral Assumptions, Motivation, and Leadership Style

Numerous factors and conditions operate to create **behavioral assumptions** that influence a person's perception of another individual or situation. Physiological factors such as age, health, fatigue, biological cycles, and hunger affect one's image of people and the environment. Cultural differences, social roles (gender, occupation), self-concept, and ideals people share also influence perception. People are often influenced by what is most obvious, cling to first impressions, and assume that others think and feel the way they do (Adler & Towne, 2002).

Behavioral assumptions about people and how to motivate them influence leader behavior. If a leader harbors false assumptions about people, the beliefs can cause a leader to use inappropriate motivational techniques with followers. Correct behavioral assumptions can result in positive outcomes (Fournies, 2000). Although many behavioral assumptions and their accompanying models for direction and control of human beings were developed for managerial personnel, the concepts apply to leaders as well. Therefore, the discussion in this section will address the models in terms of these assumptions as they relate to motivation and leadership style.

Theories X, Y, and Z

One of the most widely quoted models for recognizing and distinguishing assumptions about motivation was developed by Douglas McGregor in the 1950s. In his classic work, *The Human Side of Enterprise,* McGregor (1960) explored theoretical assumptions about human nature and human behavior as it relates to ethics, management, leadership, and motivation. McGregor proposed that two sets of leadership or managerial assumptions regarding human behavior appeared to exist. He referred to the traditional view of leadership and managerial direction and control as **theory X** and the view that leadership and management should be based on the integration of individual and organizational goals as **theory Y.** Theory X includes the following leadership and managerial assumptions:

- The average human being has an inherent dislike of work and will avoid work if possible.
- Because of the dislike for work, most people must be coerced, controlled, directed, or threatened with punishment to get them to put forth adequate effort toward the achievement of objectives.
- The average human being is self-centered, prefers to be directed, wishes to avoid responsibility, has relatively little ambition, and wants security above all.

McGregor suggested that theory X leaders and managers did not account for critical factors associated with motivation. These factors include a few simple generalizations about human beings. First, human beings are "wanting" animals. As soon as one need is satisfied, it is replaced with another. Second, human needs are organized in a hierarchy of importance. Third, a satisfied need is not a motivator of behavior. According to McGregor, theory X leaders and managers ignore these generalizations. They direct and control through the exercise of authority (McGregor, 1960).

Theory Y leaders and managers, on the other hand, operate with a different set of assumptions regarding human behavior. Theory Y assumptions include the following:

- The expenditure of physical and mental effort in work is as natural as play or rest.

- External control and the threat of punishment are not the only means for bringing about effort toward objectives. People will exercise self-direction and self-control in the service of objectives to which they are committed.
- Commitment to objectives is a function of the rewards associated with their achievement.
- The average human being learns, under proper conditions, to accept as well as seek responsibility.
- The capacity to exercise a relatively high degree of imagination, ingenuity, and creativity in the solution to problems is widely, not narrowly, distributed in the population.
- Under the conditions of modern industrial life, the intellectual potentialities of the average human being are only partially realized (McGregor, 1960).

Theory Y assumptions are dynamic rather than static and represent significantly different implications for leadership and management than do theory X assumptions. Theory Y assumptions focus on human growth. Theory X leaders and managers blame followers and workers for failure to achieve goals. Theory Y implies that poor productivity is more often the result of poor leadership and management. Theory Y focuses on the integration of goals: the creation of conditions through which members of a group or organization may achieve their own goals as well as the goal of the enterprise. Thus, motivation, the potential for growth, the ability to assume responsibility, and the readiness to work toward individual as well as group goals are present in all people. The leader's responsibility is to recognize, harness, and channel these characteristics toward common goals by creating a climate and methodology conducive to success (Baker, 2000; Hellriegel, Jackson, & Slocum, 2002; McGregor, 1960).

An adaptation of theory Y, called **theory Z,** was created by William Ouchi in the early 1980s. Theory Z is a leadership and management style that advocates trusting followers and employees and creating an environment in which followers and employees feel as though they are an integral part of the group or organization. According to theory Z, a relationship of trust promotes increased productivity and goal achievement (Lewis, Goodman, & Fandt, 2001; Ouchi, 1981).

The Managerial Grid

The **managerial grid** developed by Robert Blake and Jane Mouton (1985) identifies five leadership styles that integrate varying degrees of concern for people with concern for production and goal achievement.

Blake and Mouton's five leadership styles are arranged on a grid. The impoverished leadership style (1,1) demonstrates low concern for people,

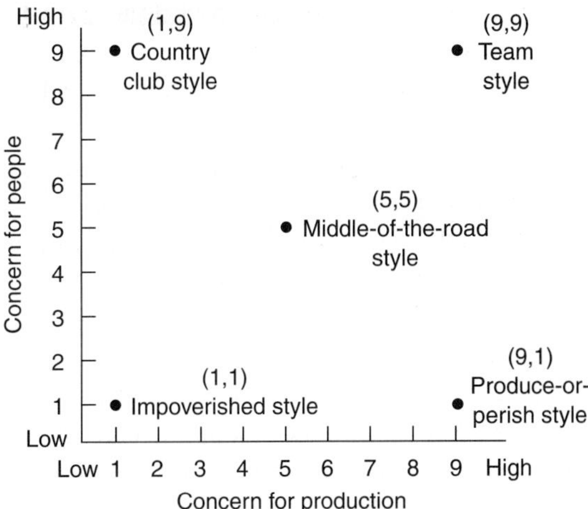

FIGURE 7–5 The Managerial Grid.
Illustration by Dorie Savage.

production, and goal achievement. Leaders utilizing this style exert minimal effort and wish to maintain the status quo. Through the country club style (1,9) leaders demonstrate high concern for people but low concern for production and goal achievement. Leaders create a secure and comfortable environment in the hope that followers will produce. Low concern for people and high concern for production and goal achievement characterize the produce-or-perish leadership style (9,1). Leaders use coercive powers to achieve results and show little concern for the personal needs of followers. Through the middle-of-the road style (5,5), leaders strive to balance follower personal needs with a concern for productivity and goal achievement. Through the team style (9,9), leaders demonstrate high concern for people as well as productivity and goal achievement. Blake and Mouton believed that 9,9 was the optimal style. The 9,9 approach is consistent with McGregor's theory Y. Leaders at 9,9 strive for teamwork and commitment to goal achievement among team members (Blake & Mouton, 1985).

TESTED IN OTHER TEXT

The Situational Leadership Model

Paul Hersey and Ken Blanchard created a **situational leadership model** that suggests that supportive (people-centered) and directive (production and goal-centered) leadership behaviors should be contingent on the readiness level of followers and workers (Hersey & Blanchard, 1982; Hersey, Blanchard, & Johnson, 2001). Supportive leadership behavior is consistent with open communication links between a leader and followers. Leaders listen, encourage, and involve followers in decision making. Directive leadership behaviors are consistent with situations requiring structure, control,

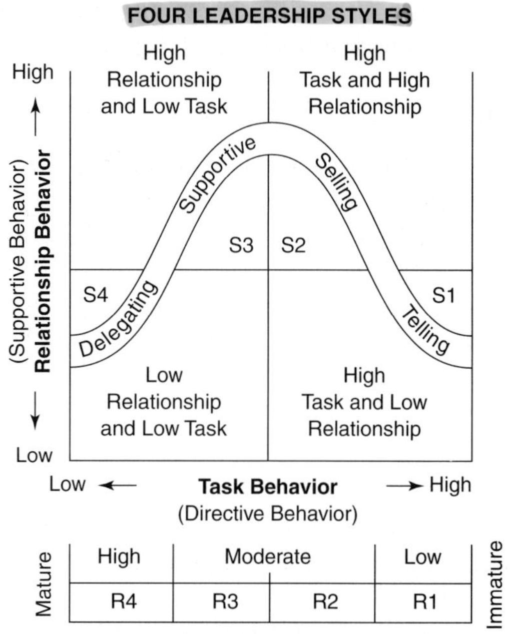

FIGURE 7–6 Situational Leadership Model.
Illustration by Dorie Savage.

direct supervision, and a reliance on one-way (leader to follower) communication. Follower readiness (maturity, experience, expertise) determines the follower's ability to set high and attainable task-related goals and willingness to assume responsibility for achieving the goals. The level of supportive or directive leadership behaviors is dependent on different levels of follower readiness. According to the situational leadership model, leaders use a delegating, supportive, selling, or telling style, depending on follower readiness.

Leaders use a delegating style when they view followers as mature, competent, and motivated. The supportive style is used to encourage, assist, and maintain open communication links between leader and follower. Through the telling style, the leader provides direction, encourages two-way communication, helps build confidence, and motivates the follower. The telling leadership style is used when clear and specific instructions are necessary (Hersey & Blanchard, 1982; Hersey, Blanchard, & Johnson, 2001). Although the model has limitations (requires leaders to adjust style frequently and does not account for different performance levels when followers have same level of readiness), it does encourage leadership style flexibility. In addition, the model suggests that leaders should promote and assist with follower growth and development, thus improving follower readiness and satisfaction (Hellriegel, Jackson, & Slocum, 2002).

Vroom-Jago Time-Drive Leadership Model

As a prescription for leadership style choice, the **Vroom-Jago time-drive leadership model** focuses on seven motivator contingency variables a leader should consider when selecting a leadership style. Victor Vroom created a Windows-based computer program (Expert System) that enables leaders to record the presence of the contingency variables in a given situation. A five-point scale ranging from five (high presence) through three (moderate presence) to one (low presence) is used to determine the presence of the variables in a particular problem situation. The seven contingency variables include the following:

- Decision significance.
- Importance of follower commitment to goal achievement.
- Leader expertise and competence to understand the nature of the problem.
- Likelihood of follower commitment.
- Team support and goal sharing.
- Team expertise to understand the problem and select the best solution.
- Team competence to resolve conflicts among competing preferred solutions and handle the decision-making process.

The Vroom-Jago leadership model includes five leadership styles that vary in relationship to follower decision-making ability and participation:

- The Decide Style: The leader decides on the best course of action and directs followers.
- The Consult Individually Style: The leader decides after consulting with followers individually rather than in a group.
- The Consult Team Style: The leader decides subsequent to an open meeting with all followers.
- The Facilitate Style: The leader facilitates problem solving and decision making through team (leader and follower) consensus building.
- The Delegate Style: Representing the highest level of follower participation and discretion, the delegate leadership style allows followers to arrive at a decision within limits prescribed by the leader.

Utilizing a matrix that incorporates the seven contingency variables and five leadership styles, the leader formulates a judgment on which leadership style is appropriate to the situation. Given the reality of decision time

Problem	Decision Significance	Importance of Commitment	Leader Expertise	Likelihood of Commitment	Team Support	Team Expertise	Team Competence	Suggested Style
	H	H	H H	H	----	----	----	Decide
				L	H	H	H	Delegate
							L	Consult Team
						L	----	
					L	----	----	
			H	H	H	H	H	Facilitate
							L	Consult Individually
						L	----	
					L	----	----	
			H	L	H	H	H	Facilitate
							L	Consult Team
						L	----	
					L	----	----	
		L	H	----	----	----	----	Decide
			H	----	H	H	H	Facilitate
							L	Consult Individually
						L	----	
					L	----	----	
	L	H	----	H	----	----	----	Decide
				L	----	----	H	Delegate
							L	Facilitate
		L	----	----	----	----	----	Decide

NOTE: An "H" indicates a high level of importance with that contingency variable, an "L" indicates a low level of importance, and a dashed line (----) indicates "not a factor."

FIGURE 7–7 Vroom-Jago Time-Drive Leadership Model.
Illustration by Dorie Savage.

constraints (some solutions are extremely time sensitive and the Vroom-Jago model may be inappropriate) and a leader's ability to diagnose contingencies correctly, the leader can utilize the matrix to identify the most appropriate leadership style (Hellriegel, Jackson, & Slocum, 2002; Vroom 2000).

Path-Goal Motivational Leadership

Although many leadership theories include motivation of others as an objective, the stated purpose of **path-goal motivational leadership** is to enhance performance and satisfaction by focusing on motivation as a primary ingredient of leadership. As discussed in Chapter 3, the underlying assumption of path-goal leadership theory is that followers will be motivated if they believe that they are capable of performing tasks assigned, that their efforts will culminate in a certain result, and that the rewards for completing the tasks are worthwhile.

Through the application of path-goal theory, the leader's challenge is to select and implement a leadership style that best meets a follower's motivational needs. Leaders exhibit the behavior necessary to complement or supplement information, rewards, or other elements a follower needs to accomplish a goal. Leadership motivates when it: increases or enhances rewards that followers receive from accomplishing a goal; makes the path to the goal clear and easy through direction and coaching; removes obstacles; and makes the process of accomplishing the goal personally satisfying for the follower. By selecting and implementing the most appropriate leadership style, leaders increase follower expectations for success and satisfaction (House, 1996; Northouse, 2001).

Although complex, the application of the path-goal theory of leadership achieves follower motivation through careful consideration of leadership behaviors, follower characteristics, and task characteristics. The theory suggests that each type of leader behavior (directive, supportive, participative, or achievement-oriented) has a different impact on the follower. Which leadership behavior is motivating is contingent on follower and task characteristics. Follower characteristics determine how a leader's behavior is interpreted by the follower. For followers who are dogmatic, authoritarian, or work in uncertain situations, path-goal theory suggests a directive leadership style because it provides structure and task clarity. Directive leadership makes the path to a goal less ambiguous. Authoritarian followers enjoy a greater sense of certainty in structured, directive leadership environments. According to path-goal theory, a directive leadership style also works well for followers with an external locus of control—they believe fate, chance, or outside forces determine a course of events. However, as followers' perceptions of their own abilities and competence increase, their need for directive leadership decreases. Thus, directive leadership becomes redundant, and excessive control by the leader could irritate followers and negatively impact morale and motivation.

A follower who has a strong desire for affiliation prefers a supportive (friendly and considerate) leadership style. Followers with an internal focus of control (they believe they have control over events in their lives) prefer a participative leadership style. Followers with an internal locus of control find their leader's behavior more satisfying if the followers are part of the decision-making process and possess relative independence with respect to completion of tasks and achievement of goals.

In addition to leader behaviors and follower characteristics, task characteristics must be considered in path-goal leadership theory motivational dynamics. Task characteristics include the amount of formal authority in the group or organization, the design of the task, and the follower's primary peer or working group. Situations in which tasks are clearly structured and strong group norms and an established authority exist, followers find paths apparent and goals foreseeable. Leaders are not required to clarify paths or goals, or needed as much to coach followers. In other situations,

FIGURE 7–8 Path-Goal Motivational Model.
Illustration by Dorie Savage.

tasks may be ambiguous and goals not clearly defined. Under these circumstances, more extensive leadership involvement is necessary. Also, situations in which tasks are repetitive, authority is weak or not clearly delineated, and group norms are not supportive, leadership helps make paths and goals clear, builds cohesiveness and group solidarity, and helps define roles and responsibilities (Northouse, 2001).

Path-goal motivational leadership helps followers overcome obstacles to enhance follower expectations and satisfaction through motivation toward goal achievement. R. J. House expanded his original concept of path-goal leader behaviors to eight. In addition to directive, supportive, participative, and achievement-oriented behaviors, House's expanded classifications include work facilitation, group-oriented decision processes, work-group representation and networking, and value-based leadership behaviors (House, 1996).

Theoretically, path-goal leadership theory provides a set of assumptions about how leadership styles interact with follower and task characteristics to affect motivation of followers. Leaders chose a style that is consistent with the needs of followers and the tasks at hand. Practically, path-goal leadership theory provides direction for leaders on how to motivate followers. The theory reminds leaders that their central purpose is to motivate and assist followers with goal definition and achievement in the most efficient manner possible (Northouse, 2001).

THE ETHICAL LEADER AS MOTIVATOR

True leadership is not a by-product of position, rank, or title. Leadership results when people possess, develop, or acquire skills to motivate others to achieve (Kokkelenberg, 2001). From a decision-making perspective, motivation supports choices that leaders make to influence the behavior of others (Adler, 2002). The ethical leader makes morally correct choices. The ethical leader motivates by inspiring and influencing others in attitude and demeanor, eliciting excellent performance, recognizing contributions, and celebrating success (Anderson & King, 1996a, 1996b).

Some descriptions of leadership focus on the leader's ability to motivate others to achieve goals. A consequence of this description is that the output (goals achieved) is often limited to the vision and ability of the leader rather than the shared vision and sum total of the energy of all people involved in goal achievement. A more effective leader, however, focuses on harnessing and releasing the creative energy of the people being led (Knowles, 1990).

Effective leaders are not controlling. Rather, they are much more positive in their approach. They have faith in people, offer them challenges, and delegate responsibility (Knowles, 1990; McGregor, 1960). Effective leaders assume that people are committed to a decision in proportion to the extent that the people believe they have participated in the decision-making process. Effective leaders believe that others strive to live up to the leader's expectations of them. Effective leaders value individuality, stimulate and reward creativity, are committed to the process of continuous change, and are skilled change managers. Effective leaders emphasize intrinsic (internal) motivators (achievement, recognition, fulfillment, responsibility, advancement, and growth) over extrinsic (external) motivators (organizational policy, administration, supervision, working conditions, salary, and status) (Herzberg, 1959). Finally, effective leaders encourage others to be self-directed. Effective leaders believe that the maturation process involves movement from a state of dependency toward states of increasing independence (Knowles, 1990).

An ethical leader achieves the greatest fulfillment by improving the quality of life for self and others (Peter & Hull, 1969). Successful leaders enjoy learning, seek challenges, value effort, and persist in the face of obstacles. Successful leaders are not always the ones who are the most accomplished or those with the highest intelligence levels. Even people who are not skilled or intelligent can be very successful. They appear to seize challenges and are energized by obstacles and setbacks. Rather than claim they cannot accomplish a goal because of limited intelligence, many less-intelligent people use some form of self-instruction and self-monitoring designed to aid their performance. Successful people do not view failure as an indictment of themselves. They do not feel helpless or inadequate. They simply summon their resources and apply themselves to the task at hand (Dweck, 1999).

Motivation is not an inborn trait. Nor can motivation be taught or developed simply. However, motivation as well as the ambition that accompanies and supports it can be learned through experience and appropriate mentoring. Proper attitude and motivation are sometimes difficult to achieve. Some people are highly motivated while others are not. Inappropriate levels of motivation can lead to negative outcomes. Lack of motivation and ambition can result in underachievement. Excessive motivation and ambition can result in overextension. One must seek an appropriate balance that enables people to realize their potential and achieve personal and professional goals (Champy & Nohria, 2000).

To achieve an appropriate level of motivation and ambition, one must seek to examine one's own sensibilities and sharpen the awareness of one's own actions. Honest self-examination and application of lessons learned will assist an individual with the determination of an appropriate motivational level for self and others. To accomplish this seemingly vague and insurmountable task, ethical leaders should diligently seek to identify their own strengths and weaknesses as the foundation for achieving their full potential. Factors relating to motivation and ambition adapted from Champy and Nohria (2000) may help to arm an ethical leader with necessary motivational skills.

First, through the discovery of fresh insight, ethical leaders strive to observe or imagine what others may not. Ethical leaders achieve ambitious goals by thinking beyond contemporary ideas and mental conventions. They unite in their ability to visualize the world and the future clearly. They confront disbelief, pursue worthy goals, begin with the possible to accomplish the impossible, demonstrate courage in the face of adversity, and acknowledge that the quest for improvement means recognizing that few "constraints" are permanent.

Second, success is often the result of numerous failures that are confronted and overcome. Ethical leaders follow a steadfast path. Leadership requires perseverance, optimism, and hope for a better future. Ethical leaders possess determination and an appetite for learning, accept failure and modest gains toward goal achievement, and build on success.

Third, ethical leaders seize the moment when opportunity presents itself. Leaders are motivated to risk failure lest they ignore a window of opportunity. Ethical leaders are prepared, seek and acquire appropriate knowledge, are alert for different forms of opportunity, identify trends, initiate action in a timely manner, confront and make painful choices, and create opportunities.

Fourth, ethical leaders temper ambition and motivation by gaining momentum without losing balance. Ambitious goals will not be achieved unless they are balanced with disciplined execution of measurable objectives to reach the goals established. Ethical leaders temper ambition and motivation with common sense grounded in reality. They realize that knowledge does not always bring wisdom. They are prudent and recognize that lack of balance can lead one to repeat mistakes. Ethical leaders realize that ambition and practicality are compatible, that ambition can be undone by ego and greed, and that overreaching failure can destroy motivation in self and others.

Fifth, ethical leaders inspire others by creating a greater purpose for action. Leaders transform and expand personal ambition and motivation to include a noble cause toward and through which others can contribute and identify. The greatest purpose is one that empowers its pursuer to motivate others. The right meaning for the greatest purpose goes beyond the leader's personal power and authority. It drives achievement in self and others. Purposefully correct ambition and motivation survives hardship. The greatest purpose is achieved by a pursuit of excellence, creating value, empowerment of others, improving the human condition, the celebration of high achievers, using rewards for the common good, and improving the quality of life for everyone.

Sixth, ethical leaders never violate core values. Although shortcuts to goal achievement are often tempting, leaders do not let compromise lead to dishonest or unethical behavior. The strength of core values prompts correct action. Adherence to core values helps establish purpose, dilutes ethical dilemmas, promotes integrity, generates followers, guides principled people, and guards against rationalization of moral lapses.

Seventh, ethical leaders keep and maintain control by sharing control with others. Ethical leaders do not retain control through force, fear, or intimidation. Fear stymies creativity and destroys motivation. Great leaders benefit when followers are high achievers. Thus, great leaders are not threatened when followers assume control and achieve desirable outcomes. Ethical leaders recognize that others can match the leader's competence and vision. The ethical leader realizes that sharing power and control unleashes high levels of performance in others, that partnerships prove to be stronger than the sum of the product when individuals work alone, that complex problems and situations cannot be resolved from a single perspective, and that lack of the perception of control can destroy initiative.

Eighth, ethical leaders embrace change. They constantly reinvent themselves and realize that internal and external environments are not static. The conditions that led to the leader's assent may change in favor of another. Thus, ethical leaders accept and derive meaning and wisdom from shifts in leadership and changing circumstances. Ethical leaders harness the dynamics of disharmony change creates, reorganize after failure, are global rather than provincial in thinking, know when and how to act, and are alert to change even when all is well. Ethical leaders do not develop quickly. Rather, they accumulate power and experience gradually. They use failure, without regret, as inspiration for future success.

Finally, ethical leaders exit gracefully when their mission is complete. Ethical leaders do not seek an immortal legacy for themselves. Although ethical leaders utilize ambition and motivation to achieve great ends, they realize that immortality is achieved in history, not in one's own life.

The ageless human motivator is ambition to create and achieve. Generally, human beings strive to improve their world and, hopefully, the world of others. As motivators, ethical leaders harness human ambition and direct the energy of others toward achievement of goals established for the common good (Champy & Nohria, 2000).

MOTIVATION GUIDELINES FOR ETHICAL LEADERS

The ability to motivate others is based, to a greater or lessor extent, on three factors: the leader's position or resources, follower motives relating to willingness to be influenced, and the methods used to motivate. The methods used to motivate are critical to outcome determination. Direct methods of influence include communication mediums such as ordering, telling, persuading, commanding, requiring, rewarding, and punishing. Indirect methods are sophisticated and subtle. They include evasion, avoidance, humor, modeling, and acquiescence. Intentional indirect methods of influence used by a leader can be viewed by the target person as unintentional. Thus, indirect influence becomes a source of strength for the leader. Asking followers to do something, rather than commanding them, may help overcome follower resistance. Although indirect methods for motivation are not always appropriate, they can be used when circumstances indicate followers are defensive or resistant (Tingley, 2001).

Attempts to influence others directly is not valued in many cultures. In these cultures, implicit (indirect) influence is preferable to explicit (direct) influence. Middle Eastern and many Asian cultures, for example, prefer a more indirect approach to influence and motivation (Tingley, 2001). Indirect attempts to motivate can be problematic, however. People very often mean more than what they communicate through a message. It is left to the message's receiver to infer meaning from the message.

To ensure that intended meaning and influence is received through the message, a leader should use communication, whether direct or indirect, that presents sufficient quality, quantity, clarity, and relevance. Quality of a motivational message refers to its truthfulness. Quantity refers to the amount of communication used. The message should not be over-informative or under-informative. Clarity is achieved if the manner through which the message is presented is unambiguous and clear. Relevance addresses the relationship between intended meaning, the message itself, and the behavior that is desired by the motivational influence (Holtgraves, 2002).

Leaders with knowledge of motivational theories and strategies as well as what motivates people as individuals possess the ability to diagnose and rectify motivational problems. To motivate effectively, leaders should:

- Design activities to create high motivating potential.
- Communicate desired outcomes and explain how performance will be rewarded.

- Provide frequent constructive feedback.
- Diagnose and remove barriers to performance.
- Provide rewards people value.
- Provide equitable rewards for desired outcomes (Hellriegel, Jackson, & Slocum, 2002).

Behavior that is followed by positive reinforcement to the individual demonstrating the behavior will tend to repeat itself. Alternatively, behavior that is followed by a negative consequence (negative reinforcement), such as punishment, is likely to cause a decrease in the behavior. Inappropriately administered negative consequences can lead to apprehensiveness or aggression (Fournies, 2000).

Leaders are also cautioned that the elimination of dissatisfaction or barriers to goal achievement may not always result in satisfaction. According to studies conducted by Frederick Herzberg (1959), relationships or factors that lead to dissatisfaction are entirely different than those that lead to satisfaction. Herzberg suggested that workers tend to derive dissatisfaction from organizational policy administration, supervision, poor working conditions, and inequitable or low salary. Satisfiers include achievement, recognition, the satisfying nature of the work itself, and responsibility. Thus, environmental factors surrounding a job tend to demotivate, while recognition and satisfaction for a job well done tend to motivate (Herzberg, 1959; Thurman, Zhao, & Giacomazzi, 2001). Therefore, because of individual differences and the apparent lack of relationship between satisfiers and dissatisfiers, leaders may wish to focus on emphasizing desired behavior rather than punishment of undesirable behavior (Fournies, 2000).

Recent research has called Herzberg's findings into question, however. Research demonstrates that people sometimes continue a course of action because they made a public commitment to it, not because it is rewarding. Similarly, some people, who claim intrinsic satisfaction at the beginning of an activity, switch to extrinsic motivators to explain their behavior after they receive an extrinsic reward for their efforts. What motivates people depends on cultural considerations and often on the context or situation in which a person is to be motivated (Adler, 2002).

Regardless of the research suggesting or questioning a particular theory of motivation, theoretical knowledge assists a leader to identify and value the factors that motivate in a particular environment. Motivating factors in a group activity or on the job, for example, include characteristics associated with the nature of the activity or work and an organizational context that promotes positive feelings among members of the group or workforce. An acceptable level of responsibility, challenging activities, recognition, achievement, and personal and professional growth are all motivating factors. The presence of these factors does not ensure productivity or goal achievement, however, since motivators promote outstanding performance only if no dissatisfiers are present (Hellriegel, Jackson, & Slocum, 2002).

MOTIVATION AND BURNOUT

The term **burnout** has become popular in recent decades. Most often, the term is applied to the image of people who develop a negative relationship with their occupation or the overwhelming nature of the tasks to be accomplished. The scenario usually includes circumstances in which people enter into an activity or occupation with positive expectations, enthusiasm, and the motivation to achieve desirable goals. Over time, however, circumstances change and people sense overwhelming exhaustion, frustration, anger, ineffectiveness, failure, cynicism, and anger. The initial flame, the fire within that existed in the beginning, has burned out. The burnout syndrome impairs personal, social, and professional functioning. As time progresses, people resign their positions, retire early, or simply continue the activity or employment with minimal productivity (Maslach & Leiter, 1999). An assumption prevails that burnout can happen to overachievers (workaholics) as well as underachievers (incompetent individuals or unmotivated slackers). Thus, burnout promotes negative as well as positive side effects. However, the assumption supposes that there is something fundamentally wrong with the person who burns out. A more rational approach might focus on the occupation or context in which burnout takes place. Although the nature of work-related stressors can lay a foundation for burnout (constant crises, conflict with others, the chronic nature of high job demands), it may be more beneficial to view burnout from the context of one's total environment.

Burnout involves a sense of exhaustion, cynicism, and ineffectiveness that results from chronic stressors. Exhaustion relates to an individual's feelings of overextension and depletion of personal emotional and physical resources. The primary sources of exhaustion are overload and personal conflict. Cynicism develops as an interpersonal emotional buffer of detachment. The detachment can lead to dehumanization of others. The ineffectiveness (inefficacy) component of burnout results from an individual's feelings of incompetence, low achievement, and poor productivity. This lowered sense of self-worth is compounded by lack of resources, social support, or opportunities for professional development. Burnout involves a prolonged process of psychological and physical erosion of people that stands in contrast to energetic, involved, and engaged individuals. The erosion diminishes a burned out person's commitment, and causes personnel absenteeism, attrition, and physical illness.

Because of the stressful nature of police work and the many factors that make such work difficult, attention to burnout among officers and how to prevent it is extremely important. A better understanding of burnout and its implications involves an appreciation for the phenomenon based on a framework that integrates the person and the environment. Addressing the person or the environment in isolation underestimates the value of the person-environment relationship. When one addresses the degree of fit (congruence) between a person and the environment, it may be easier to motivate and enhance a person's adjustment to the circumstances, and seek to reduce the stress that leads to burnout.

As a motivator, the ethical leader should seek to fit the individual (follower) to the environment. Recalling that burnout occurs long after a person's initial contact with the activity or environment, the leader as motivator must not leave critical issues unresolved or change an environment in a way the follower finds unacceptable. The activity-person fit (congruence) is achieved when: activity demands do not exceed human limits, people have some control over the tasks they perform, people are appropriately rewarded, people connect with others in the group, leaders are perceived as fair, and people are not required to perform in an unethical manner (Maslach & Leiter, 1999; Stojkovic, Kalinich, & Klofas, 2003).

SUMMARY

Motivation provides the reason for a course of action. Motivational skills are vital for success as a police officer in contemporary society. The context for motivation refers to factors that one must consider when motivation of others is sought. A leader must consider intrinsic as well as extrinsic motivators. The leader must maintain a proper attitude (mental commitment) and consider individual differences. Several theories articulate how individual differences impact motivation. Numerous theories also describe how motivation is affected by leadership style and assumptions regarding human behavior. As a motivator, the ethical leader inspires and influences others by modeling appropriate behaviors, designs activities to create high motivating potential, and seeks to eliminate obstacles that lead to follower exhaustion, cynicism, and ineffectiveness.

KEY TERMS AND CONCEPTS

Alderfer's ERG theory
attitude

behavioral assumption
behavioralistic (process) motivational theorist
burnout
context for motivation
expectancy theory
extrinsic motivation
humanistic (content or need) motivational theorist
intrinsic motivation
managerial grid
Maslow's hierarchy of needs
McClelland's learned needs theory
motivation
path-goal motivational leadership
situational leadership model
theory X
theory Y
theory Z
Vroom-Jago time-driven leadership model

Discussion Questions and Exercises

1. What motivates an individual? A group?
2. How do contextual factors affect motivation?
3. How do individual differences affect motivation?
4. How do assumptions about human behavior influence leader behavior?
5. How can ethical leaders motivate others?
6. A police officer is addressing a community group at a public meeting. The purpose of the meeting is to identify and create solutions to community crime and disorder problems. The officer asks for input but the community members sit in silence. How can the officer motivate the citizens to participate?

Chapter 8

Ethical Decision Making and Problem Solving

Learning Objectives

After completing this chapter, the reader should be able to:

- describe an ethical decision-making process.
- demonstrate problem-solving techniques.
- describe the SARA problem-solving model.
- present an overview of the organization and operation of a problem-solving effort.
- develop procedures for problem solving in groups.
- conduct a community needs assessment.
- utilize community crime mapping.
- explain the need for evaluation processes.
- discuss the methods for measuring and evaluating performance.
- discuss the concept of quality assurance and common errors made in quality assurance initiatives.
- identify, critically analyze, and develop solutions to problems in management.
- analyze the effectiveness of the components of a problem-solving effort.
- evaluate major global and societal trends that impact policing.
- develop strategies for improving the effectiveness of police services.
- identify barriers to effective problem solving.

INTRODUCTION

The nature of policing demands ethical decision making and the use of problem-solving techniques. Although policies and standard operating procedures exist, the many different situations encountered by a police officer often have unique features. Thus, standardized approaches must often be modified to account for the multitude of situational variables. In fact, one of the major differences among police officers is how they make decisions in the various situations they encounter. Problem-solving skills, as a set of skills possessed by those with competence in leadership, assist with appropriate decision making. Coupled with aspirations toward a code of ethics, problem-solving ability can promote ethical decisions that are lawful, humane, and fair (Pollock, 1998).

For years, policing experts have recognized that the best way to educate the police to embrace and take advantage of change is to use knowledge to solve problems (Sherman, 1978). The theoretical foundation for problem solving in police work was laid by Herman Goldstein. In his classic work, *Problem-Oriented Policing,* Goldstein (1990) formulated a model for policing that drew heavily from decision-making theory. Goldstein's conception includes a logical progression of rational decision-making processes that include problem identification and definition, development of alternative courses of action, selection and implementation of the most appropriate action plan, and evaluation and follow-up. Goldstein suggested that, in addition to handling incidents, police officers should group incidents as problems, systematically analyze the underlying causes that contribute to the problems, and devise appropriate actions to prevent reoccurrence of incidents. In doing so, the police, acting as problem solvers, can achieve ambitious crime, disorder, and fear reduction goals (Goldstein, 1990, 2001; Vinzant & Crothers, 1998).

Whether they want to be or not, police officers are problem solvers (Peak & Glensor, 2002). Individual citizens, business leaders, and community groups expect, and even demand, that the police solve crimes and regulate noncriminal conduct. As such, the citizenry expects the police to identify and analyze problems, employ situational strategies, evaluate constituent needs, and provide the means for attaining crime reduction and other community goals. The police are expected to mediate disputes and negotiate settlements between adversaries in noncriminal domestic arguments and landlord-tenant disputes. Problems also arise within and between police organizations. Therefore, the police professional must deal with internal as well as external problems.

Often, the police must act instinctively to diagnose problem situations and prescribe appropriate courses of action. Without critical-thinking, ethical decision-making, and problem-solving abilities, which are the keys to the sound analysis of situations, problems will not be identified and creative solutions to problems will not be discovered. Problem-solving skills are important for self-management and crisis management, and they also lie at the heart of conflict de-escalation and resolution. If the ultimate goal is to solve the problem, police officers should, resources permitting, strive to provide or at least assist in locating the means for problem identification and solution development. Police officers in a community policing environment must also work to mobilize the community into partnerships with others to identify and create solutions to problems (Kingsley & Pettit, 2000; Ortmeier, 1996).

Most police officers in the United States, especially those assigned to patrol duties, are rarely under the direct control of a supervisor. Therefore, police officers can often exercise an enormous amount of discretion with respect to decisions that impact the lives of other people (Goldstein, 2001). Except for enforcement of major violations of the criminal law, an individual police officer may opt to strictly enforce traffic laws, while a peer on patrol in an adjoining area may not. In addition, police work often requires independent judgment in individual cases. Thus, discretion in the exercise of police authority is commonplace and often necessary if justice is to be served (Fyfe, 1996; Kleinig, 1996a; Lyman, 2002).

Since unsupervised independent decision making is the method of operation for most police officers, initial and advanced training for police officers should focus on the development of independent problem-solving and decision-making skills. Accordingly, many experts agree that a great deal of police training, especially in the academies, is inconsistent with the police mission. In *Policing in the Community*, Champion and Rush (1997) state:

> Clearly, the overemphasis on lockstep obedience found in many police academies will not serve to provide new hires with a productive and independent frame of reference for performing their jobs. This is not to suggest that stress or the handling of stressful situations should not be part of law enforcement training. Clearly, police officers may well find themselves in very stressful positions while performing their duties, and it would be only prudent to evaluate their abilities to function under simulated stressful conditions. But a heavy reliance on close-order drill and other group exercises does not promote individuality and proves to be of little value in the actual performance of police duties. Moreover, stress does not belong in the classroom, as it impedes the learning process. It would be difficult to try to teach a student a concept while the student is wondering whether his or her bed has passed inspection (p. 135).

As noted, problem solving and decision making are an integral part of police work. However, traditional police training methods may actually inhibit the development of critical-thinking and problem-solving abilities. Ethical decision making and problem solving are emerging as new trends in police training, particularly in programs described variously as problem-based, scenario-based, or facilitation-based (California State Commission on Peace Officer Standards and Training, 2001; Massachusetts Criminal Justice Training Council & the Regional Community Policing Institute for New England, 1997). Traditional police training methods emphasize cognitive (knowledge) and psychomotor (skills) learning. Problem-based training adds a dimension that attempts to move learning to the higher-level domains of analysis, synthesis, and evaluation. Cadets learn about the cognitive aspects of policing early in the training process. This is followed by skills training. Later, the cadet, working individually or in a group, is immersed in a series of scenarios in which the cadet must draw on knowledge and problem-solving skills in specific types of situations (Conser & Russell, 2000). In this chapter, the reader is introduced to this form of ethical decision making and problem solving.

ETHICAL DECISION MAKING

A police officer is offered free coffee and snacks at a convenience store. The store owner stated that the free refreshments were a form of compensation for the officer's service to the community. In another situation, a police officer witnessed unethical conduct on the part of a colleague. The colleague entered false information about a suspect's behavior into a crime report. Subsequently, the false information was used to convict the criminal suspect. Should the officer in the convenience store refuse special treatment, even in the absence of any law or agency policy forbidding acceptance of gratuities? Does acceptance of the gratuity enhance a relationship with a community member or a store owner? Would refusal of the gift invite ill-feeling from the store owner? Should the officer-witness in the second instance intervene or at least report the unethical conduct?

The police officers in each of these situations have encountered a **dilemma.** Are unsolicited minor gratuities, given and accepted in good faith without any future expectations, to be viewed as compensation for providing a community service? If an officer who witnesses unethical police conduct reports such conduct, is the officer-witness subject to informal punishments and rejection by peers within the police subculture? If the officer-witness does not report inappropriate conduct, does the officer risk disciplinary action, public humiliation, and a personal moral struggle associated with dishonesty that could lead to a loss of self-respect?

These and similar situations appear to be no-win situations. They form the foundation for dilemmas. The intrinsic nature of a dilemma is that it does not lend itself to a simple solution. When confronted with a real dilemma, decision making can be extremely difficult because any decision associated with the dilemma results in negative as well as positive consequences. Thus, decisions associated with dilemmas often defy a perfect solution. The decision maker experiences pain as well as pleasure, punishment as well as reward (Jones & Carlson, 2001).

When faced with an ethical dilemma, an appropriate solution may not be apparent. In many situations, unethical decisions may not be the product of intentional human actions. Some experts speculate that many unethical decisions may actually be the result of faulty views or beliefs about the world, other people, and the unethical decision makers themselves (Johnson, 2001). As stated previously, true dilemmas generally defy simple solutions and are often viewed as no-win situations. Although the perfect solution is not apparent, one can be guided to the best solution by considering and practicing techniques consistent with the moral decision-making process. Utilized appropriately, ethical decision-making techniques can assist with the development of an ethical solution—a determination of the correct response. This is the essence of **ethical decision making.** The techniques include limit setting and consideration of the principles of ethics, benefit maximizations, and equal respect.

Limit setting involves communication to others of what one's personal limits are prior to any involvement in a potentially compromising situation. An officer may simply indicate to colleagues what types of behavior are not acceptable or will not be tolerated. The limit setting can be applied to behavior and situations such as use of excessive force, violation of rights, dishonest reporting or testimony, sleeping or intoxication on duty, acceptance of gratuities, and uncivil treatment of the civilian population. Setting and communicating one's personal limits may cause another officer to reconsider when contemplating unethical conduct. Although limit setting may be problematic for some peers, most trainees and junior officers, if approached diplomatically, discover that the technique may earn respect for the limit-setting officer.

Other techniques involve thoughtful consideration of ethical principles prior to any communication or action. These techniques involve the actual application of ethical principles to case situations. Paramount among these ethical principles are the principles of benefit maximization and equal respect. The principle of benefit maximization involves a projection of potential and probable consequences of any decision. According to this principle, an appropriate and ethical decision is the one that will probably lead to the most benefit for the greatest number of people. Caution must be exercised when practicing this principle. The principle could be misconstrued as providing the foundation for rationalizing certain types of behavior.

Violating a known career criminal's rights under the Constitution for the sake of obtaining a conviction—protecting the public from the known criminal's illegal behavior—is not a legitimate rationalization. When used in conjunction with the principle of equal respect, however, the principle of benefit maximization can lead to ethical decisions and worthwhile outcomes (Jones & Carlson, 2001; Pollock, 1998).

By far, the vast majority of police officers are committed to fairness and justice for all, the essence of the principle of equal respect. These officers appropriately concentrate, or at least attempt to concentrate, on treating human beings equally and respectfully. This principle may be difficult to practice, especially when a criminal suspect resists arrest or a motorist is belligerent regarding a traffic citation. The ever-present potential for danger in arrest situations and motorist stops for traffic violations does not lend itself to the type of rational thinking and objectivity an officer might experience while on a lunch break at a restaurant. However, regardless of the difficulties associated with the practice of equal respect, police officers should strive to practice the principle. The legal concept of due process of law, one of the concepts a police officer swears to uphold and protect, is derived from the principle of equal respect. Accordingly, police officers should strive to treat others fairly, consistent with officer safety and the interests of morally and ethically acceptable behavior (Jones & Carlson, 2001).

In the final analysis, a police officer's decisions are subject to the scrutiny of a wide variety of people, organizations, and special interests. When confronted with ethical dilemmas, an officer should focus on what ought to be done, basing decisions on sound ethical principles and how the outcomes will be viewed after the officer's actions have been scrutinized. Close and Meier (1995) suggest the following questions should be addressed when making duty-related decisions:

- Does the action violate another person's rights under the Constitution, including the right of due process?
- Does the action involve treating another only as a means to an end?
- Is the considered action illegal?
- Can one predict that more negative than positive consequences will result for all those affected by the action?
- Does the proposed action violate an agency policy or professional duty?

Close and Meier's ethical decision-making procedure incorporates a sensitivity to the due process protections lacking in many other decision-making schemes. The element of due process, at least in terms of police-citizen interaction, is often missing when police officers commit unethical acts. In another form, the questions to consider when faced with developing a response to an ethically charged dilemma include the following:

- Does the decision affect another?
- Will the decision injure another?
- If roles were reversed, would the decision maker want to be the recipient of the impact of the decision?
- Can the decision maker take pride in the decision because it is correct and honorable (Pollock, 1998)?

Discretion assumes a vital role in the police ethical decision-making process because officers have the opportunity to exercise wide discretion when confronted with issues and problems (Fyfe, 1996; Kleinig, 1996a; Lyman, 2002). Although many police procedures are standardized, each situation encountered by officers may present unique challenges. Therefore, ethical decision making as a leadership skill cannot be viewed as a linear process through which decisions are made. Rather than emphasize a routine approach to decision making, the nature of police work necessitates a *thinking style* that assists with the development of alternative choices in crisis situations. Thus, discretionary decision-making ability provides a general framework for thinking about the choice alternatives police officers create and how the legitimacy of their choices are evaluated (Vinzant & Crothers, 1998).

The relationship between discretion and ethical decision making can be described in terms of the processes (how to resolve a situation) and outcomes (goals to be achieved) associated with one's ability or authority to exercise discretion in a particular situation. Different situations create differing challenges along with numerous opportunities for exercising discretion, ethical decision making, and leadership. Different situations include those involving: limited or no discretion, choices regarding process, decisions about outcomes, or choices relative to processes and outcomes.

Rigid concepts of administrative procedure leave a person with little or no discretion over how to handle a situation (process) or the goals to be achieved (outcomes). Situational leadership is appropriate when a person has substantial discretion over process but not outcomes. A police officer may be required to arrest a criminal law violator (outcome) but exercise considerable discretion over the mechanics of the arrest (process) based on the level of violator resistance. Transformational leadership skills may be required when an officer can exercise discretion regarding outcomes but not process. Once an officer decides a vehicle driver is intoxicated, for example, officer discretion is severely restricted; the officer is obligated to effect an arrest. If the driver is not intoxicated, the officer is obligated to release the driver if no other violation is apparent.

Finally, some situations provide opportunities for officers to exercise considerable discretion over outcomes and process. When confronted with a nonviolent domestic dispute, a police officer may exercise discretion whether or not to arrest a disputant (outcome) as well as determine the level of force or collaboration necessary to resolve the situation (process). In these situations, police officers can demonstrate situational as well as transformational leadership competencies because two major decisions are required: what to achieve and how to achieve it (Lyman, 2002; Vinzant & Crothers, 1998).

PROBLEM SOLVING

A problem can be defined as the presence or absence of someone or something that contributes to the discomfort or suffering of an individual or group (Welsh & Harris, 1999). A problem involves a discrepancy between current and desired conditions. **Problem solving** is a comprehensive planning process used to move a situation from an unsatisfactory to a desirable condition. Problem solving should not be confused with decision making. The latter refers to the act of choosing between alternatives and is part of the problem-solving process. Problem solving involves the creation and discovery of alternatives and requires numerous decisions. The problem solver's goal is to solve the problem, not implement a particular solution (Harris, 2002). Preventing the development of a problem is a problem solution. Problem solving involves the use of processes, approaches, procedures, methods, tactics, strategies, policies, products, technologies, and structures as tools for corrective action (Memory, 2001).

All problems consist of three components: an existing condition that is unsatisfactory, goals, and the obstacles that inhibit goal achievement. Recognition of the unsatisfactory condition or situation is the incipient stage of a problem. In other words, one recognizes that a problem exists. The goal or goals include a perception of a desirable situation, one aligned with the comfort associated with a satisfactory condition. Obstacles represent anything or anyone that interferes with achievement of the goal (satisfactory condition). Examples of obstacles may include lack of funding or personnel (Brilhart & Galanes, 1998).

Problem solving is inconsistent with traditional **incident-driven policing.** With incident-driven policing, the reactive posture of the police encourages superficial responses. Responding to and handling the incident quickly, filing a report, and returning to patrol duty are the cornerstones of incident-driven policing. However, in a policing environment, the **community problem,** rather than a specific incident, should be the main focus of police work. A community problem involves two or more incidents of a similar nature within a community. Problem solving is the process used to address the community problem (Bynam, 2001; Goldstein, 1990, 2001). According to the California Department of Justice, Office of the Attorney General (1996), problem solving is defined as: the process of identifying problems and priorities through a community-coordinated community-police needs assessment; collecting and analyzing information concerning the problem in a thorough, but uncomplicated manner; developing or facilitating responses that are innovative and tailor-made with the best potential for eliminating or reducing the problem; and evaluating the response to the problem to determine its effectiveness.

Problem solving can be used to examine crime and disorder problems, analyze underlying causes, develop a range of solutions to address these problems, select appropriate solutions, and evaluate the effectiveness of the solutions over time (Measuring what matters—part two, 1997). Problems must also to be analyzed from the standpoint of the community so solutions can be adapted to meet community needs (Kingsley & Pettit, 2000; Lyman, 2002; Sampson, 2001; Sampson & Scott, 2000; Scott, 2001). The analysis may include both quantitative (objective) and qualitative (subjective) data and information (Ortmeier, 1999; Peak & Glensor, 2002).

Quantitative analysis involves the use of objective measurements, while qualitative analysis focuses on the use of subjective measurements (Patton, 1990). Examples of objective measurement tools include statistical and investigative reports, surveys, and inspections. Subjective measurements include forecasting, the use of expert opinion, and the Delphi Technique. The latter is a process whereby several experts or individuals provide input on an issue or problem and ultimately arrive at a consensus on desirable alternatives, priorities, and goals. The **Delphi Technique** may be the most appropriate problem-solving and decision-making vehicle when emotions are high, or when a few members of the problem-solving group tend to dominate the process.

There are two general approaches to problem solving. The convergent approach solves problems systematically by utilizing a series of logical steps. These steps define the problem, generate solutions, assist with the selection of appropriate solutions, implement a course of action, and evaluate the outcome. A less-structured, more creative method for problem solving involves the divergent approach. This approach calls on intuition and innovation and encourages spontaneity. Brainstorming is an example of the divergent approach.

Whether problems are solved logically or creatively, the goal is to arrive at the most appropriate solution. Both approaches may be used separately or conjunctively (Caroselli, 1997). When a single solution is required, the convergent approach is best. A series of burglaries committed by a single individual may require an approach that leads to the suspect's arrest and successful prosecution. When multiple solutions are necessary, as when multiple burglaries are committed by numerous individuals, a divergent approach to problem solving (with multiple solutions) may be more appropriate.

Herman Goldstein, often referred to as the father of **problem-oriented policing,** has spent over 40 years studying police operations. In the 1970s,

Goldstein suggested that police agencies should shift their focus from an inward orientation (number of officers, staffing patterns) to an outward orientation (the agency's impact on crime and disorder). As such, Goldstein (1990, 2001) advocates moving from the traditional efficiency model of policing to an effectiveness model, placing less emphasis on statistics and number of arrests, and more emphasis on strategic initiatives to eliminate the problem. The key to problem solving in a community policing environment involves an analytical inquiry into the problem before devising solutions. Problem solving in this sense does not mean troubleshooting or guesswork. Rather, it involves planning as the systematic, step-by-step approach to problem resolution. Problem-oriented policing (POP) is simple, yet complex. It incorporates a way of thinking that helps to define the police function to assist with problem solving in the community (Goldstein, 2001). Problem-oriented policing:

> is an approach to policing in which (1) discrete pieces of police business (each consisting of a cluster of similar incidents, whether crimes or acts of disorder, that the police are expected to handle) are subject to (2) microscopic examination (drawing on the especially honed skills of crime analysis and the accumulated experience of operating field personnel) in hopes that what is freshly learned about each problem will lead to discovering a (3) new and more effective strategy for dealing with it. POP places a high value on new responses that are (4) preventive in nature, that are (5) not dependent on the use of the criminal justice system, and that (6) engage other public agencies, the community and the private sector when their involvement has the potential for significantly contributing to the reduction of the problem. POP carries a commitment to (7) implementing the new strategy, (8) rigorously evaluating its effectiveness, and, subsequently, (9) reporting the results in ways that will benefit other police agencies and that will ultimately contribute to (10) building a body of knowledge that supports the further professionalization of the police (Goldstein, 2001).

THE SARA PROBLEM-SOLVING MODEL

Problems can be resolved through the application of step-by-step approaches to creative problem solving (Harris, 2002). Several models have emerged to assist agencies with community policing and problem-solving efforts. Virtually all models trace their origin to Goldstein's problem-oriented policing (POP) model (Goldstein, 1990). The U.S. Department of Justice sponsored program is Operation Weed and Seed (Simons, 2002). The Royal Canadian Mounted Police (RCMP) follow a systematic approach to proactive and

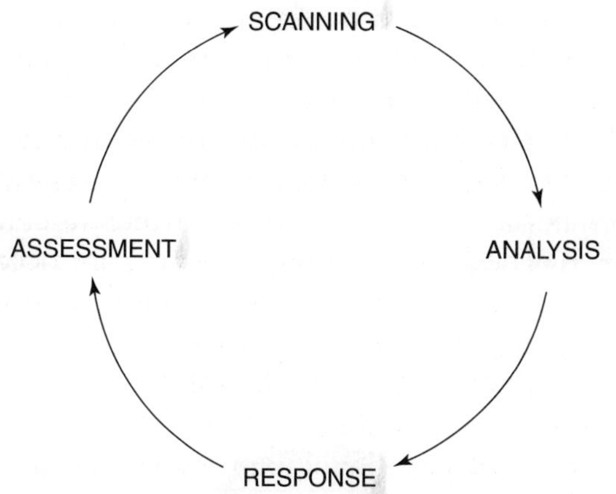

FIGURE 8-1 The SARA Problem Solving Model
Illustration by Dorie Savage.

reactive policing situations. The RCMP model focuses on clients, acquiring and analyzing information, partnerships, response, and assessment (CAPRA). The Florida Department of Law Enforcement developed a model that focuses on safety, ethics, community, understanding, response, and evaluation (SECURE). The Scanning, Analysis, Response, Assessment **(SARA) problem-solving model,** discussed next, appears to be the foundation for these models (Conser & Russell, 2000). The Oxnard, California, Police Department expanded the POP SARA model by establishing the "Five Cs" of advanced community policing: collaboration, cooperation, commitment, compassion, and concern (Simons, 2002).

The SARA technique is used by many police agencies throughout the United States. It integrates the convergent and divergent approaches to problem solving. The SARA model is a creative problem-solving process (Kidd & Braziel, 1999) that was first developed and implemented by police officers and researchers in Newport News, Virginia, in 1984 (Peak & Glensor, 2002). Although several problem-solving methods exist, the SARA model is presented here as an example of one approach to problem solving.

Scanning

Scanning involves problem identification. It refers to the identification of patterns or persistent problems within a community. Two or more similar incidents constitute a community crime, fear, or disorder problem. Utilizing this strategy, community crime problems may be identified in ways other than through police officer observations. Community meetings, citizen surveys, one-on-one conversations with citizens, crime and community mapping, and statistical information as well as research conducted by government and private organizations may be sources of information (Community Policing Consortium, 1997b; Peak & Glensor, 2002).

Risk and needs assessments are appropriate tools for problem identification. Risk assessments are typically used to predict the likelihood of a negative outcome. High probability of rearrest subsequent to solution (intervention) implementation (conviction and sentence completion) is an example of risk. Needs assessments usually refer to instruments and processes designed to identify unmet needs. Graffiti removal and treatment for chronic drug offenders may be identified through needs assessments.

Once a problem has been identified, a working definition of the problem is created. The working definition provides the foundation for analysis and the solutions developed in subsequent stages of the SARA problem-solving model. Analysis of the situation and corrective action should focus on prevention of future occurrences.

Analysis

Analysis involves an intensive probe into all of the characteristics and factors contributing to a problem. It requires the acquisition of detailed information about people involved with the problem (offenders, victims, others), time and location of occurrence, the environment, and the outcomes of current responses. Analysis involves the discovery of problematic trends and the planning of effective responses (Bynum, 2001; Goldstein, 1990).

The persistent problems and patterns of activity within a community require careful analysis. Problems develop slowly. Hasty solutions rarely

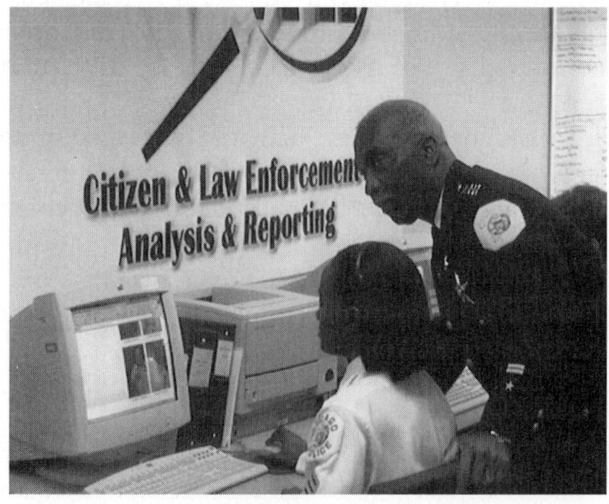

Analysis lies at the heart of the problem-solving process. Photo courtesy of Chicago Police Department.

eliminate the problem. The analysis must address the underlying causes rather than the symptoms of the problem. Although analysis lies at the heart of the problem-solving process, it is probably the most difficult step in the SARA model. Analytical processes are also difficult for police officers to learn and apply (Glensor & Peak, 1999). It requires a look at and through the problem. Juveniles may be loitering on the street corner, for example, and police may be dispatched to disband the group. Eventually, the juveniles will return to the street corner. The reason for the loitering may be that the juveniles have no other place to congregate; thus, the underlying cause of the loitering is a lack of resources for the youth in the community. Therefore, participants in the problem-solving process must carefully analyze the situation and think critically to identify the underlying causes.

Critical thinking involves a process through which an individual or group examines information to determine if a logical connection between facts exists. Critical thinking resists emotional appeals. Conclusions are based on a logical progression of ideas formed from available evidence rather than feelings or guesswork.

Many characteristics differentiate the critical from the uncritical thinker. The critical thinker acknowledges ignorance, is open-minded, takes time to reflect on ideas, pays attention to those who agree and disagree, and looks for good reasons to accept or reject expert opinion. Additionally, the critical thinker is concerned with unstated assumptions and what is not said in addition to what is stated outright, insists on getting the best evidence, and reflects on how well conclusions fit the circumstances. Alternately, the uncritical thinker does not acknowledge ignorance, is closed-minded and impulsive, jumps to unwarranted conclusions, and pays attention only to those who agree. The uncritical thinker is concerned only with what is stated, not with what is implied, ignores sources of evidence, and disregards the connection or lack of connection between evidence and conclusions (Gamble & Gamble, 1999).

Every individual is born with creative capacity, despite assertions to the contrary. Unfortunately, creativity is often suppressed. Over 90 percent of young children are very creative at age five. By college age, only about two percent of individuals tested are very creative. In American society, individuals are conditioned to respond to pre-created stimuli, rather than be creative or imaginative themselves. Fortunately, creativity can be recaptured with practice. Brainstorming in groups is very effective. Emphasis should be placed on the least as well as the most likely resources that can be used to respond and solve the problem (Caroselli, 1997).

The **problem analysis triangle** (the three factors of offender, victim, and location necessary for a crime to occur) offers a simple mechanism to visualize and analyze crime, disorder, and harmful behavior problems. Because all three sides of the triangle must be present for a problem to

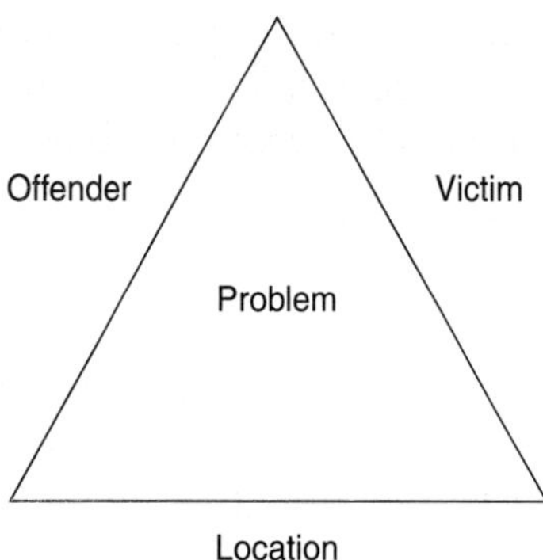

FIGURE 8–2 Problem Analysis Triangle.
Illustration by Dorie Savage.

occur, the elimination of any one of the three elements may solve the problem (Peak & Glensor, 2002). If a potential victim implements measures to eliminate the opportunity for crime to occur, the crime may be prevented. Target hardening through improved locks and lighting, for example, may deter burglaries of residences and businesses.

The sides of the problem analysis triangle may also be impacted positively by the presence of a capable guardian. The guardian controls the target and makes it less attractive to criminal activity. Possible guardians include the police, citizens, security personnel, abatement ordinances, and signs. A noise abatement ordinance can be enacted for the community. No parking signs can be posted or erected to eliminate congestion. All-night convenience store clerks can be trained to prevent robberies or minimize losses due to robberies (Community Policing Consortium, 1997b). As discussed in Chapter 9, crime prevention through environmental design (CPTED) techniques can be used to gain knowledge of the location side of the problem analysis triangle (Bynum, 2001).

Problems should be analyzed from multiple perspectives. Different stakeholders often view the problem and solutions in different ways. It is often helpful to solicit the perspective of someone (or some group) totally unrelated to the problem. Unrelated parties or experts from other disciplines are often more objective when analyzing a situation. Objectivity is crucial to the development of appropriate answers to questions that typically arise during an analysis:

- Who is impacted by the problem?
- What are the possible causes?
- Are the causes considered to be problems themselves?
- What are the circumstances surrounding the causes?
- What aspects of the circumstances are not part of the problem?
- When, where, why, and how do the problems occur?

The best solutions are created when more than one person is involved in the problem-solving process. Practical applications of decision-making processes demonstrate that the synergistic effect of group problem solving helps to create better solutions.

Response

With a clear definition and analysis of the problem in mind, participants in the problem-solving process can begin to create **responses** (solutions). Crime problems may be impacted by eliminating the problem altogether, reducing the harm caused by the problem, reducing the number of incidents, improving problem-solving methodology, or referring the problem to another authority (Community Policing Consortium, 1997b).

To be effective, responses (solutions) to a crime or disorder problem should impact at least two sides of the problem analysis triangle. Police and community members must also think creatively to develop responses that fit the community. Often, participants are eager to adopt a response that was developed for a similar problem in another community. Those involved in the process must remember that standardized solutions (i.e., replicas of what was done in other areas) are rarely appropriate.

More than one solution can be created to respond to a problem. Each alternative solution should be compared to the others. Solutions (goals) should be specific enough to solve a problem and set direction for action. Effective solutions are measurable and verifiable, realistic and achievable within a reasonable period of time, genuinely committed to and in accord with the values and beliefs of stakeholders, motivating and desirable, and subject to continuous monitoring and evaluation (Anderson, 2000; Simons, 2002). Members of the decision-making group may arrive at a consensus regarding the most appropriate solution by anonymously ranking the possible alternatives presented. The rankings are tabulated and the solution with the highest score receives the most favorable consideration.

Participants in the solution development process must also consider the consequences of any action or response implemented (Caroselli, 1997). Will the response create a more difficult problem? Could a crackdown on gang activity result in the detention of innocent law-abiding juveniles? How would these situations be handled? What impact might an inappropriate detention have on the juvenile detained, on media accounts of the incident, and in the public's perception of the police?

As consideration is given to the possible negative side effects of a solution, it may be determined that an alternative and less desirable course of action is more appropriate. At first glance, trained guard dogs locked in a business at night may discourage burglaries. The liability incurred, however, as the result of a would-be burglar entering the business without knowledge of the dog's presence could create another problem. Businesses and individuals have been successfully sued for creating hazards while protecting property. A more enlightened approach might include target hardening and installation of alarm systems to deter and detect burglars.

Implementation of the response (solution) to a problem is often difficult because it produces change. Resistance to change is a problem itself. Even those who may benefit from change are often resistant to it. Therefore, the initial step to response (solution) implementation is to communicate the need for change to those who might be affected. One should anticipate opposition and be prepared to explain the rationale for any change in policies and procedures. Effective persuasion includes an explanation on how the opposition will benefit (Caroselli, 1997). Restrictions on freedom of movement, for example, may help to create a safer environment. Metal detectors in schools can prevent weapons from endangering students, faculty, and staff.

The problem-solving process can be applied in virtually any situation. It has been applied successfully to problems associated with street prostitution (Scott, 2001), false burglar alarms (Sampson, 2001), graffiti (Lamm Weisel, 2002), thefts in parking facilities (Clarke, 2002a), shoplifting (Clarke, 2002b), bullying in schools (Sampson, 2002), panhandling (Scott, 2002a), rave parties (Scott, 2002b), and burglary of retail establishments (Clarke, 2002c).

Two Vallejo, California, police employees used problem solving to develop programs to assist needy people with noncriminal as well as crime-related problems. The Vallejo Community Outreach Program (VCOP) utilizes volunteers to collect donations that are used by police officers to assist needy citizens. Funds are used to pay utility bills, purchase food, and assist stranded individuals by providing short-term motel accommodations. Another program, the Vallejo Elder Abuse Advocacy Outreach Program, includes a registry of local Alzheimer patients. The list assists police officers seeking to find a lost Alzheimer victim's home or primary care giver. The elder abuse advocacy program has also been instrumental in the prevention and investigation of fraud and abuse cases involving the elderly (Taylor, 2002).

Assessment

No problem-solving process is complete without an **assessment** (evaluation) of the impact of the responses (solutions) to problems. Assessment is an ongoing process and should be considered during the other three stages of the SARA problem-solving model. **Qualitative** (subjective) as well as **quantitative** (objective) **measures** may be used to assess the impact of a response (Thurman, Zhao, & Giacomazzi, 2001). The assessment measures or tools should address several fundamental evaluative questions. In addition to crime reduction or elimination, how do the participants view the success, or lack of success, of the entire operation? Are the citizens within the community, as well as the police, satisfied with the outcome? Has the outcome clearly addressed the goals initially established by the community partnership? If responses to these questions are not acceptable, the assessment can identify what does not work and create an environment where alternative solutions can be created (Community Policing Consortium, 1997b; Measuring what matters—part two, 1997).

Assessment has forward-looking and after-the-fact aspects. Through the forward-looking aspect, the evaluator attempts to anticipate and prevent potential sources of deviation from established standards and considers the possibility of undesirable outcomes. Crime prevention is an example of forward-looking evaluation. After-the-fact evaluation analyzes why an event or deviation from established standards has occurred and determines what corrective action is required. Determining the cause(s) of a number of reported burglaries in a particular neighborhood is an example of after-the-fact evaluation.

The first step in the assessment and control process is to measure performance based on the objectives established during the response stage of the SARA problem-solving process (Community Policing Consortium, 1997b). These objectives, or standards, are units of measurement that serve as reference points for evaluating results. Standards can be either tangible or intangible. Tangible standards are quite clear, concrete, specific, identifiable, and generally measurable. These standards measure quantity and quality of the responses. They may be used to assess the impact of any corrective action taken.

Tangible standards can be categorized as numerical, monetary, physical, or time-related. Numerical standards are expressed in numbers such as crime statistics, percentage of successful calls, or number of personnel required for an operation. Monetary standards are expressed in dollars and cents. Examples of monetary standards include predetermined (planned) costs, actual costs, and budget analyses. Physical standards refer to quality, durability, size, weight, or other factors related to items such as equipment and supplies required for the response. Time standards refer to the speed with which the task should be completed (Ortmeier, 1999).

Intangible standards are not expressed in terms of numbers, money, physical qualities, or time since they relate to human characteristics that are difficult to measure. They take no physical form. Yet, they are just as important as tangible standards. Examples of intangible standards include desirable attitude, high morale, ethics, cooperation, and the organization's reputation. In policing, assessment through the use of intangible standards goes beyond traditional success measurements such as number of arrests and reductions in crime rates. Intangible standards complement tangible standards to create a better understanding of a program's impact (Crime statistics don't tell the whole story, 1999).

Performance may be measured through personal observation, written or oral reports of subordinates, automatic methods, and inspections, tests, or surveys. Some members of the organization may resent performance measurements. This resentment often results from the use of efficiency experts and supervisors who set unrealistic standards of performance. Managers within an organization must remember that performance standards should be based on realistic targets.

Sometimes, the most thoughtful effort fails to meet performance standards or achieve desirable results. Identification of the cause(s) of failure rather than the symptoms is extremely important if any additional corrective action is to be taken. It is important to consult with those closest to the situation to determine why the performance standards are not being met. Participation by all affected members of the organization and the community is an essential ingredient in this process (Clemmer, 1992).

Time is also essential to the assessment process. The sooner a deviation from a standard is identified, the sooner the situation can be corrected. Assessment, therefore, must be continuous and viewed as a thread that runs through all stages of the SARA process.

If no deviations from an established goal occur, the evaluative check has been fulfilled. However, after a careful analysis, deviations from a performance standard may be identified and additional corrective action may be necessary. Modifications, adjustments, and alterations to the original plan should not be viewed negatively. After all, objectives and standards as stated in the original plan are often based on forecasts. If the deviation from the standard is extreme or exceptional, it may be necessary to evaluate the approach used in the problem-solving process itself.

Before any corrective action is taken, the actual causes of the deviation should be analyzed carefully. Knee-jerk reactions may cause greater harm to occur. There may be many reasons why a deviation from an established standard has occurred (Haberer & Webb, 1994). It is possible that:

- The standards could not be achieved because they were based on faulty forecasts or assumptions or because an unforeseen problem arose that distorted the anticipated results.
- Failure had already occurred in some other activity that preceded the activity in question.
- The persons who performed the activity either were unqualified or were not given adequate directions or instructions.
- The persons who performed the activity were negligent or did not follow required directions or procedures.

Assessment can help assure quality or, at the very least, improve the quality of life. However, quality can be an elusive concept. It means different things to different people. In the context of assuring consumer satisfaction, quality may be defined as a phenomenon associated with products, people, services, processes, and environments that meet or exceed expectations. Quality assurance, continuous quality improvement, and total quality management (TQM) initiatives involve approaches that attempt to maximize effectiveness (or competitiveness) of an organization through the continual improvement of the quality of its people, processes, products, and environment (Goetsch & Davis, 1995). Quality assurance initiatives should involve all community constituencies in the process of identifying and improving aspects of community life.

Quality assurance initiatives should be based on: decisions founded on fact rather than intuition, taking personal responsibility for quality, improving teamwork and commitment, and a focus on end users and service. Quality assurance initiatives also involve goal setting, trust, building cohesion, developing problem-solving skills, increasing information flow, and resolving conflict. At a minimum, a total quality assurance approach includes: customer focus (internal and external), obsession with quality, use of the scientific approach in decision making and problem solving, long-term commitment, and teamwork. Total quality assurance focuses on involvement and empowerment, continual improvement, bottom-up education and training, freedom from control, and unity of purpose.

Quality assurance initiatives are not a quick fix. Rather, they are an entirely new approach to administration that requires new management styles, long-term commitments, unity of purpose, and specialized training (Tos, 2000). The police must commit to quality as well as quantity of service. Quality service may be addressed through appropriate quality assurance initiatives such as TQM (Peak & Glensor, 2002). Although TQM should not be viewed as a cure for the vast array of police and community problems, concepts associated with TQM can be adapted to the police service. Problem-solving processes, such as the SARA model, can be accomplished through TQM strategies (Thurman, Zhao, & Giacomazzi, 2001). Through quality assurance initiatives, police agencies can:

- Address the needs of internal and external customers (police personnel and citizens).
- Focus less on competitive individual officer performance measures and more on customer (officer and citizen) satisfaction. Most individual performance measures are based on organizational expectations (number of arrests, citations issued) rather than customer needs.
- Strive toward constancy of purpose and the desire for continuous improvement by all employees.

- Evaluate and measure performance on the basis of team accomplishments.
- Rely on providing the best possible service in the first instance rather than inspections to monitor services provided.

With quality assurance in mind, police officers strive, as a team, to ensure high-quality customer service and satisfaction rather than focus on personal achievements within the organization (Stevens, 2002).

PROBLEM SOLVING IN GROUPS

A group is a collection of people who interact with each other to achieve a common purpose. A number of people present at a specific location at the same time do not necessarily constitute a group. If these people interact with each other, establish common goals, and have a structure and a pattern of communication, then a group exists. Every member of a group usually has a personal stake in the outcome of the group's effort.

In many of the situations a police officer encounters, problem solving and decision making rests squarely on the shoulders of the individual officer. These situations require immediate identification of the problem, intuitive evaluation of the circumstances, the development of viable alternatives, and an instinctive reaction to resolve the problem. However, some problems develop over an extended period of time, are pervasive within a neighborhood or community, and create a situation in which hasty decisions and actions may have an unpopular, and sometimes disastrous impact on the citizen stakeholders. These situations lend themselves to a **group problem-solving** process. When involvement of a group is appropriate, the synergistic effect of group problem solving often leads to better results than does problem solving by an individual.

Groups are an excellent medium for identifying and solving problems (Kidd & Braziel, 1999). However, working in groups can be frustrating as well as rewarding (Gamble & Gamble, 1999). It can be frustrating because group work tends to encourage laziness and conflicts may develop between personal and group goals. A few individuals may dominate the group and stubbornness on the part of certain members may lead to deadlock. Group work is futile if members are obstinate and refuse to be open to different points of view. Reaching a decision may also require more time in a group setting. On the positive side, group work facilitates the sharing of resources, makes errors more recognizable, and tends to increase motivation. Decisions are often better received and personal rewards much higher in group settings. Yet, conflict within a group can develop.

Methods for resolving conflict can take many forms. Through win-lose problem solving, one side uses power or authority (rank, physical force, intellectual ability) to overcome an opponent. In lose-lose problem solving, neither side is satisfied. As two sides attempt to win, both can suffer tremendous losses. Compromise offers an opportunity for both parties to achieve some of what they want. Partial satisfaction is better than no satisfaction at all. However, the best approach is to strive toward full satisfaction of all parties, a win-win situation. Although win-win problem solving is not appropriate in all situations, it does offer opportunity for creative solution development (Adler & Towne, 2002; Whisenand & Ferguson, 2002).

Cohesion within teams and problem-solving groups can result in negative consequences. Cohesive groups can suffer from **group think,** which is symptomatic of groups or teams that give priority to unanimous agreement over reasoned problem solving. Groups suffering from group think fail to: consider all alternatives, gather enough information, reexamine failing action plans, weigh risks, develop contingency plans, or discuss important moral issues. This type of cohesiveness can lead to overconfidence, closed-mindedness, and group pressure to conform (Flippen, 1999; Janis, 1989; Johnson, 2001).

In view of the advantages and disadvantages of working in groups, when is group work most appropriate? According to Gamble and Gamble (1999), the formation of a group to identify and solve problems is indicated when most of the following conditions exist:

- The problem is complex.
- The problem is multifaceted.
- No single person possesses all information relevant to the problem.
- A division of responsibility for the problem-solving process is necessary.
- Several alternative solutions to the problem are desirable.
- Diverse opinions are essential to solution development.
- Activities are task related.

Problem solving and decision making in groups may be accomplished through a variety of different strategies. Taking the least offensive alternative, allowing the leader to decide, majority rule, relying on expert opinion, or total deferral of the decision are methods commonly used. The least offensive position may be politically correct and garner public support, but may not provide the best solution. In some situations, the group leader retains decision-making power and only confers with other group members. Majority rule is a common strategy in elections as well as the legislative process. However, majority rule may not effectively serve the needs of the minority. Experts often provide viable alternatives, but reliance on experts may not promote acceptance by the stakeholders. Total deferral to another authority may be appropriate under certain conditions but may not absolve the group from responsibility and accountability with respect to any outcomes.

PROBLEM SOLVING THROUGH GROUP CONSENSUS

In an ideal scenario, a group will identify and confront a problem directly, assume responsibility for it, and become actively involved in the development of alternative solutions to the problem. In this best case, the most effective problem-solving and decision-making strategy is decision by consensus. When **consensus** is achieved, all members of the group help to formulate, support, and agree on the decision. Decisions made by a leader or expert, or through majority rule, may be less time consuming. Also, many problem-solving situations may not lend themselves to a group consensus model. However, in most situations, the quality of decision making is better and the satisfaction of the participants is higher when a consensus strategy is used. The consensus model, when appropriately used, facilitates interaction and permits open discussion and effective use of resources.

Building group consensus can be a formidable task for anyone, especially for police officers in situations where emotions are high and the group is heterogeneous. Opinions and goals may be extremely diverse. For group problem solving to work in real-life environments, certain guidelines must be established, understood, and adhered to (Gamble & Gamble, 1999, p. 282):

- Group goals are not to be imposed by a few. Rather, group goals are cooperatively formulated and easily understood.
- All ideas and feelings are valued and all group members are encouraged to freely communicate these ideas and feelings.
- When a decision is necessary, input from all members is sought and group members seek to reach consensus.
- Equal weight is given to goal achievement and the well-being of group members. In other words, quality decisions are as important as how well members maintain themselves as a group.
- Group members are motivated to provide input, share ideas, listen to others, and engage in a team effort to develop the best solutions to the problem.
- The group's efforts are objectively evaluated to identify the strengths of the group's style as well as the flaws in the group's problem-solving process.

One excellent method for consensus building that prevents domination of the group by a few, and provides equal opportunity for input, is the Delphi Technique mentioned earlier in this chapter. The technique was developed by Olaf Helmer and several of his associates at the Rand Corporation in the 1950s in an effort to respond to urgent national defense problems. The technique is used to predict the future, to assess current trends, to gain expert consensus while clarifying minority opinion, and as a teaching technique. It has been applied in such diverse areas as public safety, national defense, economic forecasting, and the analysis of educational needs. It is a creative and futuristic tool that gives each participating individual equal input into the reaching of consensus, although that person may be miles from and perhaps unacquainted with the other participants (Bunning, 1979). The technique also provides documentation including the recording of dissenting opinions of group members (Rasp, 1974; Stahl, 1992). In 1984, FBI Special Agent William Tafoya, a Ph.D. candidate at the University of Maryland, used the Delphi Technique to conduct research for his dissertation on the future of policing (Tafoya, 1986). Ortmeier (1996) used the Delphi Technique while conducting research to identify essential leadership competencies for line-level police officers.

Basically, the Delphi Technique is a method for collecting and organizing knowledge and opinion on a subject in an effort to produce a group consensus. The convergence of group consensus is accomplished through a series of three or more questionnaires dealing with a variety of questions on a single subject (Bunning, 1979). Statements regarding the topic are formulated and the respondents, consisting of a panel of people, are asked to respond to the statements in questionnaire form according to their own perceptions (Gomez, 1985). The results of the first round of anonymous questioning are summarized and returned to the individual group members with a request that they reconsider the appropriateness of their initial responses. On each succeeding round, panel members whose responses deviated from consensus, and who wish to remain outside consensus, are requested to justify their responses (Brooks, 1979).

The exact procedures of the Delphi Technique may vary depending on the type of study. The typical procedure is as follows:

- The area of concern or policy is selected and defined (Stahl, 1992).
- Background information on the particular topic, problem, or policy issue is gathered and combined into a set of basic statements—each of which will become an individual item to be rated on a questionnaire (Stahl, 1992).
- If not accomplished in step two, a panel of participants is identified. No guidelines exist that describe the most appropriate number of panel members to select for the Delphi process. Various studies have

employed anywhere from 15 to 20 to more than 140 well-selected respondents. Panels consisting of between 17 and 29 members appear to be the most advantageous for data management purposes (Dalkey, 1969).

- An initial questionnaire, or survey instrument, is developed. The number of questions or items should be limited to as few as possible. The questionnaire should also provide space in which the participants may include additional items (Bunning, 1979). Designed to collect both closed and open-ended data, the initial as well as subsequent questionnaires may utilize a combination opinion/questionnaire format. Determination of averages based on a Likert scale of one as not important to seven as extremely important may be used to establish a rating for each question.
- The questionnaires are coded (to help provide a sense of anonymity) and distributed to the participants.
- After the first and each succeeding questionnaire, the ratings for each item are tabulated and a composite rating, or consensus, is computed. The composite rating for each item is written on the subsequent questionnaires so all members of the panel can view their own ratings and the composite rating of the group.
- The second questionnaire is distributed to the participants to provide the panel with a second opportunity to rate the original statements as well as any additions. The questionnaire each person receives informs the person as to how the original statements were rated by the entire group as well as how that specific person rated all the statements included in the first round.
- The responses to the second questionnaire are tabulated and a third questionnaire is distributed to the participants to provide the panel with a final opportunity to rate the original statements as well as any additions.
- The rated responses to the third questionnaire are tabulated and the mean (average) value score of each item is calculated for presentation with the findings. The Delphi Technique formally ends with the analysis and interpretation of the results of the final round of questionnaires. Consistent with standard Delphi practice, final reports from the data usually contain a ranking of the statements by priority and a listing or summary of the minority opinions (reasons for remaining outside consensus) of the panel members (Stahl, 1992).

The extensive process and lengthy nature of the Delphi Technique make it more appropriate for major problems, for which the solution will have a long-standing effect.

COMMUNITY MAPPING

The problem-solving process involved in rebuilding troubled communities and improving the quality of life in others necessitates mechanisms for assessing needs and identifying assets. Needs assessment and asset identification can be accomplished through the use of comprehensive **community mapping** tools. The applications for mapping are almost limitless (Bynum, 2001). A needs map helps to identify problem areas and deficiencies within a neighborhood. Some communities have more deficiencies than others. Impoverished neighborhoods are typically more needy than their more affluent counterparts. However, no matter how poor a neighborhood might be, it often contains valuable assets, usually in the form of law-abiding citizens, organizations, and institutional resources.

A thorough mapping of a community begins with an identification of its assets as well as its deficiencies. The asset map will include an inventory of the skills and capabilities of the community's residents. These assets are indispensable tools for creative development. They can be mobilized along with other resources to address problems, deficiencies, crime, and disorder (Kingsley & Pettit, 2000; Kretzmann & McKnight, 1999).

One of the most sophisticated methods for anticipating, recognizing, and appraising a crime risk involves the use of computer mapping and **geographic information system (GIS)** technology. Commonly referred to as crime mapping, GIS software can be used to map and display reported crime and predict future occurrences within a community. Public agencies routinely collect and maintain data that include location information. Police databases contain addresses of reported crime and arrests. Court and corrections files contain addresses of offenders. Other agencies manage property, street, physical infrastructure, and public health data. Computer mapping and GIS technology combine these multiple databases into one display so law enforcement agencies can isolate and treat factors contributing to crime, manage resources more efficiently, and evaluate the effectiveness of any crime prevention action taken (Peak & Glensor, 2002).

Mapping is not new nor is it limited to policing. For years law enforcement agencies analyzed crime patterns by inserting pushpins into paper maps taped on walls. Similarly, medical researchers use mapping to investigate disease and illness rates among different geographic locations (Bynum, 2001). Computerized mapping is new and today's technology allows much more detailed information to be superimposed over a map. Crime analysts can use the database to quickly identify crime hot spots, problem areas, and resource distribution (Rich, 1999).

BARRIERS TO PROBLEM SOLVING

A study conducted to determine the extent to which federal Community Oriented Policing Services (COPS) grantees implemented problem solving according to COPS funding requirements revealed that most grantees engage in problem solving. However, the form and visibility of problem solving varies greatly among agencies. Some of the most notable problem-solving efforts include:

- The evolution of problem solving from special operations to complex activities that attack disorder and fear of crime, and require police to search for noncriminal interventions.
- Administrative systems that recognize problem solving at different levels within agencies.
- Broad-based and widely distributed authority to initiate problem-solving projects.
- The development of evaluative systems to assess and learn from problem-solving projects.
- Law enforcement agency ability to engage other organizations and government agencies in defining and solving community problems (Roth & Ryan, 2000).

However, **barriers to** effective **problem solving** can develop in almost any situation. As with any planned change or revision, barriers or resistance to problem solving can be social, political, physical, economic, educational, legal, technological, organizational, or cultural. Social factors in a community associated with class, gender, or race can produce inequality that is not easily corrected. Political groups with power can promote change in favor of themselves. The physical environment can inhibit implementation of crime prevention strategies. Economically, sufficient financial resources may not be available. Community members may lack sufficient education to understand the nature of the problem and thus will be unable to assist with the creation and implementation of a solution. Legal restrictions can inhibit police ability to solve some types of problems. Technologically, more sophisticated communications and information systems may be necessary to implement the solution to a problem (Welsh & Harris, 1999). Organizationally, members of a group may resist the change that will inevitably result from the implementation of a problem's solution. Finally, problem solving across cultures creates profound ethical questions that leaders must confront as they attempt to maintain integrity while making culturally appropriate decisions (Adler, 2002).

In some jurisdictions, traditional enforcement activities are labeled "problem solving" when the activities are directed toward problems identified by the community. However, enforcement-based solutions to problems are likely to be short-lived because activities dominated by enforcement actions rarely advance the strategic objectives of community policing. Enforcement actions alone are unlikely to eliminate underlying causes of crime and disorder or attract community support for long-term solution maintenance. The growing trend to zero-tolerance policing, for example, although based on some community input, may alienate potential community partners who were unable to provide input when the zero-tolerance policies were developed (Roth & Ryan, 2000).

Other barriers to effective problem solving exist. Police officers engaged in community policing and problem solving often express concern over the difficulties encountered when they attempt to translate problem-solving theory into practice. Despite the success potential associated with the problem-solving strategy as well as the financial resources available to support the effort, police officers who are able to solve problems in training sessions often experience application difficulties in the field. Problem solving is complex. It is not an easy task. This is especially true when working with groups whose membership consists of people from diverse backgrounds. Furthermore, citizens as well as police officers must realize that the police cannot prevent or eliminate every problem.

Many police agencies are failing or are progressing too slowly toward implementing community policing and problem-solving concepts because officers lack ethical decision-making and problem-solving skills. Failed attempts and slow progress fosters resistance and encourages many officers to regress into inefficient and obsolete traditional policing methods. Success in the community policing effort requires competence to explore and define problems with specificity and assist with problem ownership (Anderson, 2000).

A thorough exploration of the circumstances of a problem situation facilitates problem identification. Hunches, personal feelings, bias, emotion, and premature evaluations must be set aside in favor of a patient identification and examination of the facts and causal connection between the symptoms and the negative consequences a problem creates. The more thoroughly a problem is explored, the more likely a high-impact solution will be developed.

Problem exploration requires a complex set of human qualities and competencies. In addition to patience and creative thinking, problem exploration requires the ability to craft and use a language that defines the problem clearly. The ability to define a problem with specificity is difficult to master. Thus, many police officers are reluctant to engage in problem-solving efforts. Supervisors may view the reluctant officer as uncooperative and malcontent. The reality is that the officer may feel uncomfortable when transitioning from traditional to community policing. The transition is aggravated when officers are exposed to the concepts of community policing but do not have the benefit of proper training in the practical realities of its implementation. Officers are expected to view crime and disorder problems from multiple perspectives. As a result, an officer's job can become more difficult. Rather than prescribed by a supervisor or traditional procedure, a police officer's actions in a community policing environment depend on the officer's problem-solving competence. An officer is expected to be less reactive and more proactive, preventing crime and disorder with community-based problem-solving strategies (Anderson 2000).

The barriers to effective problem solving in the police service can be summarized as follows:

- Lack of Training. Problem-solving strategies represent a complete paradigm shift from traditional policing in which officers simply respond to radio calls or reported incidents. However, problem-solving skills can be learned with good, extensive, and ongoing training by qualified personnel. Short-term training sessions are not enough.
- Lack of Leadership. Police administrators often fail to support line officers in the problem-solving effort. In addition, line officers themselves have not acquired the leadership skills necessary to engage and work with community members.
- Confusion. Police executives and line officers often confuse community policing and problem solving with community relations. Although good police community relations are important, problem solving involves the added dimension of community participation.
- Lack of Clearly Defined Roles. Police officers in a community policing and problem-solving environment often experience an identity crisis. The crisis results when agencies do not clearly define the mission and values of the organization and fail to identify the roles and responsibilities of police executives, midlevel managers, frontline supervisors, and field officers. Often the problem-solving activities are relegated to a few specialized community relations patrol units. The problem-solving effort should permeate the entire agency.
- Lack of Resources. The social agencies, community groups, and other necessary services outside the police department—which are needed to deal with aspects of the problem that are beyond the jurisdiction or capabilities of the police—are not readily available or are insufficient.
- Lack of Technological Support. Except for major crimes and arrest and conviction data, the information necessary for effective problem solving is not readily available to the officers in the field. Integrated information systems that incorporate incident data with crime mapping programs are essential to the problem-solving effort and are desperately needed.

- The Fad Complex. Programs and concepts in policing come and go in agencies that view new ideas as fads or passing political fancy. To be successful, the concept of community policing and problem solving requires long-term commitment, support, and integration of the strategy into every functional area of the police organization.
- Lack of Legitimacy. For the past half century, police strategy and tactics have focused on the identification and apprehension of criminals. As a result, police officers question the legitimacy of the police role in crime prevention.
- Lack of Effective Outcome Assessment. A major criticism of community policing and problem solving is the lack of structured evaluations to assess the effectiveness of problem-solving efforts. Although anecdotal success stories are publicized, effective assessment methods and instruments have yet to be devised.

It is apparent that the barriers to problem solving in a community policing environment include training and information deficiencies, existing organizational cultures, and lack of leadership and understanding. Until these issues are addressed fully, barriers to effective problem solving will continue to exist (Glensor & Peak, 1999; Lyman, 2002; Ortmeier, 2002; Peak & Glensor, 2002; Thurman, 2002).

SUMMARY

The nature of policing demands ethical decision making and problem solving. Decisions should be based on sound ethical principles. Police officers are problem solvers and although problem solving is a major portion of police work, traditional police training methods may actually inhibit the development of ethical decision-making and problem-solving ability. In policing, the community problem rather than a specific incident should be the main unit of police work. Problem solving involves the use of quantitative as well as qualitative data and analysis. Although many problem-solving models are available and appropriate, the police problem-solving model most commonly used today consists of four major components: scanning, analysis, response, and assessment (SARA).

To work effectively with neighborhoods and communities to address crime and disorder problems, the police must develop the skills necessary to work with diverse groups of people. Included in a community problem-solving effort are techniques and processes for community mapping. The police must also be aware of the numerous barriers to effective problem solving.

KEY TERMS AND CONCEPTS

Define, describe, or explain the importance of each of the following:

analysis
assessment
barriers to problem solving
community mapping
community problem
consensus
critical thinking
Delphi Technique
dilemma
ethical decision making
geographic information system (GIS)
group problem solving
group think
incident-driven policing
intangible standard
problem analysis triangle
problem-oriented policing
problem solving
qualitative measures
quality assurance initiative
quantitative measures
response
SARA problem-solving model
scanning
tangible standard

DISCUSSION QUESTIONS AND EXERCISES

1. Outline and describe the elements of the planning process.
2. Identify and describe the four components to the SARA problem-solving model.
3. How would one apply problem-solving techniques when working with a group of people?
4. Conduct a community needs assessment for a neighborhood. Review crime rates as part of the needs assessment and create a map that identifies high-crime-rate areas within the neighborhood.
5. What are the barriers to effective problem solving?
6. Discuss the role of evaluation in the planning process.

Chapter 9

Planning, Organization, Implementation, and Evaluation

Learning Objectives

After completing this chapter, the reader should be able to:

- define and explain the need for planning.
- list and describe types of plans.
- contrast mission and vision statements.
- articulate the steps in the planning process.
- differentiate organization as a process or function from organization as an institution.
- design a crime prevention strategy utilizing crime prevention through environmental design (CPTED) techniques.
- explain how organization is aligned with planning, leading, and controlling.
- list and describe the four major elements of the organizing function.
- compare public organizations with private organizations.
- evaluate the relationship between organizational complexity and span of control.
- create an organizational structure.
- contrast the relationship between organizational leadership and learning and performance in organizations.
- demonstrate ability to select and implement an action plan.
- evaluate progress toward meeting measurable objectives.
- design a strategy for human resource management.
- contrast policies and procedures.
- select assessment tools appropriate for evaluating outcomes.

INTRODUCTION

At the core of community-centered, problem-oriented policing is the ability to plan a strategy, organize community resources, implement an action plan, and evaluate progress and outcomes. To promote positive change, police officers must possess the ability to assist others in the creation and maintenance of a vision for improvement in the quality of life. Community-oriented policing is dynamic, changing continuously to meet the needs of the client. Officers must help to define objectives, maintain goal direction, and prioritize and assign tasks effectively. As veteran police officers will testify, circumstances and situations change very quickly. Given the conflicting demands placed on contemporary policing, the ability to be flexible and reprioritize is critical to any community problem-solving effort. As leaders, officers must also provide for and maintain the group process by helping to create a psychologically safe environment that encourages open, honest, and frank communication. Safe environments and open communications can engender necessary attitudinal changes among participants.

In many instances where community problems exist, the police officer may be the only person in a position to plan activities and organize community energy to implement a plan and evaluate outcomes. Officers are often required to work with groups that do not possess inherent planning or organizing ability. Team building and maintenance is difficult. However, once the group is established and trained, motivational skills can be used to encourage group self-sufficiency with little energy expended by the police (Ortmeier, 1996). As stated in Chapter 8, problem solving in police work follows a logical progression through rational decision making that includes problem identification and definition, the development of alternative courses of action, selection and implementation of an action plan, and evaluation (Goldstein, 1990). This chapter reinforces and expands the problem-solving techniques discussed in Chapter 8.

PLANNING

Planning is central to the scanning and analysis elements of the SARA problem-solving model presented in Chapter 8. The need for proper planning cannot be overemphasized. It is probably the most crucial ingredient to the success of any activity. Planning involves a definition of group or organization mission and vision based on core values (Johnson, 2001; Peak & Glensor, 2002) and includes an analysis of the current situation, a forecast of future events, the establishment of objectives and priorities, and a decision as to which course of action will most appropriately achieve the mission. To be effective, planning must precede all other management and administrative functions. Thorough planning results in better resource utilization. It promotes efficiency, reduces costs, and eliminates waste.

There are several types of plans. Some are single-use, while others are repeat-use. Other types include tactical, strategic, and contingency plans. **Single-use plans** are no longer needed once the objectives of the plan are accomplished. Budgets and special projects are examples of single-use plans. **Repeat-use** (standing) **plans** may be used again and again. They are followed each time a given situation or incident occurs. Unless modified, repeat-use plans change little over time. Examples of repeat-use plans include policies, procedures, and methods for achieving objectives. **Tactical plans** are short range and are scheduled to be executed within a short period of time. **Strategic plans,** on the other hand, are long range and may involve plans that are scheduled to be implemented over a period of years (Peak & Glensor, 2002). **Contingency plans** are those that will be implemented only if certain events, such as natural disasters or emergencies, occur.

There may be several versions of each type of plan. Contingency planning, for example, requires a different plan for each kind of emergency. Some plans are simple, while others are complex. The response to an accident requiring basic first aid may be relatively simple, while a response to a natural disaster may be very detailed and complex. Natural disasters may affect an entire community or region (Ortmeier, 1999).

Preliminary to planning, organization, implementation, and evaluation activities is the need for the creation of an **organizational mission** as well as an **organizational vision** based on the fundamental values. Often perplexing to clarify and articulate, values represent the foundation upon which organizational activity is based. Values include integrity, honesty, compassion, respect, professionalism, and accountability (Johnson, 2001). Individual values must be aligned to form the collective conscience of the enterprise. The mission of the organization represents the tactical (short-term) and operational focus of the organization's resources. Vision portrays an image of a desirable future (Anderson, 2000). In unison, values help to operationalize an action plan (mission) designed to realize the image of a better future (vision). Organizational values, mission, and vision are commonly documented in statements.

Planning processes contain up to ten steps. Wilson (1952) outlined five steps to the planning process:

- Recognize the need for a plan.
- Formulate a statement of objectives.
- Collect and analyze relevant data.
- Develop details of the plan.
- Obtain agreement from the operational units that will eventually carry out the plan (Wilson, 1952).

Anderson (2000) identifies eight steps:

- Assessment of needs, wants, problems.
- Clarification of need for change.
- Exploration of readiness for change.
- Exploration of potential for readiness in working together as a team.
- General goal setting.
- Specific objectives to be achieved.
- Action plans for achievement of objectives.
- Evaluation and reporting of results (Anderson, 2000).

Regardless of the number of steps involved in a single planning scheme, common elements exist in all planning processes. These include: a **needs or risk assessment,** the development of **alternative courses of action,** and **action plan selection.**

Needs and Risk Assessments

The first step is to establish the need or frame of reference for a plan, which may be the accomplishment of a desired result or the elimination of a risk or threat. What is the group's or organization's mission and vision? Clear, concise, yet comprehensive, mission and vision statements help establish a frame of reference. The creation of shared mission and vision statements should involve all key stakeholders (Peak & Glensor, 2002; Whisenand & Ferguson, 2002). All officers within an agency as well as citizens and other community clients of the police should be involved in the development of the agency's mission and vision.

Next, it is necessary to collect and analyze relevant data. This involves a needs or risk assessment. A needs assessment refers to research conducted to determine if a problem or need exists. A risk assessment is used to determine if a known or foreseeable threat (crime, natural disaster, etc.) exists. Data may be collected utilizing both subjective and objective measurements. Subjective measures include the use of forecasting, expert opinion, and the Delphi Technique. Objective (empirical) measures may include audits, marketing, operations research, statistical reports, threat assessment, investigations, risk analysis, inspections, and surveys (Ortmeier, 1999; Peak & Glensor, 2002). For example, a survey may be used for school safety and security planning purposes. The survey involves a critical, objective, on-site analysis of the organization's entire safety and security system. The survey instrument (checklist) used should address:

- The general area or neighborhood surrounding the facility. Consideration should be given to area crime rates, aesthetic qualities, and susceptibility to catastrophic events such as floods.

- The perimeter near the facility should also be evaluated in terms of its parking, fencing, landscaping, and signs.
- Building points of entry, exits, access control, locks and keys, alarm systems and lighting, and vulnerability to intrusion.
- Restricted areas within the facility.
- An analysis of procedures used in the protection of people, property, and information.
- Strategies for accident prevention.
- The indoctrination and education of all stakeholders regarding safety and security policies and procedures.

Developing Alternative Courses of Action

After the mission and vision of the organization are defined and the needs (goals) are identified, objectives for meeting the needs are outlined. This involves the development of alternative courses of action (action plans) that include measurable objectives (Parshall-McDonald & Greenberg, 2002). Alternative course of action development requires identification of necessary resources, budgeting, the creation of procedures for acquiring or reallocating resources, specification of dates by which plan implementation tasks will be accomplished, the development of mechanisms for self-regulation (orienting participants and coordinating activities), strategies for management of resistance and conflict, and strategies designed to create and maintain support for action plan implementation (Welsh & Harris, 1999). Each alternative must be evaluated to determine probable undesirable as well as desirable consequences. The decision-making process and the decisions made may not always be popular. The impact the decision will have on an organization, its people, its clients, and the community will require careful consideration. If well thought out, each decision may be viewed as an opportunity for development, progress, and advancement of individual, organizational, and community goals and objectives.

The financial impact of each alternative course of action must be determined. This requires a **budget** for each action plan. Although viewed by some as a laborious task, budget preparation should be viewed as an integral part of the planning process. It is an essential planning tool and must be tied to the established goals and objectives that were developed as alternative courses of action. The budget is a comprehensive plan, expressed in financial terms.

Areas to consider in budget preparation include past operations, present conditions, and future expectations. Revenue forecasts, client population demands, and projected expenditures to meet the demand are all part of budget preparation. The budget process should be continuous, flexible, and responsive to the changing needs of the organization. The elements of a budget should include provision for personnel, operating expenses, supplies and materials, capital expenditures, and miscellaneous expenditures (Ortmeier, 1999; Whisenand & Ferguson, 2002).

Action Plan Selection

Action plan selection depends on several factors. Of course, a major consideration will focus on available resources, financial and otherwise, to implement the action plan selected. Other factors include the social, political, legal, and physical environments as well as the educational and technological sophistication and support of all stakeholders and participants. The existence of these factors must be recognized, and their impact analyzed, to reveal critical sources of resistance and support for any planned change. Leaders as planners must also analyze the organizational environment within which the action plan is to be implemented (Baker, 2000; Welsh & Harris, 1999; Stojkovic, Kalinich, & Klofas, 2003). Key stakeholders within the organization may prefer maintenance of the status quo.

To select the most appropriate action plan, participants in the budget process must analyze the capabilities of the organization and compare the plan to the organization's mission. In other words, a determination must be made of available resources and the value the plan contributes to the goals of the group, organization, and community.

Support must be generated for the action plan recommended. The types of support needed for effective implementation include the following:

- Organizational—Appropriate members of the organization must be involved in the decision-making process or, at the very minimum, they should be informed as to the nature of, and reason for, future plans. Traditional police agency organizational structure presumes that those in higher ranks possess greater wisdom and creativity than line officers. This is not the case, however. All members of a police agency, including line personnel, possess decision-making potential (Parshall-McDonald & Greenberg, 2002).
- Community—When a community will be impacted by the implementation of the plan, information should be disseminated, on a need-to-know basis, to generate public support. This may be accomplished through the media (Otto, 2000), public speaking engagements in community forums, and at meetings of professional organizations.
- Consumer—Who are the consumers of the action plan? Regardless of who the consumers are, it is important that those who might be considered clients of the plan be informed as to its nature, scope, and intent.
- Entity responsible for approval of the budget—Who is responsible for approving the budget? Is it management, the legislature, the city

council, a department head, a foundation, or granting agency? A strategy must be developed to justify the budget to all the major stakeholders. It, or they, will want to know what value the plan, if implemented, will contribute to the goals and objectives of the organization, agency, and community.

- Other organizations—If the plan involves other organizations and agencies, liaison should be established with them. For example, an agency may require assistance from other jurisdictions to implement the plan. Similarity, if resources are to be shared through a consortium, the planning process must involve the other organizations impacted by the plan (Ortmeier, 1999).

CRIME PREVENTION THROUGH ENVIRONMENTAL DESIGN (CPTED)

Crime and disorder prevention involves the anticipation, recognition, and appraisal of a crime or disorder risk and the initiation of action to remove the risk to an acceptable level. Police officers can anticipate crime risks by becoming intimately familiar with crime patterns and the procedures for gathering information from citizens who live and work in the area. Some conditions in an area (24-hour businesses, shopping centers, automatic teller machines) may pose a higher risk than others. Police officers must be able to recognize which conditions pose the highest risk, appraise the situation, and predict where conditions are favorable for crime to occur.

After high-risk areas are identified, officers can work collaboratively with businesses, residents, government agencies, and other community members to remove or reduce opportunities for potential law violators. Access control, utilization of alarm systems, directed patrol, selective enforcement, and neighborhood watch programs are examples of target hardening mechanisms that can be recommended and used to reduce opportunities for crime (California State Commission on Peace Officer Standards and Training, 1999; Zelinka & Brennan, 2001).

An excellent mechanism for problem resolution as well as preventing crime and disorder is **crime prevention through environmental design (CPTED)** (Bynum, 2001). CPTED supports a movement toward problem-oriented policing. Alternately, problem-oriented policing reinforces the concepts of CPTED (Scott, 2000). CPTED is based on the theory that the environment can be protected and crime prevented through the proper design of buildings, neighborhoods, and communities. CPTED also reduces fear of crime and the perceptions of crime risks (Peak & Glensor, 2002; Robinson, 2002). Emphasis is placed on architecture, building codes, and

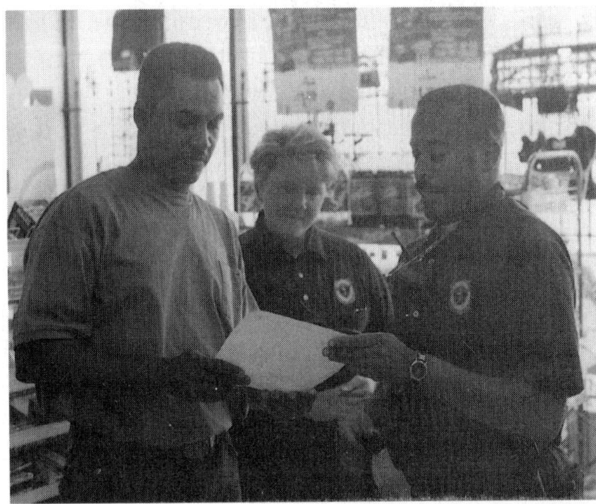

CPTED can be applied in business as well as residential environments.
Photo courtesy of Cobb County, Georgia, Police Department

defensible space. It requires that security and safety concepts be incorporated into the planning of a facility or community. Although long in coming to policing, when used in conjunction with community policing programs, CPTED may be applied to residential and business areas to increase public safety and reduce citizen fear of crime (Kroeker, 2001).

Public safety and security planning through CPTED and the implementation of the recommendations developed as a result of such planning have been very effective in preventing and deterring crime. Conversely, poor security planning not only fails to prevent and deter but also encourages crime because the facility or neighborhood design attracts criminal activity.

Crime prevention and CPTED are not new concepts (Robinson, 2002). In prehistoric times, cave dwellers cleared areas in front of their caves and stacked rocks around the perimeter to designate private space and warn intruders. In ancient Greece, temple designers used environmental concepts to affect and control behavior. The temples were built of a type of stone that contained phosphorus and reflected a golden light shortly after dawn and just before dusk. During medieval times, height was used as a defensive tactic. Sleeping quarters were high above ground level and whole communities were walled in. Louis XIV, king of France from 1643 to 1715, was the first to use outdoor lighting in the form of torches and fires to reduce crime. Napoleon III (1808–1873) authorized his chiefs of police to demolish hideouts for criminals.

Since the 1970s, the National Institute of Justice has sponsored research and promoted crime prevention strategies that focus on using

CPTED and community policing to make neighborhoods safer. Research results indicate that proper design of the physical environment can and does control crime (Robinson, 2002). Private individuals and businesses working in conjunction with the police have also reduced fear of crime, deterred criminals, and utilized government building codes and inspection power to discourage illicit drug use and other criminal activity.

Assuming that criminal offenders are influenced by the vulnerability of a potential target and the possibility of being apprehended, a CPTED perspective suggests four approaches to making an environment more resistant to crime and crime-related problems:

- Appropriate housing design and block layout can make it more difficult to commit crime.
- Creating safer land use and circulation patterns in neighborhoods can reduce routine exposure to potential threats.
- Encouraging the use of territorial features and signs at the residential block level indicate that residents who are vigilant can deter would-be criminals.
- Controlling the physical deterioration of an environment may reduce criminal offender perception that an area is vulnerable and not well protected.

The conceptual thrust of CPTED is that the environment can be manipulated to produce behavioral effects that reduce the incidence and fear of crime, and improve the quality of life. The environment includes people and their physical and social surroundings. Design includes all those activities, structures, and policies that seek to positively impact human behavior as people interact with their environment. As such, CPTED focuses not only on the physical aspects of the environment but also on what social scientists, public safety and security personnel, and community organizations can do to safely meet the needs of legitimate users of a space (Crowe, 2000; Robinson, 2002).

CPTED utilizes traditional target-hardening techniques such as natural and artificial barrier systems, access control, and surveillance to reduce the threat from a criminal offender. It also involves strategies developed, implemented, and evaluated by security personnel, law enforcement, and the community to allow for the least-restrictive human interface with the barrier systems. Appropriate land use and environmental design strategies, human activity and programming considerations, and management and maintenance of safe areas combine to enhance public safety (Zelinka & Brennan, 2001).

CPTED is based on assumptions of how space is to be designed and used (Crowe, 2000). All human space has some designated purpose; it has social, legal, cultural, or physical definitions that prescribe desired and acceptable behaviors; and it is designed to support and control these desired behaviors. The basic concepts of territorial reinforcement, access control, and surveillance are inherent in these assumptions. These basic concepts may be accomplished through any combination of the following:

- Provide a clear border definition of the controlled space. Public and private spaces must be clearly delineated.
- Provide for clearly marked transitional zones. The user must acknowledge movement into the controlled space.
- Relocate gathering areas. Formally designate gathering areas in locations with good access control and natural surveillance capabilities.
- Place safe activities in unsafe locations. Safe activities serve as magnets for normal users and communicate to abnormal users that they are at greater risk of detection.
- Place unsafe activities in safe locations. Vulnerable activities should be placed within tightly controlled areas to help overcome risk and make normal users feel safer.
- Redesignate the use of space to provide natural barriers. Conflicting activities may be separated by distance and natural terrain to avoid fear-producing conflict.
- Improve the scheduling of space. The effective use of space reduces risk as well as the perception of risk for normal users.
- Redesign space to increase the perception of surveillance. Perception is more powerful than reality.
- Overcome isolation and distance. Design efficiencies and improved communication systems increase the perception of surveillance and control (Crowe, 2000).

Good planning will dictate the tactical implementation of CPTED strategies (Robinson, 2002). Crime analyses, demographic and land use information, and resident or user interviews should be used with CPTED in mind. CPTED is not a panacea nor is it a substitute for a comprehensive crime prevention program. However, CPTED may reduce the opportunity to commit crime when implemented in the context of a program designed to prevent crime while providing freedom from interference for legitimate users. Each situation is unique. No two environmental settings are exactly the same. Yet, virtually all human functions are amenable to the use of CPTED concepts and strategies. Their adaptation to produce a safe and secure environment is virtually unlimited (Crowe, 2000).

ORGANIZATION

Organization involves the function or process of creating a relationship structure that enables participants to implement plans and meet objectives and goals. Through organization, leaders as managers coordinate, integrate, and utilize human, financial, physical, and informational resources efficiently and effectively. Within a group, organizing is aligned with the functions of planning, leading, and controlling (Hellriegel, Jackson, & Slocum, 2002). The discussion of organizations presented in this section will focus on organization as a process as well as social units or institutions.

The four major elements of the organizing function are specialization, standardization, coordination, and authority (Daft, 2001). **Specialization** involves the identification of specific tasks and assignment of those tasks to individuals, units, teams, departments, or divisions. **Standardization** is the development of uniform practices that individuals and groups can follow to complete tasks. Standardization assists with the creation of procedures, job descriptions and specifications, instructions, and expected behaviors. Recruitment procedures and application processes and documents are used to standardize selection of personnel. Training and education programs standardize skills. Standardization also assists leaders and managers in the assessment of personnel performance in relation to established performance indicators (Hellriegel, Jackson, & Slocum, 2002).

Through **coordination,** leaders as managers align and integrate personnel activities and organizational units. The desired level of coordination is achieved through the use of procedures, rules, directions, and formal goals that are used, in some degree, in all groups and organizations. As an organization's hierarchy becomes more vertical by increasing the levels of personnel, coordination becomes more difficult and decision-making time increases.

Authority involves a person's right or power to make decisions of varying importance that impact an individual, group, or organization. Individuals toward the bottom of an organizational hierarchy usually possess limited authority. As one moves vertically through the hierarchy (chain of command), authority typically increases. In some cases, however, tremendous authority can be vested in those at the lower end of an organization's structure. In a community policing environment, for example, a great deal of decision making is decentralized, with line officers granted authority to make decisions based on problem-solving goals and objectives established in concert with citizens at the neighborhood or community level.

Organizations as social units or institutions (human groupings) emerge from the need for individuals to cooperate with others on complex, difficult, or multiple tasks to achieve common goals of an agency, business, community, or society (Whisenand & Ferguson, 2002). The motivation to cooperate may be based on a reward system that is intrinsic, extrinsic, or both. One could argue that public sector personnel are motivated by intrinsic rewards such as service, while private sector personnel rewards are more extrinsic (motivated by the potential for high compensation levels).

However, all people, whether public or private sector personnel, or volunteers, may be motivated by various combinations of intrinsic and extrinsic rewards.

To understand and appreciate the nature of organizations, it may be helpful to review the characteristics of public and private organizations generally as well as the principles of organization and management specifically. Generally, **public organizations** are:

- Public affairs oriented. They focus on the administration of public agencies and organizations.
- Impartial and fair. All citizens are entitled to a particular government service and must be treated in a uniform manner.
- Apolitical. The policies of government may be political but the detailed execution of these policies is administrative.
- Public service oriented. Government organizations exist to serve the public and profit is not a motive for operations.
- Publicly funded. Funds for public organizations are appropriated by law and derived from tax revenues.
- Publicly documented. Administrative records and financial documents are public information that must be made available for review by all citizens.
- Accountable to the public. They are subject to legislative and judicial review at all times.
- Selectively staffed. Qualified personnel are selected on the basis of demonstrated merit through civil service examinations.
- Hierarchical. Public organizations are formal and consist of levels of positions.

Private organizations are generally distinct from public organizations. Private organizations tend to support or focus on:

- Private enterprise. They exist to fulfill a private rather than public obligation or interest.
- Private and corporate ownership. They are owned by a private individual, group, or stockholders.
- Competition. The organization may be in competition with other enterprises engaged in producing the same product or service.
- A profit incentive. Except for certain nonprofit private organizations, the incentive is to generate net profit.
- Financing regulated by market price. Revenue is based on ability to sell the product or service.
- Privacy of information and records (within limits). Information is proprietary and is the property of the owner(s).

- Accountability to owners and stockholders. The organization and its employees are held accountable to the owners rather than the public.
- Some freedom in selection and termination of members. The organization is not bound by civil service rules in the hiring or termination of employees.
- Freedom in regulating work methods and organization. The organization is not bound by civil service regulations (Perry, 1996).

As time passes, the distinction between public and private organizations becomes increasingly blurred. In some cases, the characteristics of public and private administration are merged or blended and a single organization or agency may assume the characteristics of private as well as public organizations. Examples include some nonprofit organizations as well as quasi-governmental institutions.

The level of complexity within an organization is dependent upon the amount of horizontal and vertical differentiation that exists. Horizontal differentiation is usually based on activity. This activity may be associated with the type of clientele, style of service, geography, time, or process. Vertical differentiation, on the other hand, is based on levels of authority.

Complexity within an organization is not always based on size. Small departments, agencies, or businesses may be very complex in organizational design. Some organizations have narrow spans of management control with tall structures and many levels. Other organizations increase the span of control and shorten the organization structure, thus reducing levels of management. There is no one-size-fits-all structure and there are advantages and disadvantages associated with each. Tall organizations with narrow spans of control, for example, place fewer demands on supervisors while increasing problems with communication.

Components within organizations may be differentiated by line, staff, function, or project orientations. Line refers to those elements that perform the tasks for which the organization was created. Staff refers to those elements that support the line, such as communications and laboratory facilities. Functional structures, although complex, improve communication between elements because delegation of management authority extends beyond normal spans of control. Intelligence activities in a police department, for example, may cross all lines of authority. The essence of the project structure is that elements from various segments of the organization or from several organizations may be assigned to task forces to work on specific problems or situations.

The structural component of an organization is usually represented in the form of an **organizational chart.** In the latter half of the twentieth century, however, computer technology changed the methrodology through which many institutions operate. Many institutions moved away from the hierarchical or military structural model to a flatter, more collegial organization built around shared information. As a result, middle management, which in the past has functioned as the conduit between chiefs, CEOs, and line personnel, has been eliminated. The organizational structure becomes more decentralized. With decentralized control, power is shared. The organization is less bureaucratic and hierarchical, and more agile (Peak & Glensor, 2002; Whisenand & Ferguson, 2002). Each member of the organization becomes the member of a team that is more innovative, participatory, flexible, and adaptable. The resurrection of team policing and its transformation to community policing illustrates this trend. In a community policing environment, for example, the line police officer operates with less direct supervision and is much more directly involved with assisting the community client in the identification and development of solutions to community problems (Lyman, 2002; Ortmeier, 1999; Swanson, Territo, & Taylor, 1998).

The fluid and dynamic process of organization focuses on the principles of management. There are clear differences between leadership and management (Baker, 2000; Stojkovic, Kalinich, & Klofas, 2003). However, an integration of the two concepts provides a clear view of what is required for goals to be accomplished in an appropriate manner. Leadership emphasizes a people and process orientation while management emphasizes a task and results orientation (Anderson, 2000). The relationship between leadership and management can be expressed in terms of the primary functions of leadership and management activity. In an organizational sense, both activities are necessary.

Leadership: People and Process Orientation
- Creatively applying research information
- Motivating and rewarding others
- Relationship and culture building
- Team building and team development
- Creative planning and shifting
- Envision end-states process
- Personnel selection, orientation, performance management
- Future focus for accomplishing a higher purpose

Management: Task and Results Orientation
- Evaluation, research
- Decision making
- Planning systems
- Problem solving
- Data-based decisions
- Specifying procedures
- Administering policy

- Day-to-day operations
- Present focus to ensure results (Anderson, 2000)

ORGANIZATIONAL LEADERSHIP, LEARNING, AND PERFORMANCE

Why Organizations Fail

As early as 1921 experts recognized that the uneven development of American police organizations appeared to be caused, more than any other factor, by the lack of intelligent leadership (Fosdick, 1921). The often-quoted Dr. Laurence Peter stated that exceptional leadership competence in most cases cannot develop in the established hierarchy of an organization. Most hierarchies are encumbered with traditions, policies, regulations, and rules so that true leadership development is often stymied. In many public agencies, the organization and its employees are so restricted by public law, that even the highest ranking employees do not lead anyone anywhere, at least in the sense of creating a vision and setting the pace of activity. Those with rank simply follow precedent, obey the rules, and move at the head of the crowd. In such situations, the genuine leader (any person, regardless of rank, who demonstrates leadership competence) is resented and feared. Dr. Peter refers to this fear as "hypercanino-phobia" (top-dog fear) and its accompanying "hypercanino-phobia complex" (fear that the genuine leader will become the top dog) (Peter & Hull, 1969).

Organizations fail because they allow too much complacency, do not create powerful guiding coalitions, underestimate and undercommunicate the power of vision, and permit obstacles to block vision. They fail because they do not create short-term successes, they declare victory prematurely, and they neglect to anchor changes firmly in the organization culture (Kotter, 1996). Police agencies as organizations experience a great deal of difficulty when: members have no shared values, mission, or vision; they neglect planning; or they lack leadership competence (Peak & Glensor, 2002; Whisenand & Ferguson, 2002). In the twenty-first century, successful police agencies will be those that challenge the traditional organizational culture by implementing proactive leadership strategies (Bill Blackwood Law Enforcement Management Institute of Texas, 2000).

Leadership Organizations

A leadership organization creates and sustains a leadership-centered culture (Baca, 2002), through which the organization's members are equipped to develop additional leaders at all levels of the organization as well as within personal relationships and the community. Leadership development occurs because learning occurs. Learning occurs because the leaders are caring, competent, creative, and honest. Fully functioning police leaders successfully initiate community policing initiatives, engage in problem solving, and build a police organization that is responsive to community needs. A leadership organization is committed to leadership development for all personnel. It provides opportunities for personal, financial, physical, career, emotional, intellectual, and spiritual health and growth. The leadership organization realizes that human leadership development maximizes personnel and organizational performance (Anderson, 2000).

Leadership organizations differ from traditional organizations in several respects. The leadership organization:

- is codesigned by its members rather than controlled by the organization's design.
- assumes that what is best is always changing.
- responds to change immediately.
- anticipates change rather than clings to old paradigms.
- utilizes systems rather than linear approaches.
- promotes collegial team relationships.
- views work as meaningful self-expression rather than monotonous repetition.
- focuses on an ideal future rather than the past or present.
- views people as collaborators rather than cogs in wheels.
- is oriented toward continuous improvement.
- is people- and idea- rather than bureaucracy-oriented.
- operates through leadership competence rather than management by objectives.
- recognizes and rewards competence rather than reinforce traditional rank and compensation systems.
- creates credibility through leadership rather than manage through position (rank) power.
- prevents or processes rather than attacks problems.
- fosters creative problem solving rather than conformity to rules.
- uses team decision making.
- stresses accountability to the team rather than the supervisor.
- is quality and customer service-oriented.
- promotes human development as well as high performance.
- distributes rewards based on contribution rather than position (Anderson, 2000).

Leadership organizations are created from the top down and the bottom up. Those in senior positions make a commitment to long-term leadership development (Whisenand & Ferguson, 2002). They learn to become better leaders and develop other leaders directly through their own mentoring as well as through organization-wide programs that promote leadership development for all individuals. Leadership development for all is vital to the long-term health of any organization. However, a large-scale and long-lasting transformation from a traditional organization to a leadership organization is not easy. The organization's members must realize that the transformation involves a commitment to successful completion of several identifiable steps. The organization and its members must:

- Shift paradigms from managing the status quo to leading teams toward a preferred future.
- Involve all members in the development and communication of an inspiring vision of a preferred future that will motivate individuals and performance teams.
- Assess the needs, wants, problems, and fears of the organization's internal and external customers.
- Use a systems approach to change management and set realistic, achievable goals that will help realize the preferred future.
- Plan and implement measurable objectives while removing obstacles to progress.
- Identify and train those who are willing and able to develop leadership competencies in all members of the organization.
- Assess outcomes of change initiatives, reporting results in a timely manner, so accomplishments can be celebrated and unexpected obstacles to progress removed or managed.
- Intentionally engage in continuous learning that promotes personal, professional, team, organization, family, and community development (Anderson, 2000).

Organizational Learning

Organizations face continuous and rapid change. It is no wonder that organizations also face the need for continuous learning. Leaders must do more than simply encourage members to learn. They must establish mechanisms for system-wide learning. To be successful, all members, units, and departments of the agency must be involved in the organizational learning process (Johnson, 2001).

Organizational learning is based on information. Information is generated as individuals in the group or agency interact with the external environment or experiment to create new information internally. The new information is integrated into the group or agency. As all available information related to an issue is collectively interpreted, action is taken based on the interpretation. The action generates feedback, and the feedback helps members generate new information. The process can assist members in the discovery of new problems, solutions, and opportunities (Ortmeier, 1999).

The basics of a learning organization cannot be installed without first creating leaders capable of developing other leaders who can execute the systems willingly and competently. Therefore, leadership must be developed before an organization can become a learning organization. Although a learning organization promises to deliver high quality, productivity, efficiency, and morale, few, if any, traditional organizations contain the leadership talent necessary for a successful transition from control to learning. Leadership skills form the foundation for individual success as personal and interpersonal development builds effective team members and leadership in others. As leaders build high performance teams, the teams build successful learning organizations that build healthy communities (Anderson, 2000).

Performance in Organizations

In the 1960s, Robert Townsend was employed as CEO of AVIS Rent-a-Car Company. AVIS had not earned a profit in its 13 years of existence. Three years after Townsend's arrival, AVIS posted a $9 million profit. Townsend's success was attributed to his management and leadership style. Townsend stated that most organizations are administered, not led, as individuals are treated as personnel, not people. Thus, people within an organization are treated as a means to an end. According to Townsend, leaders come in all shapes and sizes. Some are poor administrators and some are not very intelligent. However, the genuine ethical leader in an organization can be recognized because the leader's followers consistently perform well (Townsend, 1970).

In an effort to determine why performance is unsatisfactory, a leader should ask the following questions:

- Do members of the group (followers) know what the goals are?
- Do they (followers) know their performance is not satisfactory?
- Do they know how to achieve the goals?
- Do they know why goals should be achieved?
- Are there obstacles beyond the follower's control?
- Do followers believe the path to goal achievement will work?
- Do followers subscribe to a different path toward goal achievement?
- Do followers have different priorities than the leader?
- Are positive and negative consequences appropriately sanctioned?
- Are a follower's personal difficulties interfering with goal achievement? (Fournies, 2000).

High **performance in organizations** is usually found in leadership and learning organizations that focus on values, mission, vision and a community culture. In such environments, leaders understand that their key role is to provide conditions that enable group member productivity. High performance organizations can be identified when:

- Anyone in the group can articulate its mission and values.
- It is always looking into something new.
- Its customers' satisfaction level is high.
- A failure is considered a learning experience.
- Its members frequently work in teams.
- The leader is a partner to the staff members.
- Others study and write about it, and everyone wants to take credit for its accomplishments.
- It can give relevant information on its program results.
- It is a laboratory and its own best model.

Productivity and performance are high in a group whose leader helps to provide a clearly defined and articulated mission, focuses on the client, enables members with avenues for input on decision making, and fully involves members in managing their work (Ortmeier, 1999).

Creating and sustaining superior performance in a fast-paced, rapidly changing world presents a very real challenge. It is a challenge because staying on the cutting edge means dealing with constant instability. The alternative is maintaining the status quo, being lured too far into the future, or becoming trapped in too much bureaucracy. Consistent superior performance also depends on one's ability to keep up with change. High performance involves a dynamic equilibrium when the equilibrium point (balance) is constantly shifting. Finally, superior performance means staying ahead of the competition. Today's winners may be tomorrow's losers. Complacency may result in a loss rather than a gain (Brown & Eisenhardt, 1998). As competitors, career criminals with some level of sophistication are quick to identify new criminal schemes designed to penetrate weaknesses in law enforcement and justice system processes. Therefore, police officers and other system personnel must stay ahead of the competition.

IMPLEMENTATION

Some people argue that the ability to create a vision for improvement, as well as the skill to implement the vision, is much too sophisticated for police officers to understand or develop. This may be true in a traditional, military-style police organization. Often referred to as the professional model of policing, the traditional organization assumes that individual officers lack the ability to think and, therefore, must be told what to do and when to do it. However, when individuals are allowed to exercise and cultivate their intellect to create and implement solutions, great success may be celebrated. Granted, patrol officers may have little discretionary time in many agencies. However, the investment of additional resources in the short term can help to create efficiencies and solve problems so the problems will not reappear in the long term. To this end, if they are allowed to implement a vision into action, police officers may demonstrate the capacity to represent different interests simultaneously while completing multiple projects on schedule. As officers work with individuals and community groups to implement plans and evaluate progress toward meeting measurable objectives, all involved parties become stakeholders, thus unleashing the synergism that leads to success (Ortmeier, 1996).

Described as a response in the SARA problem-solving model presented in Chapter 8, **implementation** is the action phase of problem solving and program administration. The first step in the implementation of the action plan selected is to organize the operation as discussed previously. Many organizational structures in the latter half of the twentieth century became more collegial. As a result, middle management was reduced and subordinates and supervisors functioned more as colleagues. Whether based on traditional or more collegial principles, the organizational structure or framework of a group or agency will vary depending upon its size, location, budget, and methods of operation. Additional considerations for implementation of an action plan include the human resources required, the development of policy statements, use of contract vendor services, and operations. Further, the suggestions presented in this section can be applied in an employer-employee relationship or in a setting where volunteers are utilized.

Human Resource Management

Regardless of the type of organization, basic elements exist in the management of human resources. These elements are included in the process of determining how many people are required, what they will do, and how they will be employed, trained, led, and evaluated. Areas to consider when staffing any project or organization include the following.

Occupational (Job Task) Analysis

After the number and types of persons or employees required is determined, it is necessary to conduct an analysis of the tasks the person in each position is expected to perform. The analysis can be accomplished through direct observation or by comparing the position with similar positions in or outside the group or organization. The tasks may be identified by interviewing current group members, management, and other employers.

The **occupational (job task) analysis** identifies the job functions (duties) a person is expected to perform. After the duties are identified, desired behaviors are evaluated to determine future training needs. Finally, each behavior must be analyzed in terms of the actual performance of the behavior—in other words, how the person's behaviors will be measured.

Job Description

A **job description,** often referred to as a position description, is a written description of the principal duties of the position. It identifies the principal elements, scope of authority, and responsibilities involved in the position. Tabulating the results of the task analysis and reviewing the results with appropriate staff will assist in this process. The job description should be reviewed and revised annually.

Job Specifications

Closely aligned with the occupational analysis and job description are the **job specifications.** Whereas the job description describes the major duties of a position, the job specifications outline the specific skills, competencies, and personal qualifications that are necessary to perform the job adequately. The job description and job specifications may appear in the same document.

Recruitment

Recruiting candidates to fill a position vacancy can be accomplished in a variety of ways. Internally, it may be accomplished through promotion, transfer, or upgrading the position itself. Externally, recruiting may take place through a variety of sources, include media advertising, career fairs, civic groups, employment agencies, charitable organizations, the Internet, labor organizations, colleges and universities, former associates, and resumes or applications on file.

Instruments used as applications should be objective, uniform, consistent, and job-task related. Caution should be exercised in the development of application forms to ensure that information is not requested in violation of any state or federal statute. Items that might create an illegal or potentially illegal inquiry include address, age, birthplace, race, citizenship, religious affiliation, and arrest or conviction information. Public organizations, such as law enforcement agencies, may request information that would be illegal for a private organization to request or collect. For example, as a general rule, private organizations have access to conviction data but not arrest records because conviction records are public information.

Selection

The selection process begins with a preliminary screening of the applicants. This involves a review of each application packet to ensure that the candidate meets the qualifications and specifications for the position. The preliminary screening may also involve preemployment aptitude tests, physical ability tests, medical examinations, criminal history and credit checks, and a legally permissible polygraph examination. Selection personnel must exercise a great deal of care in the screening process. Although candidates for police positions cannot be expected to be morally superior to anyone else in the general population (Cohen & Feldberg, 1991), failure to exercise "due diligence" in the preemployment process may establish a liability connection between the candidate and the group, agency, or organization if the candidate is employed. The last phase of the selection process involves an interview and a background investigation (Lyman, 2002; Ortmeier, 1999; Whisenand & Ferguson, 2002).

Training

Personnel training falls into three broad categories: pre-service, in-service, and career enhancement. Some specialities require prescribed **pre-service training** prior to employment. For example, public safety employees, such as those found in police, fire, and corrections agencies, have specific detailed pre-service training requirements. **In-service training** may be formal or informal. It may involve apprenticeships, internships, or on-the-job training. **Career enhancement training and education** includes those types of training and educational experiences that focus on specific job-related training as well as those experiences that promote the personal and professional development of the individual. Substantial returns on the training investment may be realized if the group, agency, or organization focuses on individual personal and professional growth. Benefits in terms of increased productivity, improved morale, and loyalty to the group or organization are the positive by-products of an individualized training program.

Ethics instruction should be a part of any training program. Most people agree that ethics instruction is important in education and training environments, especially in justice education generally and practitioner training specifically. This is particularly important when training new police recruits. Creating an awareness of ethics early in a career helps to hold a seasoned officer accountable for unacceptable behavior later. However, a distinction should be made between teaching ethics *per se*, and providing an opportunity to learn about ethics and moral decision making. In other words, instilling a specific *ethos* into the minds of learners is one thing, raising the level of awareness about morality and ethical issues is quite another

(Jones & Carlson, 2001; Massachusetts Criminal Justice Training Council & the Regional Community Policing Institute for New England, 1997).

Instructors and supervisors are necessarily in positions of power (Jones & Carlson, 2001). Both have a certain amount of power over learner or subordinate performance appraisal. Since most police academy instruction and all supervised field training is provided by in-service police officers, senior to the recruits, trainees receive instruction from individuals who derive power from two sources: academic and supervisory. Thus, academy cadets can be easily influenced by the attitudes, beliefs, values, ethics, and behaviors of the academy instructors and field training officers who are senior to the cadets (Jones & Carlson, 2001). As a result, bad habits and bad attitudes can be passed on from one generation of police officers to the next (Ortmeier, 1995, 1996, 1997, 2002). The danger associated with the provincial thinking and beliefs of some officers and agencies is illustrated by the following.

In May 2001, one of the authors witnessed a recruitment presentation sponsored by one of the largest police departments in the United States. The presentation was conducted by two professional, articulate, and experienced officers. A prospective recruit from the audience asked if previous police academy training with a different agency could be used to fulfill any basic training requirements for the agency represented by the recruiters. One of the recruiters responded by stating that no previous training is considered adequate. The recruiter went on to state that the agency has always preferred recruits without previous training so they (the recruiting agency) could "grow their own" in the agency's image. The danger associated with "growing one's own" is that learning may be limited to the scope, knowledge, values, and ethics of the subculture of the agency. The police recruiters represented an agency that experienced tremendous upheaval during the early 1990s and was involved with the most costly riot in American history. The agency was also responsible for one of the largest corruption scandals in police history. The negative side effects of the scandal created a strained relationship between the agency and its community.

The instructor-learner dynamic is critical to ethics education and training because of the natural tendency for learners to view instructors and supervisors as experts. The challenge for those in positions of authority is to create a climate in which subordinates are secure from retaliation for expressing ideas about morality and ethics that may be inconsistent with the superior's. A problem exists when traditional learner-instructor and worker-supervisor relationships do not encourage open and honest exploration of ideas. Thus, learners and subordinates are intimidated and conditioned to respond in a prescribed manner (Jones & Carlson, 2001).

Despite the shortcomings of traditional instruction methodology, morality and ethics can be learned without indoctrination by an instructor or supervisor. Although intimidation may not be totally eliminated, learners can be encouraged to think critically and independently about morality and ethics. Instructors and supervisors must be made aware that the teaching and learning of morality and ethics requires an approach that is radically different from teaching and learning less abstract subjects such as officer survival and police patrol operations. Survival tactics and patrol procedures are based on years of experience and are not open to interpretation. Morality and ethics instruction, on the other hand, should not focus on the indoctrination of the learner. Rather, ethics instruction should equip the learner with the skills necessary to increase their capacity to think critically about ethical issues and moral judgments (Jones & Carlson, 2001). As the President's Crime Commission stated in 1967, the use of experienced police officers to train new recruits and provide in-service training is obvious and necessary. Experienced officers are thoroughly familiar with the nature of police work. Certain subjects, however, could more appropriately be taught by non-sworn civilians with expertise and talent in specific areas (President's Commission on Law Enforcement and Administration Justice, 1967).

Scheduling

Personnel should be scheduled according to a plan that is based on need and productivity requirements. Schedules are generally based on the assumption that individuals are willing to work at 100 percent capacity. However, people cannot be expected to work continuously at full speed. Therefore, adequate personnel must be assigned to a set of tasks to ensure that personnel productivity needs are met. Caution should be exercised to account for absences and to reduce the need for overtime. Nontraditional scheduling arrangements and the use of part-time, contract, reserve, or volunteer workers may be used as alternatives to full-time regular personnel.

Performance Appraisal

A **performance appraisal** involves the systematic assessment of how well people are performing. A performance appraisal should focus on performance, not the person, on strengths as well as weaknesses, and should be designed to enhance performance. The ideal appraisal or evaluation process includes, at a minimum, the supervisor's evaluation of the employee and a self-evaluation made by the employee. In addition, some formal appraisal processes include peer evaluations and evaluations of the workers by clients or consumers of the worker's services.

Many, if not most, evaluations of police performance typically focus on traditional productivity measurements such as increases or decreases in crime rates, number of arrests, or citations issued. Traditional measures alone, however, fail to recognize or value many other dimensions of police work. In a community-oriented policing environment, for example, many activities do not lend themselves to quantitative measurement. Officers may be involved with organizing community groups, planning, facilitating meetings, and problem solving. These activities tend to be process-oriented and many address quality of life issues. Thus, the scope of police performance measurement should be expanded to include process as well as productivity dimensions (Thurman, Zhao, & Giacomazzi, 2001).

Promotion

Promotion should serve as an incentive for people to perform better. Those with the best records for production, quality of work, and cooperation should be the ones promoted. Additional promotion criteria should address the individual's activities that assist with an improvement in the quality of life for the community.

Discipline

The purpose of disciplinary action is to improve performance and behavior rather than to punish or seek revenge. **Discipline** is related to the word disciple, which means "follower." Follower is derived from the Latin word *discere,* which means "to learn." Therefore, the disciplinary process should serve to educate the employee. Hopefully, systems designed to identify potentially problematic officers are in place. Intervention through appropriate counseling and training may prevent officer misbehavior (Walker, Alpert, & Kenney, 2001). If disciplinary action is warranted, it must be based on an objective standard. Questions to ask prior to any such action include the following:

- Were people forewarned concerning consequences?
- Was the task or rule reasonable?
- Did the agency verify the violation prior to disciplinary actions?
- Was the investigation thorough and fair?
- Was there substantial evidence of guilt?
- Were rules and penalties enforced uniformly?
- Was the disciplinary action appropriate to the situation?

Criticism leveled against disciplinary procedures often underscores a lack of clarity in the guidelines or that disciplinary actions are not applied in a uniform manner. A model disciplinary code is one that is clear, concise, yet specific, applied consistently, and provides the mechanism for progressive discipline. A system for progressive discipline includes a verbal warning, written warning, written reprimand, suspension, demotion, and dismissal (Halle, 1994; Peak, 1995; Thibault, Lynch, & McBride, 1998; Whisenand & Ferguson, 2002).

Equipment and Facilities

In most cases, personnel services will be the most expensive budget item. Unless volunteers are used, the cost of human resources may be as high as 80 percent in many operations. Equipment and facilities also represent high dollar cost items on the budget. Careful planning may avoid the pitfalls of overextension. A lease arrangement, for example, may be a viable alternative to purchase (Peak & Glensor, 2002).

Examples of equipment typically utilized in a public safety environment include such items as communications equipment and vehicles. The quality and expected life span of each item as compared to price should also be a consideration. Competitive bidding, references, as well as a requirement for performance and service contracts are essential ingredients to successful equipment and facilities acquisitions.

Policy and Procedure Statements

In essence, written policies and procedures provide uniform guidelines for handling various types of situations. Policy statements typically describe organizational rules and how anticipated situations should be handled. Procedures outline a series of steps to be followed consistently in a definite order.

Policy statements are many and varied. They may focus on a wide range of personnel issues, such as selection, discipline, promotion, and termination. They may address behavioral issues such as chemical abuse, sexual harassment, discrimination, and use of force. Most existing organizations already have numerous policy statements in place. However, these policies must be revised to accommodate new variables and additional policies may be required as new situations arise. Procedures outline specific operational protocol and describe detailed responses to incidents or events.

When planning or revising a policy or procedure, leaders must help define and select target populations, articulate the skills and training required, identify the responsible authority, provide direction on what is to be accomplished, and develop procedures for objective and goal achievement (Baker, 2000; Welsh & Harris, 1999). Is the target population an individual, organization, or community? With respect to skill development and training, what types of academic and occupational education must those impacted by the policy or procedure receive? Who is the authority responsible for ensuring policy or procedure implementation and evaluation? Who will develop guidelines for meeting objectives and goals? Many well-prepared policies and procedures fail due to lack of appropriate guidance and methodology for achievement of desirable outcomes.

Contract Services (Outsourcing)

Contract service organizations provide services, such as maintenance and preemployment screening services, for a contracted fee. If a contract service is appropriate for certain types of services, the following items should be included in the contract:

- Wage rate specifications—If a premium wage rate (a rate above the prevailing wage) is specified, the contractor should be audited to ensure payment of the premium rate.
- Insurance coverage specifications—The contractee should consult with an insurance expert to determine the type and amount of insurance to be required of the contractor. Many contractors are underinsured and underfinanced and they may not have the resources to withstand a lawsuit.
- Indemnity/hold harmless clause—The client of the contractor is held harmless in the event of a wrongful act by a contract employee.
- Preemployment screening (of contract employees)—Procedures should be specified in the contract.
- Audit rights—The client should reserve the right to audit to prevent unscrupulous activities on the part of the contractor.
- Performance standards and training—These should be included in the contract.
- Adjustment of compensation clause—This clause allows the client to reduce compensation to a contractor for failure to meet obligations spelled out in the contract.
- Letters of authorization—For the outside contractor to act on client agency's behalf, the letters should spell out the contractor's limits of authority.

Operations

The allocation and deployment of human, financial, and physical resources should always be based upon need. Too many agencies allocate resources without giving special attention to where the greatest return on investment may be derived. A careful survey and analysis of high risk areas and hazards, along with continuous monitoring and evaluation of results, will ensure that the group or organization receives the highest return on investment.

EVALUATION

Evaluation flows from the control function prescribed in the management process (Hellriegel, Jackson, & Slocum, 2002). **Evaluation** is used to monitor implementation and to assess outcomes, and forms the fourth element of the SARA problem-solving model discussed in Chapter 8.

Evaluation is not simply an after-the-fact assessment of the impact or outcomes of a plan's implementation. A plan must also be monitored as it is implemented. Several different types of data collection techniques are available for monitoring implementation of an action plan: observational data, service records (documents), service provider (staff) input, and target population (consumer) data.

Through observation, trained personnel participate in or observe the program or policy in operation. The main observational techniques include the narrative, data-guide, and structured-rating methods. Through the narrative method, the observer maintains a detailed chronological record of events. The narrative method is the least structured of the observational techniques but it can provide rich detail during implementation. Through the data-guide method, evaluators provide specific questions to the observers. Through the structured-rating scheme observational method, observers are asked to rate behaviors on a standardized scale. If observers want to rate behaviors of the suspect being arrested, for example, a rating scale of one to five, with one representing "nonresistant" to five representing "very resistant," could be used to evaluate suspect behavior.

Service record data include any type of documentation (handwritten, typed, or computerized) created and maintained by personnel in the course of employment. Service record data are inexpensive to collect and easy to obtain. However, service record data often do not present enough detail for a thorough evaluation. Service provider (staff) input is obtained from staff directly through structured interviews, surveys, or questionnaires. Although often subjective in nature, staff input can provide detailed, firsthand information. Target population (consumer) data are collected from those who receive agency or organization services. Citizen surveys are examples of target population data collection techniques (Welsh & Harris, 1999).

The evaluation of outcomes can be accomplished through impact assessments, continuous evaluations, or efficiency analyses. An impact assessment compares actual outcomes with desired outcomes (objectives). To be effective, the impact assessment's objectives must be measurable. Crime rates are measurable. Thus, a decrease in the crime rate for a community is a desirable outcome.

Continuous evaluation (an outcome-based information system) is used to collect and assess outcome information over time. Continuous evaluation provides an opportunity to adjust methodology to maximize outcome realization. Frequent assessment (testing) of a trainee's knowledge and skills acquisition, for example, provides opportunity for intervention and behavior modification.

Efficiency analyses include cost-benefit and cost-effectiveness analyses. A **cost-benefit analysis** seeks to determine if the outcome produced (benefit) is worth the cost of resources expended to achieve the outcome. A **cost-effectiveness analysis** compares different programs and policies intended to produce similar outcomes. Heavy expenditures to reduce crime may not result in significant crime reduction (benefit). The cost may not be supported by the benefit. Through cost-effectiveness analysis, the expensive program can be compared to a different crime reduction program. If the latter program sustains better results, it is more cost-effective. Incarceration of offenders may be compared to probation for similar offenses. Typically, incarceration is more expensive than probation. Comparing outcomes (rates of recidivism) between incarcerated offenders and probationers is a measure of the effectiveness of the resources (costs) associated with both programs (Welsh & Harris, 1999).

SUMMARY

Planning, organization, implementation, and evaluation skills are critical to officer effectiveness in a policing environment. Through planning, a mission and vision for a group or agency is created based on core values. Several types of plans may be required. However, every plan includes a needs or risk assessment, the development of alternative courses of action, and selection of the most appropriate action plan. Crime prevention through environmental design (CPTED) is an appropriate tool for community and facility crime prevention planning purposes.

Organization is a function, process, or institution designed to create a relationship structure that enables participants to implement plans and meet objectives and goals. Public as well as private organizations benefit from the elements of the organizing function: specialization, standardization, coordination, and authority. Organizational complexity depends on the existence of horizontal and vertical differentiation. Leadership and effective management are critical to the organization function. Successful operations result in leadership-centered organizations that focus on organizational learning and quality performance.

Implementation of an action plan may involve human resource management, the acquisition of equipment and facilities, the creation of policy and procedure statements, the use of contract services, and the allocation and deployment of resources. Continuous evaluation is necessary to monitor plan implementation progress as well as to evaluate outcomes.

KEY TERMS AND CONCEPTS

Define, describe, or explain the importance of each of the following:

action plan selection
alternative course of action
authority (as element of organizing function)
budget
career enhancement training and education
contingency plan
continuous evaluation
contract service
coordination (as element of organizing function)
cost-benefit analysis
cost-effectiveness analysis
crime prevention through environmental design (CPTED)
discipline
evaluation
implementation
in-service training
job description
job specification
leadership organization
needs assessment
occupational (job task) analysis
organization
organizational chart
organizational learning
organizational mission

organizational vision
performance appraisal
performance in organizations
planning
pre-service training
private organization
public organization
repeat-use plan
risk assessment
single-use plan
specialization (as element of organizing function)
standardization (as element of organizing function)
strategic plan
tactical plan

DISCUSSION QUESTIONS AND EXERCISES

1. List and describe the three common elements to the planning process.
2. What is the relationship between values and a group or organization's mission and vision?
3. Utilizing CPTED concepts, design a crime prevention and reduction program for a neighborhood.
4. Define organization and describe the major elements of the organizing function.
5. To what extent does the structure of an organization enhance or inhibit group or organizational efficiency and effectiveness?
6. Why do organizations fail? What is the relationship of leadership and organizational learning to high performance and success in organizations?
7. What must be considered when implementing an action plan?
8. When should evaluation of program, policy, or action plan implementation occur? Is there one best method for evaluation purposes?

CHAPTER 10

ETHICAL LEADERSHIP IN THE CONTEXT OF POLICING A COMMUNITY

LEARNING OBJECTIVES

After completing this chapter, the reader should be able to:

- define community policing.
- describe personal qualities and competencies necessary for a police officer in a community policing environment.
- analyze the context for community policing.
- discuss techniques for working with diverse populations.
- discuss the roles and responsibilities of the police and the community in the policing effort.
- describe the process for building police-community partnerships.
- create effective police-community partnerships.

INTRODUCTION

In early American colonial communities, policing tasks were carried out by citizens. To avoid control by a central government, American policing was meant to be shared with community members. In the nineteenth century, as a result of Robert Peel's reforms in Great Britain, law enforcement in the United States became more formalized and public police agencies were created in England, America, and elsewhere (Cronkhite, 1995). In the early twentieth century, public police agencies became concerned primarily with crime control. As a result, the public as well as law enforcement's perception of police work has been thought of in terms of the enforcement of criminal law

(Kleinig, 1996b; Germann, Day, & Gallati, 1988; Law Enforcement Assistance Administration, 1976; Lyman, 2002; Michelson, 1999; Nichols, 1998).

In the second half of the twentieth century, policing was based on a crime control model. To combat police corruption, this period was also characterized by an apolitical philosophy, centralized administration, pinpointed responsibility, and strong discipline (Wilson, 1963). Some police agencies also developed an organizational culture that emphasized crime control, insisting that aggressive enforcement, detection of major crimes, and rapid response to calls for police intervention represented the mission of the police (Independent Commission on the Los Angeles Police Department, 1991). Police organizational goals were based primarily on arrest statistics and clearance rates, both of which are inadequate measures of effective police performance (Skolnick, 1994).

Contemporary policing involves far more than the control of crime. It involves peacekeeping, order maintenance, and numerous related responsibilities that in many instances make policing different from most occupations in America today (Coffey, 1990). Yet, even under the best of circumstances, police agencies have several peculiar characteristics that make them especially difficult to administer. Police officers are deployed over large areas, not subject to direct supervision. As a result, individual officers exercise enormous authority, including the authority to deprive people of their liberty and, even more awesome, of their lives (Lyman, 2002). In addition, difficult and often unpredictable situations are inherent in policing. Many of the people with whom the police must deal are antisocial, frequently despicable, and sometimes violent (Goldstein, 1990).

Policing in the twenty-first century faces many challenges. Contemporary policing has become increasingly complex, yet the **traditional policing model** remains authoritarian and paramilitaristic. This model aspires to predictability in performance, assumes that police officers are incapable of making independent judgments, and establishes prescriptive training and highly supervised field relationships (Goldstein, 2001; Meese & Kurz, 1993). The dominant form of policing in many jurisdictions continues to view police officers as automatons. Despite an awareness that officers exercise broad discretion, they are held to account strictly for what they do and how they do it. In procedural matters, they are required to adhere to detailed regulations. In many large police agencies, rank-and-file police officers are often treated impersonally and kept in the dark regarding policy matters. Under these conditions, officers learn that rewards go to those who conform to expectations—that nonthinking compliance is valued. However, modern policing requires an approach that is more community- and problem-oriented. It must focus directly on the substance of policing—on the problems that constitute the business of the police and on how to handle them

(Goldstein, 1990, 2001). In light of the need to focus on a different policing strategy, considerable attention must be given to the type of individual who joins the police service and how that person is trained and educated. It requires individual qualities and competencies such as leadership, initiative, and imagination that have traditionally been associated with higher-ranking officers. The police officer in a twenty-first-century agency must possess many skills, including those of information processor, community organizer, crime analyst, counselor, street corner politician, arresting officer, school liaison, and community leader (Murphy, 1989). Thus, police agencies must deploy innovative, self-disciplined, and self-motivated officers directly into the community as outreach specialists and community problem solvers (Goldstein, 1990, 2001; Haberfeld, 2002; Kelling & Moore, 1991; Lyman, 2002; Meese, 1993; Meese & Kurz, 1993; Ortmeier, 1995, 1996, 1997, 2002; Trojanowicz & Carter, 1990; Whisenand & Ferguson, 2002).

The most important element for successful police-community partnerships is ethical police leadership. Lack of ethics and effective leadership skills results in unsuccessful policing efforts (Dantzker, 2002). In a contemporary policing environment, officers with ethical leadership skills:

- Embrace change.
- Think creatively.
- Demonstrate decisiveness.
- Promote trust.
- Delegate responsibility.
- Decentralize decision making.
- Take action.
- Communicate well.
- Share command.
- Articulate a vision.
- Demonstrate integrity.
- Demonstrate commitment (Stevens, 2002).

Major research regarding the nature of policing was first undertaken in the 1950s (Petersilia, 1989). Until then, both the public and the police made certain assumptions about how the police should operate (Boydstun, 1977; The Police Foundation, 1981). These assumptions were often taken as descriptive of police operations even though police practice differed sharply (Goldstein, 1990). In the early 1970s, the Kansas City Preventive Patrol Experiment questioned the effectiveness of preventive police patrol operations (Kelling, 1974). Later, studies of response time undermined the premise that rapid response was effective in making arrests (McEwen, 1984; Sparrow, Moore, & Kennedy, 1990). Further research indicated that officers and detectives, by themselves, are limited in their ability to successfully investigate crimes (Eck & Spelman, 1987; Goldstein, 2001;

Greenwood, 1979; Kelling & Bratton, 1993; Ortmeier, 1996; Peak & Glensor, 2002). The lessons drawn from these studies indicate that the police erred in investing a disproportionate amount of police resources in a limited number of practices (Hughes, 2000; Rand Corporation, 1999; Truth, DARE and consequences, 1998). Goldstein identified five reasons why existing police resources are insufficiently utilized:

- The police field is preoccupied with management and efficiency.
- The police devote most of their resources to responding to calls instead of acting on their own initiative to prevent or reduce community problems.
- The community itself, as a major resource with enormous potential for problem identification and resolution, is largely ignored.
- Rank-and-file officers' time and talent have not been used effectively.
- Efforts to improve policing have often failed because of the overall dynamics and complexity of the police organization (Goldstein, 1990, 2001).

Numerous experts agree that contemporary policing requires a philosophy and a strategy that is inconsistent with the traditional model of policing. These experts suggest that the philosophy and strategy that focuses on engagement and solutions to community-based problems can improve the image, efficiency, and effectiveness of the police service (Community Policing Consortium, 1994; Goldstein, 1990, 1993, 2001; Lyman, 2002; Peak & Glensor, 2002; Whisenand & Ferguson, 2002). Commonly referred to as community policing, this renewed policing philosophy and strategy requires the officer to possess a wide variety of technical, cognitive and affective skills. Essentially, the **community policing philosophy** reassesses who is responsible for public safety, redefines the roles and relationships between the community and the police, strengthens community-based efforts, and increases understanding and trust (California State Department of Justice. Office of the Attorney General, 1996). A **community policing strategy** involves a plan of action that promotes community engagement, participation, and problem solving (Ortmeier, 1996, 1997, 2002).

COMMUNITY POLICING DEFINED

In many ways, community policing is a concept in search of a definition. In its broadest context, **community policing** embodies the essence of policing, that is, a relationship between the public and the police (as representatives of the public) that promotes community welfare. Viewing citizens as customers (Thurman, Zhao, & Giacomazzi, 2001), community policing optimizes democracy in action. It is part of the network of people and organizations that constitute a focus on **community-oriented government,** a philosophy and strategy that mirrors community policing by promoting broad-based government-community partnerships (Kidd & Braziel, 1999).

Community policing may actually defy a specific definition. Community policing is both a philosophy and a culture based on shared police-community values. Thus, community policing is often difficult to describe in definitive terms. In a narrow sense, community policing is about partnerships and problem solving. Through personal and professional relationships, the philosophy and culture of community policing guide and empower police, citizens, public institutions, and private organizations as they collaborate to prevent crime and disorder, reduce fear of crime, and improve the quality of life for everyone.

Unilaterally, the police service has been unable to respond to the changes in a nation characterized by diverse social, cultural, economic, and political units (Earle, 1988; Thurman, 2002). This lack of responsiveness and the underlying problems associated with traditional police practices were addressed by several national commissions that studied and assessed the status of policing: the President's Commission on Law Enforcement and the Administration of Justice (1967), the National Advisory Commission on Civil Disorders (1968), the National Advisory Commission on the Causes and Prevention of Violence (1969), the President's Commission on Campus Unrest (1970), and the National Advisory Commission on Criminal Justice Standards and Goals (1973) (Goldstein, 1990). These and other studies revealed that the basic strategies of the traditional model of policing—motorized patrol, rapid response, and follow-up investigations—are, by themselves, limited in dealing with the substantive problems that face individual communities (Goldstein, 1993; 2001; Sheehan & Cordner, 1989). In addition, the bureaucratic and autocratic nature of most police organizations appears less likely to satisfy citizens as well as the organization's police officers (Couper & Lobitz, 1991; Lyman, 2002). As a result, there are several problematic realities facing police organizations in the twenty-first century:

- The police are having a very tough time dealing with crime by themselves.
- Effective crime control depends on an effective working partnership between the police and citizens in the communities they serve.
- The public police are losing market share in the safety and security business.
- The public police should be able to contribute to the quality of life in their communities in many ways other than by controlling crime.
- The administrative instruments now being used to ensure accountability and control of police officers cannot reliably do so.
- The police are routinely held accountable for the fairness and economy with which they use force, authority, and money.

- Rather than seek insulation from political interference, it is more appropriate for police agencies to make themselves more accountable to political institutions and citizens alike (Moore & Stephens, 1991).

In response to these problematic realities, a variety of police strategies have been developed (U.S. Department of Justice, 1994). Names associated with these strategies include:

- Citizen-Oriented Police Enforcement (COPE)
- Code Blue
- Community-Based Policing (CBP)
- Community-Oriented Policing (COP)
- Community-Oriented Policing and Problem Solving (COPPS)
- Community Patrol Officer Program (CPOP)
- Neighborhood-Oriented Policing (NOP)
- Police Area Representative Policing (PAR)
- Problem-Oriented Policing (POP)
- Quality Policing
- Target-Oriented Policing

Regardless of the label attached to these strategies, the primary focus is on community engagement and problem solving (Community Policing Consortium, 1994). The main themes included in this approach are increased effectiveness, reliance on the creativity and expertise of line officers, and closer involvement with the public (Spelman & Eck, 1987). The approach focuses on neighborhoods, problem solving, effective listening, and mobilization of community energies (A LEN interview with Police Chief Mark A. Kroeker of Portland, Ore., 2002).

In a traditional policing environment, emphasis is placed on limiting police discretion, reducing opportunities for corruption, separation of policing from politics, and improved performance through efficiency measurements. Often referred to as the professional model of policing, traditional policing methodology promotes distance between the police and the public, resulting in less emphasis on the social function of the police (Lyman, 2002). In a traditional policing environment, the police work *for* a community, reacting to incidents and calls for service (Whisenand & Ferguson, 2002).

In a community policing environment, emphasis is placed on decentralization, a recognition that crime control is only one function of the police, and on the development, through police-community engagement, of a more intimate relationship between the police and the public. In a community policing environment, officers work *with* a community, proactively assisting with the development of solutions to community problems (Whisenand & Ferguson, 2002). Although the professional model of traditional policing is still valued, it is supplemented with an understanding

Community policing involves community engagement, participation, and problem solving. *Photo courtesy of Portland, Oregon, Bureau of Police.*

that the police serve the community as well as enforce the law. Problem solving is a key ingredient in community policing (Gaines, Kaune, & Miller, 2000). Still, a major problem associated with the implementation of community policing is the realization that changes in policing are necessary (Goldstein, 1993, 2001). Both community engagement and problem solving call for behaviors that are different from those that police officers have traditionally been trained and educated to demonstrate (Meese & Kurz, 1993; Ortmeier, 1995, 1996, 1997, 2002). Additional training and education that focuses on ethical leadership skill development is necessary.

Community policing is about partnerships and problem solving. Partnerships help create allies in a mutual quest to prevent and control crime and disorder through problem solving. Partnerships are created with citizens and other community agencies. Sometimes partnerships extend beyond international borders. Officers from the Maine State Police (MSP) and the Royal Canadian Mounted Police (RCMP) joined forces to ride along with each other in areas of Canada and the United States contiguous to the Canada-Maine (U.S.) international border. The Maine Community Policing Institute's International Patrol Exchange has become a model program that many other agencies with distinct jurisdictional boundaries seek to replicate (March, 2001).

What Community Policing Is Not

Community policing, as a philosophy, strategy, and practical solution to community-based problems, has been the subject of a great deal of criticism and resistance (Manus, 2002; Mastrofski & Worden, 1991; Peak & Glensor, 2002), particularly from the law enforcement profession itself. Many line officers as well as police supervisors and command staff are part of the resistance movement. Each group appears to have its own reasons for not wholeheartedly adopting the community policing model. Some reasons are self-serving. Others represent sincere concerns regarding the erosion of effective police practices that took years to develop. Many agencies are cited as models, although these programs have struggled with the ebb and flow of chief executive support for community policing. Additional conflicts occasionally develop with mayors and city councils regarding budgets and concerns that too much police contact with the public infringes on the political process (Jones & Wiseman, 2001).

Community policing is not a detailed, coherent program whose elements can be checked off by any novice assuming a community policing stance (Skolnick, 1994). Those who believe that community policing is simple to achieve are doomed to fail. In some situations, excessive enthusiasm for community policing, coupled with impatience (Goldstein, 1993) and unrealistic expectations of what can be accomplished (Manus, 2002) through implementation of the model, has led agencies to abandon community policing efforts altogether. Much of the criticism is based on misconceptions about community policing. Thus, before describing what community policing is, it may be best to describe what community policing is not.

First, community policing is not radically different from what the public police mission was originally conceived to be. In 1829, Robert Peel envisioned and helped to implement a police service that worked closely with the community to identify and find solutions to community problems. This original strategy focused on crime prevention. Peel contended that the police are the public and the public is the police. He intimated that the police are only members of the public who are compensated in return for giving full-time attention to duties that are incumbent on every citizen to promote a community's welfare and existence (California State Department of Justice Office of the Attorney General, 1996, 1999).

Second, community policing is not so radically different from traditional policing that it requires a total reorganization of every police agency. Even the most traditional police agencies engage in community policing to some extent. If some restructuring is required, it would not be the first step in the implementation of community policing. In addition, traditional police skills are still required. The new skills required of a police officer in a community policing environment are designed to supplement, not replace, traditional police techniques and practices.

Third, community policing does not permanently increase a line officer's workload. A considerable amount of most officers' patrol time is uncommitted. Patrol officers in a community policing environment still respond to dispatched calls and engage in preventive patrol. However, by utilizing uncommitted time, police officers take the initiative to establish partnerships with the community. When, because of heavy workloads, police officers do not experience the luxury of uncommitted time, community policing can be practiced with each police-citizen contact. Community policing should not be limited to a few specialized units within a police agency either. This split force approach does increase nonspecialized officer workloads. All officers should be involved in the community policing effort. Eventually, the synergistic effect of a partnership with the community can reduce crime and disorder, thus reducing patrol officer workload.

Fourth, community policing does not distract officers from doing authentic police work and thus increase the likelihood of crime. Crime is multicausal. Crime rates increase or decrease for a variety of reasons. A decrease in the crime rate may be attributable, in part, to the presence of the police. However, police presence is not the sole determining factor. In fact, the crime rate has increased in some areas where the police practice traditional aggressive crime-fighting patrol techniques. In a community policing environment, patrol officers still enforce the law and cite and arrest violators. In fact, community policing, appropriately implemented, can be tougher on crime than traditional policing efforts. In community policing, the focus is not on what the police should do, but why and how they do it. The police are not street-level bureaucrats. Rather, they are street-level criminologists (California State Department of Justice Office of the Attorney General, 1996, 1999).

Fifth, community policing does not transform police officers into social workers. Even if it did, social work is important to the alleviation of pain and suffering. Social workers should be natural allies of the police, particularly when they possess and employ skills and services beyond the jurisdiction or capabilities of police agencies. The police mission is not limited to catching bad guys. The police have a much broader role in society. The mission also involves order maintenance and service (Watson, Stone, & DeLuca, 1998).

What Community Policing Is

By the middle of the twentieth century, the prevailing view in police management was the belief that police agencies should adopt an operational style that called on officers to be distant and unemotional. The belief was due, in part, to a commonly held belief that police officers would be less corruptible. To deal with rampant police corruption in the first half of the twentieth century, organizational rules, policies, and deployment practices limited police discretion and restricted officers' activities to prescribed assignments. Defining the resulting police behavior as professional and objective, this philosophy often led to perceived, and sometimes real, police insensitivity to the needs of the community. Contemporary wisdom, however, refutes this thinking. Accordingly, community policing is evolving as a way to use a sense of vision to meet the need for shared responsibility for public safety (Brann, 1999). To accommodate community needs, police agencies must change, both structurally and philosophically, and ethical leadership skills are required of police officers at all ranks (Anderson, 2000; Ortmeier, 1995, 1996, 1997, 2002).

Community policing requires not only a mere restructuring of some police organizations, but an orientation by the police toward an entirely different way of thinking and operating (Goldstein, 2001; Sparrow, 1988). It goes much further than placing officers in storefronts, on foot patrol, or riding on bicycles. It is a comprehensive philosophy, management style, and organizational strategy that involves all employees of the police agency and promotes proactive problem solving and police-community partnerships (Goldstein, 2001; Ortmeier, 1996, 2002; Parker, 1993; Peak & Glensor, 2002; Skolnick, 1994). It is different from traditional policing because it causes a revolution in the way police departments interact with the public as well as in the way police agencies are organized (Trojanowicz & Bucqueroux, 1990). And, although some view as ill-conceived the notion of allowing the community to be involved in the definition of the police role (Goodbody, 1995; Manus, 2002), many experts view community policing as a mandatory rather than optional policy strategy (Goldstein, 1993; Meese & Kurz, 1993; Thurman, Zhao, & Giacommazi, 2001).

Though some view it as a soft approach to law enforcement, concrete experience in numerous agencies demonstrate that community policing can achieve ambitious crime control objectives, even with existing resources (Kennedy, 1993). In addition, community policing is seen as a powerful tool to increase community support for, and the public image of, the police. Both are essential ingredients to effective policing (Coffey, 1990; Ortmeier, 1995, 1996, 1997, 2002). Community policing focuses directly on the substance of policing, the police role as peacekeepers. In a broad context, it is a comprehensive strategy for deploying resources that gives high priority to substantive problems and reshapes the police agency by influencing changes in personnel, organization, and procedures (Goldstein, 1990, 2001). In essence, the community problem, rather than a single incident, becomes the main unit of police work (San Diego Police Department, 1993). Performance measures are not based solely on arrests, response time, and clearance rates but also on citizen involvement, reduced fear of crime, improved quality of life, and solutions to chronic community problems (Trojanowicz, 1990).

The philosophy and strategy for community policing in no way suggests that police officers should become social workers. On the contrary, those who violate the criminal law must receive whatever is due them.

Criminal offenders should not be coddled. However, a vast majority of the people with whom the police come in contact are not criminals. Even in the most crime-infested blocks of a city, 90 percent of the residents are law-abiding citizens. The responsible citizen should not be treated the same as the criminal offender. The practical application of the community policing strategy means that responsible citizens and the police will work together to be tougher on crime.

Definitions of community policing are many, varied, and constantly evolving. Community policing means different things to different people. The simplest definition for community policing evolves from the Golden Rule: The police should police others as they would have themselves policed (Thurman, 2002). One state attorney general's office defines to it as a philosophy, management style, and organizational design that promotes proactive problem solving and police-community partnerships to address the causes of crime and fear as well as other community issues (California State Department of Justice Office of the Attorney General, 1996). After extensive research on the definitions and subject matter of community policing, one of the authors developed the following definition: a philosophy and a strategy that promotes community engagement, participation, and problem solving; action that leads to the discovery and implementation of solutions to community problems (Ortmeier, 1996, 1997, 2002).

In spite of numerous attempts to define community policing, an agreed-upon definition continues to elude authorities on the subject (Palmiotto, 2002). The concept of community policing may not require a definition. Rather, the elasticity associated with the concept of community policing may be the most appropriate as community-oriented policing efforts are customized to meet citizen-group needs. Thus, a specific uniform definition for community policing is not necessary.

Oversimplification of the concepts of community policing into a simple definition may, in itself, be problematic. Policing is very complex. Communities as well as the police should not expend an inordinate amount of energy attempting to create a perfect model (Goldstein, 1993). It is critical to remember that community policing should not be viewed as an outcome (end). Rather, community policing provides a means to more efficient and effective policing (Ford, Boles, Plamondon, & White, 2000).

Community policing is defined by what the police and citizens in a given community want it to mean. Community policing is what policing is all about. The bottom line is that the philosophy and strategy for community policing embody several principles that relate to different ways of thinking about, organizing, and managing police agencies. These principles were summarized very effectively by the Office of the Attorney General, California Department of Justice (1996).

- Community policing reassesses who is responsible for public safety and redefines the roles and relationships between the police and the community to require shared ownership, shared decision making, and shared accountability. The police and the community must collaborate to identify problems and develop proactive community-wide solutions. The police must acknowledge that they cannot do the job of public safety alone and recognize that they have valuable resources available to them in the community. Shared ownership does not mean that the community takes the law into its own hands. Nor does this approach diminish the role of the police who are in a unique position to facilitate problem solving.
- Community policing strengthens and empowers community-based efforts. A new view of community is emerging in society—a view that advances the importance of using an asset-based model. The model recognizes that communities are naturally resilient and have the ability to identify and solve some of their own problems.
- Community policing increases understanding and trust between police and community members. Inherent in any successful partnership is a sense of equality, mutual respect, and trust. Assigning officers to one beat for extended periods of time (beat integrity), and promoting ongoing daily, direct, and positive contact—including partnership efforts—between the police and the community, fosters understanding and trust. Establishing mutual trust between the police and the community results in less fear and fewer public complaints about use of excessive force by the police.
- Community policing shifts the focus of police work from responding to individual incidents to addressing problems identified by the community as well as the police, emphasizing the use of proactive problem-solving approaches to supplement traditional law enforcement methods. Shifting from an incident orientation to a problem orientation requires looking for underlying conditions, as well as patterns and relationships among incidents, that might identify common causal factors. These underlying problems, rather than individual incidents, become the main units of police work. Community-oriented policing is not soft on crime. On the contrary, with increased community support and communication, good arrests often increase.
- Community policing requires a sustained commitment from the police and the community to develop long-term, proactive programs and strategies that address the underlying conditions causing community problems.
- Community policing establishes new public expectations of, and measurement standards for, police effectiveness. The public and the

police must have realistic expectations of what the police can and cannot do to achieve community health and well-being. Community policing is not a panacea that will correct all social problems and resolve all crime and violence. The public must be aware of the reality of police limitations and the related importance of public involvement. Police efforts are reprioritized to focus on customer service and satisfaction. Qualitative as well as quantitative approaches are used to measure officer and agency effectiveness.

- Community policing requires the buy-in of top management of the police and other local government agencies as well as a new leadership style that makes most effective use of human resources within a community. It requires vision, strategic planning, teamwork, and problem solving.
- Community policing requires constant flexibility to respond to all emerging issues. By most estimates, only 25 percent of police work actually involves enforcing the law or arresting people. Traditional law enforcement equips the police with very few tools, other than the authority to arrest and incarcerate, to deal with the broad scope of police business. Prevention and intervention alternatives available to police need to be greatly expanded. The focus should be on developing creative, tailor-made responses to specific problems and incorporating such prevention and intervention efforts into the mainstream of policing.
- Community policing requires knowledge of available community resources and how to access and mobilize them as well as the ability to develop new resources within the community. Being resource-knowledgeable is a unique skill that enhances community policing efforts.
- Community policing decentralizes and de-specializes police services, operations, and management wherever possible. It relaxes the traditional chain of command and encourages innovation and creative problem solving by all. While specialization is necessary in some instances, such as the investigation of child abuse and gang activity, de-specialization can often free up personnel for community beats and improve officer communication, innovation, and ownership of beat areas.
- Community policing requires new recruitment, hiring, and promotion practices and policies. The community policing model requires new skills and duties for police officers. Community police officers must be able to assess situations, analyze problems, and evaluate strategies.
- Community policing requires a commitment to developing additional officer skills through training and education. Officers must possess a global perspective and receive personal satisfaction from helping oth-

ers. The new skills include essential problem solving, networking, mediation, facilitation, and conflict resolution abilities along with cultural competency and literacy and quality ethical leadership skills.

A community policing model is an appropriate vehicle to restore police and community relations. It places emphasis on service to the public and crime prevention as the primary roles of the police in a democratic society. Rather than placing primary emphasis on arrest statistics, community policing emphasizes community-based problem solving and active citizen involvement in those matters that are of importance to the community (Independent Commission on the Los Angeles Police Department, 1991).

CONTEXT FOR COMMUNITY POLICING

Community policing is a philosophy and a strategy that governs how citizens and police work together to identify, address, and solve crime and disorder problems within a community. As such, community policing consists of two core elements: **community participation** and **problem solving.** Both elements must be given equal consideration and emphasis. When priority is given only to the development of police-community partnerships, the result is a negligible impact on crime. When priority is given only to the problem solving half of the equation, police-community relations are strained. A community policing model is designed to supplement and complement, not necessarily replace, traditional policing models. However, change in philosophy and strategy is required because of changes in the level and nature of crime, the character and diversity in American communities, family structure, resources available to fight crime, and levels of public safety (California State Commission on Peace Officer Standards and Training, 1999; California State Department of Justice. Office of the Attorney General, 1999).

Role of the Community

The phrase community policing is derived from two words: the community and the police. In a community policing environment, the role of the community is a powerful one and community involvement is vital to success. In community policing, citizens assume two important roles. They are consumers of police services and they function as coproducers of policing itself. As community policing promotes greater **citizen-police cooperation,** it also presents an excellent opportunity to enhance police-community relations (Mastrofski, Parks, Reiss, & Worden, 1999; Ramsey, 2002).

The community must have equality with the police. The community needs the police and the police need the community. The community cannot be viewed as an advisory group or silent partner to the police. In fact, the essence of the police role is to reinforce and support informal crime and disorder control mechanisms of the community itself. Without committing enormous public safety resources, the police cannot be a substitute for community involvement and informal control (Kelling, 1999; Wilson & Kelling, 1982). Yet, despite the critical role of the community in the community policing effort, research and literature regarding community involvement is generally lacking. Most of the research available focuses on the role of the police officer.

One problem encountered when trying to determine the community's role involves defining what a **community** is. Communities are variously defined in terms of territory, like-mindedness, shared beliefs and feelings, cultural identity, lifestyle, and interaction on a continuous basis (Palmiotto, 2002). Communities include apartment complexes, neighborhoods, cities, counties, church and business groups, government agencies, schools and colleges, Internet chatrooms, and homeless shelters. They include gangs, crack houses, and organized crime families. Yes, communities are not always law abiding and police interaction with each community will obviously be different.

In addition, the composition and goals of individual communities are constantly shifting. As membership and environmental changes occur, problems that need to be addressed by the police also change. Thus, from a community-oriented policing perspective a community may be defined as any collection of people who share common concerns or attitudes toward crime and disorder problems. Law-abiding residents of a neighborhood where crack houses exist share one view of the situation. Drug addicts and dealers who frequent the crack houses have a different view. Police strategies with both groups must differ also (Oliver, 1998). The police can expect law-abiding citizens to support a crack house eradication effort. The illegal drug community will resist it.

Although police strategies among groups may differ, the police should not entertain preconceived notions regarding community desires. Some law enforcement personnel may not believe people living in impoverished areas care as much about crime as do citizens from affluent neighborhoods. The belief suggests that the street culture in poor neighborhoods finds crime, disorder, and drug use acceptable. However, there is no difference in attitudes toward violence among races, ethnic groups, and social classes. A study conducted in Chicago revealed that Blacks and Latinos are even less tolerant of deviance than are their White counterparts (Sampson & Bartusch, 1999).

Community policing fits well into suburban and rural areas as well as urban environments. Community initiatives often begin because citizens are dissatisfied with existing conditions and the criminal justice system is viewed as too formal and slow to respond to problems. In some cases, invocation of the system is not viewed as an appropriate and fair response. This appears to be especially true in many rural communities where carefully crafted alternatives to criminal sanctions are preferred. In truancy cases, for example, nonsystem alternatives, such as parental involvement and peer pressure, may be more effective than system-issued truancy citations.

Police personnel are in a unique leadership position in rural communities to engage and encourage citizens to participate in a broader inquiry into community needs and desires. These communities are built around shared values. The police can assist communities with the creation of opportunities and rewards based on these shared values. Law enforcement, interdiction, and negative sanctioning of law violations tend to ignore rewards for abiding by the rules. Especially in situations involving juveniles, the police and the community can collaborate to create opportunities and rewards for young people who demonstrate positive behavior.

Additionally, since many rural communities now exhibit a multicultural dimension due to an influx of minorities and non-native-born individuals, the police and the community can strive to honor differences while reinforcing shared community values. Participation from private as well as public organizations is often easier to muster in rural areas. As public servants serving the broader community, local police and sheriff's deputies can use their position of authority to seek assistance from state and federal agencies, private foundations, and professional associations. By adopting a problem-solving approach, law enforcement officers in rural areas can lead communities to enjoy safety and improvements in the quality of life (Dickey & McGarry, 2001).

To date, most feedback from the public regarding community policing efforts has been favorable. Recent research reveals that the public believes community policing is beneficial to their neighborhoods. One positive side effect is the improved relationship between the public and the police. Therefore, the police should promote increased involvement of the community in the policing effort. More attention must also be given to the education of the public and inclusion of citizens in the evaluation of community policing efforts. Responsible citizens are not apathetic, they simply may be unaware of what their role is. Generally, the public has been excluded from the dialog regarding police work for the last 50 years. And, although a great deal of research has focused on officer attitudes toward community policing, more studies should include a focus on citizen attitudes and knowledge of community policing. Such studies can assist policymakers in the development of an understanding of the role of the community in policing (Webb & Katz, 1997).

The concept of government agencies working in partnership with a community (community-oriented government) is not new to the United

A goal of community policing is an improved relationship between the public and the police. *Photo courtesy of Cobb County, Georgia, Police Department.*

States. Since the time of the Revolutionary War, citizen participation has been the foundation for a democratic form of government. However, as societies grow in terms of the number of citizens and economic conditions force government agencies to become more centralized, continuous participation by the populace in partnership with public officials becomes more sporadic. As a result, government agencies, including the police, become more isolated and removed from the citizens they are obligated to serve. In a community policing environment, the police must reverse the process of centralization. This process involves a return to a more democratized decision-making strategy. The role of the citizen and the community should shift from an advisory capacity to one of more authoritative action (Oliver, 1998).

Community members, groups, businesses, and institutions are responsible for voicing concerns regarding neighborhood crime and disorder, reporting crimes and other problems, providing information, helping to convict criminal offenders, employing crime prevention measures, and exercising parental authority over juveniles. Community constituents also assume responsibility for working with the police and solving some of the community problems on their own (Ortmeier, 2002).

Role of the Police

The second part of the community policing partnership equation involves the role of the police. In a community policing environment, police officers still respond to calls, write traffic citations, and make arrests. However, patrol officers use uncommitted time more efficiently and effectively. In a community policing environment, the police also participate in community groups and activities, establish and support crime prevention programs, and prioritize and help solve community problems (Parker, 1999). Community policing acknowledges the value of the patrol function as well as the individual police officer. The patrol officer is viewed as a responsible, versatile problem solver rather than a mere automaton who responds to supervisors' orders and dispatched calls for service. Supervisors operate as facilitators rather than ranking officers with unquestioned authority. As one senior police official stated, patrol officers must learn, and be encouraged, to supervise themselves because there will never be enough ranking supervisors (Baca, 2002).

Many police officers tend to be very skeptical, especially when anyone suggests changing policing philosophy or strategy. Most people and organizations, even police officers and their agencies, are resistant to change. Why should a police agency or its officers change radically from what they were originally trained to do? Will the change in philosophy and 180-degree shift in strategy benefit the agency and the individual officer? These are extremely important questions. They require practical as well as abstract answers although most in-service community policing training programs for line officers focus on the abstract.

Transformational change also requires creativity, innovation, and acceptance by the most senior officials in the police agency. Senior officials in the organization, especially chiefs, sheriffs, and commissioners can enhance partnerships with external groups, reengineer operating systems, restructure organizational hierarchy, align human resources to fit community policing efforts, and adopt perspectives that seek continuous improvement of police services (Ford, Boles, Plamondon, & White, 2000).

Benefits to the agency and the individual officers include the possibility as well as the probability of increased productivity and improvement in the police public image. Other benefits, especially from the standpoint of the individual line police officer, include more freedom in decision making, improved management support, better working conditions, and higher pay (Oliver, 1998). Yes, community policing may benefit officers in the form of higher pay. One major urban city converted its entire police operation to the philosophy and strategy of community policing. The change generated tremendous community support for the police. In fact, the citizens were so pleased one year that police officers were the only city employee group to receive a pay raise even though the municipality was experiencing serious financial difficulties.

One of the greatest benefits of community policing to a police officer's career, however, may be expressed in terms of the officer's satisfaction. Community policing can improve the quality of the responses police make to community problems. The improvement is a positive change. It responds to the critical need to treat line police officers as mature individuals, demonstrate more confidence and trust in them, give officers more responsibility, make officers stakeholders in the outcomes of their efforts, and give them a greater sense of fulfillment in a job well done (Goldstein, 1990).

Community policing is implemented in different ways. One size does not fit all. Problems and priorities vary from city to city, community to community. Although every bit as applicable in small towns and rural communities as it is in urban and suburban areas, community policing must fit the community it serves (Cordner & Scarborough, 1999). The point is that the police and the community being served work together to create solutions to community-based problems and improve the quality of life for all of a community's citizens (Community Policing Consortium, 1997a; Ortmeier, 2002; Parshall-McDonald & Greenberg, 2002; Ramsey, 2002).

WORKING WITH DIVERSITY

Demographic changes in the population cannot be overstated. Immigration to the United States and the growth in minority populations in general has dramatically changed the face of America. The United States accepts approximately 1 million new immigrants each year. Close to one-third of American children are Black, Hispanic, or Asian. In addition, one-half of all marriages end in divorce and over one-quarter of the nation's households are headed by women. The population is also aging. By 2010, 25 percent of Americans will be 55 or older. These groups form special interest constituencies. As the various groups are forced to compete for limited resources, the police may become involved when competition and intergroup rivalries develop (Lyman, 2002; Muraskin & Roberts, 2002; Peak, 1995; Peak & Glensor, 2002).

Individuals and groups in America also tend to share a common culture based on a national heritage of democratic principles and personal freedom. Although not a homogeneous population, Americans tend to adhere to basic societal customs and laws built on consensus. Thus, America is a melting pot as well as a complex mixture of diverse groups. This **diversity** affects police-community relations in numerous ways. Culture influences human behavior and the police cannot ignore cultural differences. There is strength in diversity. Understanding and appreciating individuals and groups within a cultural context can expand and strengthen police-community relationships and provide new opportunities for open communication, increased mutual respect, and common goal achievement.

People behave in culturally defined ways. Thus, interpersonal communications and interactions are understood in terms of the cultural context through which the interaction takes place. It is possible to have excellent communications skills, yet apply these skills in culturally inappropriate ways. It is possible to make decisions that are consistent with law and policy, yet commit acts that are inappropriate and inhumane. Misunderstanding can lead to misinterpretations of the intentions of others. Many new immigrants, for example, suffered great abuse at the hands of the police in their native countries. In America, these law-abiding people may distrust the police and flee at the sight of a police officer.

Everyone has biases and prejudices regarding others. These preconceptions are based on past experiences and beliefs acquired within one's own culture. However, to interact fairly and objectively with others in a diverse society, police officers must be sensitive to the cultural differences of others. It is important to remember that a society is comprised of one culture as well as many subcultures. Each member of a society shares common beliefs and goals with other members. Each member of a society is also a member of a subculture within the societal culture. An appreciation of the reality of diversity can assist police officers to creatively overcome communication and interaction barriers (Mayhall, Barker, & Hunter, 1995; Muraskin & Roberts, 2002; Palmiotto, 2002; Walker, Spohn, & DeLone, 2000).

BUILDING COMMUNITY PARTNERSHIPS

Community policing involves an outreach to the community, an outreach designed to promote partnerships with the community that reduce crime, enhance public safety, and improve the quality of life for the community's inhabitants (Baker, 2000; Skogan, Hartnett, DuBois, Comey, Kaiser, & Loving, 1999; Stevens, 2001, 2002). Unfortunately, many community policing initiatives are limited to changes within a police agency or on community-oriented programs that have little impact on the basic functions or structure of police activity in the community. The failure of these initiatives can lead some to believe that the concept of a **police-community partnership** is flawed because a community is not a single entity but a group of competing interests (Manus, 2002). Yet, partnering and collaboration with a community is of value to policing, as evidenced by successes of the past quarter century (Parshall-McDonald & Greenberg, 2002). Participants are cautioned to remember that notable success with community policing efforts can be achieved only when both the police and citizens change their attitudes and work collaboratively to identify and solve community problems (Baker, 2000, Dubois & Hartnett, 2002; Sampson, 2001; Scott, 2001).

Researchers often report resistence to change and mistrust on the part of the police as well as the citizenry. Police resistance can be traced to the police subculture, numerous organizational barriers, and recalcitrant personnel who simply wish to wait until change initiatives, such as community policing, pass. Likewise, citizens and community groups often resist change and lack enthusiasm without prior positive experiences that demonstrate that change is necessary and worthwhile. Despite some poll results to the contrary, many citizens also distrust the police. Police and citizen support for and participation in the community policing effort must go beyond motivation sessions and behavioral reinforcement. Implementing community policing requires substantial education and reeducation of the parties involved. Additionally, both sides must commit to a substantial amount of personal contact so trust and cooperation can develop (Dubois & Hartnett, 2002).

The police cannot solve all community problems on their own. Finding solutions to community-based problems requires community participation and power sharing. Police-community partnerships form a core component of community policing (Whisenand & Ferguson, 2002). Typically, however, residents and business people within a community are not aware of all the resources at their disposal. If citizens were aware of such resources, there might be far fewer inappropriate calls for police services. In a traditional policing environment, the police try to reduce crime and disorder without soliciting a great deal of community assistance. However, various agencies and organizations within a community can be very useful resources. Government, not-for-profit, nonprofit as well as for-profit organizations, and health, education, welfare, housing, public works, and social services agencies can be very helpful (Palacios, Cromwell, & Dunham, 2002). The police can also mobilize citizens to form neighborhood crime prevention groups.

Communities differ in the types and number of organizations within them (Muraskin & Roberts, 2002; Walker, Spohn, & DeLone, 2000). Impoverished areas tend to have less community involvement than more affluent areas. Regardless of the type of community, citizens must realize that the police cannot resolve problems associated with crime and disorder alone. Residents and business persons must organize and mobilize for the problem-solving effort. For most order maintenance and restoration issues, resources exist, if not in the immediate vicinity, then at the city, county, state, or federal levels. Although the police are not social workers, the police should know how to contact and solicit the support of social services agencies and resources when necessary.

Without question, community participation is essential to any community policing effort. Unfortunately, there is no known magic formula for securing, and sustaining, participation by a community. Developing community involvement can be just as difficult as involving police officers. To secure and maintain a community's participation, the citizens of a community must be:

- Convinced that participation will improve community conditions.
- Organized, not randomly selected.

- Trained and guided through the community policing effort.
- Aware of the risk of inequitable outcomes. Those who really need community policing may be the most difficult to convince. Many residents of poor and disenfranchised neighborhoods may have been disappointed in the past. Those who generally support the police may also be skeptical. Reports of police abuse, misconduct, and corruption, true or not, can result in citizen mistrust of the police (DuBois & Hartnett, 2002).

In many areas where community policing strategies can have the most significant impact, the community and the police often have a history of antagonistic behavior. In these areas, the police may be viewed as arrogant and uncaring, as the enemy rather than partners. On the community side of the equation, citizens may not demonstrate support for the police or have a history of not cooperating with police officers. Additionally, these areas often lack the organizational infrastructure conducive to community involvement. In high crime neighborhoods, citizens may distrust and be hostile toward each other as well as the police. They may also fear retaliation from neighborhood drug dealers and gangs. In economically and ethically diverse communities, suspicion may divide citizens along class and racial lines, creating inevitable cohesiveness problems and pressure the police to choose between competing community factions (DuBois & Hartnett, 2002; Lyman, 2002; Walker, Spohn, & DeLone, 2000).

The challenges involved in securing and maintaining community participation are significant but not insurmountable. Ethical police leadership at the line officer level can help to achieve positive results even against what appears to be insurmountable odds. Competent rank-and-file police personnel, skilled in the art of leadership and supported by agency command staff, can assist a community with an articulation of a vision for an improved quality of life and lead citizens in a communal effort to identify and solve community problems. In summary, the police can solicit and encourage community participation by:

- Creating meaningful roles for the community and training citizens on these roles.
- Customizing community policing program efforts to meet the needs of various community constituency groups.
- Promoting active community involvement rather than simple awareness.
- Focusing recruitment efforts toward existing community organizations.
- Ensuring that community meetings are worthwhile (DuBois & Hartnett, 2002).

Community engagement and **mobilization** starts with the identification of leaders within that community. Leaders include those affiliated with educational, religious, and business organizations, public officials, and office holders. Some leaders can emerge from unexpected sources. Informal and volunteer organizations typically do not appear at the forefront of a community. If the community is experiencing a problem with gang-related activity, gang leadership must also be identified. The police must create an environment in which the leadership mass within the community can work together toward a shared vision. These leaders may not, and probably will not, reach agreement on all major issues. However, they can arrive at consensus on many issues and resolve many problems facing the community.

Leaders and other interested parties within a community can be brought together at a community meeting. The community meeting should not be viewed as simply a police public relations effort. Rather, a meeting presents opportunities to learn about citizen and community concerns and develop strategies for problem analysis and problem solving. Leadership skills for the police officer are critically important in this effort.

The police should consider several key points when attempting to mobilize a community and build partnerships. The police can facilitate community mobilization and help to create community organization where none exists. Alternatively, the police can limit their role when existing community organizations are accomplishing agreed-upon goals. When a crime prevention program must be established, the police can work with others in the early stages and later function as a resource to support program participants. The best leaders are those who can mobilize and influence others to identify and solve problems on their own. Line officer ethics and leadership competence are essential in this area. The most effective community organizations tend to be those that are independent of the police. Many community organizations also appear more credible if they are not seen as adjuncts to government agencies. However, communication between the police, public agencies, and community leaders must be developed and maintained. Thus, the community, in collaboration with the police and other community organizations, will create an organization that addresses undesirable conditions (Community Policing Consortium, 1997a).

The most effective police-community partnerships are initiated by three factors: a crisis that mobilizes people to action, adequate funding, and the dynamic personalities of the members. To be sustainable, a community partnership must share a common vision, develop good relationships, have adequate resources and internal operating procedures, possess leadership and commitment, generate community support, be accountable for its actions, and adaptable to change (Phillips & Pack, 1999).

Community partnerships must also be advertised and marketed. It is important to deliver the message of good works. Several communication channels may be utilized for this purpose. Mass media include radio, television, newspapers, cable systems, and the Internet. Other communication media include flyers, brochures, letters, and newsletters. Direct communication involves town meetings and speakers' bureaus. Special events make excellent forums for public speaking engagements. Public ceremonies may provide a venue to honor people for their personal commitment to the betterment of the community.

Communication channels present opportunities to develop creative tactical and strategic alliances. Partnerships must go beyond those who are within the community and the criminal justice system. These alliances may originate from nontraditional sources. The police and community members might partner with like-minded groups and individuals who share common concerns. Partnerships may also be developed with non-like-minded groups such as synagogues or churches that may sponsor seminars on crime prevention. In some cases, alliances can be established with those who appear to be at odds with the community policing mission. If the community is experiencing a high number of incidents involving gun violence, it might appear that gun store owners would not be interested in an alliance. However, gun store owners can be encouraged to sponsor gun safety seminars and work with the community organization to prevent gun theft and violence (Campbell, 1999).

COMMUNITY PARTNERSHIPS IN ACTION

Examples of effective community partnerships in community policing environments are numerous. In several communities throughout the country, Drug Abuse Resistance Education (DARE) has been introduced through collaborative efforts on the part of the police and local school districts. Officers leave patrol duties to enter schools and educate young people about the dangers of drug use. Although DARE has its critics, it demonstrates how creative partnership initiatives can be developed to meet the growing citizen demands for change, resource accountability, and improvement in the quality of life (Carter, 1995; Truth, DARE, and consequences, 1998). Other partnership initiatives include the following cited by the President's Crime Prevention Council (1997):

- Allegheny County, Pennsylvania: Juvenile Crime Prevention throughout the county. As a response to an increase in violent juvenile crime,

Allegheny County, which includes the city of Pittsburgh, launched a county-wide antiviolence campaign. The campaign's first step was to form two groups. The Law Enforcement Agency Directors and the Youth Crime Prevention Council were created to develop a strategy to focus resources toward youth violence. The coalitions, through coordinated efforts, reduced juvenile violence through community-driven prevention efforts.

- Columbia, South Carolina: Community Coordination. Columbia, South Carolina, has been involved in a multiagency crime prevention initiative since the mid-1990s. Columbia, through a massive planning and assessment effort, identified the causes of violence and criminal activity in the community and is now engaged in coordinating community services to achieve goals identified in the plan.
- Flint, Michigan: Funding Neighborhood Activities. In Flint, Michigan, crime prevention begins at the neighborhood level. Small neighborhood groups develop tailor-made strategies for protecting the city block by block. The Neighborhood Violence Prevention Collaborative coordinated the efforts of existing agencies and assessed the causes of violence within the community.
- Fort Peck Indian Reservation, Montana. The tribes on the Fort Peck Indian Reservation experienced a homicide rate 13 times higher than that of the state of Montana. Unemployment, poverty, and multi-jurisdictional issues aggravated the problem. Tribal Strategies Against Violence was developed by a reservation planning board to reduce crime, violence, and substance abuse. The program is bringing people and resources together for the first time.
- Jacksonville, Florida. The State Attorney General's Office implemented a comprehensive plan to combat juvenile crime by balancing early detection, prevention, and intervention programs with aggressive violent offender prosecution. Over a four-year period, the number of murders committed by juveniles dropped 72 percent in Jacksonville.
- Portland, Oregon. In 1989, Oregon developed a state-wide plan to improve the quality of life for citizens of the state. After a series of gang-related murders, the Portland Bureau of Police developed a task force that included community organizations that provided gang prevention services or would benefit from reduced gang activity.
- Salinas, California. Between 1984 and 1994, murders committed by juveniles increased by 200 percent. Fifteen hundred documented gang members in over 20 gangs dominated this farming community. The Salinas Police Department began its Youth Firearms Violence Initiative in 1995, funded through a grant from the U.S. Department of Justice's

Office of Community-Oriented Policing Services. The $1 million grant funded a Violence Suppression Unit. The mission of the unit was to remove firearms from young people and gang members. The program had a positive impact and reduced youth gun violence.

- San Antonio, Texas. The San Antonio Crime Prevention Commission represents education, religious, business, police, media, and local government organizations. The group has been charged with the responsibility for creating and implementing a comprehensive crime prevention plan for the city. Based on the commission's recommendations, San Antonio passed several ordinances that focus on gang and crime suppression. Even the clergy became involved by presenting over 800 sermons in one week that supported the need for everyone to get involved in the crime prevention and suppression effort. The San Antonio program consolidates and coordinates resources and, since full implementation in 1992, overall crime within the targeted areas has decreased over 30 percent.

Community participation and problem-solving efforts are much more comprehensive and extensive in some jurisdictions than in others. The extent to which community policing is incorporated into the fabric of a community and its policing agency depends on local circumstances and philosophical orientation. In cities such as Chicago, Houston, St. Petersburg, San Diego, Seattle, and Madison the philosophy, strategy, and problem-solving efforts permeate the community to a greater extent than in many other cities (Wycoff & Oettmeier, 1994; Wycoff & Skogan, 1994).

In Chicago, for example, new police recruits spend a great deal of time developing problem-solving skills and the entire patrol division is involved in the Chicago Alternative Policing Strategy (CAPS). Residents take an active role in solving problems and are encouraged to meet with the police regularly. The CAPS program also includes other municipal services such as the Department of Streets and Sanitation. Major changes have occurred in the way citizens view their city. Abandoned vehicle and trash complaints as well as drug and gang violence problems, once major issues with residents, have declined sharply (Harnett & Skogan, 1999).

The San Diego Police Department has been involved with community policing and problem-solving strategies for a number of years. San Diego's Neighborhood Policing Program began in 1973 when the San Diego Police Foundation sponsored a Community Profile Development Project. The goal of the project was to improve patrol practices by encouraging officers to systematically analyze their patrol districts to identify and solve local problems. However, the early model lacked support. In 1988, the United States Bureau of Justice Administration selected San Diego as one of five cities for a pilot project to use community-oriented policing to address neighborhood drug problems. In 1993, San Diego implemented the Neighborhood Policing Restructuring Project. Its purpose was to realign the department to expand and strengthen the department's community policing throughout the city.

The San Diego community policing program has several components through which police officers, community groups, and the public as well as private agencies create meaningful partnerships. The components include citizen volunteer groups, nuisance and drug abatement teams, a revitalized Neighborhood Watch Program, safe streets initiatives, juvenile and domestic violence units, crime prevention through environmental design (CPTED) strategies, homeless outreach, police satellite facilities, and an analytical approach to reducing crime (California State Department of Justice Office of the Attorney General, 1999).

San Diego's comprehensive community policing and problem-solving program has generated positive results. Overall crime declined almost 50 percent during the 1990s. Citizen surveys also give the San Diego Police Department high marks. In a survey conducted in 1999, nearly 70 percent of the community respondents rated the police department's performance as good to excellent. Only six percent indicated the police were performing poorly (Nguyen, 1999).

The community policing initiatives cited in this section in no way represent all of the major community policing and problem-solving efforts throughout the United States or elsewhere. On the contrary, commendable and progressive community policing practices are located in numerous large and small communities. Notable examples of the success of community policing are located in Nashua, New Hampshire; Charleston, South Carolina; and San Jose, California (Thurman, Zhao, & Giacomazzi, 2001). Other examples of notable programs can be found in Austin, Texas; Fort Lauderdale, Florida; St. Louis, Missouri; Fresno, Hayward, and Arroyo Grande, California; Lincoln, Nebraska; Eugene and Gresham, Oregon; Grand Rapids, Michigan; Reno, Nevada; Savannah, Georgia; Spokane, Washington; Tempe, Arizona; Elmhurst, Illinois; Arlington County and Abington, Virginia; and numerous state and federal jurisdictions (Peak & Glensor, 2002).

Community policing must progress beyond mere lip service. It must include positive relationships, community participation, pooled resources, and shared responsibility. It must include problem solving as a process for carefully identifying crime and disorder problems and priorities, collecting and analyzing information, developing solutions (responses), and evaluating responses to determine their effectiveness. Community policing and the problem-solving process can help to promote meaningful community contact, sincere communication, trust, and the exchange of relevant information critical to community-oriented government (Ortmeier, 2002).

SUMMARY

Policing in the twenty-first century faces many challenges. Although contemporary law enforcement has become increasingly complex, the model for policing remains authoritarian and paramilitaristic. A different approach that complements, and in some cases replaces, the traditional police model, is referred to as community policing. Although difficult and probably impossible to define in specific terms, community policing is a philosophy and a strategy that promotes community engagement, participation, and problem solving. It involves action that leads to the discovery and implementation of solutions to community-based problems. Community policing is what policing is.

A community policing environment requires the introduction of new and different police officer competencies and skills. Within the framework of community policing, the community plays a major role in efforts to reduce crime and disorder. The police must learn to work with diverse populations and build partnerships with communities. To accomplish their mission, police officers must possess and practice ethical leadership competence.

KEY TERMS AND CONCEPTS

Define, describe, or explain the importance of each of the following:

citizen-police cooperation
community
community engagement
community mobilization
community-oriented government
community participation
community policing
community policing philosophy
community policing strategy
demographic change
diversity
police-community partnership
problem solving
traditional policing model

Discussion Questions and Exercises

1. Create a definition for community policing. Include the core elements of community policing in the definition.
2. Do the qualities and competencies or skills required of a police officer differ between traditional and community policing environments? Why, or why not?
3. Discuss the framework for community policing, describing the role of the police as well as the community.
4. Describe techniques for engaging diverse groups and the procedure for building police-community partnerships.
5. Conceptually, what is the philosophy of community policing?
6. Does community policing compete with or complement traditional policing? Is a community policing strategy designed to replace traditional policing efforts?

CHAPTER 11

THE VISION FOR CHANGE

LEARNING OBJECTIVES

After completing this chapter, the reader should be able to:

- identify and discuss critical issues in contemporary policing.
- describe technical, social, economic, political, and legal trends that challenge the police.
- evaluate the effectiveness of community policing.
- identify and analyze obstacles to full implementation of community policing.
- create a vision for policing in the twenty-first century.
- present a rationale for ethical leadership competence for all police officers.

INTRODUCTION

The police face challenging trends, problems, issues, and changes. As the twenty-first century progresses, policing will become more demanding and delicate as new law enforcement-related problems and issues emerge and community demand for protective services increases. Police officers in the twenty-first century are expected to be more responsive to community needs, maintain a high standard of ethics, provide better leadership, and be accountable for their performance (Meadows, 2002).

Tremendous leaps in technology will continue to transform societies around the world in the twenty-first century. The new nature of crimes, crime scenes, and criminals will also impact policing and the criminal justice system in a critical way (Balint, 2000; Boni & Kovacich, 2000; China's piracy plague, 2000; Coleman, 1994; Global crime cartels are tech-savvy, 2000). Preference for punishment of criminals will be balanced with treatment of offenders as societies seek to reduce recidivism as a tool for crime prevention. As technological, social, economic, political, and legal advances precipitate and respond to rapid changes in the information age, the police and other elements of the criminal justice system must change as they anticipate a future that is actually occurring today. Computer-based and artificial intelligence systems along with other technologies will greatly enhance criminal justice agency abilities to: investigate crime; identify, trace, locate, and apprehend criminal suspects; monitor and treat convicted offenders; and analyze information in a quest to prevent offenses in the future. The enhancements pose potential dangers as well, particularly as technological ability encroaches on civil liberties and rights to privacy. Sophisticated programs and people are necessary to plan, implement, and evaluate police and other public safety agency projects. Policies and practices must preserve and reinforce democracy and justice based on the rule of law and respect for human rights (Muraskin & Roberts, 2002). Truly, police practitioners and other justice system personnel of the twenty-first century must possess and sustain a firm ethical foundation and demonstrate the leadership ability necessary to promote and maintain fairness and democratic ideals.

Twenty-First Century Issues in Policing

Several critical issues and problems confront the modern police officer. Obviously, crime continues as a major issue despite statistical crime reduction trends in recent decades (Dorning, 2000; Foote, 1997; Maguire & Pastore, 1998; U.S. Department of Justice, Federal Bureau of Investigation, 1997). For years, researchers have struggled to discover what police tactics have the greatest impact on crime (Sherman & Berk, 1984). There are indications that crime rates will rise again in the future (Arner, 2000; *Is LA's crime honeymoon over?*, 2000; Karmen, 2001; Maltz, 1999; Sickmund, Snyder, & Poe-Yamagata, 1997; U.S. Department of Justice, Federal Bureau of Investigation, 2001). Some issues and problems have causes beyond the control of the police, while others result from police conduct itself. Regardless of the source, each issue can be appropriately addressed, if not resolved, through the exercise of ethical behavior and effective leadership by police officers. What follows is a discussion of a few of these issues. Although the list of issues presented are by no means exhaustive, it provides a glimpse into some of the issues the police must face.

The Dynamics of Police Work

The **dynamics of police work** are reflected in the police subculture and the police working environment. Police officers often become cynical because of the conditions that surround their daily work (Kleinig, 1996b). Policing is an occupation characterized by authority, danger, and the pressure to produce (Skolnick, 1994). Officers see the worst of people and people at their worst. As a result, officers develop a subculture that is used as a mechanism for self-protection (Jones & Carlson, 2001; Lyman, 2002; Skolnick, 1994; Whisenand & Ferguson, 2002). As time progresses, officers often become alienated and isolated from most others in the community. They may begin to feel surrounded by adversaries: criminals, the courts, lawyers who appear to protect defendants, and citizens who complain about the police. As the stress associated with the job affects an officer's personal life, relationship problems with family and friends may develop. These problems cause additional stress, which is evidenced by a police divorce rate that is higher than the national average (Albanese, 2000; Cole & Smith, 2001; Inciardi, 2000).

The relationship between one's occupational environment and the way one interprets events creates a set of emotional and behavioral characteristics that can be defined as a "working personality" (Skolnick, 1994). The police subculture often produces a police **working personality** (Cole & Smith, 2001; Lyman, 2002). This can lead to the police enforcing the law according to its letter rather than its spirit. The authorization to use force becomes personalized and a disrespectful or unruly suspect is seen by the officer as an affront to the officer's authority. As a result, abuse of authority and use of excessive force become strong possibilities (Barlow, 2000; Wilson, 1968).

Civil Liability

A major concern of the police and law enforcement administrators is the **civil liability** connection among the agencies, individual officers, and civilian complainants (Bill Blackwood Law Enforcement Management Institute of Texas, 2000; Kappeler, 2001; Lyman 2002; Ross, 2003). Litigation arising from several types of situations and incidents have been costly, not only in terms of dollars, but also in terms of the public image of the police. Civil liability typically arises from complaints or situations involving use of excessive force, deaths and injuries resulting from pursuit driving incidents, sexual harassment, and discriminatory practices (Greenhouse, 1998; SWAT team may prove costly for small farm town, 1999; Thorton, 1999, February 27; Thornton, 1999, November 5; $12.5 million awarded in police-raid shooting death, 1999). Over a period of two years ending in July 1998, one major city in the United States paid $19 million to settle lawsuits against the police. Additional millions were paid out as compensatory and punitive damages awarded by juries (Krasnowski, 1998).

Part of the solution to the civil liability problem might be found in the educational level of people recruited for the police service (Baro & Burlingame, 1999; Lyman, 2002; Meese, 1993). One study indicated that highly educated officers perform in a more satisfactory manner (Roberg, 1978). In addition, police departments with high personnel education levels have fewer lawsuits filed against them and their officers (Vodicka, 1994). Reducing liability payments could result in millions of dollars available to attract better recruits into the police service and to increase police officer salaries. Ultimately, severe financial losses to police agencies, as well as individual officers, resulting from civil liability may help those in the police service realize that appropriate behavior is less expensive and more gratifying (Klockars, 1991).

Officer Safety and Survival

The physical dangers of police work are an ever-present part of the job and adds to the stress discussed above. Between 1986 and 1996, the average number of police officers killed in the line of duty each year was 166. This number decreased dramatically during the middle 1990s to the lowest level since 1960, a decline that paralleled the major decrease in crime in many large cities of the United States during that period. There were 117 federal, state, and local law enforcement officers killed in the line of duty in 1996, a 30 percent drop from the 162 officers who were killed in 1995, according to the Washington, D.C.-based National Law Enforcement Officers Memorial Fund. The last time the number was as low as 117 was in 1960, before the dramatic increase in violence that signaled the beginning of America's modern crime wave. Seventy law enforcement officers were slain on duty in 1997 and 61 were killed in 1998 (*'98 police fatalities,* 2000; Number of slain cops hits all-time low, 2000). However, officer deaths in the line of duty increased to 134 in 1999 and to 151 in 2000 (Ho, 2000). Of the 151 officer deaths in 2000, 51 were shot, 47 died in automobile collisions, 20 were struck by automobiles while outside their own vehicle, eight died in motorcycle accidents, seven were killed in aircraft accidents, six died from job-related illnesses, and 11 died from other causes (National Police Week, 2001). As 2001 came to a close, the number of job-related sworn police officer deaths increased over the year 2000, largely due to the 65 officers who died as the result of the terrorist attacks on September 11, 2001 *(Police deaths up sharply in just first half of year, 2001).*

In the law enforcement field as a whole, a field that includes corrections and security personnel, practitioners are victims of assault at a rate higher than any other occupational field *(A dangerous place to work, 2002).*

Officer safety and survival is dependent upon several factors. Critical to officer safety and survival is the need to seek out advanced technologies, procedures, and training to prevent officer injuries and deaths. Additionally, police officers should develop and practice the types of communication skills that can assist with conflict de-escalation (Lyman, 2002).

Police officers also die at an early age, and at an alarming rate, from suicide. Failure to seek help or deal appropriately with personal and professional stressors, coupled with self-imposed isolationism, contribute to self-inflicted premature death of police officers (By their own hands, 1999).

Limited Resources

Police agencies operate with **limited resources** (Goldstein, 2001). Competition for tax dollars, governmental and political priorities, and the increasing cost of public police personnel and equipment limit police resources and restrict the ability of most police departments to keep pace with the demand for law enforcement services. This is illustrated by the fluctuation in budget resources and manpower allocations. Budgetary considerations often cause hiring freezes and agencies fail to replace officers who retire or leave the department for higher-salaried positions. When the lack of police personnel results in crime increases or public dissatisfaction, departments are suddenly forced to hire more officers in a short time, which often has serious consequences in terms of both personnel quality and fiscal impact. In the 1990s, the Los Angeles Police Department placed the training costs of a new recruit at over $100,000 (Champion & Rush, 1997).

In the aftermath of the terrorist attacks of September 11, 2001, police resources have become even more strained. Prior to September 11, police agencies, for the most part, were dealing with peacekeeping, order maintenance, and traditional street crime. Subsequent to September 11, however, the police acquired additional duties. Increased patrols of government buildings, landmarks, utility and nuclear facilities, and commercial airports were required. Overtime costs, additional training, new equipment, and other elements associated with increased homeland security drain already strained police agency budgets (McDonald & Thornton, 2002).

Relations with Private Security

Private security represents the largest protective resource in the United States. Public policing and private security are complementary professions (Harr & Hess, 2003). Further, some police agencies multiply their capabilities by establishing relationships with private security organizations. Many security companies possess technology and resources that surpass their local police counterparts. Private security personnel can also assist the police by collecting and offering information, extending protective surveillance, and providing investigative services to private companies (Cunningham, Strauchs, & Van Meter, 1990; Operation Cooperation, 2001; Sniffen, 2001). The vital role played by private security in crime prevention efforts should not be overlooked. As stated in the National Advisory Commission on Criminal Justice Standards and Goals' Task Force Report on Private Security in 1976, the security professional may be the one person in society who has the knowledge and technology to effectively prevent crime. Since public police are necessarily limited in number, private agencies can help fill the gap. It may be in the best interest of public police agencies to initiate cooperative efforts with the private sector and to promote improved training of security personnel to enhance the quality of crime prevention services (Lyman, 2002; National Advisory Commission on Criminal Justice Standards and Goals, 1976).

Police Discretion

Historically, the organizational model for most police agencies has been based on the military. Both the police and military personnel wear uniforms, have a rank structure, carry lethal weapons, and possess the authority to use force as provided by law. However, military personnel usually act as part of a unit, under the direct supervision of their supervisors. Police officers, unlike military personnel, usually must act on their own and are rarely subject to the direct control of a supervisor. Police decisions usually take place before limited audiences and, when no formal action is taken, the police officer rarely creates any documentation of why a particular decision was made (Fyfe, 1996). Therefore, police officers are in a position to exercise an enormous amount of **discretion** when making decisions (Coffey, 1990; Cohen, 1996; Cohen & Feldberg, 1991; Davis, 1975; Goldstein, 2001; Lyman, 2002; Meadows, 2002; Palacios, Cromwell, & Dunham, 2002; Pollock, 1998; Walker, 2001; Whisenand & Ferguson, 2002). An officer may choose to enforce a particular law against one person and not against another person. In addition, local public policy may dictate that some laws are enforced strictly while others are not. For example, responding to community demands, the police may elect to enforce certain types of laws, such as those relating to prostitution, more strictly than other statutes (Albanese, 2000; Barlow, 2000; Wilson, 1968).

Discretionary enforcement can result in complaints of racism, sexism, and abuse (Kleinig, 1996a). A common complaint from some ethnic minorities, for example, is that they are stopped by the police with greater frequency. Although some evidence suggests that racial profiling occurs rarely (Langan, Greenfeld, Smith, Durose, & Levin, 2001), many people blame the police for the inappropriate use of profiling, a technique that uses race, age, dress, vehicle type, and other factors to identify people who the police believe may be involved in criminal activity (Lyman, 2002).

In *Varieties of Police Behavior,* James Q. Wilson wrote that the public itself may be responsible for police behavior and discretionary enforcement based on three acceptable styles of police service tolerated and accepted by the community. Under the **watchperson style,** the police view themselves, or are viewed, as community caretakers. Through the **service style,** the police are expected to provide a wide range of services to the community. Under the **legalistic style,** the police are viewed as a paramilitary force responsible for near full enforcement of the law (Wilson, 1968). Currently, with zero tolerance policing, some agencies attempt full enforcement and encourage aggressive pursuit of law violators in an effort to reduce criminal activity. In the final analysis, a community tends to receive the type of police service it supports, desires, or tolerates. The exercise of discretion need not result in negative consequences. But, it is the responsibility of police executives to develop guidelines that will shape police officers' inevitable use of discretion and it is the responsibility of middle managers and first line supervisors to ensure that the guidelines are followed (Kelling, 1999). Society must recognize that the police exercise discretion, yet there must be a means for its review and control (Goldstein, 1993). Discretionary authority can be sustained to exercise individual judgment in individual cases, but only to the extent that those who exercise discretion can be held accountable for their decisions (Kleinig, 1996a).

Police Misconduct

As discussed elsewhere in this book, **police misconduct** is manifested in many forms. Although only a small fraction of police officers engage in such behavior (Walker, Alpert, & Kenney, 2001), misconduct, when it occurs, receives great notoriety, compromises the police individually and collectively, and damages relationships with the public. Corruption and violation of rights under the Constitution represent two examples of serious police misconduct.

Police officer Frank Serpico was instrumental in uncovering pervasive, organized corruption within the New York City Police Department in the 1960s. The Los Angeles Police Department was riddled with corruption during the first half of the twentieth century (Walker, 1983). Although corruption may not be so pervasive today, media accounts of such misconduct often help to create the perception that corruption is systemic in contemporary policing. Bribery, extortion, and political favors are a constant threat in police work. Because of the nature of police business, especially when enforcing vice laws, the temptation to engage in corrupt activities and benefit financially are always present. A general definition of police corruption involves some type of official wrongdoing by a police officer in return for a gratuity or other gain. Accordingly, failure to perform a legal duty, failure to perform a legal act in a proper manner, or commission of an illegal act can constitute corruption (Albanese, 2000). Ideally, the police themselves should initiate strategies to prevent corrupt conduct and punish those who engage in it (Lyman, 2002; Whisenand & Ferguson, 2002).

Violation of rights under the Constitution also exemplifies serious police misconduct. Through the use of the due process clause of the Fourteenth Amendment and a doctrine of incorporation, the United States Supreme Court has selectively applied provisions of the U.S. Constitution's first ten amendments (Bill of Rights) to state, county, and local law enforcement. Many of the decisions impacting law enforcement were an outgrowth of the "Warren Court" during the 1950s and 1960s, when Earl Warren was chief justice of the U.S. Supreme Court. These decisions were precipitated by cases that alleged inappropriate and unconstitutional police behavior (Inciardi, 2000). In a democratic republic dedicated to liberty, it is the duty of the police officer to protect individual rights, not abuse them (Walker, 2001).

The Police Public Image

Aside from statutorily mandated authority and police agency mission statements, the police role in society is often defined and described by the public's image of the police and perceptions of what the police do. Discussions that focus on the origins of policing address the social service nature of the early police: They administered to the indigent and spurred many moral reform movements. In the twentieth century, as the police moved toward a professional model in response to increasing crime and disorder, the perception of the police changed from social service agents to crime fighters. First and foremost, the public as well as the police perceive the police role as that of law enforcement (Kleinig, 1996b). The crime fighting role de-emphasized social service and ultimately led to police detachment and isolation from the community. In more recent times, social service activities of the police have been resurrected and reintegrated into police operations. Through community policing and similar strategies, law enforcement agents, once again, are perceived as responsible for serving the public as well as fighting crime. Thus, the **police public image** and perceptions of what the police do have been transformed from "public servants" to "crime fighters" and back to "public servants" (Peak & Glensor, 2002; Pollock, 1998).

The vast majority of police officers in the United States are hard working, conscientious, ethical, and dedicated public servants. However, most citizens form their opinion of the police through personal experience as a victim, witness, or suspect. These encounters often involve less than pleasant circumstances. Media and newscasts, movies, newspapers, and television also have a major impact on the public's image of the police (Peak & Glensor, 2002; Wallace, Roberson, & Steckler, 2001; Whisenand & Ferguson, 2002).

If a police officer is identified as corrupt or is charged with using excessive force, the incident is front-page news. If more than one officer is involved, the story often appears on nationally televised newscasts. The general public may become fearful or distrustful of the police (Werner, 2000). Consequently, the police themselves must create a climate of trust and must work to improve the public image through courteous, fair, and professional contact with the public.

Police recognition of common public attitudes toward law enforcement can assist officers in the development of positive relationships with the community (Building a bridge, 1999) Many people, especially victims and witnesses, have unreasonably high expectations of the police. Citizen attitudes are influenced by negative stereotypes of the police when officers:

- are apathetic due to insensitive actions.
- engage in unethical or unprofessional conduct by accepting gratuities, abusing authority, or adhering to a code of silence.
- are prejudiced, target certain groups, or apply different standards of enforcement to different people.
- project a poor image by inappropriate appearance, demeanor, or body language.
- are unwilling to handle service calls (California State Commission on Peace Officer Standards and Training, 1999)

Politics and the Police

Although history is replete with vain attempts to remove political influences from law enforcement, politics is a reality in policing, since control of the police ultimately rests with the elected representatives of the people. The police often find themselves caught between the wishes of political leaders and the police mission to reduce crime and disorder (Whisenand & Ferguson, 2002). Conflicts also exist between budgetary realities and political promises. Thus, the police may become a political target when they are unable to control a public safety problem. Often the agency and its chief executive officer are blamed for situations that are beyond the ability of the police to control (Goldstein, 2001).

The police are ultimately responsible for and accountable to an electorate. Yet, every community has a political process that is reflective of the aspirations of community public officials. Police officials may be confronted by political leaders who wish to maintain a positive relationship with their constituents, even though those constituents' desires are inconsistent with statutory or even constitutional mandates. A successful approach to balancing politics with the police mission often involves an emphasis on the police obligation to serve all citizens well while respecting the value system of each political leader's constituency. While no single strategy works in all communities, professional and unbiased behavior on the part of the police can help to prevent capricious and destructive politically motivated activity. When the police work with community leaders to establish a climate of trust, outcomes are more likely to be positive (Coffey, 1990). The police must establish a political climate and media relations conducive to working with diverse populations (Otto, 2000; Palmiotto, 2002).

The police themselves may engage in political activity. In an effort to promote their own causes, many police unions and associations become politically active. Theoretically, budgetary constraints and political considerations should not affect policing. However, police officers who feel unappreciated and underpaid often support political causes and candidates that reflect their parochial views (Champion & Rush, 1997). Political demonstrations by officers in uniform, or inappropriate activity that confuses political action with official police work, can have a negative effect on the public and a divisive impact on the community.

The police are confronted with internal politics as well. Yet, politics within an organization or agency is not a problem. Rather, it is a situation. Problems can be solved. Situations are continuously present. If individual and organizational interests are totally self-serving, highly political situations are inevitable. Depoliticizing the situation requires the development of a shared vision and openness. Internal politics may also be associated with some police labor unions. Although developed originally to combat low salaries and poor working conditions, police unions can and should expand their efforts to help promote professionalism (Whisenand & Ferguson, 2002).

Training Content and Methods

Although the topics covered in a basic police academy do not vary widely from one academy to another, the method of training does. Many police academies still emphasize traditional military-style stress training. Yet, the objectives of military operations and civilian policing are strikingly different. Granted, recognition of stress, and training and testing of reaction to it, is necessary to measure the resolve and ability of new officers to handle the types of situations and incidents encountered on the job. But the stress encountered by police is usually different from that experienced by soldiers. Officers most often work alone and thus are required to exercise independent judgment and demonstrate effective decision-making ability without supervision. Therefore, training should focus on the development of critical-thinking and problem-solving ability (Goldstein, 2001; Peak & Glensor, 2002).

Obedience-oriented, traditional military-style training may actually be detrimental to the officer on the job. It can produce arrogance and creates militaristic attitudes among some officers (Kelling, 1999). This attitude may threaten civil liberties, constitutional norms, and the overall well-being of citizens (Study sees cause for alarm, 1999). Military-style marching and overemphasis on unquestioning obedience does not promote individual decision-making and problem-solving ability and often proves to be of little value in the performance of contemporary police duties. Military-style stress training has no place in an academy classroom when it impedes the learning process and the development of professional attitudes (California State Commission on Peace Officer Standards and Training, 2001; Champion & Rush, 1997; Lyman, 2002; Peak & Glensor, 2002). Training methodology should be problem-based, incorporating adult learning concepts. Although incorporation of problem-based instruction in academics is a challenge, training methods should simulate, as much as possible, the actual working environment of the police officer (Goldstein, 2001).

More emphasis should also be placed on post-academy field training programs. **Field training officers (FTOs),** the senior officers who provide post-academy on-the-job training, must be selected and trained carefully to ensure that they possess ethical leadership skills and have the ability to help others develop these skills. The FTO has an enormous and profound impact on how a trainee views policing and how the trainee will behave and perform in the future. If the FTO does not accept and promote ethics, leadership, and an appropriate attitude and philosophy for policing a community, it is virtually impossible for a new police officer to develop appropriate attitudes and behaviors (Ortmeier, 1997, 2002; Peak & Glensor, 2002). In response to the urgent need to emphasize community policing and problem solving, many police agencies are redesigning FTO programs. The Reno, Nevada, and Savannah, Georgia, FTO programs, for example, fully integrate community policing and problem-solving concepts throughout the field training program (Peak & Glensor, 2002).

Other training-related problems include both an agency's failure to train and negligence in the training process itself (Kappeler, 2001; Ross, 2003). Failure to train implies a lack of appropriate skill development, while negligent training involves improper training. The agency employing a police officer must ensure that the officer knows how to do the job and receives the proper equipment to do it. An officer's performance must also be evaluated to ensure compliance with training guidelines. The training must encompass the full range of possible situations a police officer may encounter. Failure to train properly may easily lead to liability accompanied by lawsuits resulting in multimillion dollar judgments against the officer and the agency (Champion & Rush, 1997). Police recruit and in-service training must address the knowledge and actual skills required of the officer on the job (California State Commission on Peace Officer Standards and Training, 1998; Haberfeld, 2002). Although critical to performance, the subjects of ethics and leadership are often overlooked or receive inadequate attention.

Urban Decay

Many urban areas in the United States are in a state of decay. **Urban decay** results when dilapidated and vacant buildings, aging infrastructure, the plight of the unemployed and homeless as well as the flight of residents and businesses to suburban areas leave few resources to maintain inner-city urban areas. Crime and disorder are often the end result and the police are tasked by the public with the responsibility for finding solutions to these problems. Obviously, the police role was never designed to correct such basic social problems.

Nevertheless, the police can develop effective responses to these problems when the problems create conditions that can lead to crime and disorder. A strategy for attacking urban blight and decay may be extracted from the "broken windows" theory. First articulated by James Q. Wilson and George Kelling, the broken windows theory supposes that urban decay results when a seemingly insignificant poor condition, such as a broken window, is left uncorrected. When the broken window is not repaired, people who are inclined to break windows are led to believe that no one cares. So, they break more windows. The result is the perception of decay in the neighborhood. Social disorder and crime will increase and law-abiding citizens will live in fear or flee the neighborhood (Wilson & Kelling, 1982, 1989). At the first sign of a broken window, graffiti, or other disorder, the police can assume a leadership position. They can muster resources within a community to have the window repaired and graffiti removed and address other issues, thus improving the aesthetic quality of the neighborhood, reducing fear, and enhancing the possibility that crime and disorder will be prevented or reduced in the future (Giuliani & Kurson, 2002; Palacios, Cromwell, & Dunham, 2002).

Use of Force

Use of force by police officers is a critical issue in contemporary American society (Ross, 2003). Incidents, such as the one that occurred in Los Angeles with Rodney King, can be used to portray the police as an aggressive and abusive "occupying army." The media also pays very close attention to reported incidents of police abuse, and the resulting negative publicity often exaggerates the actual situation. Although it may appear otherwise, police authority to use force is actually dictated by the circumstances rather than the type of crime. Contrary to common belief, the police nationally are involved in less than 3,000 shooting incidents per year. Police use of deadly force occurs rarely (U.S. Department of Justice, 1999). However, when force is used, it is seldom ruled that the police used force improperly (Kleinig, 1996b).

Fictional television police dramas and movies depict police use of force as a common occurrence. Additionally, well-publicized incidents and accompanying allegations of excessive use of force, whether true or not, heighten public concern about police use of force (Hughes, 1998, 1999). Some suggest that aggressive, "zero-tolerance" law enforcement policies in the 1990s may have encouraged abuse by the police. However, research indicates that the police actually use force infrequently. A U.S. Department of Justice-sponsored study indicated that only about 1 percent of those people who have direct personal contact with the police allege that officers used or threatened force. Furthermore, less than 20 percent of all arrest situations involve the use of any physical force. Where force is used, it occurs at the lower end of the use of force spectrum. It usually involves physical force to restrain or move a suspect. Weapons are used rarely with firearms used only two-tenths of one percent (.002) of the time. Most injuries resulting from police use of force are likely to be minor. The most common injury is an abrasion or bruise. These injuries often occur when suspects are resisting arrest (Good news, better news on use of force, 2001; U.S. Department of Justice, 1999). Ninety-eight percent of felons justifiably killed by police are male; 53 percent are between the ages of 18 and 30 (Brown & Langan, 2001).

The types of incidents that often result in use of excessive force complaints are rare. Furthermore, the police actions that arouse the public, such as fatal shootings or beatings by the police, occur infrequently and are not typical of most incidents where the police use force (Lyman, 2002; U.S. Department of Justice, 1999). Nevertheless, although incidents of wrongful use of force by the police may be rare, public outrage over perceived police brutality is not. Therefore, since public support for the police is essential, the police community itself must make every effort to educate the public regarding the facts concerning police use of force.

Working with Diverse Populations

As the United States and other societies progress through the twenty-first century, domestic and foreign populations will become wealthier, older, and more culturally diverse. In many areas, the police workforce itself has become diverse, as evidenced by early studies of gender-related issues in policing (Bloch & Anderson, 1974; Sichel, 1978). The diversity of crime will also increase and the police service must keep pace with this diversity (Muraskin & Roberts, 2002; Palmiotto, 2002).

The police and the public should view diversity as a strength.
Photo courtesy of Los Angeles Sheriff's Department

To manage effectively in diverse environments, differences must be recognized rather than ignored, and people must learn to use the differences effectively (Adler, 2002). A single culture contains values that are shared by members of a group (Crank, 1998). Yet, in the heterogenous populations of the twenty-first century, crime is more likely to flourish because diverse cultures are less likely to arrive at consensus regarding societal values (Walker, Spohn, & DeLone, 2002). Cultural differences impact everyone, directly and indirectly, in personal, regional, national, and global terms. Intragroup and intergroup relations change continually and different groups with differing values affect the whole of a society. Differences with respect to race, religion, national origin, age, gender, and culture pose tremendous challenges for the police service (Lyman, 2002).

Although national surveys appear to indicate that most Americans are satisfied with the police in their community, many citizens and police officers develop misperceptions that create tension between the police and certain groups of people. Sources of tension surround issues related to profiling and other police field practices. Many minority groups, for example, believe the police and other justice system components are biased in their treatment of minorities. These minorities may view the police as an occupying military force. Complaints associated with slow or poor police response, verbal abuse, excessive questioning, discriminatory patterns, under-enforcement of the law, and use of excessive force are common. In particular, minority group members often suggest that the police practice of profiling, stopping subjects because they meet certain criteria, favors detention of minorities (Peak & Glensor, 2002).

Intragroup and intergroup relations change continually and differing values affect the whole of society. *Photo courtesy of Portland, Oregon, Bureau of Police*

Terrorism

In the twenty-first century, the United States, along with many other modern, industrialized, information-age countries, finds itself immersed and preoccupied with the terrorist activities of weak, sometimes third-world, nations, small groups, and a few radical individuals (Maniscalco & Christen, 2002). Additionally, there is considerable disagreement over the definition of terrorism, largely because a definition depends on an interpretation of the motivation of the participants. What is terrorism to one person may be a selfless act to another (Barlow, 2000). Broadly speaking, **terrorism** involves the use of violence and threats to intimidate or coerce. Terrorism may be the product of an individual or a group. Within this context, terrorists include: idealistic and political groups; economic opportunists; urban terrorists, such as predatory, ethnic, and economic gangs; career criminals; domestic violence perpetrators; drug cartels; and some antiabortion, prochoice, animal rights, and environmental activists. Within a narrower context, terrorism is defined as an act of violence committed against an innocent person or noncombatant for the purpose of achieving a political end through fear and intimidation (Siegel, 2001).

The definition of terrorism continues to evolve as terrorists and their motives, targets, and techniques change. Terrorists, foreign and domestic, include individuals, street gangs, political and religious zealots, and highly organized national and international organizations (Maniscalco & Christen, 2002).

Command and Control Centers enhance coordination and communication among public safety agencies. *Photo courtesy of New York Police Department*

Terrorist acts can be classified as domestic or international. In 1995, Timothy McVeigh bombed the Alfred P. Murrah federal office building in Oklahoma City. A terrorist group, the Aum Shinrikyo cult, was responsible for a saran nerve gas attack in a Tokyo subway in March 1995. The attack killed 10 commuters and left nearly 5,000 ill (Gaines, Kaune, & Miller, 2001). International terrorists do not confine themselves to a nation-state. Osama bin Laden, an exiled Saudi Arabian financier, is alleged to be responsible for a worldwide terrorism conspiracy. He is implicated in the bombing of the World Trade Center in New York City in 1993, the 1998 bombings of the U.S. embassies in Tanzania and Kenya, and the bombing of the U.S.S. Cole in Yemen on October 12, 2000. Of course, the most devastating terrorist attacks to occur on United States soil took place on September 11, 2001. Terrorists believed to be followers of Osama bin Laden hijacked four commercial aircraft, two of which were flown into the twin towers of the World Trade Center in New York City, one into the Pentagon, and one into the ground in rural Pennsylvania. Subsequently, the World Trade Center towers collapsed on themselves. Deaths resulting from the attacks and downed aircraft approached 3,000.

Critics argue that public pressure to combat terrorism often results in measures designed to curtail civil liberties such as rights to privacy, due process, and freedom from unreasonable searches and seizures. However, if the pattern of terrorism continues, U.S. citizens may decide to sacrifice some liberties and freedoms in exchange for safety and security (Gaines, Kaune, & Miller, 2001). According to the U.S. Commission on National

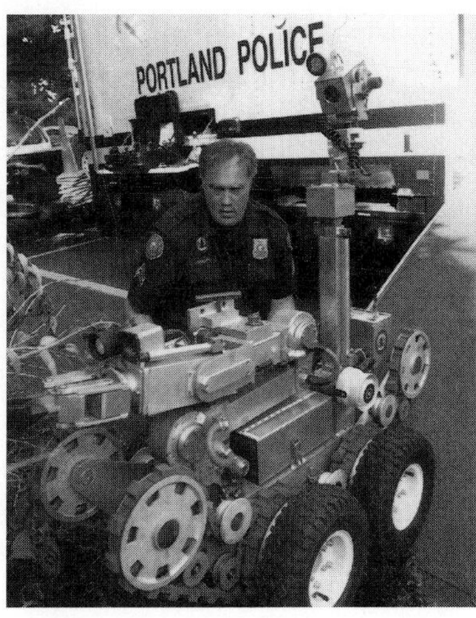

Technology can assist the police to prevent terrorist attacks and mitigate damage associated with terrorism. *Photo courtesy of Portland, Oregon, Bureau of Police*

Security, 21st Century, a new national security structure is necessary to replace the institutions that combated the threat of terrorism during the 40 years of the Cold War. Emerging technology and expanding economic growth promote new and different threats. Computer technology allows hackers to penetrate American businesses and vital public safety infrastructure databases. A foreign or domestic hacker, utilizing a computer, could manipulate and destroy vital and top secret information, create havoc with air traffic control systems, deactivate public utilities, and slow emergency communications systems. The commission predicts that people are more likely to die in large numbers on American soil if precautionary measures are not implemented. New age terrorism requires government and military capabilities characterized by stealth, speed, accuracy, mobility, and intelligence that are different from antiterrorism mechanisms used in the past. Private, nonmilitary antiterrorism strategies will be required also.

Terrorism is not a new phenomenon. Yet, few experts suggest that the threat of terrorism is not escalating. The weapons of terrorism range from traditional low technology firearms and improvised explosive devices (IEDs) to information warfare and weapons of mass destruction (WMDs), sometimes referred to as weapons of mass effect (WMEs) (Maniscalco & Christen, 2002). The threat of the use of WMDs is particularly frightening. Many nation-states as well as some non-state organizations either possess or have access to nuclear, biological, or chemical (NBC) devices that have the potential to cause loss of life and property destruction on a scale never before experienced.

As the threat and incidents of terrorism increase, the police community must assume a leadership role as it seeks to prevent terrorist attacks and mitigate damages associated with terrorism. Additionally, community policing can play a major role in the fight against terrorism (Newton, 2002).

Community policing provides a vehicle for communicating a reassuring message to a fearful citizenry and can provide a means for collecting information to assist in the investigation of terrorist activities. With full implementation of community policing along with collaborative police officer ethical leadership competence, citizens feel safer and more secure, demonstrate greater confidence and trust in the police, and are more likely to supply critical information (Nislow, 2001).

POLICING: DIFFICULTIES, CONSEQUENCES, AND GROWTH

During the last quarter of the twentieth century, many police practitioners realized that traditional reactionary policing (the professional model) was not effective as a mechanism to control crime or reduce fear of it. Community-oriented policing emerged as a viable alternative to traditional policing as the police recognized that community support and participation was necessary to prevent and control crime and disorder. Yet, substantive evidence on the **effectiveness of community policing** is still incomplete because it is difficult to determine if police agencies are actually committed to the concept of community policing or they are just attempting to be politically correct (Palmiotto, 2002).

From the earliest days of community policing, the concept has been defined generally in terms of two key ingredients: partnerships and problem solving. And, although the labels attached to community policing efforts (i.e., Neighborhood Policing, Problem-Oriented Policing) may vary among jurisdictions, partnerships and problem solving are what makes community policing fundamentally different from traditional policing strategies. However, after espousing and attempting to implement the concepts of community policing during the latter part of the twentieth century, police agencies throughout America discovered that speaking the language of community policing is a lot easier than institutionalizing and operationalizing community policing concepts. Many police agencies simply create a community policing program or unit within the agency rather than making community policing an operational reality throughout the entire organization. Nevertheless, a number of departments have achieved significant success that has been validated by both crime reduction and increases in citizen satisfaction.

Many police officers are thinking more analytically and strategically, the police and citizens are at least speaking to one another, and policing practices have improved dramatically in many quarters. Still, many problematic realities remain. Uniformed patrol officers in agencies with significant demands for service are still rushing from call to call, with little time or opportunity to develop community partnerships and engage in problem solving. Many citizens still view their role as nonparticipant observers, simply reporting crime and disorder as they see fit. In some cases, community policing efforts have been reduced to monthly meetings with sporadic participation and minimal problem solving (Ramsey, 2002).

In spite of a lack of resources and numerous shortcomings in some areas, community policing can supplement, if not replace, traditional policing efforts and still achieve ambitious goals. As a central theme of this book, the police are in an excellent position to assume a leadership role to promote and implement strategies that go beyond traditional police practices and maintenance of the status quo. If everyone was content with the traditional (professional) model of policing, rhetoric about community policing would not exist (Thurman, 2002). Community policing, as a philosophy and a strategy, exists because alternatives to it have been proven to fail (Skolnick, 1994).

Although the new age of community policing began in the late 1970s and early 1980s, evidence that community policing significantly reduces crime in a community has not been definitively established on a nationwide basis. This is because community policing has yet to be completely institutionalized throughout the nation. It is still in its initiation stage and cost-benefit analyses are difficult to apply to community policing innovations. However, most research suggests that community policing is the future model for the American police service. This model will progress and mature as it becomes more fully institutionalized (Thurman, Zhao, & Giacomazzi, 2001; Zhao, 2002).

Beyond attitudinal changes and new vocabulary acquisition, the institutionalization of community policing requires new agency mission statements, organizational change, modification of police selection standards and practices, changes in basic training for recruits, additional training for experienced officers as well as citizens, effective use of information and technology, new tools and tactics, and greater public awareness and understanding. Internally, police agencies must continue to evolve into more technologically sophisticated and community-based organizations (Goldstein, 2001; Meese, 1993; Meese & Moffit, 1997; Ortmeier, 2002; Peak & Glensor, 2002; Zhao, 2002).

Although substantial evidence suggests that community policing enhances citizen input and participation, there are certain problems that must be resolved before it becomes a universally accepted feature of American policing. For example, a great deal of progress in police accountability in the latter half of the twentieth century was achieved through traditional police management and centralized control over police discretion. In a community policing environment, by contrast, responsibility and control shifts to the line officer who is allowed to exercise more discretion than in a traditional policing environment. This juxtaposition of decentralization and accountability is one of the dilemmas that must be overcome. Despite difficulties such as this, community policing represents an important breakthrough that emphasizes police-community partnerships and problem solving (Walker, 2001). As community policing efforts blossom and become more productive, appropriately exercised police discretion can be harnessed to help achieve ambitious crime and disorder reduction goals.

Institutionalization of community policing will occur if: the philosophy and strategy becomes a formal part of patrol operations and criminal investigations, the evaluation of community policing moves beyond simply measuring citizen satisfaction, and community policing is widely accepted by the police culture. Forces that seem to favor expansion of community policing include its increasing popularity, strong federal government financial support, increased use of technology, and declining crime rates. In at least one major urban area, a citizens' committee recommended that the city's police agency culture be changed from an aggressive, command and control culture to one emphasizing community policing (Zahniser, 2002).

Negative forces impacting a movement toward community policing include the ambiguity of community policing and largely unchanged police organizational structures. Community policing still lacks theoretical refinement. It is a loosely defined concept, with varying definitions that lead to confusion when the community policing label is attached to numerous police innovations. Further, police organizational structures have remained relatively static. To fully institutionalize community policing, agencies must increase the horizontal structure and decrease the vertical structure of their organizations (Zhao, 2002).

Community policing innovations will continue to expand in the future. However, serious questions remain as to whether community policing will be institutionalized in the police culture. Radical change in the police service is practically impossible. Although programmatic change is relatively easy to implement, the structural (organizational) changes required for full institutionalization of community policing are difficult. Flattening the organization, for example, might require the elimination of certain ranks, a move that would meet with tough resistance from many officers, police unions, and politicians (Whisenand & Ferguson, 2002; Zhao, 2002). But the success of some police departments in streamlining their hierarchal structures and decentralizing authority indicates that progress can be achieved.

A renewed focus on police **accountability** will emphasize the need for results (Gaines, Worrall, Southerland, & Angell, 2003). Most significantly, effective community policing involves preparing the community for its role and providing it with the tools necessary to meet its obligations to the police-community partnership. After community policing becomes institutionalized throughout the police agency and the communities it serves, the police cannot be simple spectators (Baca, 2002). They must continue to assume a leadership role. Without direct and consistent police involvement, citizens may regress to the comfort of their previously limited and passive role in the policing effort (Lyman, 2002; Ramsey, 2002). Further, in the leadership role, the police are positioned to promote **community-oriented government,** a concept that broadens community policing to include all government resources that can be mustered to address community problems and issues *(Community-oriented government, 1998).*

There are uncertain forces that could impact the implementation of community policing, depending on the direction in which these forces move. One uncertain force is the increase in the number of paramilitary policing units (PPUs) or special weapons and tactics (SWAT) units in police departments of almost any size. This trend may be accentuated because of the terrorist attacks of September 11, 2001. Numerous police agencies serving medium and even small jurisdictions have established paramilitary units to respond to infrequent activities such as hostage situations, acts of terrorism, high-risk searches and arrests, and civil disturbances. Some experts argue that a return to the paramilitaristic orientation of the 1970s could interfere with the community-focused, service-oriented approach that is fundamental to the new style of policing. History is replete with examples of strained police-community relations due to paramilitary police conduct, and the police cultural aspects that accompany it (SWAT team may prove costly for small farm town, 1999; Thurman, Zhao, & Giacomazzi, 2001; *$12.5 million awarded in police-raid shooting death, 1999;* Zhao, 2002).

Another uncertain force focuses on the role of police unions in a community policing environment. Research on the relationship between police unions and the organizational change required for full implementation of community policing is incomplete. Police unions, traditionally, are not advocates for change. Unions often fight for power sharing with management and increased compensation and benefits associated with terms and conditions of employment. As community policing encourages innovation and change in areas such as operational practices and shift changes, the new style can affect terms and conditions of employment, thus creating potential resistance (Thurman, Zhao, & Giacomazzi, 2001; Zhao, 2002).

Community policing has made a significant contribution to the police performance evaluation process. In a traditional policing environment, police officers are required to complete and submit reports, and maintain records of their activities. Such documents, however, are self-generated and presumably self-justifying. Thus, documents used for performance evaluation in a traditional environment represent the police view and not the citizen perspective. Community policing, on the other hand, has stimulated the recognition that traditional police data, such as arrest statistics, do not adequately measure what the police do, nor do the data address the quality of service rendered to the public (Lyman, 2002; Walker, 2001). Citizen participation in the policing process provides a new source of information on police performance as well as community needs and satisfaction.

The ability of the police to respond to demands of and issues raised by citizens is also constrained by legal, social, political, and economic considerations. By law, the police are restricted procedurally. Socially, the police are restricted by citizen expectations regarding acceptable police behavior. Politically, support by and resistance from special interest groups impact police activity. Further, it is important that unrealistic expectations not be created. Poverty, inadequate education, and other socioeconomic ills create situations that are beyond the ability of the police service to control (Thurman, 2002).

Although many technical, legal, social, political, and economic factors interact to create social ills, community policing can help alleviate some social problems. Both the public and the police are beginning to realize that crime, disorder, and fear prevention and control necessitate a partnership between the police and the community they serve. Yet more work must be done to refine this process. Clearly, there are a variety of policing styles and innovations that are referred to as community policing. It has philosophical, strategic, tactical, and organizational dimensions (Thurman, 2002). Community policing involves new police deployment methods, community revitalization, problem solving, a customer service orientation, and police legitimacy through credibility maintenance (Police Executive Research Forum, 1996). Community policing emphasizes positive interactions, police contact with other public agencies as well as private groups, and an expanded police mission (Thurman, 2002).

Realistic assessment of community policing requires that exaggerated claims be avoided. For example, some evidence suggests that funding for community policing has not produced the results that have been claimed. According to numerous studies conducted by the federal government and others, the **Community-Oriented Policing Services (COPS)** program has not definitively proved to reduce violent crime nor has it succeeded in placing 100,000 additional police officers on the street as intended. Initiated in 1994 and funded by the federal government, the COPS program to date has consumed nearly nine billion dollars and is responsible for adding fewer than 60,000 new officers to the U.S. police service. In addition, violent crime rates began a decline in 1991, three years prior to the implementation of the COPS program. The COPS program failed to demonstrate a statistically measurable effect on violent crime rates.

The analysis of the COPS program indicates that more police, increased financing, and using the language of community policing do not necessarily have a demonstrable impact on violent crime. To be effective, police officers must do more than speak the language of community policing. They must also adopt strategies designed to focus clearly on targeted crime-risk factors and high crime areas (Muhlhausen, 2001; Roth & Ryan, 2000). More money does not necessarily result in more desirable outcomes. To be effective, resources must be deployed in a manner that targets specific measurable crime and disorder reduction objectives. Although additional police officers are welcomed, significant progress with public safety can be achieved only through deployment of highly skilled officers, those with technical as well as ethical leadership competence.

In the mid-1990s, community policing strategies implemented by the Los Angeles Police Department (LAPD) served as a model for other cities in the United States and Europe. The German Police Institute proposed a nationwide Burgernahe Polizeiarbeit (community policing) and Paris, France, introduced Officers de reseau (community patrol officers) based on LAPD's model of senior lead officers (SLOs). The entire country of France now features neighborhood lead officers, recognizing LAPD's use of SLOs to unite the police department with the communities in a partnership to address crime and disorder concerns (Jones & Wiseman, 2001).

In spite of some resistance within and outside the law enforcement profession, community policing is expanding (Lyman, 2002). As the community policing approach seeks to address the causes of crime and social disorder and reduce fear of crime, more agencies are shifting from traditional reactive policing to police leadership-centered community partnerships and problem solving as a means to improve public safety (Baca, 2002). Between 1997 and 1999, state and local police agencies increased the number of officers assigned full time to community policing efforts from 21,000 to 113,000 officers. By the end of the twentieth century, a majority of local police departments serving most U.S. residents had police officers engaged full time in community policing activities. Approximately 80 percent of local police departments, serving 96 percent of all residents, were meeting with groups and 40 percent of all local agencies serving over 70 percent of all residents formed a problem-solving partnership with the community (Hickman & Reaves, 2001). And, in spite of the post–9/11/01 emphasis on terrorism-oriented problems, the problems that impact neighborhoods most must continue to be addressed by the synergy of the police and the community *(A LEN interview with Police Chief Mark A. Kroeker of Portland,* Ore., 2002).

ETHICAL LEADERSHIP CHALLENGES

The **ethical leadership challenges** for the twenty-first century are many and varied. Leaders will be expected to communicate effectively with diverse populations. Leaders must understand the role of leadership in dynamic global and societal environments. Leaders must appreciate individual differences and demonstrate the competence to manage team and group activities. Leaders must motivate individuals to produce and achieve ambitious personal and professional goals (Lewis, Goodman, & Fandt, 2001). Leaders must also align organizational systems with the purposes of the organization (Giuliani & Kurson, 2002). As circumstances and environments inevitably change, the police must lead change initiatives (Gaines, Worrall, Southerland, & Angell, 2003).

Change can be planned or unplanned. Planned change is proactive and occurs as the result of human effort to develop or revise a policy, program, or project. **Unplanned change** is not proactive. Rather, it often results from a dramatic incident or is a reaction to an unforeseen crisis. Planned change contains an element of human control that increases the likelihood of success. Unplanned change, although well intentioned, is often ineffective and expensive. Planned change is dynamic, as are the problems and issues it seeks to address. People play a vital role as planned change is developed and implemented. Planned change increases the odds of success by explicitly considering the impact the change will have on political, social, and natural environments. Thus, good planning is specific and limited in scope, includes input from stakeholders in the planning process, and is guided by leaders who function as change agents. Effective proactive planning considers resource constraints, is accountable, and recognizes opportunities resulting from the expansion of knowledge and technology (Welsh & Harris, 1999). As exemplified by the visionary efforts of some policing experts, planned change can promote the development of ethical police leadership competence (California State Commission on Peace Officer Standards and Training, 2002) necessary to engage in proactive planning efforts.

The police service of the twenty-first century is positioned to assume a leadership role as it proactively plans to identify and meet the challenges facing modern policing (Bill Blackwood Law Enforcement Management Institute of Texas, 2000; Gaines, Worrall, Southerland, & Angell, 2003). Police credibility and productivity depend on the line officer's ability to solicit and receive community support and to participate in police-citizen partnerships. To be fully accepted, effective, and appropriately rewarded for their efforts, all police officers should possess and demonstrate the qualities and competencies inherent in ethical leadership.

SUMMARY

Policing in the twenty-first century will become more demanding and delicate as new issues and problems create challenges for the police. The issues and challenges encountered by the police will include the dynamics of police work, civil liability, officer safety and survival, limited resources, improving relations with private security, police use of discretion, police misconduct, and the need to improve and maintain a public image conducive to community support of the police service. The police must strive to avoid inappropriate political influence, revise and improve training content and methods, address urban decay, exercise restraint and effective judgment with respect to use of force, work effectively with diverse populations, and confront terrorism. Technological, social, economic, political, and legal advances will necessitate change in policing concepts, strategies, and practices. Community policing, although faced with numerous obstacles, appears to be the most viable alternative to a less effective traditional policing model. To garner necessary community support and participation in the peacekeeping ideals of a democracy, the police will be required to possess and practice ethical leadership skills.

KEY TERMS AND CONCEPTS

Define, describe, or explain the importance of each of the following:

accountability
civil liability
community-oriented government
Community-Oriented Policing Services (COPS)
dynamics of police work
effectiveness of community policing
ethical leadership challenges
field training officer (FTO)
institutionalization of community policing
legalistic style
limited resources
officer safety and survival
planned change
police discretion
police misconduct
police public image
private security
service style
terrorism
unplanned change
urban decay
watchperson style
working personality

DISCUSSION QUESTIONS AND EXERCISES

1. List and describe three critical issues in policing. How can problems associated with these issues be resolved?
2. Police practitioners and other justice system personnel of the twenty-first century must possess and sustain a firm ethical foundation and demonstrate leadership ability. Explain.
3. Is community policing effective? Why, or why not?
4. How can community policing be institutionalized?
5. Compare and contrast planned change with unplanned change.
6. Create a vision for policing in the twenty-first century. Document the vision in the form of a statement.

References

Adams, T. F. (2001). *Police field operations* (5th ed.). Upper Saddle River, NJ: Prentice Hall.

A dangerous place to work: When it comes to on-the-job perils, police have it the worst. (2002, January 15/31). *Law Enforcement News, 28* (569/570), 1.

Adler, N. J. (2002). *International dimensions of organizational behavior* (4th ed.). Cincinnati: South-Western/Thomson Learning.

Adler, R. B., & Elmhorst, J. M. (1996). *Communicating at work.* New York: McGraw-Hill.

Adler, R. B., & Towne, N. (2002). *Looking out/looking in* (10th ed.). Fort Worth, TX: Harcourt College Publishers.

Albanese, J. S. (2000). *Criminal justice 2000 update.* Needham Heights, MA: Allyn & Bacon.

A LEN interview with Police Chief Mark A. Kroeker of Portland, Ore. (2002, March 15/31). *Law Enforcement News, 28* (573/574), 9–12.

Alderfer, C. P. (1972). *Existence, relatedness and growth: Human needs in organizational settings.* New York: Free Press.

Anderson, T. D. (Ed.). (2000). *Every officer is a leader: Transforming leadership for police, justice, and public safety.* New York: St. Lucie Press.

Anderson, T. D., & King, D. (1996a). *Managerial leadership training needs assessment in justice and public safety.* New Westminster, B.C., Canada: Justice Institute of British Columbia.

Anderson, T. D., & King, D. (1996b). *Police supervisory leadership training needs assessment.* New Westminster, B.C., Canada: Justice Institute of British Columbia.

Argyris, C. (1964). *Integrating the individual and the organization.* New York: John Wiley & Sons.

Arner, M. (2000, October 16). Crime rate falling in this county and in U.S.—for now. *San Diego Union Tribune,* A1, A15.

As costs soar, questions of quality dog Mass. college for cops program. (2001, February 28). *Law Enforcement News, 27* (550), 1,8.

Baca, L. D. (2002, April 7). Address. Speech presented at Academy of Criminal Justice Sciences annual conference, Anaheim, CA.

Baker, T. E. (2000). *Effective police leadership: Moving beyond management.* Flushing, NY: Looseleaf Law Publications, Inc.

Balint, K. (2000, September 8). Copyrights take a licking on Net frontier. *San Diego Union Tribune,* A1, A23.

Barlow, H. D. (2000). *Criminal justice in America.* Upper Saddle River, NJ: Prentice Hall.

Barnard, C. I. (1938). *The functions of the executive.* Cambridge, MA: Harvard University Press.

Baro, A. L., & Burlingame, D. (1999, Spring). Law enforcement and higher education: Is there an impasse? *Journal of Criminal Justice Education, 10* (1), 57–73.

Bass, B. M. (1960). *Leadership, psychology and organizational behavior.* New York: Harper.

Bass, B. M. (1981). *Stogdill's handbook of leadership: A survey of theory and research.* New York: The Free Press.

Bass, B. M. (1985). *Leadership and performance beyond expectations.* New York: The Free Press.

Bass, B. M. (1990). *Handbook of leadership.* New York: The Free Press.

Beauchamp, T. L., & Bowie, N. E. (1988). *Ethical theory and business* (3rd ed.). Englewood Cliffs, NJ: Prentice Hall.

Beauchamp, T. L., & Childress, J. F. (1994). *Principles of biomedical ethics* (4th ed.). New York: Oxford University Press.

Bellows, R. M. (1959). *Creative leadership.* Englewood Cliffs, NJ: Prentice Hall.

Bennett, W. J. (Ed.) (1993). *The book of virtues.* New York: Simon & Schuster.

Bennis, W. G. (1961, January). Revisionist theory of leadership. *Harvard Business Review, 38* (1), 26–36, 146–150.

Bennis, W. G. (1984, September). The four competencies of leadership. *Training and Development Journal, 38* (9), 14–19.

Bennis, W. G. (1993a). *An invented life: Reflections on leadership and change.* Reading, MA: Addison Wesley.

Bennis, W. G. (1993b). Managing the dream: Leadership in the 21st century. In W. E. Rosenbach & R. L. Taylor (Eds.), *Contemporary issues in leadership* (3rd ed.) (pp. 213–218). Boulder, CO: Westview Press.

Bentham, J. (1789/1973). *Political thought.* New York: Barnes & Noble.

Bernard, L. L. (1926). *An introduction to social psychology.* New York: Holt.

Bill Blackwood Law Enforcement Management Institute of Texas. (2000). *Texas police chief leadership series.* Corpus Christi, TX: Bill Blackwood Law Enforcement Management Institute of Texas.

Bisesi, M. (1983, Fall). Strategies for successful leadership in changing times. *Sloan Management Review, 25* (1), 61–64.

Blake, R. R., & Mouton, J. S. (1965). A 9.9 approach for increasing organizational productivity. In E. H. Schein & W. G. Bennis (Eds.), *Personal and organizational change through group methods* (pp. 169–183). New York: John Wiley & Sons.

Blake, R. R., & Mouton, J. S. (1985). *The managerial grid.* Houston, TX: Gulf.

Blanchard, K., & Johnson, S. (1992). *The one minute manager.* New York: Morrow.

Bloch, P. B., & Anderson, D. (1974). *Policewomen on patrol: Final report.* Washington, DC: The Police Foundati .

Boehm, N. C. (1988). *P.O.S.T. career ethics/integrity training guide.* Sacramento, CA: Commission on Peace Officer Standards and Training.

Bogardus, E. S. (1929). Leadership and attitudes. *Sociological Society, 13,* 377–387.

Boni, W., & Kovacich, G. (2000). *Netspionage: The global threat to information.* Woburn, MA: Butterworth-Heinemann.

Boydstun, J. E. (1977). *Police staffing in San Diego: One- or two-officer units.* Washington, DC: The Police Foundation.

Brann, J. E. (1999, July). Where we've been . . . where we're going: The evolution of community policing. In California State, Office of the Attorney General, *Community-oriented policing and problem solving: Now and beyond* (pp. 11–20). Sacramento, CA: Office of the Attorney General.

Bratton, W. J. (1997). Cutting crime and restoring order: What America can learn from New York's finest. In E. Meese III and R. E. Moffit (Eds.), *Making America Safer* (pp. 87–103). Washington, DC: The Heritage Foundation.

Bratton, W. J., & Andrews, W. (1999, Spring). What we've learned about policing. *City Journal, 9* (2), 14–27.

Bridges, W. (1994, September 19). The end of the job. *Fortune, 130,* 64.

Brilhart, J. K., & Galanes, G. J. (1998). *Effective group discussion* (9th ed.). Boston: McGraw-Hill.

Brooks, K. W. (1979). Delphi Technique: Expanding applications. *North Central Association Quarterly, 53* (3), 377–385.

Brown, D. C. (2001, Spring). Cognitive and affective minds: A necessary marriage in criminal justice education. *Journal of Criminal Justice Education, 12* (1), 101–213.

Brown, J. F. (1936). *Psychology and the social order.* New York: McGraw-Hill.

Brown, J. M., & Langan, P. A. (2001, March). *Policing and homicide, 1976–98: Justifiable homicide by police, police officers murdered by felons.* Washington, DC: U. S. Department of Justice, Office of Justice Programs, Bureau of Justice Statistics.

Brown, S. L., & Eisenhardt, K. M. (1998). *Competing on the edge: Strategy as structured chaos.* Boston, MA: Harvard Business School Press.

Building a bridge to the community can begin with a better handled traffic stop. (1999, September 15). *Law Enforcement News, 25* (517), 1, 9.

Bunning, R. L. (1979). The Delphi technique: A projection tool for serious inquiry. In *The 1979 annual handbook for group facilitators* (pp. 174–181). San Diego, CA: University Associates.

Burns, J. M. (1978). *Leadership.* New York: Harper & Row.

Burns, L. R., & Becker, S. W. (1988). Leadership and decision making. In S. M. Shortell & A. D. Kaluzny (Eds.), *Health care management: A text in organization theory and behavior* (2nd ed.) (pp. 142–186). New York: John Wiley & Sons.

Byers, B. (2000, September/October). Ethics and criminal justice: Some observations on police misconduct. *ACJS (Academy of Criminal Justice Sciences) Today, 21* (3), 1, 4–7.

Bynum, T. S. (2001). *Using analysis for problem-solving: A guidebook for law enforcement.* Washington, DC: U.S. Department of Justice, Office of Community Oriented Policing Services.

Byrnbauer, H., & Tyson, L. A. (1984, September). Flexing the muscles of technical leadership. *Training and Development Journal, 38* (9), 48–52.

By their own hands: PDs grope for answers to cop suicide. (1999, June 30). *Law Enforcement News, 25* (514), 5.

California State Assembly. (1991, January). *California law enforcement training in the 1990's: A vision of excellence.* Sacramento, CA: Assembly Concurrent Resolution 58 Study Committee.

California Association of Administration of Justice Educators (CAAJE). (2002, April 25–26). *Proceedings of the CAAJE Curriculum Task Force.* San Pedro, CA: California Association of Administration of Justice Educators.

California State Community College Chancellor's Office. (1992). *Public safety curriculum project: Expanded executive summary.* Sacramento, CA: Chancellor's Office of the California Community College System.

California State Community College Chancellor's Office. (1996). *Public safety curriculum and professional development project: Law enforcement curriculum.* Sacramento, CA: Chancellor's Office of the California Community College System.

California State Commission on Peace Officer Standards and Training. (1990, November). *Syllabus: Supervisory Leadership Institute.* Sacramento, CA: POST Center for Leadership Development.

California State Commission on Peace Officer Standards and Training. (1998). *Entry-level uniformed patrol officer job analysis.* Sacramento, CA: Commission on Peace Officer Standards and Training.

California State Commission on Peace Officer Standards and Training. (1999). *Regular peace officer basic course.* Sacramento, CA: Commission on Peace Officer Standards and Training.

California State Commission on Peace Officer Standards and Training. (2001, January/February). Leadership 2000 Symposium. *POSTScripts, 3* (4), 1–2.

California State Commission on Peace Officer Standards and Training. (2002, April 10). *Proceedings of the April 10, 2002 POST Commission meeting.* Culver City, CA: California Commission on Peace Officer Standards and Training.

California State Department of Justice. Office of the Attorney General. (1996). *Community-oriented policing and problem solving: Definitions and principles.* Sacramento, CA: Office of the Attorney General.

California State Department of Justice. Office of the Attorney General. (1999, July). *Community-oriented policing and problem solving: Now and beyond.* Sacramento, CA: Office of the Attorney General.

Campbell, J. (1999, May/June). Community oriented justice: Marketing your partnerships. *ACJS (Academy of Criminal Justice Sciences) Today, 17* (6), 1, 3–5.

Carlon, P. E. (1999, Spring). Occupational outcomes of criminal justice graduates: Is the master's degree a wise investment? *Journal of Criminal Justice Education, 10* (1), 39–55.

Caroselli, M. (1997). *That's no problem: A problem-free approach to problem solving.* West Des Moines, IA: American Media Publishing.

Carter, D. L. (1995, June). *Community policing and D.A.R.E.: A practitioner's perspective.* Washington, DC: U.S. Department of Justice, Bureau of Justice Assistance.

Carter, D. L., Sapp, A. D., & Stephens, D. W. (1988). Higher education as a bona fide occupational qualification (BFOQ) for police: A blueprint. *American Journal of Police, 7* (2), 1–27.

Carter, D. L., Sapp, A. D., & Stephens, D. W. (1989). *The state of police education: Policy direction for the 21st century.* Washington, DC: Police Executive Research Forum.

Carter, L. F. (1953). Leadership and small group behavior. In M. Sherif & M. O. Wilson (Eds.), *Group relations at the crossroads* (pp. 312–322). New York: Harper.

Champion, D. J., & Rush, G. E. (1997). *Policing in the community.* Upper Saddle River, NJ: Prentice Hall.

Champy, J., & Nohria, N. (2000). *The arc of ambition: Defining the leadership journey.* Cambridge, MA: Perceus Books.

Chin, G. J. (Ed.). (1997). *New York City police corruption investigation commissions 1894–1994.* (Vols. 1–6). Buffalo, NY: William S. Hein.

China's piracy plague. (2000, June 5). *Business Week,* 44–46.

Clark, J. R. (1994, April 15). Does community policing add up? *Law Enforcement News, 20* (399), 8.

Clark, K. L. (1994). *Retrofitting the bridge between academics and business: Here is how it is done.* Paper presented to the Second Annual Conference on Global Business, Sun Valley, Idaho.

Clarke, R. V. (2002a). *Thefts of and from cars in parking facilities: Problem-oriented guides for police series no. 10.* Washington, DC: U.S. Department of Justice, Office of Community Oriented Policing Services.

Clarke, R. V. (2002b). *Shoplifting: Problem-oriented guides for police series no. 11.* Washington, DC: U.S. Department of Justice, Office of Community Oriented Policing Services.

Clarke, R. V. (2002c). *Burglary of retail establishments: Problem-oriented guides for police series no. 15.* Washington, DC: U.S. Department of Justice, Office of Community Oriented Policing Services.

Cleeton, G. U., & Mason, C. W. (1934). *Executive ability—its discovery and development.* Yellow Springs, OH: Antioch Press.

Clemmer, J. (1992, April). 5 common errors companies make starting quality initiatives. *Total Quality, 3,* 7.

Clinis, F. X., & Drew, C. (2002, October 25). Captured rifle linked to sniper shootings. *San Diego Union Tribune,* AL, A21.

Close, D., & Meier, N. (1995). *Morality in criminal justice: An introduction to ethics.* Belmont, CA: Wadsworth/Thomson Learning.

Coffey, A. (1990). *Law enforcement: A human relations approach.* Englewood Cliffs, NJ: Prentice Hall.

Cohen, H. S. (1996). Police discretion and police objectivity. In J. Kleinig (Ed.), *Handled with discretion: Ethical issues in police decision making* (pp. 91–106). New York: Rowman & Littlefield.

Cohen, H. S. & Feldberg, M. (1991). *Power and restraint: The moral dimension of police work.* New York: Praeger.

Cole, G. F., & Smith, C. E. (2001). *The American system of criminal justice* (9th ed.). Belmont, CA: Wadsworth/Thomson Learning.

Coleman, J. W. (1994) *The criminal elite: The sociology of white collar crime.* New York: St. Martin's Press.

Community-oriented government. (1998). Fort Wayne, IN: City of Fort Wayne.

Community Policing Consortium. (1994). *Understanding community policing: A framework for action.* Washington, DC: Community Policing Consortium.

Community Policing Consortium. (1997a). *Module two: Mobilizing the community for collaborative partnerships.* Washington, DC: Community Policing Consortium.

Community Policing Consortium. (1997b). *Module three: Community policing problem solving: Taking a problem-solving approach to tackling crime, fear and disorder.* Washington, DC: Community Policing Consortium.

Conser, J. A., & Russell, G. D. (2000) *Law enforcement in the United States.* Gaithersburg, MD: Aspen Publishers.

Cooley, C. H. (1902). *Human nature and the social order.* New York: Scribners.

Copeland, N. (1942). *Psychology and the soldier.* Harrisburg, PA: Military Service Publishing.

Cordner, G. W., & Scarborough, K. E. (1999, July). Operationalizing community policing in rural America: Sense and nonsense. In California State, Office of the Attorney General, *Community-oriented policing and problem solving: Now and beyond* (pp. 118–125). Sacramento, CA: Office of the Attorney General.

Cortrite, M. (2000, June 15). What's the LAPD's problem? It's the culture. *Law Enforcement News, 26* (535), 8.

Couper, D. C., & Lobitz, S. H. (1991). *Quality policing: The Madison experience.* Washington, DC: Police Executive Research Forum.

Covey, S. R. (1990). *Principle-centered leadership.* New York: Fireside.

Covey, S. R. (1998). *The seven habits of highly effective people.* New York: Simon & Schuster.

Cowley, W. H. (1928). Three distinctions in the study of leaders. *Journal of Abnormal Social Psychology, 23,* 144–157.

Crank, J. P. (1998). *Understanding police culture.* Cincinnati: Anderson.

Crank, J. P., & Caldero, M. A. (2000). *Police ethics: The corruption of the noble cause.* Cincinnati: Anderson Publishing.

Crime statistics don't tell the whole story. (1999, November/December). *Community Policing Exchange, 7* (29), 1–2.

Cronkhite, C. (1995, October–November). An eclectic approach to policing: Applying past principles to community policing. *CJ (Criminal Justice) in the Americas, 8* (5), 9–11.

Crowe, T. D. (2000). *Crime prevention through environmental design.* (2nd ed.). Woburn, MA: Butterworth-Heinemann.

Cunningham, W., Strauchs, J. J., & Van Meter, C. W. (1990). *Private security trends 1970 to 2000: The Hallcrest Report II.* Boston: Butterworth-Heinemann.

Daft, R. L. (2001). *Organization theory and design* (7th ed.). Cincinnati: South-Western.

Dalkey, N. (1969). *The Delphi method: An experimental study of group opinion.* Santa Monica, CA: The Rand Corporation.

Daniel, T. (1992, March). Identifying critical leadership competencies of manufacturing supervisors in a major electronics corporation. *Group and Organizational Management: An International Journal, 17* (1), 57–71.

Dantzker, M. L. (2002). The community in community policing: The key to success is the police and community partnerships. In D. J. Stevens (Ed.), *Policing and community partnerships* (pp. 177–185). Upper Saddle River, NJ: Prentice Hall.

Davids, M. (1995, January–February). Where style meets substance. *Journal of Business Strategy, 16* (1), 48–55, 57–60.

Davis v. City of Dallas. 777 F.2d 205 (1985).

Davis, K. C. (1975). *Police discretion.* St. Paul, MN: West.

Dempsey, T. (1992). *Contemporary patrol tactics: A practical guide for patrol officers.* Englewood Cliffs, NJ: Prentice Hall.

Desroches, F. J. (1986). The occupational subculture of the police. In B. K. Cryderman and C. N. O'Toole (Eds.), *Police, race and ethnicity: A guide for law enforcement officers* (pp. 39–51). Toronto: Butterworths.

Dickey, W. J., & McGarry, P. (2001, February). *Community justice in rural America: Four examples and four futures.* Washington, DC: U.S. Department of Justice, Office of Justice Programs, Bureau of Justice Assistance.

Dodd, C. H. (1998). *Dynamics of intercultural communications* (5th ed.). Boston: McGraw-Hill.

Dorning, M. (2000, August 28). U.S. violent crime rate dropped again last year. *San Diego Union Tribune,* A2.

Downton, J. V. (1973). *Rebel leadership: Commitment and charisma in a revolutionary process.* New York: Free Press.

Drath, W. H., & Paulus, C. J. (1994). *Making common sense: Leadership as meaning-making in a community of practice.* Greensboro, NC: Center for Creative Leadership.

Drucker, P. F. (1992, September–October). The new society of organizations. *Harvard Business Review,* 98.

Drucker, P. F. (1994, November). The age of social transformation. *The Atlantic Monthly,* 53–80.

Dubois, J., & Hartnett, S. M. (2002). Making the community side of community policing work: What needs to be done. In D. J. Stevens (Ed.). *Policing and Community Partnerships* (pp. 1–15). Upper Saddle River, NJ: Prentice Hall.

Dweck, C. S. (1999). *Self-theories: Their role in motivation, personality, and development.* Philadelphia: Psychology Press.

Dwyer, J. (2002, January 31). Chaos helped seal N.Y. firefighters' fates: Internal probe reveals erratic communications. *San Diego Union Tribune,* A1, A2.

Earle, J. H. (1988, April). Law enforcement administration: Yesterday, today, and tomorrow. *FBI Law Enforcement Bulletin, 57* (4), 2–7.

Eck, J. E., & Spelman, W. (1987, January–February). Newport News tests problem-oriented policing. *National Institute of Justice Reports,* 2–8.

Evans, M. G. (1970). The effects of supervisory behavior on the path-goal relationship. *Organization Behavior and Human Performance, 5,* 277–298.

Fiedler, F. E. (1967). *A theory of leadership effectiveness.* New York: McGraw-Hill.

Fire, police experts cite communication failures during Trade Center response. (2002, January 15/31). *Law Enforcement News, 28* (569/570), 1.

Fleissner, D., Fedan, N., & Klinger, D. (1992, August). Community policing in Seattle: A model partnership between citizens and police. *National Institute of Justice Journal*, 9–18.

Flippen, A. R. (1999). Understanding groupthink from a self-regulatory perspective. *Small Group Research 30*, 139–165.

Foote, J. (1997, August). *Expert panel issues report on serious and violent juvenile offenders.* Washington, DC: U.S. Department of Justice, Office of Juvenile Justice and Delinquency Prevention.

Ford, J. K., Boles, J. G., Plamondon, K. E., & White, J. P. (2000). Transformational leadership and community policing: A road map for change. In T. J. Fitzgerald (Ed.), *Police in society* (pp. 156–172). New York: H. W. Wilson.

Fosdick, R. B. (1921). *American police systems.* New York: The Century Company.

Fournies, F. (2000). *Coaching for improved work performance.* New York: McGraw-Hill.

Freud, S. (1922). *Group psychology and the analysis of ego.* London: International Psychoanalytical Press.

Freud, S. (1938). *The basic writings of Sigmund Freud.* New York: Modern Library.

Fuller, J. J. (2001, May/June). Street cop ethics. *The Law Enforcement Trainer, 16* (3), 6–8.

Fyfe, J. J. (1996). Structuring police discretion. In J. Kleining (Ed.), *Handled with discretion: Ethical issues in police decision making* (pp. 183–205). New York: Rowman & Littlefield.

Gaines, L. K., Kaune, M., & Miller, R. L. (2000). *Criminal justice in action.* Belmont, CA: Wadsworth/Thomson Learning.

Gaines, L. K., Kaune, M., & Miller, R. L. (2001). *Criminal justice in action: The core.* Belmont, CA: Wadsworth/Thomson Learning.

Gaines, L. K., Worrall, J. L., Southerland, M. D., & Angell, J. E. (2003). *Police administration* (2nd ed.). New York: McGraw-Hill.

Gamble, T. K., & Gamble, M. (1999). *Communication works* (6th ed.). Boston: McGraw-Hill.

Gardner v. Broderick, 392 U.S. 273 (1968).

Garrity v. New Jersey, 385 U.S. 493 (1967).

Germain, D. (1999, December 29). Clayton Moore, TV's Lone Ranger dies at 85. *San Diego Union Tribune,* A3.

Germann, A. C., Day, F. D., & Gallati, R. R. J. (1988). *Introduction to law enforcement and criminal justice.* Springfield, IL: Charles C. Thomas.

Gibb, J. R. (1961, September). Defensive communication. *Journal of Communication, 2,* 141.

Giuliani, R. W., & Kurson, K. (2002). *Leadership.* New York: Hyperion.

Glensor, R. W., & Peak, K. J. (1999, July). Complexities of the problem-solving process: Barriers and challenges to daily practice. In California State, Office of the Attorney General, *Community oriented policing and problem solving: Now and beyond,* (pp. 76–82). Sacramento, CA: Office of the Attorney General.

Global crime cartels are tech-savvy, U.S. says. (2000, December 16). *San Diego Union Tribune,* A12.

Goetsch, D. L., & Davis, S. (1995). *Implementing total quality.* Englewood Cliffs, NJ: Prentice Hall.

Goldstein, H. (1990). *Problem-oriented policing.* New York: McGraw-Hill.

Goldstein, H. (1993, December). The new policing: Confronting complexity. *National Institute of Justice: Research in brief.* Washington, DC: U.S. Department of Justice, National Institute of Justice.

Goldstein, H. (2001, December 7). Address. Speech presented at the annual International Problem-Oriented Policing Conference, San Diego, CA.

Gomez, C. C. (1985). *Emerging curricula for computer science.* Unpublished dissertation, Arizona State University, Tempe.

Goodbody, W. L. (1995, April 30). What do we expect new-age cops to do? *Law Enforcement News, 21* (422), 14, 18.

Good news, better news on use of force. (2001, March 15). *Law Enforcement News, 27* (551), 7.

Gordon, T. (1955). *Group-centered leadership—a way of releasing the creative power of groups.* Boston: Houghton Mifflin.

Gough, J. W. (Ed.). (1976). *The second treatise of government (An essay concerning the true original, extent and end of civil government and a letter concerning toleration by John Locke).* Oxford, England: Basil Blackwell.

Graen, G. B., & Uhl-Bien, M. (1995, Spring). Relationship-based approach to leadership: Development of leader-exchange (LMX) theory of leadership over 25 years: Applying a multi-level multi-domain perspective. *Leadership Quarterly, 6* (2), 219–247.

Green, M. F. (1988). *Leaders for a new era.* New York: American Council on Education/ Macmillan.

Greenhouse, L. (1998, May 27). Supreme Court eases liability of police in chases. *San Diego Union Tribune,* A1.

Greenwood, P. W. (1979, July). *The Rand criminal investigation study: Its findings and impacts to date.* Santa Monica, CA: The Rand Corporation.

Haberer, J. B., & Webb, M. L. W. (1994). *TQM: 50 ways to make it work for you.* Menlo Park, CA: Crisp Publications.

Haberfeld, M. R. (2002). *Critical issues in police training.* Upper Saddle River, NJ: Prentice Hall.

Hale, C. D. (1994). *Police patrol operations and management* (2nd ed.). Upper Saddle River, NJ: Prentice Hall.

Hanna, M. S., & Wilson, G. L. (1998). *Communicating in business and professional settings* (4th ed.). New York: McGraw-Hill.

Harnett, S. M., & Skogan, W. G. (1999, April). Community policing: Chicago's experience. *National Institute of Justice Journal,* 2–11.

Harr, S., & Hess, K. M. (2003). *Seeking employment in criminal justice and related fields* (4th ed.). Belmont, CA: Wadsworth/Thomson Learning.

Harris, R. A. (2002). *Creative problem solving: A step-by-step approach.* Los Angeles: Pyrczak Publishing.

Harrison, W. (Ed.). (1967). *A fragment on government and an introduction to the principles of morals and legislation by Jeremy Bentham.* Oxford, England: Basil Blackwell.

Hawkins, J. (2000, Summer). What exactly does ethical leadership mean these days? *Community Links, 7* (3), 3, 10.

Heifetz, R. A. (1994). *Leadership without easy answers.* Cambridge: The Belknap Press of Harvard University Press.

Hellriegel, D., Jackson, S. E., & Slocum, J. W., Jr. (2002). *Management: A competency-based approach* (9th ed.). Cincinnati, OH: South-Western/Thomson Learning.

Hellriegel, D., Slocum, J. W., Jr., & Woodman, R. W. (2001). *Organizational behavior* (9th ed.). Cincinnati, OH: South-Western/Thomson Learning.

Hemphill, J. K. (1949). *Situational factors in leadership.* Bureau of Education Research, Columbus, OH: Ohio State University.

Hersey, P., & Blanchard, K. H. (1972). The management of change: Change and the use of power. *Training and Development Journal, 26* (1), 6–10.

Hersey, P., & Blanchard, K. H. (1982). *Management of organizational behavior: Utilizing human resources.* Englewood Cliffs, NJ: Prentice Hall.

Hersey, P., Blanchard, K. H., & Johnson, D. E. (2001). *Management of organizational behavior: Leading human resources* (8th ed.). Upper Saddle River, NJ: Prentice Hall.

Herzberg, F. (1959). *The motivation to work* (2nd ed.). New York: John Wiley & Sons.

Hess, K. M. (1997, December). The ABCs of report writing. *Security Management, 41* (12), 123–124.

Hess, K. M., & Wrobleski, H. M. (1993). *Police operations.* St. Paul, MN: West.

Hickman, M. J., & Reaves, B. A. (2001, February). *Community policing in local police departments, 1997 and 1999.* Washington, DC: U.S. Department of Justice, Office of Justice Programs, Bureau of Justice Statistics.

Ho, D. (2000, December 29). 151 police officers killed this year, up 11% from 1999. *San Diego Union Tribune,* A15.

Hobbes, T. (1649/1950). *Leviathan.* New York: E. P. Dutton.

Holtgraves, T. (2002). *Language as social action: Social psychology and language use.* Mahwah, NJ: Lawrence Erlbaum Associates.

Homans, G. C. (1950). *The human group.* New York: Harcourt Brace.

Homans, G. C. (1958). Social behavior as exchange. *American Journal of Sociology, 63,* 597–606.

House, R. J. (1971, September 16). A path-goal theory of leadership effectiveness. *Administrative Science Quarterly, 16* (3), 321–328.

House, R. J. (1976). A 1976 theory of charismatic leadership. In J. G. Hunt & L. L. Larson (Eds.), *Leadership: The cutting edge* (pp. 189–207). Carbondale: Southern Illinois University Press.

House, R. J. (1996). Path-goal theory of leadership: Lessons, legacy, and a reformulated theory. *Leadership Quarterly, 7* (3), 323–352.

Hughes, J. (1998, July 18). Police shootings—a question of perception vs. reality. *San Diego Union Tribune,* B3.

Hughes, J. (1999, December 8). Suicide by cop may be trend. *San Diego Union Tribune,* A1.

Hughes, J. (2000, January 21). Ketamine-related drug arrests on the rise at border. *San Diego Union Tribune,* B1, B3.

Inciardi, J. A. (2000). *Elements of criminal justice* (2nd ed.). New York: Harcourt College Publishers.

Independent Commission on the Los Angeles Police Department (Christopher Commission). (1991). *Commission report.* Los Angeles: Los Angeles Police Department.

International Association of Chiefs of Police. (1985). *Police supervision.* Arlington, VA: International Association of Chiefs of Police.

International Association of Chiefs of Police. (1991a, October). *Law enforcement code of ethics.* Washington, DC: International Association of Chiefs of Police.

International Association of Chiefs of Police. (1991b, October). *Police officer code of conduct.* Washington, DC: International Association of Chiefs of Police.

Is LA's crime honeymoon over? Gangs blamed for surge in violent crime rate. (2000, July/August). *Law Enforcement News, 26* (537–538), 8.

Janis, I. (1989). *Crucial decisions: Leadership in policymaking and crisis management.* New York: Free Press.

Jennings, H. H. (1944). Leadership—a dynamic re-definition. *Journal of Educational Sociology, 17,* 431–433.

Johnson, C. E. (2001). *Meeting the ethical challenges of leadership: Casting light or shadow.* Thousand Oaks, CA: Sage Publications.

Jones, A. A., & Wiseman, R. (2001, September). Community policing: Fights for its life in LA. *Community Links, 7* (3), 1–4.

Jones, J. R., & Carlson, D. P. (2001). *Reputable conduct: Ethical issues in policing and corrections* (2nd ed.). Upper Saddle River, NJ: Prentice Hall.

Kappeler, V. E. (2001). *Critical Issues in Police Civil Liability* (3rd ed.). Prospect Heights, IL: Waveland Press.

Karmen, A. (2001). *Crime victims: An introduction to victimology.* Belmont, CA: Wadsworth/Thomson Learning.

Kelling, G. L. (1974). *The Kansas City preventive patrol experiment: A summary report.* Washington, DC: The Police Foundation.

Kelling, G. L. (1988, June). Police and communities: The quiet revolution. *Perspectives on Policing No. 1.* Washington, DC: National Institute of Justice.

Kelling, G. L. (1999, October). *"Broken windows" and police discretion.* Washington, DC: National Institute of Justice.

Kelling, G. L., & Bratton, W. J. (1993, July). *Implementing community policing: The administrative problem.* Washington, DC: National Institute of Justice and Harvard University.

Kelling, G. L., & Moore, M. H. (1991). From political reform to community: The evolving strategy of police. In J. R. Green & S. D. Mastrofski (Eds.), *Community policing: Rhetoric or reality,* (pp. 14–15, 22–23). New York: Praeger.

Kennedy, D. (1993, January). The strategic management of police resources. In *Perspectives on policing* (pp. 4–5). Washington, DC: U.S. Department of Justice, Office of Justice Programs, National Institute of Justice and Program in Criminal Justice Policy and Management of the J.F.K. School of Government, Harvard University.

Kidd, V., & Braziel, R. (1999). *Community oriented policing cop talk: Essential communication skills for community policing.* San Francisco: Acada Books.

Kingsley, G. T. & Pettit, K. L. S. (2000, October). Getting to know neighborhoods. *National Institute of Justice Journal,* 10–17.

Kitchener, K. S. (1984). Intuition, critical evaluation and ethical principles: The foundation for ethical decisions in counseling psychology. *The Counseling Psychologist, 12* (3), 43–45.

Kleinig, J. (1996a). Handling discretion with discretion. In J. Kleinig (Ed.), *Handled with discretion: Ethical issues in police decision making* (pp. 1–12). New York: Rowman & Littlefield.

Kleinig, J. (1996b). *The ethics of policing.* New York: Cambridge University Press.

Kleinig, J., & Zhang, Y. (Eds.). (1993). *Professional law enforcement codes: A documentary collection.* Westport, CT: Greenwood Press.

Klockars, C. B. (1991). The Dirty Harry problem. In C. B. Klockars & S. D. Mastrofski (Eds.), *Thinking about police: Contemporary readings* (2nd ed.). (pp. 413–423). New York: McGraw-Hill.

Klockars, C. B., Ivkovich, S. K., Harver, W. E., & Haberfeld, M. R. (2000, May). The measurement of police integrity. *National Institute of Justice: Research in brief.* Washington, DC: U.S. Government Printing Office.

Knickerbocker, I. (1948). Leadership: A conception and some complications. *Journal of Sociology Issues, 4,* 23–40.

Knowles, M. S. (1990). *The adult learner: A neglected species* (4th ed). Houston, TX: Gulf Publishing Company.

Kokkelenberg, L. D. (2001, February 14). Real leadership is more than just a walk in the park. *Law Enforcement News, 27* (549), 9.

Komives, S. R., Lucas, N., & McMahon, T. R. (1998). *Exploring leadership: For college students who want to make a difference.* San Francisco: Josey-Bass.

Kotter, J. P. (1990). *A force for change.* New York: The Free Press.

Kotter, J. P. (1993). What leaders really do. In W. E. Rosenbach & R. L. Taylor (Eds.), *Contemporary issues in leadership* (3rd ed.) (pp. 26–35). Boulder, CO: Westview Press.

Kotter, J. P. (1996). *Leading change.* New York: AMACOM (American Management Association).

Kouzes, J. J., & Posner, B. Z. (1993). The credibility factor: What people expect of leaders. In W. E. Rosenbach & R. L. Taylor (Eds.), *Contemporary issues in leadership* (3rd ed.) (pp. 57–61). Boulder, CO: Westview Press.

Kouzes, J. J., & Posner, B. Z. (1995). *The leadership challenge: How to keep getting extraordinary things done in organizations* (2nd ed.). San Francisco: Jossey-Bass.

Krasnowski, M. (1998, June 1). Lawsuits against cops continue to add up to millions for LA. *San Diego Union Tribune,* A4.

Krasnowski, M. (2000, January 26). Corruption prompts reversal of 10 verdicts. *San Diego Union Tribune,* A3.

Kretzmann, J. P., & McKnight, J. L. (1999, July). Community mapping. In California State, Office of the Attorney General. *Community-oriented policing and problem solving: Now and beyond* (pp. 97–105). Sacramento, CA: Office of the Attorney General.

Kroeker, M. A. (2001, September). Proper design helps stem crime. *Community Links, 7* (3), 15–16.

Lamm Weisel, D. (2002). *Graffiti: Problem-oriented guides for police series no. 9.* Washington, DC: U.S. Department of Justice, Office of Community Oriented Policing Services.

Langan, P. A., Greenfeld, L. A., Smith, S. K., Durose, M. R., & Levin, D. J. (2001). *Contacts between police and the public: Findings from the 1999 national survey.* Washington, DC: U.S. Department of Justice, Office of Justice Programs, Bureau of Justice Statistics.

Law Enforcement Assistance Administration. (1976). *Two hundred years of American criminal justice.* Washington, DC: U.S. Government Printing Office.

Lee, W. L. M. (1901). *A history of police in England.* London: Methuen (Oxford University Press).

Levine, A. (1982). Qualitative research in academic decision making. In E. Kuhns & S. V. Martorana (Eds.), *Qualitative methods for institutional research* (pp. 78–92). San Francisco: Jossey-Bass.

Lewis, P. S., Goodman, S. H., & Fandt, P. M. (2001). *Management: Challenges in the 21st century* (3rd ed.). Cincinnati, OH: South-Western/Thomson Learning.

Likert, R. (1961). *New patterns of management.* New York: McGraw-Hill.

Likert, R. (1967). *The human organization.* New York: McGraw-Hill.

Locke, J. (1690). *Second treatise of civil government.*

Lyman, M. D. (2002). *The police: An introduction* (2nd ed.). Upper Saddle River, NJ: Prentice Hall.

Maguire, K., & Pastore, A. L. (1998). *Sourcebook of criminal justice statistics* (p. 100). Washington, DC: U.S. Department of Justice.

Maher, G. F. (1989). Hostage negotiations. In W. G. Bailey (Ed.), *Encyclopedia of police science* (pp. 274–277). New York: Garland Publishing.

Maltz, M. D. (1999, July). *Bridging gaps in police crime data.* Washington, DC: U.S. Department of Justice, Office of Justice Programs, Bureau of Justice Statistics.

Mamalian, C. A., & LaVigne, N. G., (1999, January). *The use of computerized mapping by law enforcement: Survey results.* Washington, DC: National Institute of Justice.

Maniscalco, P. M., & Christen, H. T. (2002). *Understanding terrorism and managing the consequences.* Upper Saddle River, NJ: Prentice Hall.

Manus, R. P. (2002, January 15/31). Rethinking community policing. *Law Enforcement News, 28* (569, 570), 9–10.

March, N. (2001, September/October). Success in New England: The Maine Community Policing Institute. *The Law Enforcement Trainer, 16* (5), 12–15.

Maslach, C., & Leiter, M. P. (1999). Burnout and engagement in the workplace: A contextual analysis. In T. C. Urban (Ed.), *The role of context: Advances in motivation and achievement* (pp. 275–302). Stamford, CT: JAI Press, Inc.

Maslow, A. H. (1970). *Motivation and personality* (2nd ed.). New York: Harper & Row.

Massachusetts Criminal Justice Training Council & the Regional Community Policing Institute for New England. (1997). *Ethics, integrity, and moral decision-making: A supplement to the basic curriculum for police for all topics.* Waltham, MA: Massachusetts Criminal Justice Training Council.

Mastrofski, S. D., & Worden, R. (1991). Community policing as reform: A cautionary tale. In C. Klockars & S. D. Mastrofski (Eds.). *Thinking about police: Contemporary readings* (2nd ed.) (pp. 515–529). Upper Saddle River, NJ: Prentice Hall.

Mastrofski, S. D., Parks, R. B., Reiss, A. J., Jr., & Worden, R. E. (1999, July). *Policing neighborhoods: A report from St. Petersburg.* Washington, DC: U.S. Department of Justice, National Institute of Justice.

Mayhall, P. D., Barker, T., & Hunter, R. D. (1995). *Police community relations and the administration of justice.* Englewood Cliffs, NJ: Prentice Hall.

Mayo, E. (1945). *The social problems of an industrialized civilization.* Boston: Harvard Business School.

McCelland, D. C. (1971). *Motivational trends in society.* Morristown, NJ: General Learning Press.

McDonald, J., & Thornton, K. (2002, May 27). 9/11 aftermath drains cops: New duties overtax budgets, add worries. *San Diego Union Tribune,* A1, A16.

McEwen, J. T. (1984, September). Handling calls for service: Alternatives to traditional policing. *NIJ (National Institute of Justice) Reports,* 4–8.

McGregor, D. (1960). *The human side of enterprise.* New York: McGraw-Hill.

McGregor, D. (1966). *Leadership and motivation.* Cambridge: M.I.T. (Massachusetts Institute of Technology) Press.

McKinnie, R. L. (1995, July 6). Cops take a partner: The people-community policing aids rapport, crime control. *San Diego Union Tribune,* B1–B2.

McNamara, J. D. (2000, November 26). Blame the brass, not cops on the street, for Rampart's mess. *The Los Angeles Times,* M6.

Meadows, R. J. (2002). Legal issues in policing. In R. Muraskin & A. R. Roberts (Eds.), *Visions for change: Crime and justice in the twenty-first century* (3rd ed.) (pp. 137–157). Upper Saddle River, NJ: Prentice Hall.

Measuring what matters—part two: Developing measures of what the police do. (1997, November). Washington, DC: U.S. Department of Justice, Office of Justice Programs.

Meese, E. III. (1993, January). *Community policing and the police officer.* Washington, DC: National Institute of Justice.

Meese, E. III., & Kurz, A. T., Jr. (1993, December). Community policing and the investigator. *Journal of Contemporary Criminal Justice, 9,* 289–302.

Meese, E. III, & Moffit, R. E. (Eds). (1997). *Making America safer: What citizens and their state and local officials can do to combat crime.* Washington, DC: The Heritage Foundation.

Memory, J. M. (2001, Spring). Teaching patrol officer problem solutions in academic criminal justice courses. *Journal of Criminal Justice Education, 12* (1), 213–228.

Michelson, R. (1999). *The California criminal justice system to accompany introduction to criminal justice.* New York: Glencoe/McGraw-Hill.

Michelson, R., & Maher, P. T. (1993). *Preparing for promotion: A guide to law enforcement assessment centers.* Blue Lake, CA: Innovative Systems.

Miller, M. (1995). *Police patrol operations.* Incline Village, NV: Copperhouse Publishing.

Miskin, V., & Gmelch, W. (1985, May). Quality leadership for quality teams. *Training and Development Journal, 39* (5), 122–129.

Mitchell Robinson, D. (Ed.). (2002) *Policing and crime prevention.* Upper Saddle River, NJ: Prentice Hall.

Moore, M. H., & Stephens, D. (1991). *Beyond command and control: The strategic management of police departments.* Washington, DC: Police Executive Research Forum.

Moore, M. H., & Trojanowicz, R. C. (1988). *Corporate strategies for policing: Perspectives on policing no. 6.* Washington, DC: National Institute of Justice.

Muhlhausen, D. B. (2001, September 15). More funding for the COPS office means paying for fanfare, not effectiveness. *Law Enforcement News, 27* (561), 11, 14.

Muraskin, R., & Roberts, A. R. (Eds.). (2002). *Visions for change: Crime and justice in the twenty-first century* (3rd ed.). Upper Saddle River, NJ: Prentice Hall.

Murphy, P. (1989). Foreword in *The state of police education: Policy direction for the 21st century* by D. L. Carter, et al. Washington, DC: Police Executive Research Forum.

Nash, J. B. (1929). Leadership. *Phi Delta Kappan, 12,* 24–25.

National Advisory Commission on Criminal Justice Standards and Goals. (1976). *Report of the task force on private security.* Washington, DC: U.S. Government Printing Office.

National Commission on the Future of DNA Evidence. (2000, November). *The future of forensic DNA testing: Predictions of the research and development working group.* Washington, DC: National Institute of Justice.

National Incident-Based Reporting System. (2002). *NIBRS state profile map.* [On line]. Available: http://www.nibrs.search.org.

National Police Week. (2001, March/April). *The Law Enforcement Trainer, 16* (2), 16–18.

Nguyen, D. P. (1999, December 20). 67% give SDPD high marks, poll finds. *San Diego Union Tribune,* A1.

Newton, S. J. (2002, March). The community becomes first line of defense. *Community Links,* 1–3.

Nichols, L. D. (1998). *Law enforcement patrol operations: Police systems and practices* (3rd ed.). Berkeley, CA: McCutchan Publishing.

Niederhoffer, A. (1967). *Behind the shield: The police in urban society.* Garden City, NY: Doubleday.

'98 police fatalities down 13% from '97. (2000, January 28). *San Diego Union Tribune,* A13.

Nislow, Jennifer. (2001, October 15). Secret Weapon against terrorism? Chiefs say community policing is an ace in the hole. *Law Enforcement News, 27* (563), 1, 10.

NJSP gambles on the viability of its college degree requirement. (2000, April 30). *Law Enforcement News, 26* (532), 1, 10.

Northouse, P. G. (2001). *Leadership: Theory and practice* (2nd ed.). Thousand Oaks, CA: Sage Publications.

Number of slain cops hits all-time low. (2000, May 15/31). *Law Enforcement News, 26* (533–534), 7.

O'Hair, D., Gustav, F. W., & Dixon, L. D. (2002). *Strategic communication in business and the professions* (4th ed.). Boston: Houghton Mifflin.

O'Hara, C. E., & O'Hara, G. L. (1994). *Fundamentals of criminal investigation* (6th ed.). Springfield, IL: Charles C. Thomas.

Oliver, W. M. (1998). *Community oriented policing: A systematic approach to policing.* Upper Saddle River, NJ: Prentice Hall.

Operation cooperation. (2001, January/February). *ASIS (American Society for Industrial Security) Dynamics* (157), 1, 4.

Ortmeier, P. J. (1995, July–August). Educating law enforcement officers for community policing. *Police and Security News, 11* (4), 46–47.

Ortmeier, P. J. (1996). *Community policing leadership: A Delphi study to identify essential competencies.* Ann Arbor, MI: University Microfilms International (Bell & Howell Information and Learning) Dissertation Services.

Ortmeier, P. J. (1997, October). Leadership for community policing: Identifying essential officer competencies. *Police Chief, 64* (10), 88–91, 93, 95.

Ortmeier, P. J. (1999). *Public safety and security administration.* Boston: Butterworth-Heinemann.

Ortmeier, P. J. (2002). *Policing the community: A guide for patrol operations.* Upper Saddle River, NJ: Prentice Hall.

Orton, A. (1984). Leadership: New thoughts on an old problem. *Training, 21* (28), 31–33.

Osborn, R. N., & Hunt, J. G. (1975). Relations between leadership, size, and subordinate satisfaction in a voluntary organization. *Journal of Applied Psychology, 60,* 730–735.

Otto, P. (2000, January/February). The importance of building strong media relations: They will tell the story with or without you. *ACJS (Academy of Criminal Justice Sciences) Today, 19* (1), 8–9.

Ouchi, W. (1981). *Theory Z: How American business can meet the Japanese challenge.* Reading, MA: Addison-Wesley.

Palacios, W. R., Cromwell, P. F., & Dunham, R. G. (2002). *Crime & justice in America: Present realities and future prospects* (2nd ed.). Upper Saddle River, NJ: Prentice Hall.

Palmiotto, M. J. (2002). The influence of community in community policing in the twenty-first century. In R. Muraskin & A. R. Roberts, (Eds.), *Visions for change: Crime and justice in the twenty-first century* (3rd ed.) (pp. 124–136). Upper Saddle River, NJ: Prentice Hall.

Parker, P. A. (1993, April). Reorganize and reprioritize. *Police,* 26.

Parker, T. (1999, July). Community responsibilities in neighborhood policing. In California State, Office of the Attorney General. *Community-oriented policing and problem solving: Now and beyond* (pp. 110–117). Sacramento, CA: Office of the Attorney General.

Parker, W. H. (1957). *Parker on police.* Springfield, IL: Charles C. Thomas.

Parr, L. A. (1999). *Police report writing essentials.* Placerville, CA: Custom Publishing.

Parshall-McDonald, P., & Greenberg, S. F. (2002). *Managing police operations: Implementing the New York crime control model—CompStat.* Belmont, CA: Wadsworth/Thomson Learning.

Pasquali, A. (1997). The moral dimension of communicating. In C. Christians & M. Traber (Eds.). *Communication ethics and universal values* (pp. 24–45). Thousand Oaks, CA: Sage Publications.

Patton, M. Q. (1990). *Qualitative evaluations and research methods.* Newbury Park, CA: Sage Publications.

Payton, G. T., & Amaral, M. (1996). *Patrol operations and enforcement tactics* (10th ed.). San Jose, CA: Criminal Justice Services.

Peak, K. J. (1995). *Justice administration: Police, courts and corrections management.* Upper Saddle River, NJ: Prentice Hall.

Peak, K. J., & Glensor, R. W. (2002). *Community policing and problem solving: Strategies and practices* (3rd ed.). Upper Saddle River, NJ: Prentice Hall.

Perez, D. W., & Moore, J. A. (2002). *Police ethics: A matter of character.* Incline Village, NV: Copperhouse Publishing.

Perry, J. L. (1996). *Handbook of public administration.* San Francisco: Jossey-Bass.

Perry, T. (1994). *Basic patrol procedures.* Salem, WI: Sheffield Publishing.

Peter, L. J., & Hull, R. (1969). *The Peter Principle: Why things always go wrong.* New York: William Morrow.

Peters, T. J. (1992). *Liberation management.* New York: Alfred A. Knopf.

Peters, T. J. (1994). *The Tom Peters Seminar: Crazy times call for crazy organizations.* New York: Vintage Books.

Petersilia, J. (1989). The influence of research on policing. In R. G. Dunham & G. P. Alpert (Eds.), *Critical issues in policing: Contemporary readings* (p. 223). Prospect Heights, IL: Waveland Press.

Pfeffer, J. (1977). The ambiguity of leadership. *Academic Management Review, 2,* 104–112.

Phillips, R. G., Jr. (1988, August). Training priorities in state and local law enforcement. *FBI Law Enforcement Bulletin, 57* (8), 10–16.

Phillips, R., & Pack, C. (1999, Spring). Sustaining community partnerships: A road map for the long haul. *Community Links, 6* (2), 2–3.

Police deaths up sharply in just first half of year. (2001, October 15). *Law Enforcement News, 27* (563), 10.

Police Executive Research Forum. (1996). *Themes and variations in community policing.* Washington, DC: Police Executive Research Forum.

Police morale falls sharply. (2000, October 24). *San Diego Union Tribune,* A-3.

Polk, O. E., & Armstrong, D. A. (2001, Spring). Higher education and law enforcement career paths: Is the road to success paved by degree? *Journal of Criminal Justice Education, 12* (1), 77–99.

Pollock, J. M. (1998). *Ethics in crime and justice: Dilemmas and decisions* (3rd ed.). Belmont, CA: West/Wadsworth.

Porter, L.W., & Lawler, E. E. III. (1968). *Managerial attitudes and performance.* Homewood, IL: Irwin.

President's Commission on Law Enforcement and Administration of Justice. (1967). *Task force report: Police.* Washington, DC: U.S. Government Printing Office.

President's Crime Prevention Council. (1997). *Helping communities fight crime: Comprehensive planning techniques, models, programs and resources.* Washington, DC: U.S. Government Printing Office.

Pressed for applicants, NYPD waives two-year college standard. (2000, October 31). *Law Enforcement News, 26* (542), 1, 10.

Putnam, L. & Pacanowski, M. (Eds.). (1983). *Communication and organizations: An interpretive approach.* Beverly Hills, CA: Sage Publications.

Raffel Price, B. (1995, June 15). Police and the quest for professionalism. *Law Enforcement News, 21* (425), 8.

Ramsey, C. H. (2002). Preparing the community for community policing. In D. J. Stevens (Ed.), *Policing and community partnerships* (pp. 29–44). Upper Saddle River, NJ: Prentice Hall.

Rand Corporation. (1999). *The benefits and costs of drug use prevention: Clarifying a cloudy issue.* Santa Monica, CA: Rand Corporation, Drug Policy Research Center.

Rasp, A., Jr. (1974). A new tool for administrators: Delphi and decision making. *North Central Association Quarterly, 48* (3), 320–325.

Rawls, J. (1971). *A theory of justice.* Boston: Harvard University Press.

Reiman, J. (1990). *Justice and modern moral philosophy.* New Haven, CT: Yale University Press.

Rich, T. (1999, October). Mapping the path to problem solving. *National Institute of Justice Journal,* 2–9.

Roberg, R. R. (1978, September). An analysis of the relationship among higher education, belief systems, and job performance of patrol officers. *Journal of Police Science and Administration, 6,* 336–344.

Robinson, M. B. (2002). Crime prevention through environmental design (CPTED) in elementary and secondary schools. In D. Mitchell Robinson (Ed.), *Policing and crime prevention* (pp. 53–82). Upper Saddle River, NJ: Prentice Hall.

Ross, D. L. (2003). *Civil liability in criminal justice* (3rd ed.). Cincinnati: Anderson.

Rost, J. (1991). *Leadership for the twenty-first century.* New York: Praeger.

Roth, J. A., & Ryan, J. F. (2000, August). *The COPS Program after 4 years—National Evaluation.* Washington, DC: National Institute of Justice, Office of Justice Programs.

Russell, H. E., & Beigel, A. (1990). *Understanding human behavior for effective police work* (3rd ed.). New York: Basic Books.

Ryan, R. M., & LaGuardia, J. G. (1999). Achievement motivation within a pressured society: Intrinsic and extrinsic motivations to learn and the politics of school reform. In T. C. Urban (Ed.), *The role of context: Advances in motivation and achievement* (pp. 45–85). Stamford, CT: JAI Press, Inc.

Sampson, R. (2001). *False burglar alarms: Problem-oriented guides for police series no. 5.* Washington, DC: U.S. Department of Justice, Office of Community Oriented Policing Services.

Sampson, R. (2002). *Bullying in schools: Problem-oriented guides for police series no. 12.* Washington, DC: U.S. Department of Justice, Office of Community Oriented Policing Services.

Sampson, R., & Scott, M. S. (2000). *Tackling crime and other public safety problems: Case studies in problem solving.* Washington, DC: U.S. Department of Justice, Office of Community Oriented Policing Services.

Sampson, R. J., & Bartusch, D. J. (1999, June). *Attitudes toward crime, police, and the law: Individual and neighborhood differences.* Washington, DC: National Institute of Justice.

San Diego Police Department. (1993, February). *Neighborhood policing: A guide for building a police/community partnership.* San Diego, CA: San Diego Police Department.

Schenk, C. (1928). Leadership. *Infantry Journal,* 111–122.

Schmalleger, F. (2001). *Criminal justice: A brief introduction* (4th ed.). Upper Saddle River, NJ: Prentice Hall.

Schmalleger, F. (2002). *Criminal justice: A brief introduction* (4th ed. update). Upper Saddle River, NJ: Prentice Hall.

Scott, M. S. (2000). *Problem-oriented policing: Reflections on the first 20 years.* Washington, DC: U.S. Department of Justice, Office of Community Oriented Policing Services.

Scott, M. S. (2001). *Street prostitution: Problem-oriented guides for police series no. 2.* Washington, DC: U.S. Department of Justice, Office of Community Oriented Policing Services.

Scott, M. S. (2002a). *Panhandling: Problem-oriented guides for police series no. 13.* Washington, DC: U.S. Department of Justice, Office of Community Oriented Policing Services.

Scott, M. S. (2002b). *Rave parties: Problem-oriented guides for police series no. 14.* Washington, DC: U.S. Department of Justice, Office of Community Oriented Policing Services.

Scott, W. E. (1977). Leadership: A functional analysis. In J. G. Hunt & L. L. Larson (Eds.), *Leadership, the cutting edge*. Carbondale, IL: Southern Illinois University Press.

Scott, W. R. (1986). College education requirements for police entry level and promotion: A study. *Journal of Police and Criminal Psychology, 2* (1), 16–17.

Selecting a new breed of officer: The customer-oriented cop. (1999, March/April). *Community Policing Exchange, 6* (25), 4.

Senna, J. J., & Siegel, L. J. (2001). *Essentials of criminal justice* (3rd ed.). Belmont, CA: Wadsworth/Thomson Learning.

Shartle, C. L. (1956). *Executive performance and leadership*. Englewood Cliffs, NJ: Prentice Hall.

Sheehan, R., & Cordner, G. W. (1989). *Introduction to police administration* (2nd ed.). Cincinnati, OH: Anderson.

Sherman, L. W. (1978). *The quality of police education*. Washington, DC: Jossey-Bass.

Sherman, L. W., & Bennis, W. G. (1977). Higher education for police officers: The central issues. *Police Chief, 44*, 32.

Sherman, L. W., & Berk, R. (1984). The specific deterrent effects of arrest for domestic assault. *American Sociological Review, 49* (2), 261–272.

Sichel, J. (1978). *Women on patrol: A pilot study of police performance in New York City*. Washington, DC: U.S. Department of Justice.

Sickmund, M., Snyder, H. N., & Poe-Yamagata, E. (1997, August). *Juvenile offenders and victims: 1997 update on violence*. Washington, DC: U.S. Department of Justice, Office of Juvenile Justice and Delinquency Prevention.

Siegel, L. J. (2001). *Criminology: Theories, patterns, and typologies* (7th ed.). Belmont, CA: Wadsworth/Thomson Learning.

Simons, C. F. (2002). The evolution of crime prevention. In D. Mitchell Robinson (Ed.), *Policing and crime prevention* (pp. 1–18). Upper Saddle River, NJ: Prentice Hall.

Skogan, W. G., Hartnett, S. M., DuBois, J., Comey, J. T., Kaiser, M., & Loving, J. H. (1999). *On the beat: Police and community problem solving*. Boulder, CO: Westview Press.

Skolnick, J. H. (1994). *Justice without trial: Law enforcement in a democratic society* (3rd ed.). New York: Macmillan College Publishing.

Skolnick, J. H., & Bayley, D. H. (1986). *The new blue line: Police innovation in six American cities*. New York: The Free Press.

Smith, P. B., & Peterson, M. F. (1990, August). Leadership, organizations, and culture. *Education Administration Quarterly, 26* (3), 235–259.

Sniffen, M. J. (2001, January 6). Companies cooperate with FBI in fighting computer crime. *San Diego Union Tribune*, A11.

Solomon, R.C. (1996). *A handbook for ethics*. Fort Worth, TX: Harcourt Brace College Publishers.

Souryal, S. S. (1981). *Police organization and administration*. New York: Harcourt Brace Jovanovich.

Souryal, S. S. (1992). *Ethics in criminal justice: In search of the truth*. Cincinnati: Anderson.

Sparrow, M. K. (1988, November). *Implementing community policing*. Washington, DC: National Institute of Justice and Harvard University.

Sparrow, M. K., Moore, M. H., & Kennedy, M. (1990). *Beyond 911*. New York: Harper.

Spelman, W., & Eck, J. E. (1987, January). Problem-oriented policing. *National Institute of Justice: Research in Brief*, 2–3.

Stahl, N. (1992). Providing a data base for considering policy options: Applications of the Delphi Technique using an illustrative case study. In N. L. Haggerson & A. C. Bowman (Eds.), *Informing educational policy and practice through interpretive inquiry* (pp. 83–109). Lancaster, PA: Technomic.

Stech, E. L. (2001). Psychodynamic approach. In P. G. Northouse, *Leadership: Theory and practice* (2nd ed.) (pp. 189–213). Thousand Oaks, CA: Sage Publications.

Stern, M. (1999, July 3). INS computer system in spotlight following release of wanted man. *San Diego Union Tribune*, A1.

Stevens, D. J. (2001). *Case studies in community policing.* Upper Saddle River, NJ: Prentice Hall.

Stevens, D.J. (2002). Community policing and police leadership. In D.J. Stevens (Ed.), *Policing and community partnerships* (pp. 163–176). Upper Saddle River, NJ: Prentice Hall.

Stogdill, R. M. (1948). Personal factors associated with leadership: A survey of the literature. *Journal of Psychology, 25*, 35–71.

Stogdill, R. M. (1950). Leadership, membership and organization. *Psychology Bulletin, 47*, 1–14.

Stogdill, R. M. (1959). *Individual behavior and group achievement.* New York: Oxford University Press.

Stojkovic, S., Kalinich, D., & Klofas, J. (2003). *Criminal justice organizations: Administration and management (3rd ed.).* Belmont, CA: Wadsworth/Thomson Learning.

Strapped for personnel, Portland kills four-year degree requirement for recruits. (2001, January 15/31). *Law Enforcement News, 27* (547, 548), 1.

Study sees cause for alarm as police adopt a more paramilitary posture. (1999, October 15). *Law Enforcement News, 25* (519), 1,9.

Swanson, C. R., Territo, L., & Taylor, R. W. (1998). *Police administration: Structure, processes and behavior* (4th ed.). Upper Saddle River, NJ: Prentice Hall.

SWAT team may prove costly for small farm town. (1999, April 6). *San Diego Union Tribune*, A3.

Tafoya, W. L. (1986). *A Delphi forecast of the future of law enforcement.* Ph.D. dissertation: University of Maryland.

Tafoya, W. L. (1991, May/June). The future of law enforcement? A chronology of events. *Criminal Justice International*, 4.

Tannenbaum, R., & Schmidt, W. H. (1958, March–April). How to choose a leadership pattern. *Harvard Business Review, 36* (2), 95–101.

Taylor, F. W. (1911). *The principles of scientific management.* New York: Harper & Brothers.

Taylor, G. (2002, Spring). Untraditional police programs. *California Police Recorder, 22* (2), 26.

Tead, O. (1935). *The art of leadership.* New York: McGraw-Hill.

Thaiss, C., & Hess, J. E. (1999). *Writing for law enforcement.* Boston: Allyn & Bacon.

The Police Foundation. (1981). *The Newark foot patrol experiment.* Washington, DC: The Police Foundation.

Thibault, E. A., Lynch, L. M., & McBride, R. B. (1998). *Proactive police management* (4th ed.). Upper Saddle River, NJ: Prentice Hall.

Thornton, K. (1999, February 27). Tragedy stirs debate over police pursuits. *San Diego Union Tribune*, A1.

Thornton, K. (1999, November 5). Cops rarely charged in shootings, experts say. *San Diego Union Tribune*, A1.

Thurman, Q. C. (2002). Contemporary policing in a community era. In W. Palacios, J. Cromwell, & R. Dunham (Eds.), *Crime & justice in America: Present realities and future prospects* (2nd ed.) (pp. 111–121). Upper Saddle River, NJ: Prentice Hall.

Thurman, Q., Zhao, J., & Giacomazzi, A. L. (2001). *Community policing in a community era: An introduction and exploration.* Los Angeles: Roxbury Publishing.

Tichy, N., & Ulrich, D. (1984). The leadership challenge—a call for the transformational leader. SMR Forum, *Sloan Management Review, 26* (1), 59–68.

Tingley, J. C. (2001). *The power of influence.* New York: AMACOM (American Management Association).

Tos, D. (2000, January/February). A fortune 500 police department. *Community Policing Exchange, 1* (30), 5.

Townsend, R. (1970). *Up the organization.* New York: Alfred A. Knopf.

Trautman, N. E. (2002). *How to be a great cop.* Upper Saddle River, NJ: Prentice Hall.

Trojanowicz, R. C. (1990, October). Community policing is not police-community relations. *FBI Law Enforcement Bulletin, 59* (10), 6–11.

Trojanowicz, R. C., & Bucqueroux, B. (1990). *Community policing.* Cincinnati: Anderson.

Trojanowicz, R. C., & Carter, D. L. (1990, January). The changing face of America. *FBI Law Enforcement Bulletin, 59* (1), 9.

Truth, DARE and consequences: What impact is anti-drug effort having? (1998, April 15). *Law Enforcement News, 24* (487), 1, 10.

$12.5 million awarded in police-raid shooting death. (1999, March 16). *San Diego Union Tribune,* A3.

U.S. Congress. (1968). *Omnibus Crime Control and Safe Streets Act.* Washington, DC: U.S. Government Printing Office.

U.S. Congress. (1994). *Violent Crime Control and Law Enforcement Act of 1994.* Washington, DC: U.S. Government Printing Office.

U.S. Department of Justice. (1988). *Uniform crime reporting: National incident-based reporting system, Vol. 1: Data collection guidelines.* Washington, DC: U.S. Government Printing Office.

U.S. Department of Justice. (1993, November). *NIJ outreach confirms support for multidisciplinary collaborative approach.* Washington, DC: Office of Justice Programs.

U.S. Department of Justice. (1999, October). *Use of force by police: Overview of national and local data.* Washington, DC: Office of Justice Programs.

U.S. Department of Justice. Bureau of Justice Statistics. (1992). *Criminal victimization in the United States, 1991.* Washington, DC: U.S. Department of Justice.

U.S. Department of Justice. Bureau of Justice Statistics. (1992, December). *Drugs, crime and the justice system.* Washington, DC: U.S. Government Printing Office.

U.S. Department of Justice. Bureau of Justice Statistics. (1994). *Neighborhood-oriented policing in rural communities: A program planning guide.* Washington, DC: U.S. Government Printing Office.

U.S. Department of Justice. Federal Bureau of Investigation. (1997). *Uniform crime report.* Washington, DC: U.S. Government Printing Office.

U.S. Department of Justice. Federal Bureau of Investigation. (2001). *Uniform crime report.* Washington, DC: U.S. Government Printing Office.

U.S. General Accounting Office. (1998, May). *Report to the Honorable Charles B. Rangel, House of Representatives, Law Enforcement: Information on drug-related police corruption.* Washington, DC: U.S. Government Printing Office.

Urban, T. C. (Ed.). (1999). *The role of contest: Advances in motivation and achievement.* Stamford, CT: JAI Press, Inc.

Velasquez, M. G. (1992). *Business ethics: Concepts and cases* (3rd ed.). Englewood Cliffs, NJ: Prentice Hall.

Vinzant, J. C., & Crothers, L. (1998). *Street-level leadership: Discretion and legitimacy in front-line public service.* Washington, DC: Georgetown University Press.

Vodicka, A. T. (1994, March). Educational requirements for police recruits: Higher education benefits officers agency. *Law and Order, 42* (3), 91–94.

Vollmer, A. (1936). *The police and modern society.* Los Angeles: University of California Press.

Vroom, V. H. (1964). *Work and motivation.* New York: John Wiley & Sons.

Vroom, V. H. (2000, Spring). Leadership and the decision-making process. *Organizational Dynamics,* 82–94.

Walker, S. (1983). *The police in America: An introduction.* New York: McGraw-Hill.

Walker, S. (2001). *Police accountability: The role of citizen oversight.* Belmont, CA: Wadsworth/Thomson Learning.

Walker, S., Alpert, G. P., & Kenney, D. J. (2001, July). Early warning systems: Responding to the problem police officer. *National Institute of Justice: Research in brief.* Washington, DC: U.S. Department of Justice, National Institute of Justice.

Walker, S., Spohn, C., & DeLone, M. (2000). *The color of justice: Race, ethnicity, and crime in America* (2nd ed.). Belmont, CA: Wadsworth/Thompson Learning.

Wallace, H., Roberson, C., & Steckler, C. (2001). *Written & interpersonal communication methods for law enforcement* (2nd ed.). Upper Saddle River, NJ: Prentice Hall.

Watson, E. M., Stone, A. R., & DeLuca, S. M. (1998). *Strategies for community policing.* Upper Saddle River, NJ: Prentice Hall.

Webb, V. J., & Katz, C. M. (1997). Citizen ratings of the importance of community policing activities. *Policing: An International Journal of Police Strategies and Management, 20* (1), 7–23.

Weisburd, D., Greenspan, R., Hamilton, E., Williams, H., & Bryant, K. (2000, May). *Police attitudes toward abuse of authority: Findings from a national study.* Washington, DC: U.S. Government Printing Office.

Welsh, W. N., & Harris, P. W. (1999). *Criminal justice planning & policy.* Cincinnati, OH: Anderson.

Werner, E. (2000, February 27). Dishonest cops? It's no surprise. *San Diego Union Tribune,* A3.

Whisenand, P. M., & Ferguson, R. F. (2002). *The managing of police organizations* (5th ed.). Upper Saddle River, NJ: Prentice Hall.

Whisenand, P. M., & Rush, G. E. (1998). *Supervising police personnel: The fifteen responsibilities.* Upper Saddle River, NJ: Prentice Hall.

Wilson, J. Q. (1968). *Varieties of police behavior: The management of law and order in eight communities.* Cambridge, MA: Harvard University Press.

Wilson, J. Q., & Kelling, G. L. (1982, March). Broken windows: The police and neighborhood safety. *The Atlantic Monthly,* 29–38.

Wilson, J. Q., & Kelling, G. L. (1989, February). Making neighborhoods safe. *The Atlantic Monthly,* 46–52.

Wilson, O. W. (1952). *Police planning.* Springfield, IL: Charles C. Thomas.

Wilson, O. W. (1963). *Police administration.* New York: McGraw-Hill.

Wolfson, P. G. (1986). *The perceptions of corporate executives and member company general managers concerning the competencies essential for agribusiness leaders.* Carbondale, IL: Southern Illinois University.

Wulff, D. (2000, January/February). Winning strategies offered for working with different cultures. *Community Policing Exchange, 7* (30), 1–2.

Wycoff, M. A., & Oettmeier, T. N. (1994). *Evaluating patrol officer performance under community policing: The Houston experience.* Washington, DC: The National Institute of Justice.

Wycoff, M. A., & Skogan, W. G. (1994). Community policing in Madison: An analysis of implementation and impact. In D. P. Rosenham (Ed.), *The challenge of community policing.* Newbury Park, CA: Sage Publications.

You can get it in writing—LAPD finally spells out penalties for officer misconduct. (2001, March 15). *Law Enforcement News, 27* (551), 5.

Yukl, G. A. (1971). Toward a behavioral theory of leadership. *Organization Behavior and Human Performance, 6,* 414–440.

Zahniser, D. (2002, August 25). LAPD's next chief must win over rank-and-file. *San Diego Union Tribune,* A13.

Zaleznik, A. (1993). Managers and leaders: Are they different. In W. E. Rosenbach & R. L. Taylor (Eds.), *Contemporary issues in leadership* (pp. 36–56). Boulder, CO: Westview Press.

Zelinka, A., & Brennan, D. (2001). *SafeScape: Creating safer, more livable communities through planning and design.* Chicago, IL: Planners Books Service.

Zhao, J. (2002). The future of policing in a community era. In W. Palacios, J. Cromwell, & R. Dunham (Eds.). *Crime & justice in America: Present realities and future prospects* (2nd ed.) (pp. 191–204). Upper Saddle River, NJ: Prentice Hall.

INDEX